*THE SOVIET UNION
AND
THE ARAB EAST
UNDER KHRUSHCHEV*

Volume 6
THE MODERN MIDDLE EAST SERIES

Sponsored by
The Middle East Institute
Columbia University, New York

THE SOVIET UNION AND THE ARAB EAST UNDER KHRUSHCHEV

Oles M. Smolansky

Lewisburg
BUCKNELL UNIVERSITY PRESS

© 1974 by Associated University Presses, Inc.

Associated University Presses, Inc.
Cranbury, New Jersey 08512

Library of Congress Cataloging in Publication Data

Smolansky, Oles M
  The Soviet Union and the Arab East under Khrushchev.

  (The Modern Middle East series, v. 6)
  Bibliography: p.
  1. Russia—Foreign relations—Arab countries.
  2. Arab countries—Foreign relations—Russia.
  I. Title. II. Series.
  DS63.2.R9S55   327.47′017′4927   73–2890
  ISBN 0–8387–1338–6

PRINTED IN THE UNITED STATES OF AMERICA

To My Parents

Contents

Preface		9
Acknowledgments		13
Introduction	The Basic Goals of Khrushchev's Policies	15
Part I	POINTS OF ENTRY, 1955–1958	
1	The Emergence of Nasir	23
2	The Suez Crisis	34
3	The Syrian Crisis and the Creation of the United Arab Republic	59
4	The Lebanese Crisis	83
5	The Iraqi Revolution and the Rift with Cairo	102
Part II	COOPERATION AND RECRIMINATION, 1958–1963	
6	The Egyptian Crises of 1959 and 1961	125
7	Disenchantment in Iraq	157
8	Syria and Egypt after the Dissolution of the United Arab Republic	194
Part III	THE LIMITS OF RAPPROCHEMENT, 1963–1964	
9	The Ba'th Regimes in Iraq and Syria	225
10	The Grand Finale: Khrushchev's Visit to Egypt	263
Conclusion	The Ultimate Failure of Khrushchev's Policies	290
Selected Bibliography		305
Index		313

Preface

One undertakes an assessment of any aspect of Nikita Sergeevich Khrushchev's policy with more than a few qualms, for the Chairman was a man who obviously delighted in doing the bold, the sweeping, and the unexpected. When the ultimate arbiter of policy in a totalitarian society has such a personality, the task of the analyst becomes that much more difficult: he must attempt to systematize positions that are intrinsically unsystematic. Furthermore, the inaccessibility to Western observers of much of the relevant source material on Soviet foreign policy virtually precludes the use of some of the traditional modes of analysis. Since I have had no access to the persons involved in the decision-making process or to their private or official papers, I have relied almost entirely upon Soviet, Arab, and Western public sources. They include public pronouncements by Khrushchev, Gamal 'Abd al-Nasir, and other involved statesmen, as well as official documents, supplemented by secondary and tertiary materials derived primarily from books and periodicals (including magazines, journals, and newspapers). *Pravda* and *Izvestiia,* along with the *New Times* and *International Affairs* (Moscow), provided the bulk of Soviet materials, while *al-Ahram, al-Gumhuriya, Akhbar al-Yawm,* and *Ruz al-Yusif* (Egypt); *al-Thawra, Ittihad al-Sha'b, Sawt al-Ahrar, al-Hurriya* (Iraq); and *al-Ba'th* and *al-Thawra* (Syria) were among some of the Arabic sources consulted. These were supplemented by the *Egyptian Gazette,* the *Iraqi Times,* and the *Egyptian Economic and Political Review.* Western sources include the *Mideast Mirror* (Bayrut), the *Middle East Journal, Orient* (Paris), the *Economist,* the *New York Times,* and the *Times* (London).

The Khrushchev era in the Arab East naturally divides itself into two periods. In the early years of his tenure in the Kremlin, Moscow's activities in the region consisted largely of opportunistic reaction to non-Soviet initiatives, including the Western and/or Arab-precipitated crises, such as the Suez war, the Syrian and Lebanese crises, and the Iraqi revolution, as well as the creation of the United Arab Republic. Part One of this study is devoted to a detailed analysis of these events.

The remainder of the volume details the post-1958 period, which differed substantially from the first primarily because the USSR had by then acquired such a definite stake in the Arab East that a policy of simple opportunism no longer sufficed. Furthermore, the tasks of formulating a coherent policy to protect the Kremlin's newly acquired interests proved more difficult than Khrushchev could possibly have imagined at the beginning of his Middle Eastern adventure. For, in 1958, some long-smoldering feuds between various "progressive" Arab states and factions broke into the open and all too frequently forced Khrushchev to choose sides in squabbles in which he would have much preferred neutrality.

Part Two examines the various crises experienced by Moscow between 1958 and 1963 that resulted from this polarization in the Arab nationalist movement.

By the end of this second period, although some of these feuds had been apparently settled, Soviet policy-making in the area was still encountering substantial difficulties (some of which continue to plague Khrushchev's successors even in the present day). As Part Three of the study illustrates, this was the case partly because of the ascendance to power of the Iraqi and Syrian branches of the Ba'th party (with which the Kremlin had initially found itself incompatible for numerous reasons) and partly because so many aspects of the intra-Arab dispute had been merely glossed over rather than truly resolved. The final chapter describes Khrushchev's swan song in the Arab East, his 1964 Egyptian visit. The conclusion focuses closely on the essential failure of his policy.

Acknowledgments

No scholarly volume can be produced without the help of many people, in terms of both direct assistance and patient forebearance, and I wish to express here my thanks to some of the organizations and individuals who have contributed in many diverse ways to this study. My research in Soviet-Arab relations was begun during my graduate work at Columbia University and was continued subsequently at UCLA and Lehigh University. The Rockefeller Foundation and Foreign Area Study Program of the Ford Foundation provided Fellowships that enabled me to continue research in Arab sources in Egypt, Syria, and Lebanon. Additional financial assistance was generously provided by Grants-in-Aid from the Lehigh University Institute of Research and by the University's Summer Fellowship Program.

Among the colleagues who read all or parts of the manuscript are Charles Issawi of Columbia University, Ishtiaq H. Qureshi of the University of Karachi, Alvin Z. Rubinstein of the University of Pennsylvania, George Ginsburgs of the New School of Social Research, Arnold L. Horelick of the RAND Corporation, and Carey B. Joynt and Nicholas Balabkins of Lehigh University. To all of them go my thanks for their comments, suggestions, and encouragement.

The primary responsibility for exercising a checkrein on my inclinations toward excessive enthusiasm for issues only tangentially related to the book's main theme rested with Wayland W. Schmitt. His efforts have contributed much to the coherence and readability of this volume. Thanks are also due to two fine ladies, Doris Wilkinson and Helen Farrell, for typing the manuscript.

A special word of acknowledgment must go to Professor J. C. Hurewitz of Columbia University, who has performed in the ablest possible fashion all the myriad duties associated with his position as the editor of the series of which this volume is a part. His contribution to this work cannot be adequately measured in this way alone, however, for he has been a trusted and valued source of guidance and inspiration since my student days at Columbia. A simple word of thanks is a grossly inadequate expression of my debt to him.

Finally, this volume would not have been completed without the unfailing support and encouragement of my wife who, despite her numerous obligations, has always found time to lend a helping hand. To her go my expressions of deepest gratitude and affection.

Without all this assistance the book would not have been possible. Whatever flaws remain are solely the responsibility of the author.

Oles M. Smolansky
Bethlehem, Pa.

Introduction
The Basic Goals of Khrushchev's Policies

A characteristic feature of the foreign policies of most states is overriding concern with national security coupled with a tendency to predict the probable actions of an adversary in the light of his capabilities rather than his intentions. In the case of the Soviet leaders, conditioned as they had been by fear of "capitalist encirclement" and of the "inevitable" showdown between the two systems, the advent of the "cold war" in the early post-World War II period confirmed their basic distrust of the Western powers. More particularly, the Truman Doctrine and the resulting deployment in the Mediterranean of the US Sixth Fleet, the creation of the North Atlantic Treaty Organization, and subsequent efforts to establish in the Middle East a regional defense alliance—justified though these measures may have been in the minds of the Western leaders in view of Moscow's own activities in the area—merely reinforced the "encirclement complex" that Stalin and his successors seem to have shared.

There are two basic, complementary methods of dealing with perceived threats to one's national security—military and political. Since, until the mid-1960s, the United States enjoyed a heavy nuclear preponderance over the Soviet Union, political activity aimed at undermining Western positions was the only meaningful course open to the

Kremlin. Given Stalin's caution and mistrust of the "bourgeois nationalist" leaders in the emerging nations, his efforts in this sphere were relatively modest. Nevertheless, in the Middle East, he did back Arab nationalist demands for the withdrawal of French troops from Lebanon and Syria and of British forces from Egypt, while also supporting the establishment of a Jewish state in Palestine. In so doing, Stalin contributed, though in an admittedly limited and negative fashion, to the acceleration of Western withdrawal from the area. After 1948, with the exception of the Berlin and Korean episodes, Stalin had settled down to a holding action in international affairs, devoting much of his energy and resources to the consolidation of the Soviet empire and to the building of its military and industrial potential. Without a powerful base, he knew only too well, he could never hope to challenge the Western powers, or even guarantee the security of the USSR.

To his successors, and especially Khrushchev, this lackluster but relatively effective policy appeared totally devoid of imagination. Khrushchev's subsequent criticism of Stalin's Third World policies implied that they had failed to recognize changes taking place in the underdeveloped countries and thus to exploit opportunities that offered themselves for Moscow's manipulation. He noted, for example, that many of the newly independent nations were adhering to a neutralist foreign policy that brought them into a basic clash of interests with the "imperialist" West, which was anxious to retain a measure of control over its erstwhile colonies and dependencies. Furthermore, most of the countries remaining under direct Western tutelage were engaged in a struggle for political independence which, once achieved, would also contribute to the overall weakening of the "colonialist" powers. It therefore appeared to Stalin's successors that a vast untapped reservoir of "anti-colonialist" sentiment was virtually inviting Soviet exploitation and that Moscow's political entry into the Third World would inevitably lead to a further sapping of the strength of the Western powers. This did not mean that Khrushchev and his colleagues would neglect the requirements of the Soviet military-industrial complex. Rather, *in addition* to these efforts, the Kremlin would place more emphasis than ever before on political and economic competition with the "imperialist" nations, broadening the arena to include the underdeveloped world.

In this new theater Khrushchev concentrated his attention primarily on those countries which had attained political independence and were pursuing a neutralist foreign policy. In offering them economic, financial, technical, and, occasionally, military aid, the USSR was motivated primarily by determination to curtail and, wherever possible, eliminate Western political and economic influence. Power-political considerations may initially have been reinforced by ideology or, to be more precise, by a desire to persuade the leaders of the neutralist nations that the Soviet brand of "scientific" socialism provided the only effective method of rapid industrialization and modernization for economically backward societies. It is possible that Khrushchev's long-range goal was the communization of the Third World, although his early unpleasant experiences with Moscow's ideological compatriots should have given him food for thought.

In the Middle East, Khrushchev's *Sturm und Drang* was given a significant impetus by military-strategic considerations. The creation of the Baghdad Pact, the acquisition by the United States of air bases in Turkey, Pakistan, Saudi Arabia, and North Africa (Libya, Morocco), and the subsequent deployment in Turkey and Italy of US Intermediate Range Ballistic Missiles brought most of European Russia within easy reach of American planes and rockets. It was little wonder, therefore, that Khrushchev, in late 1954-early 1955, decided to thwart Washington's plans by establishing close relations with those Arab states which had, for reasons of their own, refused to join the new regional defense alliance. Egypt, the most populous and influential Arab state, was the key to Soviet success. As it happened, Cairo's disenchantment with the West, augmented by its growing fear of Israel and by the exigencies of inter-Arab politics, provided Khrushchev with the point of entry he sought.

*THE SOVIET UNION
AND
THE ARAB EAST
UNDER KHRUSHCHEV*

PART I
POINTS OF ENTRY, 1955–1958

1
The Emergence of Nasir

In late September 1955, the West was stunned by the announcement of a Czech-Egyptian arms agreement behind whose seemingly innocuous façade most competent observers had no trouble detecting the guiding hand of the Soviet government. Until that time the overthrow of King Faruq in July 1952 and his replacement by a revolutionary junta headed by General Muhammad Nagib and Colonel Gamal 'Abd al-Nasir had not led to any dramatic improvement in relations between the two countries. On the contrary, in 1952 and 1953 Moscow had branded the new "bourgeois-nationalist" leaders of Egypt "stooges of Western imperialism."[1] Yet now the Kremlin was abruptly coming to the support of the men it had vehemently denounced as recently as November 1954.[2]

---

1. For details, see Walter Z. Laqueur, *The Soviet Union and the Middle East* (New York: Praeger, 1959), pp. 151–52.
2. For Soviet condemnation of Egypt, see V. Kudriavtsev, *Izvestiia* (henceforth referred to as *Izv.*), August 8, 1954. For more details, see *ibid.*, July 30; I. Aleksandrov, *Pravda* (henceforth referred to as *Pr.*), August 8; and Y. Bochkaryov, "The Anglo-Egyptian Agreement," *New Times* (Moscow, henceforth referred to as *NT*), no. 33 (August 14, 1954), pp. 10–13. (Articles signed by "I. Aleksandrov," "Observer" or "Commentator" are believed to be written by high government or party officials and usually reflect the official

This shift can best be understood by noting that a series of complex developments in late 1954 and early 1955 had thrown the Middle East into a state of tension and confusion that offered the USSR new opportunities. Given the rapid deterioration of relations between Egypt and the Western powers, the concurrent struggle for leadership in the Arab world, and the worsening situation along the Arab-Israeli frontiers, Khrushchev found in the region fertile ground for the application of his new doctrine toward the underdeveloped world. Although this was the period of the "thaw," the meaning of his "peace offensive" rapidly became apparent. While proclaiming its determination not to unleash a nuclear war between the superpowers, the Kremlin made clear its intention to attack the capitalist West through its "colonial backdoor." Khrushchev's offensive was bolder, more dynamic and imaginative than anything staged by Stalin, who—his occasional appeals to the colonial peoples notwithstanding—was basically concerned with the conventional East-West struggle.

Ideologically, Khrushchev's position was quite sound. Having accepted Marx's assertion that the capitalist powers had acquired wealth and power partially as a result of a ruthless exploitation of colonies and dependencies, he may well have also relied on Lenin's prophecy that the inevitable collapse of the imperialist West would be speeded up by the detachment of its colonial possessions. It all appeared quite simple: by helping the emerging nations of Asia and Africa to assert their independence, the USSR would hasten the process of Western decline. For without sources of raw materials, cheap manpower, and markets for its industrial products, the capitalist West would not be able to survive economically. It was one of those typically sweeping Khrushchevian generalizations. Never worrying about details of implementation and possible consequences, the impulsive Party Secretary plunged into the unknown in the firm belief that his reasoning was sound and that he was strong enough to deal successfully with any unforeseen contingencies.

---

viewpoint of the Soviet authorities.) For Cairo's anti-Communist attitude, see Mustafa Amin, *Akhbar al-Yawm,* May 1; and editorial, *al-Ahram* (both of Cairo), May 5, 1954. See also Nasir's interview with *Newsweek,* as quoted in the *Egyptian Gazette* (henceforth referred to as *EG*), July 21, 1954.

It may be safely assumed that, in his more optimistic moments, Khrushchev was looking forward to supplanting Western with Soviet influence in the underdeveloped world. In the meantime, however, the Kremlin would encourage and aid the bourgeois-nationalist governments of the emerging nations in reasserting their independence from the imperialist powers. In deciding upon this course of action Khrushchev supplanted the time-honored Bolshevik motto "He who is not with us is against us," with "He who is not against us is with us, at least for the time being."

While courting some of the more prominent Asian statesmen who refused to ally themselves with the Western powers for fear of getting entangled in a possible East-West conflict—including Prime Minister Nehru of India and President Sukarno of Indonesia[3]—the USSR cast an eager glance toward the Middle East. In the post-World War II period, the area's strategic importance was underscored by US determination to establish in it a network of American bases. If successful, Washington would have brought most of European Russia within easy reach of its land-based missiles and aircraft.[4] Prior to 1955, Moscow found it difficult to penetrate the Middle East because of the strong anti-Soviet views prevalent in Turkey, Iran, and Pakistan and because the power vacuum created by the post-1945 elimination of French and the diminution of British influence in the Arab East had been partially filled by the United States. Ironically, however, Washington's preoccupation with the containment of the USSR, especially its help in organizing the Baghdad Pact, provided Moscow with an opportunity to enter the region.[5] Since Nasir also objected to the

---

3. For more details, including the 1955 Khrushchev-Bulganin (then Soviet Prime Minister) journey to South Asia, see David J. Dallin, *Soviet Foreign Policy After Stalin* (Philadelphia: Lippincott, 1961), Part Three, chap. 4; and J. M. Mackintosh, *Strategy and Tactics of Soviet Foreign Policy* (London: Oxford University Press, 1963), chap. 9.

4. For a contemporary analysis, see James W. Spain, "Middle East Defense: A New Approach," *The Middle East Journal* (henceforth referred to as *MEJ*) 8, no. 3 (Summer 1954): 258–66.

5. For details, see text of Dulles's "Report on the Near and Middle East" in *The Department of State Bulletin*, no. 28 (June 15, 1953), pp. 831–35; and Mackintosh, pp. 121–22.

US-sponsored Pact, it should not have been surprising that Moscow and Cairo joined forces to try to limit its effectiveness.

During the summer of 1954, Nasir had urged the West to abstain from the establishment of a regional defense organization. Throughout the area's modern history, he explained, treaties and alliances had served primarily the interests of outside powers and were therefore considered by most Arabs to be a veiled form of Western domination.[6] The question of regional defense was closely related in the minds of the Egyptian leaders to the problems of Palestine as well as of Cairo's leadership in the Arab world. Whereas Washington was bent on creating a "position of strength" against a possible Soviet attack and relegated all other issues, including Arab-Israeli hostility, to the background, most Arab states, especially Egypt, were primarily interested in establishing an Arab regional defense pact designed to discourage a possible Israeli aggression.[7] In any event, Nasir must have realized that in case of World War III the West was bound to protect the Middle East, thought vital because of its strategic position and natural resources, regardless of whether or not the countries of the area belonged to any defense organization. Furthermore, the fact that the Western powers encouraged Egypt's main rival for leadership in the Arab world, Iraq, to join the proposed defense alliance in the Middle East merely reinforced Nasir's determination to oppose the Pact.

Moscow, which alleged that the 1953 change of administration in Washington had strengthened American determination to establish in the Middle East an aggressive military pact directed against the USSR,[8] had already denounced the political, cultural, and military cooperation agreement signed by Turkey and Pakistan in 1954.[9] The Kremlin used that same opportunity to warn the Arabs that

    6. As quoted in the *New York Times* (henceforth referred to as *NYT*) September 3, 1954.
    7. For a solid analysis of Nasir's motivations, see Tom Little, *Egypt* (London: Benn, 1958), pp. 261–63.
    8. See O. Orestov, *Pr.,* September 27, 1953.
    9. See *Trud* (Moscow), February 20; Observer, *Izv.,* February 27; and the text of Soviet note to Turkey in *Pr.,* March 21, 1954.

the accord offered "unmistakable evidence that . . . the Pentagon plans to bring . . . [the Arab] countries under U.S. occupation and convert them into American bridgeheads." Needless to say, it rejected as unfounded allegations concerning a "Soviet threat" and "Communist danger" to the Middle East: the Arabs knew full well that the USSR was their trustworthy and reliable friend.[10]

Making similar criticisms of the Iraqi-Turkish treaty (February 24, 1955), Moscow promised not to "remain idle at a time when aggressive military alliances are being organized along the southern frontiers of the Soviet Union."[11] Soviet intentions to take positive action to counterbalance Washington's recent gains in the Middle East were reiterated on April 16, 1955, in the form of a "Statement by USSR Ministry of Foreign Affairs on Security in the Near and Middle East."[12] That document accused the imperialist powers of disregarding the true national interests of the Middle Eastern countries, claiming that the West aimed only at the political and economic enslavement of the region. The Soviet Union, in contrast, "from its very inception has resolutely condemned the imperialist policy of aggression and colonial oppression." For this reason, the statement continued, Moscow's policy corresponded to the basic national interests of the states of the Middle East and enjoyed the sympathy and support of the region's peoples.

The Kremlin agreed that a threat to the security of the Middle East existed but alleged that it came from the powers organizing military pacts and not from the Soviet Union. Since the formation of blocs and the creation of foreign military bases in the Middle East had a direct bearing on the security of the USSR, the Soviet government could not "remain indifferent" to these activities. Therefore, and supposedly with a view to decreasing tension, Moscow announced its determination to "develop peaceful cooperation" with all states of the Middle

10. Observer, "Friend of Small Nations," *NT,* no. 17 (April 24, 1954), pp. 5, 7; and G. Akopian, *Izv.,* April 16, 1954.
11. V. Medvedev, *Pr.,* February 27, 1955. For more details, see "Turetsko-Irakskii dogovor," *Mezhdunarodnaia Zhizn'* (Moscow), April 1955, pp. 116–17.
12. Text in *Pr.,* April 17, 1955.

East interested in "strengthen[ing their] national independence" and invited them to approach the USSR with requests for aid: "The Soviet government will take positive action toward any steps by the governments of the Near and Middle Eastern countries to strengthen the national independence of their states and to promote peace and friendly cooperation among nations."

The April 1955 Statement was a landmark in the history of Soviet-Arab relations because, in addition to expressing Moscow's anxiety over the turn of events in the Middle East, it marked the official abandonment of the policy of relative noninvolvement in the affairs of the Arab East. Spurred by Khrushchev's desire to challenge the West in the underdeveloped world and, in the particular instance of the Middle East, alarmed by the success of US Secretary of State John Foster Dulles's policy of creating a regional defense alliance, the Kremlin discarded earlier reserve and plunged into Middle Eastern politics.

The arms deal between Egypt and Czechoslovakia was merely the most dramatic outgrowth of this basic change in strategy. From Cairo's viewpoint, the Baghdad Pact was a particularly unwelcome and even dangerous development: as Iraq's prestige rose in the wake of its decision to side with the West, Egypt's political fortunes correspondingly declined. A dramatic counterstroke designed, among other things, to rekindle the enthusiasm and admiration of the Arab masses became one of Egypt's immediate priorities, and a massive guarantee of up-to-date weapons was the most logical solution to this problem of prestige. Furthermore, two other compelling reasons favored the establishment of closer contacts with the USSR.

One was the apparent success of the policy of positive neutralism practiced by some of Nasir's friends and political allies in the underdeveloped world, among them Nehru and Sukarno, as well as Yugoslavia's President Tito. In mid-February 1955, both Nehru and Tito visited Egypt. In a joint communiqué issued at the conclusion of their talks, the Indian and Egyptian Premiers reiterated their conviction that military alliances and power entanglements did not add to the security of any country but, on the contrary, tended to foster rivalries and increase tension.[13] Both voiced opposition to the Baghdad Pact, probably for fear that their respective rivals—Iraq and Pakistan—would be significantly strengthened through cooperation with the Western powers. Their mutual interest on this point was reinforced on the Egyptian side by Nasir's desire to lend more moral weight to Cairo's demands for "total emancipation" of the Arabs by couching them in terms of Nehru's political philosophy. Nasir's admiration for the Indian Premier, a statesman who had gained his country's independence by peaceful means and who then proceeded to make it one of Asia's most powerful and respected states, further facilitated close ties between Egypt and India. And both Nehru and Tito must have pointed out to Nasir that possible exploitation of the East-West rivalry for one's own purposes was, in the long run, more rewarding (both militarily and economically) than close association with either power bloc. In any event, adoption of "positive neutralism" required a degree of normalization of relations with the USSR and its allies and served as an additional impetus for accepting the Soviet aid offer.

Nasir's decision to espouse neutralism received added support when he attended the conference of Asian and African states held at Bandung (Indonesia) in April 1955. The respect and deference with which he was treated by a number of Asia's leading statesmen, including Chinese Foreign Minister Chou En-lai, strengthened his belief that, by securing Communist support for Egypt's claim of leadership in the Arab world, he could improve Cairo's bargaining position *vis-à-vis* the West. He seems to have underestimated the dangers inherent in playing one power bloc against another. Judging by his policies in late 1955–1956, Nasir apparently believed that if Egypt established and strengthened its ties with the East, this very act would produce offers of assistance from the West that would not otherwise be available.

The second factor influencing Nasir's decision to accept the Soviet aid offer was his alarm at Israel's apparent military superiority, combined with the West's reluctance to supply Egypt with modern weapons. After an Israeli force attacked and destroyed the Gaza garrison

---

13. *Chronology of International Events and Documents, 1955* (London: Chatham House), p. 112.

headquarters of the Egyptian army on February 28, 1955, killing 38 men, Nasir, too weak to retaliate militarily and open to criticism that his regime was incapable of bolstering the strength of the armed forces, turned to the Western powers with a request for weapons. With the exception of two destroyers purchased from Great Britain in July 1955, Cairo's petitions fell on deaf ears. Though the West was not unwilling to negotiate, it attached conditions that, in the view of Colonel Anwar al-Sadat (then one of Nasir's closest associates and a member of the Revolutionary Council), would have placed Egypt under Western military, economic, and political control. The United States in particular insisted on sending military missions "in an aim to place the Egyptian armed forces under American control."[14]

As a result of these pressures, Nasir, sometime during the first half of 1955, approached the USSR with a request for large-scale military assistance.[15] On September 27, 1955, he announced the signing of the Egyptian-Czech military and technical assistance agreement.[16] Although the pact was extended twice, in March and June 1956, its terms have never been disclosed. It is generally believed that Egypt received heavy armament valued at approximately $225 to 250 million, mainly on credit against future cotton shipments.[17]

14. *Al-Gumhuriya* (Cairo), October 18, 1955.
15. According to *The Baghdad Pact*, a memorandum by the Information Department of the Royal Institute of International Affairs (as quoted in Mackintosh, p. 123), Nasir told the US Ambassador in June 1955 that he had contacted the USSR concerning the arms purchase from Russia. According to a Soviet source, the initial Czech-Egyptian arms deal was concluded in February 1955 (K. Ivanov, "National-Liberation Movement and Non-Capitalist Path of Development," *International Affairs*, no. 5 (May 1965), p. 61), while Muhammad Hasanayn Haykal, editor of *al-Ahram*, claimed subsequently that it was initiated in May (*al-Ahram*, April 14, 1967). For an interesting account of the background of the arms deal, see Uri Ra'anan, *The USSR Arms the Third World: Case Studies in Soviet Foreign Policy* (Cambridge: The M.I.T. Press, 1969), Part I.
16. On July 26, 1956, Nasir revealed what most observers suspected all along: the deal was made between Egypt and the USSR, not Czechoslovakia (Mackintosh, p. 123, n. 1). For tactical reasons, the Kremlin initially refused to take the credit.
17. Estimates of the total amount vary, depending on valuation ascribed to the military goods, considered by some as totaling over $400 million. Under the terms of the agreement Cairo was to obtain Soviet MIG 15 and 17 jet

The Western powers, with exceptional bitterness, accused Egypt and the USSR of a deliberate breach of the carefully balanced arms shipment schedule to the Middle East worked out by Western experts. Both countries were suspected of aggressive designs, with Egypt serving as a Soviet puppet. Cairo countered these charges by asserting that the USSR was the only great power willing to satisfy its requirements and that, being an independent and sovereign state, Egypt was free to shape its foreign and trade policies in its own interests. Agreements with Communist countries were concluded on the basis of mutual advantage, meant an end to "foreign" (i.e., British) control, and did not signify the beginning of Cairo's dependence on the USSR. On the contrary, a strong and independent Egypt would not tolerate foreign control or yield to foreign pressure but would be better able to defend its freedom and independence.[18] Accusations concerning an alleged breach in the area's balance of power were also dismissed by the Egyptian Premier, who argued that the Western powers were not concerned with a "true balance of power" or "true peace" and that the entire concept of the balance of power in the Middle East was but another "trick" designed to keep the Arabs under imperialist control.[19]

In its statement of October 1, the Soviet Foreign Ministry said that various Middle Eastern states, notably Egypt, had recently been pressured to purchase arms from the Western powers. Cairo, it went on, regarded such pressure as "intolerable interference, damaging to Egypt's national independence and its rightful interest in defense." Moscow held that each country had the right to defend itself and to purchase arms for its defense from other states on a normal commercial basis. No government had the right "to make unilateral demands

---

fighters, Iliushin 28 jet bombers, medium and heavy tanks, artillery, submarines, torpedo boats, two destroyers, and ammunition. Under the technical aid program members of the Egyptian armed forces were to undergo training in Poland and Czechoslovakia while numerous Soviet and satellite military missions were to work in Egypt. 85th Congress. The Senate. Document no. 52, *Foreign Aid Program*, p. 724.

18. As quoted in *Pr.*, September 29, 1955.
19. *Al-Gumhuriya*, October 3, 1955. See also Anwar Sadat in *ibid.*, September 30, 1955.

2
The Suez Crisis*

The agreement by means of which the USSR had entered the Middle East may have made Cairo dependent on the Soviet Union for keeping its armed forces supplied with up-to-date weapons and essential spare parts as well as the expertise in using them, but it did not transform Egypt into a Soviet satellite or create a unity of long-range interests between the two states. Their objectives coincided only to the extent that both, for reasons of their own, wished to curtail Western influence in the Middle East. In terms of the regional politics of that time, the arms deal constituted a major short-run success for Khrushchev's policy while also enabling Nasir to assert his independence from the Western powers, but, at the same time, it set into motion a process of action and counteraction that soon threatened to destroy Egypt's Premier. Thus Moscow was placed in the unenviable position of having to choose between annulling its recent gains in the Arab East and risking a nuclear war with the United States.

The year following the conclusion of the Soviet-Egyptian military and technical aid agreement was one of the most critical in the turbu-

---

*Parts of this chapter are based on my "Moscow and the Suez Crisis, 1956: A Reappraisal," *Political Science Quarterly* 80, no.4 (December 1965): 581–605. Reprinted by permission of the publisher.

lent modern history of the Middle East. It was marked by the abortive British attempts to induce Jordan to join the Baghdad Pact; Egypt's pursuit of an independent course in international politics while it strengthened its hold on its Arab allies (Syria, Saudi Arabia, Yemen) and pressured "inter-Arab neutrals" (Lebanon, Jordan) to join its camp; mounting Arab-Israeli tension; Cairo's recognition of Communist China in response to alleged Western plans to arm Israel; Western retaliation in the form of withdrawal of the offer to finance the construction of the Aswan High Dam, and Egyptian retaliation in the form of the nationalization of the Suez Canal Company. These are merely highlights of the drama that unfolded in an area sorely torn by big-power rivalry and intra-regional disputes.

Tension was also evident in relations between the USSR and Egypt. A clear instance is their response to the Washington Declaration. After President Dwight D. Eisenhower and British Prime Minister Anthony Eden had met in Washington in early 1956, both their governments expressed concern about the growing tension in the Arab East and mentioned the possibility of dispatching British and American troops to guard the Arab-Israeli borders. Although this position was, as might have been expected, strongly criticized in both Moscow and Cairo, their respective reactions illustrate both the Soviet Union's attempts to win Western recognition of its status as a great power with legitimate interests in the Middle East and the lack of more than a superficial identity of interests between Egypt and the USSR.

The Soviet Foreign Ministry declared on February 13, 1956, that the Washington Declaration "constituted a threat to peace and security in the Near and Middle East and ... violated the independence and sovereignty" of the states involved. Commenting on the possible dispatch of Western troops to the Middle East "without the consent of the interested countries and without the sanction of the UN Security Council," the Kremlin warned that "any action leading to complications in the area of the Near and Middle East and to an increase of tension in that area is bound to be the subject of legitimate concern on the part of the Soviet government."[1] Cairo's reaction to

---

1. Text in *Izv.*, February 14, 1956.

this statement was, in contrast, curiously cautious. Most major Egyptian newspapers appeared with headlines such as: "Soviet Union warns Western powers not to meddle in the Middle Eastern affairs and not to send troops there without Security Council's approval," and "Soviet Union accuses England and America of creating threat to peace in the Middle East."[2] One looks in vain for editorial comment on the controversy.

When clashes along the Arab-Israeli frontiers prompted the UN Security Council, in early April 1956, to dispatch Secretary-General Dag Hammarskjöld to the troubled area to survey the situation and to suggest ways and means to alleviate it, the Arab governments expressed their willingness to support the Secretary-General in every possible way and warned Israel to take its "last chance" and reduce tension because the Arabs would no longer tolerate Tel-Aviv's transgressions.[3] The Soviet Union again used this opportunity to warn the West not to intervene militarily in the affairs of the Middle East while admonishing the Arabs to beware of "imperialist intrigues." A Foreign Ministry statement of April 17, 1956 described the rising Arab-Israeli tension as "one of the most dangerous [recent] developments" in the area. Moscow asserted that the trouble was fomented by the Western powers, which intended to utilize the confrontation between Tel-Aviv and its Arab neighbors as an excuse for stationing their troops in the Middle East.

Moscow not only pledged itself as prepared to render the necessary support to those UN measures which were designed to strengthen peace in the area but called upon the parties concerned to refrain from any moves that might lead to an "exacerbation of the situation and to make the necessary efforts to alleviate the difficult position of hundreds of thousands of Arab refugees deprived of their homes and means of subsistence." (This was the first time that Moscow expressed official concern for the fate of the Palestinian refugees. The problem had been conveniently overlooked in the period between 1948 and 1956.) Finally, the Kremlin stressed the need

2. *Al-Gumhuriya* and *al-Ahram,* February 15, 1956, respectively.
3. Editorial, *al-Ahram,* April 5, 1956.

for settlement of the Palestine problem by respecting the "just national interests of the parties concerned."⁴

The allusion to the "just national interests" of Israel was bound to come as a shock to the Egyptian authorities. In issuing such a statement Moscow was indicating that close cooperation with the neutralist Arab states was not tantamount to an unequivocal Soviet espousal of the Arab nationalist cause. It is not surprising that Cairo's attitude was very cool and noncommittal. Some important newspapers, such as *al-Ahram* and *al-Gumhuriya*, published no editorial comment, while *al-Akhbar* cautiously mentioned that the statement might have a "far-reaching effect" without specifying what that meant.⁵

The Soviet moves of early 1956 and the Egyptian reaction to them refuted the assumption, widely held in the West at the time, that Cairo and Moscow had formed an alliance based on an identity of Soviet-Egyptian interests. Unfortunately, the West had by that time been affected by Egypt's belligerent propaganda campaign: attempts to prompt Washington, London, and Paris to extend Nasir their full diplomatic, economic, and military support, accompanied by reports of a continuous flow of Russian arms to Egypt and Syria, led to a sharp deterioration of Cairo's relations with the Western powers. When, in early May, news flashed across the front pages of the Arab press that a joint Anglo-French-US commission was meeting in Washington to discuss arms shipments to the Middle East, a "responsible Egyptian source" asserted that the Western powers were working out a plan "to make Israel superior in arms to all Arab countries put together."⁶

On May 16, the Egyptian government, in an obvious attempt to retaliate for what it considered growing Western pressure, recognized Communist China. This was hardly a surprising move—for over two years the Egyptian press had periodically pointed to the advantages that could be secured from such recognition⁷—and though Dulles

---

4. Text in *Pr.,* April 18, 1956.
5. As quoted in *EG,* April 19, 1956.
6. *Ibid.,* May 10, 1956.
7. For example, *al-Misri* (Cairo) of February 20, 1954, advised the Egyptian government to recognize Peking. Cairo, it was held, stood to benefit most

termed it a "regrettable action," it was widely hailed in both the Egyptian and Soviet press. *Al-Gumhuriya* declared that in recognizing Peking the Egyptian government was not only admitting a reality but also choosing its friends. The Arabs wanted friends who did not conspire against them and who did not export arms to Israel on the pretext of establishing a balance of power in the Middle East.[8] Soviet publications argued that this "bold action" was not only in conformity with the interests of all peoples of the East but would also strengthen the cause of combating imperialism.[9]

Throughout the summer of 1956, relations between Egypt and the Western powers continued to deteriorate. Finally, on July 19 and 21 respectively, the United States and Great Britain announced the termination of their offer to finance the construction of the first stage of Egypt's gigantic Aswan High Dam.[10] On July 26, the newly elected President of the Egyptian Republic, using harsh and violent language, announced the nationalization of the Suez Canal Company. The revenues collected henceforth would help defray the costs of the construction of the Aswan High Dam.[11]

On the day of his momentous announcement, Nasir reached the height of his glory. To millions of his enthusiastic followers he was the symbol of the Arab ability to deal with the Western powers on a basis of equality, even though Egypt was obviously inferior to them in terms of physical power. While it is safe to assume that the enthusi-

---

from the establishment of normal diplomatic and trade relations with China. Ihsan 'Abd al-Quddus in *Ruz al-Yusif* (Cairo) came to a similar conclusion. As quoted in *Pr.*, February 20, and September 7, 1954, respectively.

8. Editorial, *al-Gumhuriya*, May 17, 1956.

9. S. Kondrashov, *Izv.*, May 25, 1956.

10. A joint US-British offer to help finance the High Dam was made in December 1955, in an attempt to offset the effect of the Moscow-Cairo arms deal and to prevent further Soviet penetration of the Arab East.

11. During Soviet Foreign Minister Dmitrii Shepilov's June 1956 visit to Egypt a rumor spread that the Kremlin had offered to finance the building of the High Dam. Whether true or false, the rumor was regarded in Washington as political blackmail. In addition, Dulles did not think that Moscow was capable of shouldering the financial burden. For details, see Wilton Wynn, *Nasser of Egypt: The Search for Dignity* (Cambridge: Arlington Books, 1959), p. 159.

asm of the Arab masses was not shared by heads of the other Arab states, the Soviet government expressed its appreciation of his motives and offered its full support. Khrushchev declared that "nothing illegal has occurred," that the Suez Canal, situated in Egypt and built by Egyptian laborers, was an Egyptian property. He emphasized the Kremlin's interest in maintaining freedom of navigation in the Canal but noted that, with Cairo's expressed willingness to keep the waterway open, there were no grounds for concern. "We are convinced," Khrushchev continued, "that the situation in the Suez Canal zone will not become tense unless it is artificially aggravated from the outside." He concluded by saying that "the question of the Suez Canal can and must be regulated by peaceful means."[12] Although strategy and tactics were still to be worked out, Khrushchev's statement might be considered the basis of Soviet policy in the Suez crisis: interested in increasing the tension in the Arab East since it would inevitably lead to further deterioration of Western influence and prestige, the Soviet government was at the same time opposed to a war in the Middle East in which it might become involved. Moscow was not prepared to risk its own annihilation for the sake of Nasir.

Great Britain and France considered the expropriation of the Canal Company the culminating point in Nasir's drive to destroy Western interests in the Arab East. Although economic considerations, connected mainly with worries about insuring an uninterrupted flow of Arab oil to West European industry centers, were of utmost importance, the whole atmosphere was charged with emotions that could not be explained exclusively in economic terms.

It was obvious from the outset that two courses of action were open to the Western powers. Provided a unanimity of opinion prevailed among them, they could either acquiesce in the nationalization of the Company and attempt to work out a mutually acceptable compromise, based on equitable compensation of the shareholders and a guarantee of the freedom of navigation in the Suez Canal to replace the 1888 Convention,[13] or they could attempt to impose on Egypt (by

12. *Pr.,* August 1, 1956.
13. An international document guaranteeing free navigation in the Suez

force, if necessary) a solution that, because of the loss of prestige involved, would eventually lead to the elimination of Nasir. Britain and France chose to adhere to the second alternative. All subsequent developments—such as the first London conference of the Canal users, with the ensuing mission to Cairo of a delegation headed by Australian Prime Minister Robert G. Menzies; Secretary Dulles's plan for a Canal Users' Association, presented and discussed at the second London conference; the UN Security Council deliberations; and, finally, the war itself—can be seen in their proper perspective only in the light of these considerations.

The official Soviet reaction to the proposed London conference came in a statement issued on August 9, 1956. Moscow insisted that the Western powers could object to the nationalization only if Cairo refused to reimburse the Company's shareholders or interfered with the freedom of navigation in the waterway in violation of the 1888 Convention. Since President Nasir had carefully refrained from any such actions, Washington and its allies, in fact, had no legal case. The reasons for Western dissatisfaction and alarm were therefore political rather than legal: fearful of losing their influence in the Arab East, the United States, Great Britain, and France had applied economic sanctions against Egypt and staged a calculated display of force in the Eastern Mediterranean. These actions, coupled with the summoning of the London conference of Canal users, were described as clear violations of the UN Charter.

Although the Western allies called the conference without prior consultation with Russia and other signatories of the 1888 Convention, Moscow agreed to attend the "imperialist-dominated" London conference on condition that participation did not impose on the USSR "any limitations or obligations which might harm the sovereign rights of Egypt."[14] It could be argued that Russia intended to protect Cairo's "sovereign rights and dignity": both countries certainly

---

Canal, signed on October 29, 1888, by Austria-Hungary, France, Germany, Great Britain, Italy, the Netherlands, the Ottoman Empire, Russia, and Spain. Text in J. C. Hurewitz, *Diplomacy in the Near and Middle East* (Princeton: Van Nostrand, 1956), 1: 202–5.

14. Text in *Pr.*, August 10, 1956. For additional information, see the Soviet press of late July-August, 1956.

shared the view that Great Britain, France, and the United States were deliberately confusing the issue of nationalization of the Suez Canal Company with the problem of freedom of navigation in the waterway and that the London conference constituted a means of generating pressure that the Western allies intended to exert on Egypt to force upon it international control over the Suez Canal.[15] This should not, however, obscure the fact that Russia's actions were aimed primarily at furthering its own interests, which did not always coincide with those of Cairo. Nasir flatly refused to participate in the conference and temporarily favored United Nations discussion of the crisis, an idea for which the USSR showed no enthusiasm.[16]

Moscow used the first London conference of twenty-two states (August 16–23, 1956) as an international forum to blast the "atavistic colonial practices" of the Western powers and to pledge its full support to Nasir and Arab nationalism. *Pravda* denounced the plan adopted by eighteen nations, which provided for the operation of the Suez Canal by an international board, because it "contradicted the principles of the United Nations and the basic tenets of international law." The USSR objected to the assertion that "a part of Egypt's territory on which the Suez Canal is situated can be regarded as territory to which Egypt's sovereign rights do not extend."[17] In contrast, the Indian plan calling for an international advisory board to help Cairo run the Canal did not violate Egyptian sovereignty and was based on the principle of noninterference in the country's internal affairs.[18] Throughout the proceedings Soviet Foreign Minister Dmitrii Shepilov justified Nasir's right to nationalize the Suez Canal Company and warned the Western powers not to use force, for an aggression on their part might lead to "a serious conflict which would encompass the whole of the Near and Middle East and, perhaps, go even further."[19]

15. Egyptian position explained in editorial, *al-Ahram,* August 13, 1956.
16. For details, see Nasir's press-conference communiqué of August 12 (text in *ibid.*) and editorials, *ibid.,* August 6; and *EG,* August 7, 1956.
17. Editorial, August 19, 1956. See also editorial, *Izv.,* August 25, 1956.
18. Editorial, *Pr.,* August 26, 1956.
19. Shepilov's speeches of August 16 and 21, in *ibid.,* August 18 and 22, 1956, respectively.

After the conference had dispatched to Cairo a subcommittee headed by Australian Premier Menzies, the Soviet government, on August 28, issued a statement designed to back President Nasir in his rejection of the initial plan. The USSR, after a "careful study of all pertinent documents," concluded that any settlement of the Suez question in accordance with the principles of the United Nations must be based on respect for the sovereign rights of Egypt. The latter, in turn, must guarantee freedom of navigation in the Canal "at all times and to all countries using [it]." This Soviet phraseology was of considerable importance—Moscow managed simultaneously to intervene on behalf of seemingly unconditional freedom of navigation in the Suez Canal while indirectly approving the continuation of the ban on Israeli ships. This was achieved by the specification of "all countries using the Canal," thus eliminating Israel.[20]

The Menzies mission was seen by Russia as a deliberate provocation, designed to bring about Egyptian rejection. Cairo would then be accused of intractability, leaving the Western allies free to take "subsequent aggressive actions."[21] The Soviet government, "alarmed" at the reported massive concentration of British and French troops in the Eastern Mediterranean, warned the Western powers that "preparations for military intervention in the internal affairs of Egypt represent an open and intolerable challenge to the peace-loving Egyptian people, to all peoples of the East, and to the cause of peace."[22] Any military action, Moscow repeated, would entail "serious international complications."[23]

The second London conference, convened in mid-September 1956 and attended by eighteen states, set up the stillborn Suez Canal Users' Association (SCUA), originally intended to operate the Canal. Moscow described the Association as an "imperialist plot" designed to ap-

20. Text in D. T. Shepilov, *Suetskii vopros* (Moscow: Gospolitizdat, 1956), appendix IV.
21. Editorial, *Pr.*, August 26, 1956. See also V. Medvedev, *ibid.*, September 3, 1956.
22. Editorial, *ibid.*, August 26, 1956.
23. V. Kuznetsov, *ibid.*, September 8, 1956.

ply political and economic pressure on Egypt.[24] In addition to this moral and political support, the USSR dispatched a number of Russian and satellite pilots to help fill the gap left after the departure of most Suez Canal pilots.[25] On September 23, Great Britain and France, obviously disappointed with the results of the conference, announced their decision to take the Suez Canal issue to the UN Security Council.[26]

By that time, the Soviet government had become seriously alarmed at the possibility of a Western military intervention in Egypt. London, Paris, and Washington had demonstrated their "predatory intentions" by freezing Egyptian capital and assets, by withdrawing the Canal pilots, and by massing troops in the Eastern Mediterranean. In its September 16, 1956, "Declaration Concerning Peaceful Settlement of the Suez Question,"[27] Moscow described these measures as "dangerous provocations intended further to aggravate the situation." Freedom of navigation in the Suez Canal must be guaranteed, but only by peaceful means, in a conference attended by both Cairo and all the Canal users. Should this well-meant advice go unheeded, however, the USSR would not stand aside because an "aggression in the area of the Near and Middle East touches on the security of the Soviet Union." Similar sentiments were expressed throughout September and most of October. Premier Bulganin in his letters to Eden and French Prime Minister Guy Mollet warned that the USSR, "as a great power which is interested in the maintenance of peace cannot stand aside from this question."[28]

Fears of a concerted Western action in the Middle East were again evident in Soviet comments on the October, 1956, Security Council deliberations. Moscow emphasized the basic unity of purpose between Washington, London, and Paris. *Pravda* dismissed allegations con-

---

24. V. Nekrasov, *ibid.*, September 22, 1956. See also Observer, "Common Sense Must Triumph," *NT*, no. 40 (September 27, 1956), pp. 7–9.
25. A. Bozhenko, *Krasnaia Zvezda* (Moscow), September 20, 1956.
26. *MEJ* 11, no. 1 (Winter 1957): 65.
27. Text in *Izv.*, September 17, 1956.
28. Letters dated September 11, 28, and October 23, 1956. Texts in *ibid.*, April 23, 1957.

cerning the "growing rift" between the United States and its allies: "The very first day of the Security Council's work showed that there were no significant differences between the positions of the United States, Great Britain, and France" as displayed by US support of the joint Anglo-French draft resolution of October 5.[29] This led to the conclusion that "the position of the ruling circles in the United States gives no evidence of a 'peaceful' and 'just' approach to the solution of the Suez problem."[30] In contrast, the "peace-loving socialist camp" offered the Arabs "disinterested and invaluable" assistance in their struggle for complete independence.[31]

Cautious optimism prevailed at the conclusion of the Security Council deliberations, because Great Britain, France, and Egypt were expected, at the end of the month, to resume negotiations presided over by Secretary-General Dag Hammarskjöld. Instead, on October 29, 1956, Israel attacked Egypt. Then, disregarding the recommendations of the Security Council and a 64-to-5 resolution of the General Assembly (November 2, 1956) that demanded an immediate cease-fire, the withdrawal of Israeli troops from Sinai, and a general embargo on the entry of military goods into the area, Great Britain and France, at dawn on November 5, 1956, landed troops in Egypt.[32]

29. The draft resolution asked the Council, among other things, to condemn the nationalization of the Suez Canal Company as a violation of Egypt's international obligations, and to pressure Cairo into negotiations on the basis of the London proposals for international control of the waterway. *NYT,* October 6, 1956.
30. October 8, 1956.
31. Editorial, *Pr.,* October 16, 1956.
32. For more information on these events, see John C. Campbell, *Defense of the Middle East* (New York: Praeger, 1960); E. N. Dzelepy, *Le Complot de Suez* (Paris: Les éditions politiques, 1957); P. Johnson, *The Suez War* (London: Pan Books, 1957); Dwight D. Eisenhower, *Waging Peace, 1956–1961* (New York: Heinemann, 1966); Herman Finer, *Dulles over Suez* (Chicago: Triangle Books, 1964); Kenneth Love, *Suez: The Twice Fought War* (New York: McGraw-Hill, 1969); Terrence Robertson, *Crisis: The Inside Story of the Suez Conspiracy* (New York: Atheneum, 1965); Hugh Thomas, *Suez* (New York: Harper, 1966); and Anthony Nutting, *No End of a Lesson* (New York: Potter, 1967). See also Alfred M. Lilienthal, *There Goes the Middle East* (New York: Devin-Adair, 1957); Guy Wint and Peter Calvocoressi, *Middle East Crisis* (London: Penguin Books, 1957); M. and S. Bromberger, *Secrets of Suez* (London: Pan Books, 1957); Peter Calvocoressi, *Suez: Ten Years Later* (New York: Pantheon Books, 1966).

Invasion was preceded by aerial bombardment of Egyptian military targets, which lasted several days.

Moscow's propaganda organs reacted violently to the news of the Israeli attack and the Anglo-French ultimatum of October 31 ordering the belligerents to cease hostilities and withdraw behind a ten-mile zone on both sides of the Canal. In a statement published in *Pravda* on November 1, the Russians accused Eden, Mollet, and Israeli Premier Ben-Gurion of collusion and premeditated aggression against Egypt. The attack, it was argued subsequently, was conceived "with the object of crushing the national-liberation movement of the Arab peoples" and was intended "to restore the colonial system throughout the Middle East and North Africa."[33] The USSR held London, Paris, and Tel-Aviv fully responsible for the "dangerous consequences which may result from [their] aggressive actions."[34] On November 1, one day after units of the British and French air forces began bombing Egyptian targets, Bulganin appealed to Nehru while Soviet President Klimentii Voroshilov asked Sukarno to mobilize the Bandung nations behind a political offensive to reinstate peace in Egypt. In the United Nations Moscow supported the US-sponsored draft resolution adopted by the Special Session of the General Assembly on November 2. Two days later, the USSR protested to Great Britain and France against closing the Eastern Mediterranean and the northern Red Sea to commercial shipping.[35]

The Soviet government seized the initiative only on November 5, dispatching the famous messages to the heads of state of the United States, Great Britain, France, and Israel, as well as to the President of the Security Council.[36]

Shepilov's cablegram to the latter suggested that Great Britain and

33. Y. Bochkaryov, "Fruits of Folly," *NT,* no. 48 (November 22, 1956), p. 3.
34. *Pr.,* November 1, 1956. For more details, see editorials, *ibid.* and *Izv.,* of the next day.
35. *Pr.,* November 5, 1956.
36. Texts of Bulganin's messages to Eisenhower, Eden, Mollet, and Ben-Gurion in *ibid.,* November 6, 1956. Text of Shepilov's cablegram to the President of the Security Council in Department of State, *United States Policy in the Middle East, September 1956–July 1957* (Washington: Department of State Publication 6505, Middle Eastern Series 25, 1957), pp. 169–71.

France be requested to order a cease-fire within the next 12 hours and that, if they refused, a joint Soviet-American force be dispatched to end the war in Egypt. Bulganin's letters to Eden, Mollet, and Ben-Gurion declared that Moscow was "fully resolved to use force to crush the aggressors and to restore peace in the Middle East." While Israel was threatened with outright annihilation, the messages to the United Kingdom and France contained a veiled threat to use nuclear weapons against London and Paris in case of their noncompliance with UN resolutions demanding an immediate cease-fire and the withdrawal of foreign troops from Egypt. The letter to President Eisenhower was of a distinctly different character. Premier Bulganin proposed a joint Soviet-American armed intervention against the United Kingdom, France, and Israel—an idea that was instantly rejected by the United States in a strongly worded statement. Washington not only declined to participate in an anti-allied military venture but threatened nuclear retaliation in the event of an attack on London or Paris.

By this time Great Britain and France were exposed to a variety of pressures that they could not hope to withstand for any protracted period of time. Both superpowers threatened reprisals: Washington privately warned of economic sanctions at the time when all Western Europe was faced with an acute oil shortage, while the USSR hinted at the possibility of subjecting London and Paris to a nuclear attack. In addition, the British government was confronted with an increasing opposition in the parliament and criticism in the press. Various members of the Commonwealth openly condemned the invasion of Egypt. The same was true of world public opinion, as evidenced by the General Assembly votes. Faced with almost complete isolation, Eden and Mollet, on November 6, ordered their troops to cease fire and stop their advance along the Suez Canal.

On November 11, the Soviet government expressed its satisfaction with the cease-fire but warned Great Britain and France that, should hostilities be resumed, "the Soviet Union will not prevent the departure of Soviet citizens—volunteers—who wish to participate in the struggle of the Egyptian people for its independence."[37]

37. Text in *Pr.*, November 11, 1956. This was not the first time the subject

It is not easy to evaluate Soviet moves during the military phase of the Suez dispute, but it appears that in the period between October 29 and November 5—in other words, during the *eight* days embracing the Israeli invasion and occupation of the entire Sinai peninsula, the Anglo-French ultimatum of October 30, the bombardment of Egyptian military installations by British and French air force units, the UN General Assembly resolution of November 2 and the Anglo-French refusal to comply, the resolution of November 4 for the dispatch of a UN force into the area, and, finally, the actual landing of the British and French troops on Egyptian territory—the USSR government was unwilling to commit itself in any way to the active defense of Cairo. The TASS statement of October 30, Bulganin's and Voroshilov's letters to Nehru and Sukarno, and Moscow's support of the UN resolution to dispatch an emergency force to the Middle East were merely routine moves without any material significance.

It has been argued that the USSR failed to take a strong stand in Egypt because of its concerted drive to crush the Hungarian revolution. The backbone of the resistance appeared broken by November 5, only then allowing Moscow to transfer its attention to the Suez war.[38] But this view fails to take into account that throughout the Suez crisis Soviet freedom of action was profoundly limited by the position of the United States which, in the last analysis, was the only great power able to influence the outcome of the conflict. Given its over-

---

of "volunteers" had come up. On August 23, at a reception held in the Rumanian Embassy in Moscow, Khrushchev threatened the use of "volunteers" in case of an attack on Egypt. The remark was not reported in the Soviet press but was reproduced in Cairo. See J. M. Mackintosh, *Strategy and Tactics of Soviet Foreign Policy* (London: Oxford University Press, 1963), p. 186.

38. See Mackintosh, p. 187. As noted by David Dallin in *Soviet Foreign Policy After Stalin* (Philadelphia: Lippincott, 1961), p. 414: "To 'expose' the enemies of Egyptian independence while at the same time suppressing a popular movement for independence in the heart of Europe; to call for United Nations action against the 'aggressors' in North Africa while barring the United Nations from Hungary; to advocate a 'peaceful solution' of international conflicts while solving its own international problems by means of battalions and tanks—this was more than even the cynical climate of world politics could tolerate. Russia in Hungary paralyzed Russia in Egypt."

whelming preponderance of military and economic power over all other countries, including the USSR, an American decision to oppose the tripartite invasion of Egypt would be quite sufficient to tip the scales in favor of President Nasir. Moscow must have been well aware of that and was not prepared to move until it could be quite certain of Washington's attitude toward both the Hungarian and Suez crises.

Washington's position *vis-à-vis* the Middle East situation was particularly difficult to assess. In the UN Security Council the United States took the initiative in attempting to forestall the landing of the British and French troops on Egyptian territory but was thwarted by its allies' veto; in the General Assembly Washington, on November 2, pressed for a resolution demanding a cease-fire and the withdrawal of foreign troops from Egypt, but Great Britain and France refused to discontinue air attacks on Cairo's military installations. Could the US have been playing the game at which the Russians themselves excelled —talk much, do little? Moscow could not be sure. Not until November 4, when the General Assembly, strongly backed by Ambassador Henry Cabot Lodge, adopted a resolution setting up a UN Emergency Force to secure and supervise the cessation of hostilities in and the withdrawal of foreign troops from the Middle East, could the USSR be certain that the Eisenhower administration had committed itself to the defense of Nasir.[39] Having achieved its initial objectives in Hungary by then, the Soviet Union could dispatch to the governments of the United States, Great Britain, France, and Israel messages intended to reap as much benefit as possible from a situation where the eventual political defeat of the aggressors could be easily foreseen.

In its note to the United States as well as in Shepilov's letter to the Security Council, the Kremlin proposed a joint use of Soviet and American armed forces to crush the invaders. It appears that, although the odds against Washington's acceptance of the Russian offer were indeed considerable, the prevailing anti-British and anti-French climate in Washington, combined with the strong anti-aggression sentiments shared by the majority of pro-Western and noncommitted

---

39. See *The Record on Suez: A Chronology of Events* (Compiled and published by the *Manchester Guardian,* November 1956), p. 15.

nations, may have justified some measure of Soviet optimism. While many observers tend to discard the note as an empty and meaningless gesture, it was nevertheless a skillful diplomatic device: by making their proposal the Russians stood to improve their position without taking any appreciable risks. American acceptance of the offer would signify a success beyond Moscow's wildest expectations. In the short run, by pitting Washington against its two European allies, the USSR would drive still another wedge between the Western powers. In the long run, Soviet-American cooperation in the Middle East might well be expected to deal a mortal blow to the Western alliance. In addition, the Russians would have gained for themselves in that region a dominant position to be shared only with the United States. A deal between the two superpowers dividing the Middle East into Soviet and US spheres of influence—an idea that was probably dear to Khrushchev's heart—would thus have been brought into the realm of possibility.

Even if the United States could not be drawn into a joint military effort against Great Britain and France, the USSR stood to gain important, albeit not easily measurable, benefits. Washington's refusal to employ force against its allies could be interpreted as an indirect approval of the Anglo-French-Israeli aggression against Egypt. Its "guilt by association" could be contrasted with Moscow's willingness to render Cairo all-out military support. The United States would thus be depicted as a stumbling block in the path of justice, morally responsible for the hardships suffered by the Egyptian people at the hands of the aggressors. As noted in an authoritative USSR Academy of Sciences publication:

> The USA did not accept the Soviet offer and in so doing confirmed their participation in the military adventure against Egypt. During the entire period of the Suez crisis the USA did its best to conceal its true role of a participant and even organizer of the campaign against Egypt, hiding behind declarations of anti-colonialism and hypocritical criticism of the British and French colonialist policy in the Near and Middle East.[40]

40. Akademiia nauk SSSR. Institut vostokovedeniia, *Araby v bor'be za nezavisimost'* (Moscow: Gospolitizdat, 1957), p. 194. Similar accusations

Khrushchev himself later asserted that he had no reason to doubt the rejection of his proposal in view of Washington's "actual role" in the tripartite aggression. But "by turning down our proposal the US ruling circles exposed their insincere policy and showed that it [the policy] was designed to mislead the Arab world and to create the impression that the USA was prepared to protect the Arab countries."[41] It is difficult to assess precisely how successful the Soviet propaganda machine was in pounding home this theme, but it is safe to assume that anti-American seeds planted by Moscow in 1956 fell on fertile ground in some parts of Asia and Africa.

In the ensuing years Moscow developed an elaborate argument designed to "prove" that its "determined" stand taken on November 5, 1956, was the decisive, albeit not the only, factor in halting armed aggression against Egypt. The Soviet government, it was asserted, had demonstrated its ability and determination to defend the trampled rights of a small, underdeveloped nation in the face of the gravest of all dangers—the threat of an all-out nuclear war.[42]

While Moscow, for political and propanganda purposes, clearly overstated its case, the official *ex post facto* views expressed by some of the leaders of the anti-Egyptian coalition tend to minimize the effect and possible significance of the Soviet moves. Prime Minister Eden, in describing British reaction in his memoirs, refers the reader to the strongly worded reply accusing the USSR of cold-blooded extermination of countless anti-Communist Hungarians. Premier Mollet's answer was similarly stern.[43] Prime Minister Ben-Gurion, replying to

---

were also made in another authoritative study, Akademiia nauk SSSR. Institut narodov Azii, *Politika SShA na Arabskom Vostoke* (Moscow: Izdatel'stvo vostochnoi literatury, 1961), pp. 28–29.
41. Khrushchev's interview with Muhammad Hasanayn Haykal. Text in *Pr.*, November 26, 1956.
42. See, for example, Vysshaia partiinaia shkola pri TsK KPSS, *Mezhdunarodnye otnosheniia i vneshniaia politika SSSR, 1917–1960* (Moscow: Izdatel'stvo VPSh i AON pri TsK KPSS, 1961), pp. 454–55. Another authoritative publication said: "All the world knows that it was precisely the Soviet warning that forced England, France, and Israel to stop their aggression against Egypt." Akademiia nauk SSSR, *Politika SShA . . .* , p. 275.
43. Sir Anthony Eden, *Memoirs: Full Circle* (London: Cassell, 1960), pp. 619–22. Text of Mollet's note in Department of State, pp. 204–5.

the Soviet government, expressed "surprise and sorrow at the threat against Israel's existence" contained in Bulganin's note but asserted that his country's foreign policy was dictated by "our essential needs . . . [and] would not be decided by any foreign factor."[44]

Interestingly enough, the official attitude of President Nasir was surprisingly similar to that of Eden, Mollet, and Ben-Gurion. In an interview with the Columbia Broadcasting System, held on April 7, 1958, the Egyptian President commented on the failure of the Anglo-French venture designed to remove him from the Arab political scene: "I gave first credit to the Egyptian people who fought at Port Said and I gave credit to Arab peoples who cooperated in frustrating aggression. I thanked President Eisenhower for his role in upholding principles. I also thanked Russia for intervening to stop the aggression and expressed the appreciation of the Egyptian people to the United Nations."[45] The Soviet threat against Great Britain, France, and Israel was thus considered merely one, and definitely not the decisive, factor. What Nasir really thought about Moscow's extravagant claims became apparent in his speech delivered in Damascus on March 22, 1959. Noting that it took the Soviet government nine (it was actually eight) days to make up its mind, he said that in that period "we had not the slightest intimation of support from any foreign state, even the Soviet Union. We relied on God and ourselves. . . . Had it not been for our firm stand during those nine days, our whole country would have now been dominated by imperialism."[46]

Judging from the aforementioned sentiments displayed by Eden, Mollet, Ben-Gurion, and even Nasir, it is tempting to dismiss the Soviet intimidation as a meaningless propaganda gesture, but a clear distinction must be made between the immediate reaction to and

44. David Ben-Gurion, *Israel: Years of Challenge* (New York: Holt, Rinehart and Winston, 1963), p. 140.
45. Text in *President Gamal Abdel Nasser's Speeches and Press-Interviews, 1958* (Cairo: UAR Department of Information, n. d.), p. 383.
46. *Ibid., 1959,* p. 172.

subsequent analysis of the move. During a few dramatic hours the leaders of the Western world must have desperately searched their souls in an "agonizing reappraisal" of Moscow's real intentions. It appears that Washington and probably London and Paris as well, were initially surprised and alarmed at the severity of the Soviet notes. Edwin L. Dale, Jr., of the *New York Times,* reported that "it would be difficult to exaggerate the extreme tension which gripped the United States Government" from late afternoon on November 5, when the texts of Bulganin's messages had become available, until 1:00 A.M. of the next day, when Great Britain and France had announced the cease-fire in Egypt.[47] According to Herman Finer, both the President and his advisers were "terrified" at the possibility of "serious Soviet aggression." Eisenhower "even expected an attack."[48] Robert Murphy, America's "diplomatic star quarterback," while denying that fear had gripped Washington, asserted that Eden was affected by the Russian threat more than he cared to admit.[49]

The burden of this argument is that, bluff or not, during the late afternoon and evening of November 5, nobody outside the Kremlin could be *positively* sure of the true nature of Soviet intentions. Paradoxically, just as with regard to joint intervention, the attitude of the United States remained the crucial factor. The Soviet note achieved its primary objective: it stopped the British and French incursion into Egypt by driving Eden into the hands of the United States. The only way he could make certain that Moscow's menace remained a dead letter was to secure full American backing. This the Eisenhower administration was prepared to offer but only at the price of abandonment of the Egyptian policy upon which the British Prime Minister had staked his political reputation and career. Yet it appears that Moscow missed a unique opportunity to further widen the split, which in late 1956 paralyzed the North Atlantic alliance.

47. As quoted by D. F. Fleming, *The Cold War and Its Origins, 1950–1960* (Garden City, N. Y.: Doubleday, 1961), 2: 829–30.
48. For more details, see Finer, 417–18. This is corroborated by the President. See Eisenhower, *Waging Peace, 1956–1961,* p. 90.
49. Robert Murphy, *Diplomat among Warriors* (Garden City, N.Y.: Doubleday, 1964), p. 391.

On the other hand, the November 11 statement threatening the dispatch of Soviet volunteers can be dismissed as outright bluff. It was issued at a time when Great Britain and France were obviously not in a position to resume hostilities and was intended merely as an additional illustration of Soviet sympathy with the Arab cause. Each Soviet move points to careful thinking and cold calculation: there is no hint of haste, misinformation, or unnecessary risk-taking. Although some misjudgment did occur—for example, Moscow seemed to have been caught by surprise at the speed and efficiency of the Israeli thrust into Sinai—the Kremlin deserves credit for keen evaluation of the situation and for taking full advantage of the opportunities presented to it by Great Britain, France, and Israel.

Nevertheless, far from providing "the solid foundation" of the "Soviet-Egyptian alliance,"[50] the Suez crisis touched off a slow process of deterioration in Moscow-Cairo relations. The Soviet leaders could not help but question the military value of their newly acquired friends in the Arab East. Further, Egypt must have come to the painful realization that Russia, like any other great power, was primarily interested in securing its own interests and would not hesitate to step on Nasir's toes should the circumstances so require. Above all, Soviet reluctance to act at the decisive moment demonstrated to Arab nationalists that the USSR was in no position to challenge the preponderant nuclear power of the United States.

Cairo appears to have learned its lesson well: never again were the Western powers antagonized to the extent that they would consider using armed force to redress grievances. Nasir basically revised his anti-Western brand of neutralism along more "positive" lines. As early as mid-November 1956, Cairo's press asserted that the country's foreign policy was based on the principle of neutralism and noninvolvement. Soviet support of Arab nationalism, combined with improved economic and cultural relations, created good will but did not lead to political subordination: "Egypt is aware, from bitter experience, of the danger of any form of depending on a more powerful

---

50. Walter Z. Laqueur, *The Soviet Union and the Middle East* (New York: Praeger, 1959), p. 229.

nation, and does not accept without extreme caution the promises of any one of the big powers."[51] Thus, mutual dissatisfaction with each other's performance in the Suez crisis initiated a gradual and not immediately visible process of deterioration in Soviet-Egyptian relations, which eventually culminated in the crisis of 1959. More concretely, the Soviet and Egyptian attitudes toward problems arising from the Suez war—among them the role of the United Nations Emergency Force (UNEF),[52] the withdrawal of Israeli troops from occupied territory, and the freedom of navigation in the Gulf of 'Aqaba and the Suez Canal—shed light on the delicate nature of Moscow-Cairo relations.

The Kremlin had little to gain and much to lose from the elimination of tension along the Egyptian-Israeli border and abandoned its initial opposition to UNEF only after Egypt wholeheartedly embraced the project.[53] Soviet comments on the question of the evacuation of Israeli forces show that Moscow was interested more in persuading the Arabs of American "double dealing" and "foul play" than in bringing about an Israeli evacuation of the Gaza Strip and the Gulf of 'Aqaba region. How could Israel defy the United Nations, *Pravda* asked, only to answer: "Influential circles in the United States gave every possible encouragement to the Israeli military circles to attack Egypt," and have continued to extend their support ever since. Now, "after the condemnation of the aggressors by all peace-loving peoples, the American imperialists do not dare to come out openly in support of Israel. In the present situation they prefer to play a two-faced game."[54] While Cairo was primarily concerned with achieving

51. Editorial, *EG*, November 18, 1956.
52. For details, see United Nations, *Yearbook of the United Nations, 1956* (New York: Columbia University Press, 1957), pp. 31–32, 40–43.
53. The *Egyptian Gazette*, for example, greeted the formation of UNEF as "an event of the greatest importance in the development of the ordered comity of nations towards which this country's political ideas are striving." Editorial, November 11, 1956. For Russian view, see *Izv.*, November 16, 1956, and editorial, *Pr.*, November 17, 1956.
54. Editorial, February 25, 1957. For more details, see N. Karev, *Izv.*, February 24; B. Strel'nikov, *Pr.*, March 4; and Y. Bochkaryov, "U.S. Double Game," *NT*, no. 11 (March 14, 1957), pp. 14-15.

the withdrawal of Israeli forces behind the prewar lines, Moscow centered its attention on discrediting the United States.

In the same vein, Moscow refused to believe Israel's March 1 announcement of unconditional withdrawal from the occupied territories and Dulles's statement of the same date denying that any concessions had been made to Tel-Aviv in exchange for the troop pull-out.[55] Here its attitude was very similar to that of Egypt, though, once again, it was Washington, anxious "to tear the Suez Canal away from Egypt," that was behind all attempts "to prolong as long as possible the occupation of Egyptian territory by the UN troops."[56] In addition, Cairo's stand on the future status of the Suez Canal was warmly supported by the USSR. Addressing the UN Security Council on April 27, 1957, Soviet delegate Arkadii Sobolev said that Egyptian declarations were equivalent to international documents, which contained all the necessary guarantees for a free use of the Canal. Sobolev urged the United Nations not to allow the imperialist powers to force upon Cairo a solution that would infringe on Egypt's sovereign rights while providing them with an opportunity to interfere in the internal affairs of Egypt.[57] In order to maintain its influence in the region, the Soviet government had to extend full moral and diplomatic support to Egypt's endeavors to keep Israel from using both the Straits of Tiran and the Suez Canal. Western support of the Israeli determination to secure free passage in the two waterways was used as an additional "proof" of the "predatory" aims of the imperialists.

It is not surprising that the events of the summer and fall of 1956 should have prompted the United States to review its policy in the Middle East. On January 5, 1957, President Eisenhower asked the Congress to endorse a set of principles expressing unqualified American support for the sovereignty and independence of all the nations of the Middle East. In particular, the President requested authority to use US forces to protect the integrity and independence of any

55. *MEJ* 11, no. 2 (Spring 1957): 171.
56. F. Orekhov, *Pr.*, March 13, 1957.
57. *Ibid.*, April 28, 1957. See also *Izv.*, of the same date; "The Boycott That Failed," *NT*, no. 18 (May 1, 1957), p. 18; and G. Mirsky, "The Blockade That Failed," *ibid.*, no. 25 (June 20, 1957), pp. 4-6.

nation threatened with or exposed to aggression by "international Communism," and to extend Middle Eastern countries American economic, technical, and military aid.[58]

Although the Eisenhower Doctrine, as the declaration is known, has subsequently been criticized on numerous grounds, the United States had seized the diplomatic initiative at a time when Western influence in the Middle East had reached an all-time low. It was eminently predictable that the USSR would attempt to neutralize the impact of Washington's move by some dramatic gesture of its own. As Moscow's press blasted America for seeking "exclusive, undivided supremacy in the area,"[59] the Soviet government, in a statement of January 12, 1957, argued that the Eisenhower Doctrine, "which foresees the possibility of employing US armed forces in . . . [the Middle East]," might lead to "dangerous consequences for which the US government must bear full responsibility."[60] It was obvious that a vague warning would not deter Washington from implementing its policy, however, and that other steps would have to be taken by the Kremlin to maintain its prestige and influence in the Arab East. In some respects the situation was similar to that of early November 1956: it called not so much for a clarification of the Soviet position as for a demonstration to the Arabs of what Washington was or was not willing to do, in spite of its numerous allegations of sympathy for the Arab cause.

In its February 12 notes to the United States, Great Britain, and France, the Soviet Union pursued this objective by proposing to negotiate and adopt "Basic Principles of Declaration by the Governments of the USSR, the USA, Great Britain, and France on the Question of Peace and Security in the Near and Middle East and Non-Interference in Internal Affairs of the Countries of the Area." As a preliminary step to establishing a "lasting and stable peace," the Kremlin suggested that the Western powers announce their determination to abide by the following principles: (1) preservation of peace in the Middle East through settling controversial questions by peace-

58. For details, see Campbell, chap. 9.
59. B. Leont'ev, "U.S. Imperialism in the Middle East," *NT*, no. 3 (January 17, 1957), p. 3.
60. *Pr.*, January 13, 1957.

ful means; (2) nonintervention in the internal affairs of the Middle Eastern countries, and respect for their sovereignty and independence; (3) renunciation of all attempts to involve these countries in military blocs organized and supported by great powers; (4) liquidation of foreign bases and withdrawal of foreign troops from the territory of the Middle Eastern states; (5) reciprocal refusal to deliver arms to the Middle Eastern countries; and (6) promotion of the economic development of the Middle Eastern nations without any political, military, or other preconditions incompatible with the dignity and sovereignty of these countries.[61]

In a sense, the Kremlin was taking a calculated risk in announcing its proposals. Not only had former great power proposals concerning peace in the Middle East been emphatically rejected by the Arabs, but the provision on an arms embargo to the Middle Eastern countries was certain to arouse Arab anxieties.[62] However, the Soviet government must have calculated that, in view of the certain Western rejection of its proposal, the Arabs would concentrate on drawing parallels between the Moscow Declaration and the Eisenhower Doctrine. Such a comparison was very likely to produce another propaganda victory for the USSR. (This is indeed what happened. The Declaration, even though described as a "propaganda move," was praised in Cairo's publications because it brought to public attention the issues that were ignored or distorted in the West. In addition, it was hoped that the Soviet initiative would force Washington to clarify its aims in the Middle East.[63]) Furthermore, and even more important, the Soviet declaration was intended to counterbalance the effects of the Eisenhower Doctrine by underscoring the Kremlin's determination to participate actively in the affairs of the Middle East regardless of Washington's feelings in the matter.

All in all, however, it is difficult to escape the conclusion that the

61. *Ibid.*, February 13, 1957.
62. As it turned out, Moscow's proposal was indeed criticized by Cairo. For instance, *al-Qahira* said: "It is really strange that both East and West should draw up schemes . . . about the Middle East behind the backs of the peoples of the region. . . . Both East and West are . . . vying with each other in formulating schemes of cold war and . . . in both cases the gains sought by both sides are at our own expense." As quoted in *EG*, February 15, 1957.
63. See editorials, *ibid.*, February 14 and February 17, 1957.

nationalization of the Suez Canal Company and the ensuing events forced the USSR to be on the defensive. Having abandoned the initiative that it had seized as a result of the Egyptian arms deal, Moscow had no choice but to react to the drama that unfolded in the Middle East, and over which it had little or no control. This conclusion is reinforced by an examination of the Soviet actions in 1957 and 1958, when the Middle East was once again plunged into the turmoil of several major crises. The most prominent among them were the eruptions in Jordan, Lebanon, and Iraq, and the conflict between Turkey and Syria.

3
The Syrian Crisis and the Creation of the United Arab Republic*

After the events of the summer and fall of 1956, the Soviet Union for two years pursued a policy of extreme caution in the Arab East. Its efforts were directed primarily at spreading Soviet influence economically, not politically. As correctly noted by J.M. Mackintosh,[1] the success of this approach was predicated on political stability—a rather rare commodity in the highly volatile Middle East—and as a result Moscow was forced to go about its task in an atmosphere of high tension over which it had little or no control.

President Nasir had emerged as the undisputed hero of the Arab nationalist masses throughout the region, personifying their yearning for political self-esteem, independence, economic progress, and social equality. His appeal was particularly strong among Palestinian refugees who, in 1957, constituted more than one-third of the population of Jordan and who regarded him as a modern Saladin, the only Arab leader capable of driving the hated interlopers from their land. Ideas

---

*Parts of this chapter are based on my "Moscow-Cairo Crisis, 1959," *Slavic Review* 22, no. 4 (December 1963): 713–26. Reprinted by permission of the publisher.

1. J. M. Mackintosh, *Strategy and Tactics of Soviet Foreign Policy* (London: Oxford University Press, 1963), p. 221.

of Arab unity and strength also found adherents among Jordan's officers and civil servants, including Prime Minister Sulayman Nabulsi and Chief of Staff of the army, General Abu Nuwwar. In the spring of 1957, a plot to overthrow King Husayn was allegedly uncovered in 'Amman. The conspirators, including Nabulsi and Abu Nuwwar, were reportedly backed by Cairo and Damascus and had aimed at uniting Jordan with Egypt and Syria in an Arab federation. In the ensuing turmoil a number of leading anti-monarchists fled the country and Jordan came dangerously close to a civil war. In the end, the bedouin units, which remained loyal to the King, succeeded in breaking up violent anti-Husayn demonstrations that took place in most of Jordan's major cities, and by late April 1957 a semblance of order had been restored.[2]

One may be reasonably certain that the USSR was not in any way involved in the Jordanian crisis. The latter was a spontaneous upsurge of violent anti-Westernism that swept the entire Arab East in the wake of the Suez war and that, in the particular case of Jordan, was skillfully directed by Cairo and Damascus into anti-monarchist channels.[3] The Soviet press did report widely on the Jordanian events, applauding the efforts of the "progressive elements" to rid the country of what was described as a reactionary, pro-imperialist, and even pro-Israeli monarchy. Once the crisis occurred, there can be no doubt that the Kremlin would have welcomed the overthrow of King Husayn and the advent to power in Jordan of Arab nationalist, neutralist elements who could be relied upon further to undermine US influence in the Arab East and to establish closer working relations with the USSR.[4] Judging by its press commentaries, however, the Kremlin was determined to let the Jordanian events take their own course.

One of the reasons that Moscow never went beyond expressing its customary "serious concern" over the situation in Jordan and extend-

2. For details, see Raphael Patai, *The Kingdom of Jordan* (Princeton: Princeton University Press, 1958), pp. 64–70.
3. For more information, see *ibid.*, pp. 70–72.
4. Premier Nabulsi openly announced his intention to establish diplomatic relations with the Soviet Union in the spring of 1957. Mackintosh, p. 222.

ing the "progressive elements" its moral and political support[5] was doubtless the fact that, from the strategic and even the political standpoint, Jordan was not nearly so important to Russia as were Egypt, Syria, or (later) Iraq. In addition, despite a constant barrage of accusations charging the United States with staging, directing, and financing Husayn's campaign to oust Nabulsi and his collaborators, there appeared at the time little likelihood of Western military intervention in the affairs of Jordan.[6]

The crisis that erupted in and around Syria soon after had more crucial implications. Having gained its independence from the French in 1946, Syria, after an initial experiment with parliamentary democracy, was governed by a succession of military dictators who, in the period between 1949 and 1956, followed each other at such a dazzling rate that even the most cynical observers of the Syrian scene were amazed.[7] By the early fall of 1955, it had become evident that the People's party, which advocated close ties between Syria and Iraq and favored the West in the big-power conflict, was definitely on the decline. By mid-1957, it was supplanted by an uneasy coalition of the National party, the Ba'th, and the independents, supported by the

5. "Statement by USSR Foreign Ministry," *Pr.*, April 30, 1957.
6. For Soviet press comments, see V. Borovskii and S. Vishnevskii, *ibid.*, April 15; the above "Statement" (see n. 5); S. Nikolaev, *Izv.*, May 19; and "TASS Statement," *Pr.*, May 26, 1957. For discussion of subsequent events in Jordan, see the Soviet press of November 14, 1957, *et passim*. See also L. N. Kotlov, *Iordaniia v noveishee vremia* (Moscow: Izdatel'stvo vostochnoi literatury, 1962), pp. 194–224; Akademiia nauk SSSR. Institut narodov Azii, *Politika SShA na Arabskom Vostoke* (Moscow: Izdatel'stvo vostochnoi literatury, 1961), pp. 210–11; E. Orlov and N. Sashko, *Gosudarstvennyi stroi Iordanii* (Moscow: Gosudarstvennoe izdatel'stvo iuridicheskoi literatury, 1961), pp. 15–17; Leningrad. Gosudarstvennyi Universitet, *Noveishaia istoriia stran zarubezhnoi Azii i Afriki* (Leningrad: Izdatel'stvo Leningradskogo universiteta, 1963), pp. 570–72. It is noteworthy that none of the subsequent publications commented on Moscow's stand toward the Jordanian events of the spring and summer of 1957, underscoring the Soviet desire to remain detached from the situation in that country.
7. For detailed accounts of Syrian politics in the years 1945 to 1958, see Patrick Seale, *The Struggle for Syria* (London: Oxford University Press, 1965) and Gordon H. Torrey, *Syrian Politics and the Military, 1945–1958* (Columbus: Ohio State University Press, 1964). See also Nicola A. Ziadeh, *Syria and Lebanon* (New York: Praeger, 1957).

Syrian Communist party. They succeeded in creating a united front and appeared determined to steer Syria along the path of domestic reform and positive neutralism.[8] Behind this façade of unity, however, the struggle for power between the Baʻth and the Communists soon became discernible. Other groups, lacking mass followings, played a subordinate role in this contest. The army harbored adherents of both parties, but it was the predominance of the Baʻth in the armed forces that was responsible for its eventual triumph over the Communists.

The Arab Socialist Renaissance party, otherwise known as the Baʻth, which had come into existence in 1953 as a result of a merger between the Arab Renaissance (Baʻth) party, founded by Michel ʻAflaq and Salah al-Din al-Bitar ten years earlier, and Akram al-Hawrani's Arab Socialist party, organized in 1950, rapidly gained ascendancy by promising a "new deal" to intellectuals, workers, and peasants alike.[9] Young intellectuals and army officers both in Syria and elsewhere in the Arab world were also attracted by the militant anti-Israeli attitude of the Baʻth leaders and the stress that the party laid on ideas of Arab nationalism, unity, and strength. Branches of the party were organized in Jordan, Lebanon, and Iraq, and its influence reached even into the oil-rich shaykhdoms of the Persian Gulf, most notably Kuwayt.

Because of its anti-Westernism and socialist inclinations, the Baʻth was occasionally accused in the West of performing the tasks of a Communist fellow-traveler. No one denied such allegations more vehemently than the Baʻth leaders themselves. Discussing the nature of the party's cooperation with the Communists, Bitar said: "Circum-

---

8. It is noteworthy that the strength of the Baʻth and of the Communist party could not have been determined on the basis of their performance in the 1954 parliamentary elections. Only one Communist, Secretary-General of the party Khalid Baqdash, was elected to the parliament and the party was not represented in the government. The Baʻth had elected 17 deputies and secured two seats in ʻAsali's coalition cabinet. Still, these two parties were the only well-organized and tightly knit groups, representing, together with the army, Syria's only really effective and cohesive political forces.

9. Domestically, the Baʻth advocated far-reaching social reforms. In an interview with *Newsweek* magazine, ʻAflaq said that "agrarian reform, distribution of land to peasants, an end to feudalism and capitalist domination" were among the party's main goals. *Newsweek*, no. 15 (October 7, 1957), p. 48.

CREATION OF THE UNITED ARAB REPUBLIC

stances sometimes dictate cooperation, or a truce. We are now in a state of emergency. The Communists are part of our emergency coalition."[10] Moscow responded in kind. While applauding the outspoken anti-Westernism of the Ba'th leadership and its tolerance of Communist activities in Syria, the Soviet government never lost sight of the fact that the Ba'th was basically a "national-bourgeois" party that reflected the interests of the nationalistically minded petty bourgeoisie.[11]

The crisis of 1957 was caused, in part, by the Western (especially US) reaction to the events that had taken place in Syria in 1956–1957 and that had given rise to fears that the USSR, in gaining ascendancy in Damascus, was on its way to creating the first Soviet satellite in the Middle East. Another contributing factor was the Syrian fear, shared by Moscow, that the United States, determined to maintain Western influence over the Arab countries, would intervene in Syria in an attempt to restore to power the People's party, known for its openly pro-Western outlook.

Secretary Dulles's conviction that the Kremlin was bent on communization and sovietization of Syria was reinforced by a series of steps designed to tie Damascus closer to the USSR by increasing Soviet political and economic influence in Syria.[12] A trade agreement between Syria and the USSR was signed in November 1955, and on July 1, 1956, Syria recognized Communist China. In late June, Soviet Foreign Minister Shepilov arrived in Damascus at the invitation of the Syrian government. In a joint communiqué, made public at the conclusion of his visit, the two countries pledged to expand their economic and cultural relations. The cultural cooperation agreement of August 20, 1956, provided for an "all-round development of cultural relations between the Soviet Union and Syria, [and] a wide exchange of experience and achievements in the spheres of literature, arts, sciences, higher and public education, physical culture, sports, and other areas."[13]

10. See the statements by Bitar and 'Aflaq, *ibid.*
11. Akademiia nauk SSSR. Institut vostokovedeniia, *Araby v bor'be za nezavisimost'* (Moscow: Gospolitizdat, 1957), p. 237.
12. For details, see Seale, pp. 283–91.
13. Akademiia nauk SSSR, *Araby v bor'be . . . ,* p. 270.

In September 1956, a delegation of the Supreme Soviet visited Syria and on October 30, one day before the Israeli attack on Egypt, President Shukri al-Quwatli arrived in Moscow on a state visit. At a Kremlin reception shortly before his departure, he praised the Soviet attitude toward Syria: "During our visit in your country we have become convinced of the friendship felt for us by the Soviet Union. We have found here open, honest, and sincere hearts. We have found readiness to support us, to help us in our hour of need."[14] Though Quwatli's enthusiasm was no doubt prompted by his sense of urgency at the need for continued Soviet backing in the immediate aftermath of the Israeli attack on Egypt, the statement was viewed in some Western quarters as an additional indication of Syria's growing subservience to the USSR. Western apprehension increased also as a result of the steadily improving economic relations between Damascus and the Communist-bloc countries. Since 1955, Syria had entered into numerous trade and payments agreements with the USSR, Czechoslovakia, Rumania, Poland, East Germany, and Communist China.[15]

On July 24, 1957, a Syrian delegation headed by Khalid al-'Azm, then Minister of Defense, a millionaire and a leading "independent," arrived in Moscow.[16] The contents of the Soviet-Syrian talks were not made public, but the joint communiqué's reference to an extensive Russian-aid program to Syria[17] reinforced rumors that high Soviet and Syrian officers had reached an agreement on extensive Russian military aid to Damascus. It is indeed highly probable that the Syrians had come to Moscow mainly to purchase Soviet arms. Commenting on the purpose of the delegation's visit, 'Azm said at a reception attended by Khrushchev that Syria was determined to build a strong army and a healthy economy: "This is the reason why we came to you —with the intention of increasing cooperation between our countries in these areas by means of extended trade relations."[18] The Syrians

14. *Ibid.*, pp. 270–71.
15. *Ibid.*, p. 266.
16. *Pr.*, July 25, 1957.
17. *Ibid.*, August 7, 1957.
18. *Ibid.*, August 6, 1957.

were not disappointed. Their ambassador to the USSR was quoted by the Damascus press as saying on August 5: "I am now in a position to state that Syria's military requirements will be fulfilled."[19]

These, from the Western standpoint disquieting, developments were followed, in August 1957, by two unrelated but ominous events reinforcing the conviction held by some circles in Washington that Syria was on the verge of turning into a Soviet satellite. On August 13, Damascus accused three US diplomats of efforts to overthrow the Syrian government and ordered them to leave the country. This was followed, on August 17, by the removal of Chief of Staff General Nizam al-Din, known for his conservative and pro-Western views, and his replacement by Colonel 'Afif al-Bizri, suspected of Communist affiliations.[20]

As the governments of Turkey, Iraq, Jordan, and Lebanon pressed for the destruction of the "Communist" regime in Damascus, "the Middle East broke into a diplomatic furor approaching panic." According to Eisenhower, these pro-Western regimes were given prompt assurances of Washington's benevolence and support—promises of accelerated arms shipments were accompanied by a decision to reinforce US Air Force units stationed in southern Turkey and to dispatch the Sixth Fleet to the Eastern Mediterranean. In addition, the United States secured a promise from Israel not to avail itself of the opportunity to expand at the expense of its neighbors while Syria was being "restored to Syrian rule."[21]

In late August, Loy Henderson, Deputy Undersecretary of State and the Department's chief trouble-shooter, went to the Middle East on what was described as a "fact-finding mission." After conferring with officials in Turkey, Lebanon, Jordan, and Iraq, Henderson asserted that "the Syrian situation might have serious effects on the security of the whole free world."[22] On September 7, Secretary Dulles said that President Eisenhower had "expressed hope that interna-

19. As quoted by Mackintosh, p. 224.
20. For details, see Seale, pp. 292–300 and Torrey, pp. 360–64.
21. For more details, see Dwight D. Eisenhower, *Waging Peace, 1956–1961* (Garden City: Doubleday, 1965), pp. 196–99.
22. *MEJ* 11, no. 4 (Autumn 1957): 412–13.

tional Communists would not push Syria into any acts of aggression." It was clear from his statement that Dulles feared that Damascus might be slipping irretrievably into the Soviet orbit. As tension continued to grow, Turkey was reported massing troops along the Syrian border and a number of frontier incidents occurred.[23]

In applying pressure against Syria, Washington probably hoped that its total effect would be to force Damascus to review and change its pro-Soviet stand. On September 10, however, Dulles issued another statement expressing hope that the Syrian situation would be worked out peacefully and that nothing would happen in the Middle East to require "direct armed intervention by the United States." It was suggested at the time that Washington sounded retreat because the "Syrian rush toward the Communist orbit" had been "slowed."[24] But the Ba'th had continued to consolidate its power internally at the expense of both the conservative elements and, to an extent, the Communists. In its relations with the USSR the Syrian government continued to adhere to an independent, neutralist policy. Even if, for the sake of argument, it is assumed that in August and early September Syria displayed a marked inclination to move closer to the Soviet orbit, there were no indications that this trend was reversed between September 7 and 10, when Washington revised its initial assessment of the Syrian situation. A more likely explanation is that the reaction of some of the pro-Western Arab governments convinced Dulles that the Henderson report may have overstated the danger of the Communist threat in Syria.[25]

On September 11, immediately after the United States had publicly disclaimed any intention to pressure Syria into submission, Damascus inquired, in official notes to Iraq, Jordan, and Lebanon, whether these countries had expressed anxiety over the situation in Syria. The move

23. *NYT,* September 15, 1957.
24. *Ibid.*
25. King Sa'ud, for example, warned President Eisenhower that US concern over the Syrian situation was "exaggerated" and counseled moderation. Washington, incidentally, denied this but acknowledged that the King had cautioned the President "to avoid any action that might draw Russia more deeply into the Middle East." *Ibid.*

was an astute diplomatic maneuver, which paid handsome political dividends. In their replies, all three governments publicly repudiated whatever private apprehensions they may have expressed to Henderson by assuring Syria that no Arab state would attack another and that Damascus had every right to strengthen its defenses against "Zionism and imperialism." None saw any threat emanating from Syria, and all promised assistance in case of an aggression.[26] The paradoxical and unexpected outcome of the strong position taken by the United States was thus the public rallying of the pro-Western Arab governments to Syria's support.

The USSR had displayed no signs of alarm at the developments in Damascus and the Western reaction to them until the Henderson mission was under way. Then a massive diplomatic and propaganda campaign designed to block a possible outside intervention in Syrian affairs was mounted. Simultaneously, the Kremlin used this opportunity to undermine Washington's influence and to raise its own prestige in the Arab East by posing as a friend and protector of the neutralist Arabs. In its initial comment on the Henderson mission, *Pravda* expressed confidence that

> neither the Arab nations nor the peoples of the world will permit the imperialists to treat the Syrians as the colonialists treated the peoples of the East not so long ago. In their struggle for the right to manage their own affairs as they choose, the Syrian people has the unqualified support of all freedom-loving peoples.[27]

When American pressure showed no signs of subsiding, the Soviet government, on September 3, sent notes to the United States, Great Britain, and France accusing the Western powers of attempts to subvert the independence of the Arab countries and proposing the adoption by the great powers of a set of principles that would ensure peaceful settlement of disputes arising in the Middle East. As the initial step toward the normalization of relations in the area, the USSR suggested that the four powers condemn the use of force in the

26. Osgood Caruthers, *ibid.,* September 29, 1957.
27. D. Kraminov, *Pr.,* August 24, 1957.

settlement of controversial problems, renounce interference in the internal affairs of Middle Eastern countries, and assume a mutual obligation to terminate arms shipments to the Middle East.[28]

Although it would be difficult to deny that this note was intended, in part, to serve Moscow's propaganda purposes and that it did indeed accomplish this objective,[29] it was one of the few instances where the Soviet Union offered to negotiate a halt to weapon deliveries to the Middle East. One may wonder whether it was not in the long-range interest of the United States to explore Moscow's intentions. Given the climate of opinion that prevailed in Washington at the time, however, it was not surprising that Dulles dismissed the Soviet initiative as a ploy to gain Western recognition for Russia's great power status in the Middle East. The Secretary of State rejected Moscow's offer on the ground that it contained nothing not already provided for in the Charter of the United Nations. As might have been expected, Dulles's "cynical excuse" aroused a storm of indignation in the Soviet press, coming as it did from "those whose actions in the Middle East represent a gross violation of the Charter."[30]

Foreign Minister Andrei Gromyko's press conference of September 10 was the highlight of Moscow's diplomatic effort in the Syrian crisis.[31] In a blistering attack he accused the United States and its allies of organizing a conspiracy to destroy the "progressive" government in Damascus and requested that an end be put to "imperialist encroachments" on the independence of all the Middle Eastern coun-

28. Text in *ibid.,* September 5, 1957.
29. Said *al-Gumhuriya:* "The peoples of the Middle East fully support the proposal. All these peoples want is to be left alone to live in peace and tranquility and concentrate on building their future. . . ." Noninterference by the big powers in the affairs of the Middle East, it was concluded, "would not only serve the peoples of the area, but also the cause of world peace." Editorial, September 5, 1957.
30. Editorial, "Dangerous Recommendations," *NT,* no. 37 (September 12, 1957), p. 1.
31. Gromyko replaced Shepilov in June 1957, after the "anti-party" group's unsuccessful attempt to oust Khrushchev. Shepilov had opposed Khrushchev on numerous grounds. For details, see my "Moscow and the Suez Crisis, 1956," *Political Science Quarterly* 80, no. 4 (December 1965): 600–602.

tries. The Soviet Foreign Minister concluded by saying that Moscow would not remain idle in case of an armed attack on Syria.[32]

Formal charges against the United States and Turkey were leveled in a note that Soviet Premier Bulganin dispatched to his Turkish counterpart, Adnan Menderes, on September 10. In it, Moscow warned Ankara not to attack Syria and threatened retaliation in case of an aggression. With an eye on the United States the note said:

> In our day, in view of the present world situation and especially the development of weapons of war, the danger of local conflicts developing into a big conflagration has become much greater. Once they have started, military operations in such a locality could at any moment develop into an extensive conflict. It would then be difficult to limit action to a given area.[33]

Further tension arose when Khrushchev, in an October 7 interview with the *New York Times,* charged the United States with preparing a war against Syria and repeated earlier Soviet warnings that the Kremlin would intervene in the defense of Damascus. Four days later, the Soviet Premier addressed an appeal to the socialist parties of Great Britain, France, Italy, and a number of other West European countries, requesting their aid in an attempt to forestall what was described as an imminent attack on Syria. In the ensuing couple of weeks, the pages of Soviet publications were filled with reports of the Turkish troop movements and of military clashes along the Turkish-Syrian border.[34] Meanwhile, Syria, Egypt, and the USSR were attempting to drum up public support for their anti-Turkish and anti-US stand at the United Nations. Finally, in what turned out to be a grand but meaningless finale, Marshal Konstantin Rokossovskii, Deputy Minister of Defense and one of the heroes of World War II, was appointed commander of the Trans-Caucasian military district bordering on

32. Text in *Pr.,* September 11, 1957.
33. Text in *Izv.,* September 14, 1957.
34. For examples, see V. Ardatovskii, *Sovetskaia Rossiia,* October 12; "*TASS* Statement," *Izv.,* October 19; I. Plyshevskii, *Pr.,* October 21; editorial, "Syria's Friends and Foes," *NT,* no. 42 (October 17, 1957), p. 17; and editorial, "Avert the Danger," *ibid.,* no. 43 (October 24, 1957), pp. 1–2.

Turkey and Iran, a post not ordinarily considered important and usually reserved for officers of lesser rank and stature.[35]

According to Mackintosh, the Syrian crisis had reached its peak on October 24[36] and subsided a few days later. On October 29, Khrushchev signaled the real end of the crisis by attending a reception at the Turkish embassy in Moscow.[37]

In its attempt to make as much propaganda capital as possible out of the Syrian crisis, the Kremlin had worked on various parallel, interrelated themes. Its basic objective had been to undermine Western influence in the Middle East and to build up Soviet prestige by posing as a friend and protector of the neutralist Arabs. As in the past, the US government was accused of predatory determination to gain complete and undivided control over the entire Middle East. To accomplish this end, the United States allegedly endeavored to eliminate British and French influence from the area, to prevent Arab unity, and, eventually, to remove from power those Arab leaders who were pursuing an independent foreign policy.[38]

In emphasizing the temporary nature of the Western alliance and warning London and Paris to beware of Washington's determination to "destroy the competing British and French imperialism" in the Middle East, the Soviet government was attempting to drive a wedge between the Western powers so as to weaken the US position in the area. It is noteworthy that the USSR also made a distinct effort to undermine the British and French governments from within by appealing to the socialist parties of these countries. Thus Khrushchev's letter to the Labour party warned the British public that London's support of the United States and Turkey would drive the country into the "abyss of a new destructive war" with "terrible consequences for the population of the British Isles." In order to avoid the "looming catastrophe," the Soviet government asked "fellow Socialists" to prod

35. For more details, see Mackintosh, pp. 227–29.
36. *Ibid.*, p. 229.
37. David J. Dallin, *Soviet Foreign Policy After Stalin* (Philadelphia: Lippincott, 1961), p. 471.
38. For more details, see Observer and N. Pastukhov, *Pr.*, August 23 and 31, 1957, respectively. See also I. Plyshevskii, *ibid.*, August 16, 1957.

their governments into accepting the Soviet-sponsored nonaggression pact in the Middle East.[39]

The prevention of Arab unity was another US strategic objective in the Middle East, Moscow insisted. As demonstrated by the position of Iraq, nothing could split the Arab ranks more effectively than adherence to an "aggressive Western military pact." The Kremlin appealed to the Arabs to remain vigilant and to defeat Washington's determination to force Jordan, Lebanon, and Saudi Arabia to join the Baghdad Pact.[40] This propaganda line was clearly intended to isolate Iraq from the rest of the Arab world while widening the gap between the pro-Western government of Nuri al-Sa'id and its nationalistically minded subjects. It also served as a warning to the pro-Western governments of Lebanon, Jordan, and Saudi Arabia not to follow the Western lead.

Simultaneously the Soviet government admonished Cairo and Damascus that "one of the basic aims of American diplomacy" in the Middle East was to isolate them from the rest of the Arab world. Time and again Egypt and Syria were reminded that the United States was working to wipe out their governments, employing the methods of provocation, sabotage, blackmail, and conspiracy. These were averred to be the cornerstones of American policy designed to cancel all the gains of the Arab liberation movement.[41]

At the same time, the Soviet government attempted to improve its own image in the Arab East by extending to Damascus its full diplomatic and moral support and by constant reminders that the foreign policy objectives of Syria and the USSR were identical. Charges of the "sovietization" of Syria were resolutely rejected. *Pravda* angrily asserted that Syria was not a Communist state and that no Communist propaganda emanated from it. Damascus was merely upholding its sovereignty and independence against Western encroachments, and

39. Text in *Izv.*, October 16, 1957.
40. See "TASS Statement on Events in Oman," *Pr.*, August 21, 1957.
41. I. Yermashov, "Eisenhower Doctrine: First Results," *NT*, no. 35 (August 29, 1957), p. 6. See also editorial, "Trouble-Shooting Diplomacy," *ibid.*, no. 36 (September 5, 1957), p. 2.

the USSR was prepared to support it in this endeavor.[42] The Soviet-Syrian rapprochement of the past few years was a "perfectly normal and logical development," even though the two countries were "travelling along different routes." The Soviet state was building a "communist society," while Damascus was consolidating its independence "within the framework of a bourgeois republic." But in the sphere of foreign relations both were poetically described as "heading towards . . . the same oasis, the name of which is 'peace.' " Both opposed the "arms drive, aggressive military blocs, and colonialism" and advocated "international peace and cooperation." These common goals brought Damascus and Moscow close together, giving rise to an "identity of views on a number of vital international questions."[43]

The Soviet press dismissed as ridiculous allegations that Syria was being turned into Moscow's "arsenal" and that Soviet military bases were under construction on Syrian territory. Admitting "commercial" sale of arms to Damascus, the *New Times* quoted Khalil Kallas, Syrian Acting Foreign Minister: "Syria purchases only what her army requires. The assertion that Syria is being turned onto a Soviet arsenal is absurd and those who make it know perfectly well that they are telling lies." As for Soviet military bases, "they are being built and equipped only on the pages of certain Western newspapers, whose editors have apparently lost all sense of honour."[44]

As for the Soviet Union itself, it only wanted the Arab states to be "free, independent, peaceable states, with no one interfering in their affairs." But it could not help being concerned about the Syrian situation. On the one hand, the USSR sympathized with the Arab struggle for freedom and independence. It was also "bound to be disquieted by sinister machinations" in the vicinity of its southern border.[45] In his September 20 speech before the UN General Assembly, Foreign Minister Gromyko declared that joint Western-Turkish

42. N. Pastukhov, *Pr.*, September 28, 1957.
43. A. Baturin, "The Truth About Soviet-Syrian Relations," *NT*, no. 44 (November 1, 1957), p. 29.
44. *Ibid.* See also P. Demchenko, *Pr.*, October 10; S. Kondrashov, *Izv.*, October 23; and M. Stepanov, *ibid.*, October 31, 1957.
45. Editorial, "Trouble-Shooting Diplomacy," *NT*, no. 36 (September 5, 1957), p. 2.

CREATION OF THE UNITED ARAB REPUBLIC 73

activities in the Middle East infringed on the security of the Soviet Union and warned that Moscow would not stand idly by while a "permanent hotbed" of intrigues and military conflicts was being created in the "immediate proximity of Soviet territory."[46]

The Kremlin repeatedly promised Syria its full support and expressed belief in the "inevitability" of the victory over the "forces of imperialism."[47] Assurances of Russian good will, supplemented with substantial military and economic aid, were designed to strengthen the Syrian government in its anti-Western and pro-Soviet attitude. The violent flare-up of anti-Western feelings in the Arab East, Moscow fully realized, was bound to result in a further decline of Western influence in the region and, in the last analysis, that alone would have justified the magnitude of its propaganda effort during the crisis of 1957.

When it became obvious that no outside power was planning to attack Syria, Arab neutralists contended that the Western powers had to back down because they had not reckoned with "the revolutionary awakening of all Arab peoples who are standing on their guard against any imperialist move designed to shatter Arab nationalism."[48] In contrast and not surprisingly, Soviet publications emphasized the importance of various Russian moves. According to one source, Moscow played an "enormous part in preventing an armed conflict" in the Middle East.[49] Others spoke of Moscow's "firm position"[50] and of the "decisive role" it played in the liquidation of the crisis,[51] arguing that it was the "prospect of the Soviet action in support of Syria [that] forced the imperialist powers to back down."[52]

For all its "tempest-in-a-teapot" qualities, the Syrian crisis fore-

46. *Pr.*, September 21, 1957. See also editorial, *ibid.*, October 21, 1957.
47. For details, see D. Kraminov, *ibid.*, August 24. See also V. Maevskii, *ibid.*, October 15, 1957.
48. Editorial, *al-Gumhuriya,* November 9, 1957.
49. Akademiia nauk SSSR. Institut mirovoi ekonomiki i mezhdunarodnykh otnoshenii, *Mezhdunarodnyi politiko-ekonomicheskii ezhegodnik, 1958* (Moscow: Gospolitizdat, 1958), p. 543.
50. Akademiia nauk SSSR, *Politika SShA. . .* , p. 111.
51. O. E. Tuganova, *Mezhdunarodnye otnosheniia na Blizhnem i Srednem Vostoke* (Moscow: Izdatel'stvo "Mezhdunarodnye otnosheniia," 1967), p. 73.
52. *Ibid.*, p. 74.

shadowed future conflicts that were to have far-reaching repercussions both in and beyond the Middle East. For instance, it is not too far-fetched to argue that the crisis substantially weakened the pro-Western governments of Iraq, Jordan, and Lebanon by forcing them to adopt an openly pro-Syrian and, by implication, anti-American stand. It is also significant in that Soviet influence in the Arab East may have reached an all-time high during and immediately after the crisis. Yet, paradoxically, the events also served to underscore the divergence of basic interests between Moscow and the neutralist Arabs. At the height of this apparent triumph of Soviet diplomacy in the Middle East, the neutralist Arab governments turned to the United States with a plea to improve relations. Washington was summoned to recover its lost prestige by "giving up the policy of pacts, military bases, domination over other states, and interference with other peoples' affairs." The United States would again be held in "high esteem" if it extended a "helping hand to the peoples engaged in liberation struggles." Russia, it was said, "may be on its way to the conquest of space but America can certainly conquer people's hearts."[53]

Political, economic, and military backing of the neutralist Arabs conferred upon Moscow neither the right nor the power to influence their decisions, even if those decisions affected what the USSR regarded as its vital interests in the Middle East. In this respect, the position in which the Soviet Union found itself did not differ substantially from that of the Western powers. The limitations of Soviet influence were again dramatically demonstrated in early 1958, when Egypt and Syria, in a swift and dramatic move, joined to form the United Arab Republic.

During November 1957, in an interview with the Italian Communist newspaper *l'Unita,* President Nasir spoke approvingly of Cairo's close association with the USSR, arguing that their cooperation had greatly enhanced Egypt's economic progress and international position. He saw no danger in a close association with Moscow and asserted that during the last three years he had "noticed absolutely

53. Editorial, *al-Ahram,* November 6, 1957.

nothing which would confirm the suspicion that the Soviet Union might want to intervene in the internal affairs or influence our politics in a certain direction." It was Egypt that asked the USSR for aid and "each time help was immediately given to us and without political conditions."⁵⁴

In the same month, General 'Abd al-Hakim 'Amir, Commander-in-Chief of the Egyptian armed forces, visited the Soviet Union to conduct high-level political, military, and economic negotiations. These political discussions, 'Amir stated subsequently, were designed to secure Soviet support for some of the basic principles underlying Cairo's foreign policy.⁵⁵ The details of the arms talks were not disclosed. 'Amir said merely that the Egyptian military were awarded "most valuable opportunities," and it appears that he scored his biggest success in the economic sphere. Moscow granted Cairo a twelve-year loan of some $200 million and agreed to furnish technical assistance for the development of major industrial projects. Egyptian publications were overjoyed.⁵⁶ For its part, Moscow continued to profess its respect for the independence and sovereignty of the Arab states and its support of their policy of noninvolvement in the East-West conflict.⁵⁷

Such close cooperation and outward friendliness could not conceal the fact that serious strains were beginning to appear in the relations between the USSR and Egypt. Cairo's loud and insistent emphasis on positive neutralism could be cited as one example, and occasional comments on the nature of Communism and the Soviet reaction to them supplied additional evidence. Egypt's numerous expressions of

54. As quoted in *EG,* November 25, 1957. See also an article by the pro-Soviet chief editor of *al-Masa'* (Cairo) Khalid Muhyi al-Din in *NT,* no. 43 (October 24, 1957), pp. 9–10; and a statement by Muhammad Hasanayn Haykal, editor of *al-Ahram* and a confidant of President Nasir, as quoted by Y. Bochkaryov, "The Soviet Union and the Arab East," *NT,* no. 1 (January 1, 1958), pp. 12–13.
55. Text of 'Amir's report on the mission to the Egyptian National Assembly in *EG,* November 26, 1957.
56. For details, see editorials, *al-Ahram,* November 21, and *EG,* November 22, 1957.
57. See Y. Bochkaryov, "The Soviet Union and the Arab East," *NT,* no. 1 (January 1, 1958), pp. 13–14.

gratitude for Soviet aid were invariably tempered with assurances that Egypt refused "to become a slave of Western or Eastern masters," and had no intention of importing government systems from foreign countries. The influential *al-Akhbar* asserted that Egypt would never espouse the Communist creed. "While we respect every people's freedom to choose its own form of government, we nevertheless combat [Communism] in our country with the same strong determination as we have demonstrated in our struggle against any form of despotism or imperialism."[58]

Such bluntness could not escape the attention of the Soviet government. Moscow reacted by blasting "American propagandists" and their Egyptian "hirelings" for spreading "slander and lies" about the USSR and its intentions. Special attention was devoted to Cairo's book market, dumped with publications coming "from the bowels of American propaganda organizations" and written "in such a brazen and blatant tone that their authors would be the envy of Goebbels."[59] Significantly, Moscow did not accuse the Nasir regime of instigating the alleged anti-Soviet campaign, but shifted the blame to the United States and its Egyptian henchmen. This was the first indication of the remarkable degree of restraint with which Khrushchev was to treat the anti-Soviet line openly adopted by the Egyptian government at the end of 1958.

These rather minor propaganda efforts were only a prelude, however. Nothing so clearly demonstrates the apprehension that Nasir had come to feel over Soviet gains in the Middle East and the profound, though sometimes invisible, negative undercurrents in Moscow's relations with Egypt and Syria as does the creation of the United Arab Republic. Slowly but surely, following the announcement of the union, the deterioration in relations between the USSR and the UAR gained momentum, erupting into the open in December 1958, and reaching a near-crisis point early in 1959.

The influential Cairo journalist Mustafa Amin asserted that the "speedy proclamation of union between Egypt and Syria took [the

58. Editorial, *al-Akhbar,* January 18, 1958.
59. K. Smirnov, *Izv.,* December 3, 1957. Milovan Djilas's "The New Class" and Carew Hunt's "Communism: Theory and Practice" aroused Moscow's greatest indignation.

Russians] by surprise. It was a development which they had never expected." According to Amin, only twenty-four hours before the proclamation of the union, the Soviet Ambassador in Damascus dispatched a report to Moscow saying that "union rumors were absolutely unfounded, that official circles had denied them, [and] that he personally believed union was impossible."[60] Whether such a dispatch was actually sent cannot, of course, be ascertained. If it was, Western foreign offices may find some solace in the fact that they are not alone in being occasionally caught by surprise by events unfolding in the Middle East. But Amin's case appears overstated: there were numerous indications that Cairo and Damascus were seriously contemplating some kind of a federation and that the USSR was well aware of them.[61] If the Soviet government had in fact been caught by surprise, it was probably on the timing and form, but not the fact of the union itself.

Although the Arab masses strongly favored the idea of Arab unity, most Arab governments, in an effort to placate their subjects, merely paid lip service to the idea of some unspecified form of union with their "Arab brothers." At no stage, however, did any Arab government, except that of Syria in late 1957 and early 1958, seriously consider abandoning the unrestricted exercise of power within its territory for the sake of this lofty ideal. These other governments might have been expected to join a loose federation at some future date but would not consent to uniting with a centralized Arab state dominated by Egypt. In addition, Nasir must have been fully aware of the serious problems that the proposed merger faced. The two countries lacked a common frontier, and in Syria several parties were actively engaged in the country's political process, while Egypt was a one-party state. There was also a considerable difference in living standards between underpopulated, relatively prosperous Syria and overcrowded, economically unstable Egypt. It may therefore be pre-

60. *Akhbar al-Yawm*, March 29, 1959.
61. For example, in early December 1957, the Soviet press spoke approvingly of the projected Syrian-Egyptian federation, because Arab unification would mean a telling blow to the colonialist system. Y. Bochkaryov, "Cairo-Damascus Alliance," *NT* no. 49 (December 5, 1957), pp. 8–9. See also S. Kondrashov, *Izv.*, January 22, 1958.

sumed that the merger between Cairo and Damascus was carried out ahead of schedule. Furthermore, it appears that Cairo's only apprehensions were directed at the Soviet Union and the Syrian Communists and that the United Arab Republic was established with such haste and in such secrecy in order to deny them the opportunity to take effective countermeasures.

According to Nasir, the leaders of the Ba'th begged him to unite the two countries for fear that the Syrian Communists were moving to take over the government. Whether or not the threat of a Communist takeover in Syria really existed and, if so, whether the takeover was imminent, as was later alleged by the Egyptian press and some Western writers,[62] Nasir appeared genuinely worried by the extent of Soviet influence in Syria and the increased strength of the Syrian Communist party. As noted by Walter Laqueur, several important by-elections were to be contested in the spring of 1958, and the Ba'th was not confident as to their outcome. The Communists had also succeeded in increasing their influence in the army.[63] Conversely, the USSR opposed the creation of the United Arab Republic for fear that Cairo would terminate the political and economic foothold that Moscow had managed to establish in Syria during the preceding two years. The Syrian Communists, too, opposed Nasir's efforts to extend his influence in the Arab East.

Western writers have disagreed in their evaluation of Soviet intentions in the Middle East.[64] It appears, however, that, at the time, the USSR stood to gain the most by increasing its influence in Syria by means other than a Communist takeover. Previous knowledge of the timing of the merger would have given the Soviet government an opportunity to exert pressure on Syria and perhaps (although highly unlikely) to postpone or even prevent the creation of the United Arab Republic. But the timing of the union appears to have come as a

62. See Mustafa Amin, *Akhbar al-Yawm,* March 29, 1959, and Dallin, p. 469.
63. Walter Z. Laqueur, *The Soviet Union and the Middle East* (New York: Praeger, 1959), p. 260. For more details, see Seale, pp. 315–26; and Torrey, pp. 370–74.
64. See Laqueur, p. 256, and Dallin, p. 469.

surprise to Moscow, and this explains why there was no official Soviet comment on the merger for some time.[65]

The establishment of the United Arab Republic was announced on February 1, 1958. Egypt and Syria were joined into one state headed by a president. There would be one parliament, one vote in the United Nations, and a unified military command. In a plebescite, held on February 21, 99.99 percent of Egyptians and 99.8 percent of Syrians voted for the merger with Nasir as president.[66] Announced as the start of a "new era" in Arab history,[67] the UAR was described as a "brotherly national call for millions of Arabs to form with it a unity of line and action."[68]

Although the Soviet government recognized the United Arab Republic and sent congratulations on its establishment, for the first two weeks of February Moscow did not go beyond expressing the pious hope that the birth of the new state would "lead to the consolidation of peace and stability in the Middle East" and would "give fresh impetus and new strength to the peoples in their struggle for national independence against the conspiracy and intrigue of the colonialists."[69] Simultaneously, evidently hoping to preserve some of the gains made by the Communists in Syria, the USSR wished the new state more resolution in implementing the "aspirations of the people," for "the more freedom it allows for the activity of all progressive forces and trends, the stronger will be its international position and internal stability."[70]

In the end, the Soviet government decided to face the facts and to support the new state. "Observer" stated: "True to the principles of the Leninist foreign policy of peaceful coexistence and noninterference in the affairs of other countries, the Soviet Union welcomes the formation of the UAR." Every people had the right to decide its own

65. Laqueur, p. 260.
66. *MEJ* 12, no. 2 (Spring 1958): 191.
67. Editorial, *EG,* February 2, 1958.
68. Statement by Quwatli, *ibid.,* February 10, 1958.
69. S. Kondrashov, *Izv.,* February 27, 1958.
70. Editorial, "The United Arab Republic," *NT,* no. 7 (February 1958), p. 4.

national problems independently and if the peoples of Egypt and Syria chose to unite in one state, their desires should be respected. The USSR, in the past a "disinterested, loyal, and reliable friend of the independent Arab states," welcomed further strengthening of the unity of the Arab peoples because "this unity cannot but serve the interests of easing international tension and securing peace in the Arab East."[71]

If Nasir and his associates had ever believed in the "nobility" of Soviet intentions (as they often professed they had),[72] Moscow's attitude preceding and following the creation of the UAR should have opened their eyes once and for all. The Kremlin clearly disapproved of the union between Cairo and Damascus because it was detrimental to Soviet interests in the Arab East: it nullified some of the gains made in Syria by both the USSR and the indigenous Communist party. It also tended to strengthen the bargaining position of President Nasir, making him less amenable to Moscow's wishes and more immune to Soviet pressure.

Nevertheless, confronted with a *fait accompli* and with a situation over which it had no control, the Kremlin, as already noted, brushed aside its reservations and appeared to have reconciled itself to the emergence of the United Arab Republic. Instead of challenging Nasir and the forces of Arab nationalism that he then represented, Khrushchev chose to continue to protect Soviet interests in the Middle East through cooperation with, not opposition to, Cairo.

A new opportunity to enlarge its influence in the UAR presented itself to the USSR in late April 1958, when President Nasir arrived in Moscow for an 18-day state visit. Among the immediately visible consequences were a twenty-to-thirty-percent reduction in the price of arms sold by the USSR and a fifteen-percent cut in the prices of industrial equipment. Furthermore, Khrushchev presented the Egyptian government with a cotton-research plant and gave Nasir an Iliushin-14 airplane.[73] It may also be safely assumed that Soviet participation in the construction of the Aswan High Dam was among the topics discussed.

71. *Pr.*, February 15, 1958. See also *Izv.*, February 23, 1958, and Akademiia nauk SSSR, *Mezhdunarodnyi . . . ezhegodnik, 1958,* p. 457.
72. For example, see the text of Nasir's interview in *EG,* January 29, 1958.
73. *MEJ* 12, no. 3 (Summer 1958): 316.

Upon his return to Cairo, Nasir stated that his trip to the USSR reaffirmed the soundness of positive neutralism. On the one hand, Washington had informed him that the United States respected the independence and neutralism of the UAR while, on the other, Khrushchev had repeatedly expressed Soviet respect for and support of both nonalignment and the Arab drive for unity. "Thus our policy of neutralism has emerged victorious and is now recognized by the two biggest powers in the world."[74]

The Soviet government, in contrast, utilized Nasir's visit to reaffirm its determination to maintain close ties with the United Arab Republic. Khrushchev assured his guest that in giving "selfless" assistance to the countries of the Middle East, the USSR was not pursuing any "selfish aims." It did not seek to impose on the Arab states the Soviet system of government or to obtain "privileges or any other particular material advantages." Moscow was interested only in strengthening the position of the Arab peoples in their struggle against Western imperialism. The friendship between the USSR and the United Arab Republic was based on the "realization and application of the principles of mutual respect for territorial integrity, sovereignty, nonagression, noninterference in each other's internal affairs, equality, mutual benefit, peaceful coexistence, and economic cooperation." Khrushchev was gratified to note that there were "no storm clouds on the horizon" of Moscow-Cairo relations. Soviet foreign policy was recognized by an "ever-growing number of countries" as "peace-loving and selfless," he boasted. The growing Soviet prestige in Asia and Africa explained why the Western powers had resumed their attempts to destroy the ties of friendship binding Moscow with the newly independent, underdeveloped nations. "We must show vigilance in the face of imperialist intrigues and not permit them to upset the growing cooperation between the United Arab Republic, the Soviet Union, and other peaceloving countries," Khrushchev concluded.[75]

In a joint statement issued at the conclusion of their talks on May 15, the two leaders expressed their "profound satisfaction with the development of close and constantly expanding relations" between their countries and agreed to "work for [their] further strengthening

74. *The Egyptian Mail* (henceforth referred to as *EM*), May 17, 1958.
75. Texts of Khrushchev's speeches in *Pr.*, May 1 and 16, 1958.

and development." The USSR promised Nasir the aid necessary to secure Arab rights in Palestine, Yemen, and Algeria, whereas the UAR endorsed all the major planks of Moscow's foreign policy.[76] It is, therefore, not surprising that Moscow's publications struck an optimistic note in writing about the "firm foundations" upon which Soviet-Arab friendship allegedly rested and expressing the conviction that "friendly relations between the Soviet Union and the United Arab Republic will continue to develop on the basis of the principles of peaceful coexistence and mutual respect. Consolidation of these relations accords with the interests of both countries and strengthens peace in the Middle East and throughout the world."[77]

One may only wonder whether Nasir's decision to restrict pro-Communist writers in Egypt and ban Soviet propaganda pamphlets and books from the stands and bookshops throughout the United Arab Republic, taken in the wake of his trip to the USSR,[78] came as a shock to the Soviet government. But there can be no doubt that, all glowing assurances notwithstanding, this was an outward manifestation of a basic divergence of interests between Moscow and the neutralist Arabs. The rift was scarcely visible, its existence being engulfed in widely publicized manifestations of Soviet-Arab friendship, but it was there, awaiting an opportune moment to erupt into the open. The storm broke in December 1958, some six months after Nasir's return from his triumphant tour of the USSR. The impetus was provided by the Iraqi revolution and the increased restiveness of the Syrian Communists. In the meantime, however, the Arab East was once again thrown into turmoil by a crisis in Lebanon, which led, even if indirectly, to the Iraqi revolution.

76. Text in *ibid.*
77. Kh. Grigoryan, "Closer Friendly Relations," *International Affairs* (Moscow, henceforth referred to as *IA*), no. 5 (May 1958), p. 115. See also editorial, "Firm Foundation," *NT,* no. 21 (May 1958), p. 2.
78. *MEJ* 12, no. 3 (Summer 1958): 316.

4
The Lebanese Crisis

Half-Muslim, half-Christian Lebanon has been one of the most stable Arab states economically. Politically, a precarious balance has been preserved between the generally pro-Western Christian groups, organized in or sympathetic to the Phalange party, and Muslim organizations, favoring closer ties with the rest of the Arab world, notably the United Arab Republic. The Suez crisis is generally regarded as the turning point in Christian-Muslim relations in this tiny Arab state. 'Abdallah al-Yafi, the Prime Minister, and Sa'ib Salam, his deputy, resigned in protest against the refusal of the Christian President, Kamil Sham'un, to condemn the attack on Egypt and were replaced by Sami al-Sulh and Dr. Charles Malik. When, early in 1957, even prior to its approval by the United States Congress, Lebanon accepted the Eisenhower Doctrine—the only Arab state to do so—the Muslim groups condemned the act as a breach of the National Pact.[1]

Throughout 1957 and early 1958, the internal situation in Lebanon deteriorated markedly, partly because of Sham'un's determination to serve a second six-year term as President of the strife-torn country—a step that necessitated amending the Constitution. On May 8, 1958,

1. Desmond Stewart, *Turmoil in Beirut* (London: Wingate, 1958), p. 20.

Nasib al-Matni, editor of the pro-UAR Arabic newspaper *al-Telegraf,* was murdered in Bayrut. His death served as a pretext for more violence and a virulent anti-Sham'un propaganda campaign emanating from Damascus and Cairo. The President and his associates were accused of having turned Lebanon into a "center for sinister conspiracies and intrigues against Arab unity and independence and against Arab rulers inspired with a true sentiment of nationalism."[2]

On May 13, 1958, Foreign Minister Malik retaliated, accusing the UAR of inciting a revolt and aiding the rebels with men and munitions.[3] The accusation was seconded by Secretary Dulles who charged Cairo with interfering in the internal affairs of Lebanon by supplying the insurrectionists with arms and fuel.[4] The United States immediately stepped up arms deliveries to the Sham'un government and strengthened its naval units in the Eastern Mediterranean.[5]

Cairo rejected the Lebanese note on the ground that it contained nothing but "sheer fabrications and false charges" against the United Arab Republic.[6] Addressing the Secretary of State, the Egyptian press held him responsible for the "blood shed by the Lebanese people" and assured him that the "blame for all crimes committed by his agents in Lebanon" would fall "squarely on his shoulders."[7]

At this juncture Moscow recognized the opportunity to offset any gains made by Washington in the spring of 1958 and to strengthen its hold over Nasir, which was gradually slipping as a result of Cairo's determination to balance its close ties with the Soviet bloc by improving relations with the Western powers.

On May 18, 1958, an official Soviet statement accused the United States of interfering in the internal affairs of Lebanon and endangering the peace and security of the Middle East. The US embassy in Bayrut was described as "headquarters for plotting with reactionary anti-

2. Editorial, *al-Sha'b* (Cairo), May 9, 1958. For more details on the background of the Lebanese revolt, see Fahim I. Qubain, *Crisis in Lebanon* (Washington: The Middle East Institute, 1961), chaps. 1–4.
3. *MEJ* 12, no. 3 (Summer 1958): 306.
4. As quoted in editorial, *al-Akhbar,* May 22, 1958.
5. *MEJ* 12, no. 3 (Summer 1958): 306–7.
6. *EG,* May 15, 1958.
7. Editorial, *al-Akhbar,* May 22, 1958.

national elements within the country, grossly interfering in [Lebanon's] internal affairs and attempting to take charge of it as if it were a colony." In addition, the statement noted that arms were being dispatched to Lebanon and the US Sixth Fleet had been ordered into the Eastern Mediterranean. The number of American marines in the area was reported increasing rapidly, with preparations under way to land them on Lebanese soil.

Moscow dismissed as ridiculous charges that "mass actions of the population in Lebanon against foreign interference in its affairs and in defense of the independence and constitution of the country" were inspired or directed by the United Arab Republic. In contrast to the United States and its policies of "cold war, the arms race, and unrestrained expansion," the peoples of the East wished to remain "complete masters in their own homes," to live in peace and friendship with all nations. The Soviet government considered that the "settlement of questions pertaining to the Lebanese state is an inalienable right of the Lebanese people and no other state has the right to interfere in these affairs." Moscow expressed confidence that outside powers would refrain from intervening in the internal affairs of Lebanon or permitting a "dangerous hotbed of war to be created in this area."[8]

The Soviet and neutralist Arab warnings did not deter the increased US moral and material support of the Sham'un regime, which aroused even stronger indignation in Moscow and Cairo. The latter blamed the "present deterioration in the Lebanese situation" on Washington's interference in the country's internal affairs, that is, supplying the Sham'un government with "large quantities of arms to be used against the people."[9] The United Arab Republic denied any complicity in the Lebanese revolt and dismissed as false charges that men, arms, and money were being smuggled into Lebanon from Syria. Such accusa-

---

8. Text in *Pr.*, May 19, 1958. Charges that "international Communism" was at work in Lebanon were also ridiculed by Moscow. See S. Kondrashov, *Izv.*, May 30, 1958. Appraisal of events leading to the outbreak of hostilities in Akademiia nauk SSSR. Institut narodov Azii, *Politika SShA na Arabskom Vostoke* (Moscow: Izdatel'stvo vostochnoi literatury, 1961), pp. 174–88, and Akademiia nauk SSSR. Institut narodov Azii, *Noveishaia istoriia arabskikh stran (1917–1966)* (Moscow: Izdatel'stvo "Nauka," 1968), pp. 101–6.

9. Editorial, *al-Akhbar*, June 14, 1958.

tions, Egyptian sources asserted, were used to provide an excuse for the Western powers themselves to interfere in Lebanese affairs on the side of the government, which pledged to "support Western political influence to the detriment of true Lebanese independence."[10] This led to the conclusion, heartily supported by Moscow, that the Western powers feared that the Lebanese uprising might spill over into Iraq, Jordan, and other Arab countries "still ruled by imperialist lackeys."[11]

Moscow, as usual, went one step further, accusing Iraq and Jordan of determination to dispatch "volunteers" to help Sham'un combat the insurgents. Nuri al-Sa'id and King Husayn allegedly had met with Israeli Premier Ben-Gurion at the end of May and worked out an agreement to permit Iraqi and Jordanian planes, carrying arms and supplies to loyal Lebanese troops, to fly over Israeli territory. Arab nationalists, it was concluded, were confronted with an imperialist conspiracy, inspired by the ruling circles of the USA and Great Britain.[12]

Meanwhile, the situation in Lebanon continued to deteriorate. The revolt spread as arms and munitions were brought into the country from both Western and UAR arsenals. An Arab League resolution recommending a peaceful settlement of the dispute proved no more helpful than the report of a fact-finding commission dispatched to Lebanon by the UN Security Council. The Kremlin and the neutralist Arabs were gratified by the report, however, for, while finding it impossible to determine whether any of the armed men in Lebanon had infiltrated from the outside, the observers asserted that "the vast majority" of them were in fact Lebanese.[13]

In the middle of June 1958, the Lebanese government increased its efforts to exert pressure on the United States, requesting additional material aid and, possibly, direct armed intervention to help subdue

10. Editorial, *EG*, June 26, 1958.
11. Editorial, *al-Sha'b*, June 20, 1958.
12. V. Fuzeyev, "A Conspiracy Against the People," *IA*, no. 7 (July 1958), pp. 81–82. See also S. Kondrashov, *Izv.*, May 30; P. Demchenko, *Pr.*, June 4; V. Biryuzov, "The Lebanese Events," *NT*, no. 21 (May 1958), pp. 11–12; N. Khokhlov, *Izv.*, June 13; and S. Kondrashov, *ibid.*, June 14, 1958.
13. *EM*, July 5, 1958. For Soviet reaction, see editorial, "Seeking Another Instrument," *NT*, no. 28 (July 1958), p. 19.

the revolt. Following several meetings between Dulles and Malik, the Secretary of State, on June 17, renewed the pledge that the United States was ready to employ its armed forces in the defense of Lebanon's independence.[14]

On June 24, the Soviet government, apparently alarmed at the implications of Dulles's statement, issued an official declaration calling on all "peace-loving states and governments" to do their utmost to prevent the "impending imperialist aggression" against Lebanon. Attempts to "carry out armed intervention against Lebanon under whatever pretext" were in gross violation of UN principles and would inevitably lead to a serious deterioration of the international situation. The responsibility for such a "grave threat to peace," Moscow asserted, would rest on the Western powers and their Lebanese "hirelings." For this reason, the Soviet government could not remain indifferent to foreign intervention in Lebanon.[15]

The situation in Lebanon became even more serious on July 14, 1958, when the pro-Western regime of Nuri al-Sa'id was overthrown in Iraq.[16] President Sham'un addressed an urgent message to the government of the United States claiming that his regime would not survive in the face of the new impetus given to anti-Western forces by the Iraqi revolution, and formally asked that US troops be dispatched to Lebanon. Alarmed, Washington complied, and US Marines began landing on Bayrut's beaches on July 15. Two days later British paratroopers landed in 'Amman at the request of the Jordanian government, which also had reason to believe that its position was being threatened by Arab nationalist elements.

The United Arab Republic and the USSR met the US and British troop landings with a predictable wave of violent verbal indignation and criticism. On July 16, Cairo published a statement terming the "US occupation" of Lebanon "a danger to peace in the Middle East, a grave violation of the United Nations Charter and a flagrant threat

---

14. *MEJ* 12, no. 3 (Summer 1958): 309-10.
15. "TASS Statement," *Pr.*, June 25, 1958. For more information, see V. Borovskii, *ibid.*, June 7; I. Beliaev and P. Demchenko, *ibid.*, June 9; V. Maevskii, *ibid.*, June 26; and I. Aleksandrov, *ibid.*, July 8, 1958.
16. For details, see chap. 5.

to the Arab countries that [had] refused to bow down to imperialism and [had] resolved to pursue an independent policy."[17] The Soviet government used even more violent accusations to add fuel to the fire. Moscow charged that the United States and Great Britain had committed an "act of armed aggression" designed to "suppress the national-liberation movement in the countries of the Arab East." In line with its policy of undermining Western positions in the region, the USSR assailed the allies, noting that the imperialists had finally "dropped the mask and adopted the course of open aggression against the peaceable Arab peoples." The aggression explained why the US government had not accepted the Soviet proposal of February 11, 1957, stipulating noninterference by the great powers in the internal affairs of the Middle Eastern states. Washington "refused to undertake obligations whose performance would have ensured peace and relaxation of tensions in this part of the world" because it wanted to have its hands free for aggressive actions in the Middle East.

The Soviet government held that Western intervention in the Arab East had created a "serious threat to peace" and was fraught with "far-reaching consequences. The peoples cannot remain indifferent in the face of this brazen imperialist aggression, . . . [this] flagrant violation of the sovereignty and national independence of the Arab states, and the unceremonious flouting of UN principles." The USSR "insistently" urged Washington and London to cease their "armed intervention in the internal affairs of the Arab nations" and withdraw their forces from Lebanon and Jordan. In conclusion, the Western powers were warned that the Soviet government would not remain "indifferent to developments which create a serious threat in an area adjoining its borders," and reserved for itself the right to take "such measures as may be necessary in the interests of safeguarding peace and security."[18]

On July 17, President Nasir had flown to Moscow to confer with

17. Text in *EG,* July 17. For more details, see editorials, *ibid.,* July 16 and 22, 1958.
18. The above two paragraphs are based on a Statement by the Soviet government, text in *Pr.,* July 17. See also Statement of July 18, *ibid.,* July 19, 1958.

Khrushchev. A brief official announcement said that the two leaders "exchanged views on the development of the present international situation and [discussed] what is needed for the preservation of peace."[19] It was rumored in Cairo that Nasir's visit was prompted by his determination to keep the Soviet government from taking any precipitous action, unless the Western powers launched an attack against the United Arab Republic or the Republic of Iraq. According to this line of thinking, Khrushchev might have regarded a serious setback to his Middle Eastern policy, coming in the wake of the failure of his "liberal" policies in Eastern Europe, as too severe a blow to his prestige and power to accept without overt retaliation. As a result, he might be tempted to embark upon an "adventurist" policy. This explanation must be dismissed as unfounded. No matter how serious Khrushchev's apprehensions over the Middle East might have been, he would hardly have risked a showdown with the United States at a time when Washington enjoyed a clear nuclear superiority over the USSR. Put differently, mid-1958 was in this respect similar to the crises of November 1956 and October 1957; Russia was not willing to risk its own annihilation for the sake of any Third World client.

While hard evidence is not available, it is entirely possible that the US intervention in Lebanon, coupled with the entry of British troops into Jordan, appeared to Nasir to be the first stage of a concerted Western drive to destroy the nationalist governments of both the UAR and Iraq. It is much more likely, therefore, that Nasir went to the USSR in order to find out whether he could rely on Soviet military support in case of such an emergency. What he was told by Khrushchev is still shrouded in mystery, although, according to Mackintosh, "Russia declined to commit herself to military aid to . . . [Cairo] in the event of war over Iraq."[20]

Nevertheless, as tension continued to mount, Moscow made full use of the opportunity to undermine Western influence in the Arab East and, if possible, to deepen the wedge between Cairo and Washington.

19. *EM*, July 19, 1958.
20. J. M. Mackintosh, *Strategy and Tactics of Soviet Foreign Policy* (London: Oxford University Press, 1963), p. 235. This conclusion was subsequently corroborated by Haykal. See *al-Ahram,* January 22, 1965.

For example, the reasons advanced by both the US and British governments as justification for the troop landings were subjected to close public scrutiny. The fact that the United States and Great Britain had landed troops at the request of the legally constituted authorities of the countries in question did not impress the Soviet government. The Kremlin held that Lebanon and Jordan were in the grip of an internal conflict and noted that outside powers should have abided by international law, which prohibits interference in the internal affairs of other states. Washington was reminded that Americans resented foreign intervention during their Civil War. Moreover, because Sham'un's appeal for US forces had not been supported by the Lebanese parliament, it constituted a direct violation of the country's constitution. The situation in Jordan was similar: British troops were landed for the specific purpose of protecting the tottering throne of King Husayn. Having lost the support of their subjects, the rulers of Lebanon and Jordan were able to rely only on US and British forces.

In an irony not lost on some observers, Moscow reminded Sham'un and Husayn that governments and thrones cannot be maintained by bayonets. The Kremlin also dismissed the assertion that US and British troops landed in the two Arab countries for the purpose of protecting the lives and property of their respective citizens; not only had the foreigners in Lebanon and Jordan suffered no harm, but international law expressly prohibited military intervention in the affairs of another country on the pretext that one's nationals had been threatened.

The USSR was equally indignant at the use of Article 51 of the UN Charter. Self-defense could be employed only if a member-state was subjected to an armed attack and only until such time as the Security Council would take appropriate measures. In the case of Jordan, King Husayn appealed for British troops on the ground that his country was about to be attacked by the United Arab Republic. And the US and Lebanese governments had invoked the right of self-defense against an alleged outside aggression at a time when the UN Commission of inquiry had established that Lebanon was not being subjected to a foreign attack. All references to what was termed an "indirect aggression" by the United Arab Republic were dismissed as lacking any foundation. Aggression was indeed being committed in the Middle East, Moscow noted, but only in the case of the direct armed intervention by US and British imperialists in the internal affairs of Lebanon, Jordan, and other Arab states.[21]

Among the "real motives and purposes" of US and British troop landings in the Middle East exposed by the Soviet government were the fears of the "oil monopolies" for their "billion-dollar profits, which would be diminished by the triumph of the national-liberation movement in the Middle East."[22] Iraq's successful revolution was but the latest manifestation of the Arab nationalist drive toward complete independence and unity. "Observer" stated: "The chief purpose of the U.S. and British landings was to crush the [national-] liberation movement. It is not merely a matter of restoring the West's 'strategic and economic position' in the Middle East, but of preventing the Iraqi events from influencing other parts of the Arab world."[23]

The UN Security Council deliberations on the Middle East crisis, which had begun on July 15, soon reached an impasse. A US draft resolution, calling on the Secretary-General to arrange a replacement of US troops in Lebanon by a UN emergency force, was vetoed by the USSR. A Soviet draft resolution, demanding that the United States and Great Britain "cease armed intervention in the domestic affairs of the Arab states and remove their troops," was also voted down. A similar fate awaited a Swedish draft resolution, which held that the United States was not authorized to interfere in the "domestic jurisdiction" of any state and requested that the Secretary-General suspend the activities of the UN observation group in Lebanon. Before the Council recessed, both the United States and the USSR moved to

21. The preceding paragraphs are based on Statements by the Soviet government (see n. 18); Khrushchev's letter to Eisenhower, *Pr.,* July 20; and the articles by E. Litoshko, *ibid.,* August 3; and P. Tolmachov, "Colonialist Propaganda Stunts," *IA,* no. 9 (September 1958), pp. 80–83.
22. Observer, *Pr.,* July 16, 1958. For more details, see Observer, "Oil Colonialism," *NT,* no. 25 (June 1958), pp. 3–5; and editorial, *Pr.,* July 20, 1958.
23. Observer, "Middle East: What Next?," *NT,* no. 31 (August 1958), p. 3. See also Observer, "New Version of Suez," *ibid.,* no. 30 (July 1958), pp. 2–4; and a statement by various "peace" organizations, *Pr.,* August 1, 1958.

put the issue before an emergency session of the General Assembly, which opened on August 8, 1958.[24]

The intervening period was utilized by the Soviet government to stage another far-flung political and diplomatic campaign directed at the Western powers. On July 19, Premier Khrushchev addressed letters to the heads of state of the United States, Great Britain, France, and India, as well as to the UN Secretary-General, suggesting a summit meeting for the discussion of the Middle Eastern situation. Khrushchev reminded them that the Anglo-American military intervention in Lebanese and Jordanian affairs had brought the world to the "brink of disaster." In this "grim hour of history" Russia could not remain indifferent to events that were taking place "in close proximity to its border." The Western powers were reminded that the USSR, too, possessed "ballistic missiles of all kinds, including intercontinental."

Khrushchev proposed that the summit conference draw up "concrete recommendations" for terminating the military conflict in the Middle East and submit them to the Security Council, "where they should be considered with the participation of representatives of the Arab countries." In line with earlier Soviet proposals, the heads of state should also agree to cease arms deliveries to the countries of the Middle East. The proposed conference—an "inestimable contribution to the consolidation of peace and international security"—was to meet in Geneva or "any other venue, including Washington," on July 22, 1958.[25]

President Eisenhower, British Prime Minister Harold Macmillan, and French President Charles de Gaulle agreed to attend a summit meeting, but proposed that the conference be held within the framework of the Security Council, that no resolutions be submitted to the Council on which there was not complete accord, that only members of the Council and countries directly involved in the dispute participate, and that the participants discuss the entire Middle Eastern situation, not limiting themselves to the consideration of the Anglo-

24. *NYT*, July 20, 1958.
25. *Izv.*, July 20, 1958.

American intervention in Jordan and Lebanon. Khrushchev's reply of July 28 was full of abuse and overdrawn expressions of disappointment. Moscow accused the United States of going back on its original acceptance of the summit conference and insisted that the meeting take place as soon as possible. "Observer" termed Eisenhower's latest proposal a "mockery" and a "reply of those who are afraid to stand before world public opinion and account for their adventurist policies which have brought all humanity to the brink of war."[26]

On August 1, President Eisenhower told Khrushchev that the Security Council meeting must be limited to the heads of state or foreign ministers and suggested August 12 as the opening date. But by early August the Soviet government, in a complete about-face, had dropped its insistence on a summit meeting, placing the matter of the US and British "intervention" in Lebanon and Jordan on the agenda of a Special Session of the UN General Assembly. The fact that Khrushchev's initial request stipulated the convening of the summit on July 22, only three days after the invitation had been issued, may cast a legitimate doubt on the seriousness with which he was making the proposal. Similarly, in view of the abuse and violence of his letter of July 28, it is unlikely that the Soviet leader could have expected anything constructive to emerge from any ensuing conference. Thus, even if one accepts the proposition that Khrushchev was genuinely interested in a top-level meeting, he could have believed in its feasibility only in the period between July 19 and 28.

This frantic behavior may have been motivated by his desire, long thwarted by Washington and London, to gain Western recognition of Russia's status as a Middle Eastern power. Possibly the determination to arrange a summit meeting with the leaders of the capitalist great powers reflects Khrushchev's unsuccessful attempts at reconciliation with the West in the wake of his ruthless suppression of the Hungarian revolution. Finally, Moscow may simply have been intent on making as much political and propaganda capital as possible out of a situation for which the Kremlin was not responsible and over which it had little or no control. In any case, the most striking feature of Khrushchev's

26. *Pr.,* July 30, 1958. See also Observer in *Izv.* of the same date.

feverish diplomatic activity is its basic indecision, originating from the Kremlin's full realization of its inability to match Washington's and London's resolute moves in Lebanon and Jordan. Compounding Moscow's difficulties was the fear that the Western powers, encouraged by their success in Bayrut and 'Amman, would also intervene in Iraq, thus placing the United Arab Republic—and, indirectly, its friend and protector the USSR— in a very embarrassing position. Since there was no doubt in Khrushchev's mind that he would not commit his armed forces to the defense of Nasir or Qasim, the crushing of one or both would reveal to all the world the basic Soviet weakness *vis-à-vis* the West, which the Kremlin had been trying so hard to conceal.

By late July and early August, however, it had become obvious that the Western powers had decided against intervention in Iraq.[27] Further, the decision to abandon summit diplomacy and to turn the matter over to the General Assembly may also have been motivated by another consideration. On July 31, Khrushchev and a number of other Soviet dignitaries traveled to Peking for a meeting with the leaders of Communist China.[28] It is possible that Communist China resented both its exclusion from the discussion of a problem in which it claimed to be vitally interested and Khrushchev's consent to meet his Western counterparts in the Security Council, where the representative of Nationalist China occupied a permanent seat.

In any event, the Soviet propaganda apparatus in the meantime continued to extract the maximum possible advantage from the continued presence of Western troops in Lebanon and Jordan by contrasting Moscow's alleged desire to negotiate a settlement in the Mid-

27. See below, chap. 5.
28. Khrushchev met Mao and other Chinese Communist leaders at a conference, held in Peking from July 31 to August 3, 1958. In an official communiqué it was stated that the USSR and the Chinese People's Republic condemned the "flagrant aggressive actions" of the USA and Great Britain in the Middle East, demanded the immediate convening of a heads of state conference of the great powers (meaning presumably also Communist China) to discuss the situation in the Middle East, and insisted on immediate withdrawal of US and British troops from Lebanon and Jordan. Text in *Pr.*, August 4, 1958.

dle East with the provocative and unreasonable attitude of the United States and Great Britain:

> The people everywhere are tired of the cold war, and Western diplomacy has been trying to make them believe that it is working to ease international tension. Its method, a very old one, is to put the blame on the socialist camp. But the Soviet Union's energetic campaign for a summit conference to discuss pressing issues, . . . has placed the Western politicians in a predicament. They have had to resort to the old tactic of procrastination and manoeuvre, to the method of advancing patently unacceptable prior conditions.
>
> When the Soviet Union suggested an immediate conference of the heads of government to remove the danger of war in the Middle East, the West retaliated by a series of delaying tactics, evasive replies and deliberate ambiguity.[29]

The Egyptian press agreed with the USSR on the desirability of a summit conference.[30] This attitude represented a marked departure from Cairo's previous stand on the issue. It is not difficult to see why the United Arab Republic should be vitally interested in averting a major war in the Middle East. Among other things, a confrontation between the superpowers would bring about a devastation of the region and nullify all the gains made by the Arabs in their quest for social and economic development. It would also indefinitely postpone the possibility of establishing the strong and unified Arab state that Nasir was still hoping to create. Moreover, he may have hoped that Soviet and UAR political pressure would not only deter Washington and London from intervening in Iraq but also force the United States and Great Britain to stand before world public opinion branded as "aggressors." Nasir seems to have thought that massive condemnation might make Washington more receptive to Egyptian overtures, and, interestingly enough, Cairo continued periodically to express an

---

29. L. Leontyev, "The Middle East Crisis and Western Diplomacy," *NT*, no. 35 (August 1958), p. 5.
30. For details, see editorials, *EG*, July 23 and 27, 1958.

interest in friendship with the United States both before and after the Marines had landed in Lebanon.[31]

The differences in the Soviet and UAR approaches to the problem of solving the crisis became even more pronounced during the third emergency session of the General Assembly, which opened in early August. Though both Soviet and neutralist Arab publications welcomed the idea of establishing peace in the Middle East on a more permanent basis, they differed widely in their evaluation of the immediate tasks facing the special session. Moscow held that it was "the sacred duty of the General Assembly to . . . remove the war danger created by the aggressive actions of the British and American imperialists." This involved a "swift and complete cessation of armed intervention and the creation of conditions that will rid the peoples of the Middle East of foreign interference in their internal affairs."[32] Cairo predicted that numerous solutions to Middle Eastern problems would be presented to the General Assembly but indicated that its UN delegation would abide by the following rule: "Any policy not emanating from the Middle East is both wrong and rash." It was held that the Arabs, inhabiting the area, were more entitled than the outsiders, including the United States and the Soviet Union, to draw up regional policies. "Others have no right to deal with our destinies without taking into consideration our feelings, our will, and our interests," *al-Gumhuriya* asserted. If any plan approved by the United Nations for the Middle East is to succeed in alleviating tension in the area and in the whole world, the first prerequisite is that it should satisfy the feelings and aspirations of the peoples of the area."[33]

By the time President Eisenhower outlined to the General Assembly a plan for peace in the Middle East,[34] the situation in the region had improved considerably and the need for immediate Western ac-

31. See editorial in *ibid.*, August 8, 1958.
32. Editorial, "The Duty of the General Assembly," *NT*, no. 33 (August 1958), pp. 1–2. See also editorial, *ibid.*, no. 35 (August 1958), pp. 1–2; editorial, *Pr.*, August 12; and D. Kraminov, V. Strel'nikov, *ibid.*, August 15, 1958.
33. Editorial, August 12, 1959.
34. See United Nations, *Yearbook of the United Nations, 1958* (New York: Columbia University Press, 1959), p. 45.

tion was not so urgent as four or five weeks earlier. Some of his proposals, such as the establishment of a regional development institution to be directed by the Arabs and to make use of international capital, were especially formulated to appeal to Arab nationalists. The voluminous output and the violence of Soviet propaganda responses attested to Moscow's general frustration and, more particularly, to its concern with the Eisenhower plan. The Soviet government stressed the necessity of immediate and total evacuation of foreign troops from Lebanon and Jordan and scored the Western powers for their failure to comply with the wishes of "all peace-loving peoples." Referring to Eisenhower's speech, "Observer" noted that it revealed "nothing constructive, nothing which would be useful in accomplishing the first and main task—the immediate withdrawal of Anglo-American troops from Lebanon and Jordan." The plan was held to represent a program for "preserving and expanding colonialism under the UN flag, smothering the national-liberation movement in the Arab East and subordinating the peoples of this region to the rule of American and British imperialists."[35] The *New Times* called on the Arabs to reject the Eisenhower plan for the following reasons: it did not mention the withdrawal of foreign troops from Lebanon and Jordan; its provisions had no relation to the problem discussed by the General Assembly; and it "actually envisaged a 'U.N. force' to replace U.S. and British forces. But Korea proved that in practice this would mean continued U.S. and British occupation, only under a U.N. signboard."[36]

Moscow also tried to discredit the economic provisions of the Eisenhower plan. Noting prudently that raising the living standards and improving the economic position of the Arabs were "noble tasks" deserving "closest attention," "Observer" nevertheless accused the US government of attempts to divert the attention of the General Assembly from the problem of peace in the Middle East.[37] In a wider framework, Moscow struck at the "Wall Street magnates" and US "oil monopolies," whose "civilizing activities in the Middle East make

35. *Izv.*, August 16, 1958.
36. Y. Bochkaryov, "How the Aggressors Were Defeated," *NT*, no. 35 (August 1958), p. 6.
37. *Izv.*, August 16, 1958.

one wonder about the true motives of the 'philanthropists' from across the sea." Reminding the readers about the regional economic development plan presented by David Rockefeller in his speech before the annual meeting of the Arkansas Bankers' Association of May 22, 1957, *Pravda* pointed to the "striking similarity" between the two projects and termed Eisenhower's program the "second Rockefeller doctrine."[38]

After prolonged, heated, and fruitless discussions, the UN General Assembly, on August 21, unanimously adopted a draft resolution sponsored by all ten Arab members of the United Nations. It contained renewed assurances by the Arab states to respect each other's territorial integrity and political independence; urged the UN Secretary-General to continue working for the withdrawal of foreign troops from Lebanon and Jordan; and asked the cooperation of the UN members in carrying out the resolution.[39] The resolution, which pulled the General Assembly out of a seemingly hopeless predicament, was otherwise inconsequential. It did not hasten the withdrawal of US and British forces from Lebanon and Jordan; they were removed only after the internal situation in these countries had stabilized and it was recognized that their continued presence was becoming a political liability. Piously expressed hopes for future noninterference of the Arab states in the affairs of their sister countries were crushed before the year ended, and tension, in the form of a new Iraqi-UAR conflict, was already looming on the horizon. Finally, hopes for an integrated regional economic development program were inevitably dependent on a political stability clearly lacking in the area.

But these considerations did not prevent either the United Arab Republic or the Soviet Union from praising the resolution as a major achievement of the "anti-imperialist" forces. To Cairo, the united Arab action was a "shrewd step," stressing the neutrality of the Arab world and its insistence on "rejecting all forms of outside intervention

38. V. Zhukov, *Pr.*, August 18, 1958. See also D. Kraminov and B. Strel'-nikov, *ibid.*, August 16, 1958.
39. See United Nations, *Yearbook* . . . , *1958*, pp. 46–47; *MEJ* 12, no. 4 (Autumn 1958): 420. Full text in B. Shwadran, *Jordan—A State of Tension* (New York: Council for Middle Eastern Affairs, 1959), pp. 388–89.

in the area."⁴⁰ "In spite of a certain inadequacy of its formulations," the Soviet government supported the ten-power resolution because it called for an "early withdrawal of US and British forces from the Middle East." Moscow stressed the importance of the resolution as the "first international document on the Middle East accepted by all Great Powers," but warned that it would be naïve to expect the imperialists to "abandon interference in Arab affairs." The USSR, on whose initiative the special session had allegedly been convened, was a "sincere friend of the Arab nations" and wanted to see them "completely liberated from foreign control."⁴¹

Until the withdrawal of US and British units from Lebanon and Jordan was completed at the end of October 1958, both the United Arab Republic and the USSR continued to press for a speedy evacuation of foreign troops from the Middle East. The differences between Soviet and neutralist Arab publications were confined to the degree of violence with which the Western powers were attacked for their "delaying tactics" in implementing the evacuation provision of the General Assembly resolution of August 21,⁴² and to the added UAR assurances that the Arabs aspired to nothing "illegitimate" or harmful to Western interests.⁴³ In insisting on their respect for "legitimate" Western interests in the Middle East, Cairo openly stressed the divergence between the Soviet and Arab nationalist approaches to the problem of US and British presence in the area.

After General Fu'ad Shihab, the Maronite Christian Commander-in-Chief of the Lebanese army, was elected President of Lebanon, on July 31, 1958, the Egyptian press noted that the United Arab Republic had supported his election as early as May 20.⁴⁴ In his first official

40. Editorial, *al-Gumhuriya,* August 22, 1958.
41. Y. Bochkaryov, "How the Aggressors Were Defeated," *NT,* no. 35 (August 1958), pp. 6–7. See also Foreign Minister Andrei Gromyko's statement of August 22, text in *Pr.,* August 24; and editorial, *ibid.*
42. For UAR comments, see editorials in *al-Gumhuriya, al-Sha'b,* and *EG* of September 10, 16, and October 9, 1958, respectively. For Soviet comments, see O. Orestov, *Pr.,* September 4; M. Sturua, *Izv.,* September 4; S. Kondrashov, *ibid.,* September 5; and O. Orestov, *Pr.,* October 5, 1958.
43. Editorial, *EG,* October 10, 1958.
44. See *al-Ahram,* August 1, 1958.

policy statement of September 25, newly appointed Premier Rashid Karami announced that his government would ask for the immediate withdrawal of US troops from Lebanon.[45] In the sphere of foreign relations, Karami's government promised adherence to the country's "traditional policy": in the big-power struggle Lebanon's actions would be governed by the National Charter stressing independence and neutrality. Cairo expressed confidence in the new regime. By replacing a government that had forfeited the country's independence, it met the "essential requirements of the Lebanese political scene."[46]

The new government was also hailed in Moscow as "a signal success for Lebanon's patriotic forces": it removed from power the pro-US regime that had accepted the Eisenhower Doctrine, had severed Lebanon from the "independent Arab states," and had made it an "imperialist operational base in the Arab world."[47] However, while the UAR toned down its anti-US campaign once it became obvious that American and British troop landings were not directed against Cairo or Baghdad, the Soviet government exploited the presence of allied forces on Arab soil until the very day of their withdrawal. Even as late as September and October 1958, Soviet publications urged the Lebanese to insist on the immediate pull-out of foreign troops because "as long as the U.S. interventionists remain in Lebanon, there will be no peace, no order and no opportunity to carry out the national programme for which the people have shed so much blood."[48]

The importance to Moscow of the Lebanese episode was demonstrated in the editorial "Net Loss," published in the *New Times*.[49] Commenting on the Department of State announcement to the effect that the withdrawal of US troops from Lebanon was voluntary after the operation had "resulted in a net political gain," Moscow termed

45. See *MEJ* 13, no. 1 (Winter 1959): 87.
46. Editorial, *EG*, October 19, 1958.
47. Editorial, "Showing Them the Door," *NT*, no. 40 (October 1958), p. 2; and Y. Zvyagin, "Washington's Trojan Horse," *ibid.*, no. 41 (October 1958), pp. 11–12. See also V. Maevskii, *Pr.*, September 27, 1958.
48. Editorial, "Showing Them the Door," *NT*, no. 40 (October 1958), p. 2.
49. *Ibid.*, no. 45 (November 1958), p. 20. See also V. Osipov, *Izv.*, October 26, 1958.

the statement a "clumsy face-saving device." The United States had not achieved its objectives, political or military. It had failed to stifle the Iraqi revolution, had not suppressed the "popular, anti-imperialist revolt" in Lebanon, and had not prevented the collapse of the Sham-'un regime. Finally, the attempt, with Sham'un's aid, to "incite religious war as an excuse for prolonging the occupation had failed dismally."[50] But the presence of US troops in the Arab East did have some "important accomplishments," Moscow cynically asserted. It had shown the Arabs that "U.S. imperialism is just as much their enemy as British and French imperialism. The Americans have left behind a feeling of bitter resentment, but also a feeling that imperialism is no longer omnipotent and that there are forces capable of curbing its aggressive proclivities."[51]

Subsequently, Moscow claimed that it had played a major part in defeating the "Anglo-American intervention in the Arab East." As during the Suez crisis of 1956, the Soviet Union had, in its own estimate, emerged as a "powerful shield, guarding the newly liberated countries from imperialist interventions and aggressions." This, it was held, reinforced the conclusion that, in matters of national liberation, the imperialist powers, despite their contradictions, found themselves on one side of the fence, while the underdeveloped nations and the states of the "socialist camp" invariably joined forces on the other side.[52]

50. For more details, see S. Kondrashov, *Izv.,* October 17, 1958.
51. See n. 49. See also Institut mezhdunarodnykh otnoshenii, p. 608.
52. O. E. Tuganova, *Mezhdunarodnye otnosheniia na Blizhnem i Srednem Vostoke* (Moscow: Izdatel'stvo "Mezhdunarodnye otnosheniia," 1967), p. 95. See also V. A. Zorin, ed., *Vneshniaia politika SSSR na novom etape* (Moscow: Politizdat, 1964), p. 126.

5
The Iraqi Revolution and the Rift with Cairo

The Iraqi upheaval of July 14, 1958, caught by surprise not only the usually well-informed UK and US embassies in Baghdad, but also Premier Nuri al-Sa'id, himself an old hand at intrigue.[1] In retrospect, it should not have been such a surprise, however, for a number of factors favored the coup, including widespread indifference or outright hostility to the Hashimite dynasty and its pro-British backers; strong dissatisfaction with the police-state methods that kept in power a notoriously corrupt group of politicians; and extensive emotional opposition to Nuri's anti-Nasir, pro-Western policy. There also had existed, for a number of years, an underground "Free Officers" organization whose Arab nationalist, pro-Nasir leanings had become evident as early as the summer of 1956.[2]

---

1. For more details, see *MEJ* 12, no. 4 (Fall 1958): 425–26.
2. For more details, see Haykal in *al-Ahram*, January 27, 1959. For the Iraqi view, see the *Iraqi Times* (Baghdad, henceforth referred to as *TIT*), November 27, 1958. For Soviet account of the preparations for the July revolution, see B. M. Dantsig, *Irak v proshlom i nastoiashchem* (Moscow: Izdatel'stvo vostochnoi literatury, 1960), pp. 56–59. For a description of conditions leading to the outbreak of the revolution, see Akademiia nauk SSSR. Institut narodov Azii, *Politika SShA na Arabskom Vostoke* (Moscow: Izdatel'stvo vostochnoi literatury, 1961), pp. 134-50; and Akademiia nauk SSSR. Institut mirovoi ekonomiki i mezhdunarodnykh otnoshenii, *Mezh-*

According to Cairo's Middle East News Agency (MENA), the "Free Officers" acted early in July, after Premier Nuri ordered one army brigade to proceed to Lebanon to help Sham'un suppress the insurrection. Instead, on July 14, 1958, 'Abd al-Karim Qasim, the brigade's commanding officer, moved his troops into Baghdad and deposed King Faysal and the old regime. Among the first political acts of the new government were the proclamation of full support of UN and Bandung principles, annulment of Iraqi membership in the Baghdad Pact, and recognition of the United Arab Republic.[3]

At the time of the coup President Nasir was visiting Yugoslavia. According to Egyptian sources, he immediately announced that the UAR "with all its potentialities, should stand by the side of the Iraqi revolution."[4] Cairo recognized the revolutionary government on July 15, and its statement of the next day declared that any aggression against the new regime in Baghdad would be considered an attack on the United Arab Republic.[5]

As might have been expected, the Iraqi revolution was received in the Kremlin with relief. Moscow soon realized, however, that, while the coup may have solved the potential problem of an Iraqi entry into the Lebanese conflict,[6] it served as the immediate precipitant of the landings of US and British troops in Lebanon and Jordan and foreshadowed a possible allied intervention in Iraq. The gravity with which the USSR viewed the situation in the Middle East was expressed in a hastily put-together article by "Observer," who dismissed arguments that the independence and security of Lebanon were in any way threatened by the events taking place in Baghdad. On the contrary, revolution in Iraq would put an end to Nuri's interference in the affairs of other states. In any event, the revolution was an internal problem that did not warrant outside intervention.[7]

---

dunarodnye otnosheniia posle vtoroi mirovoi voiny (1956–1964), (Moscow: Politizdat, 1965) 3: 546–48.
3. As quoted by G. Mirsky, "Fall of the Middle Eastern Bastille," *NT,* no. 30 (July 1958), pp. 9–10.
4. Haykal, *al-Ahram,* January 27, 1959.
5. Text in *EG,* July 17, 1958.
6. For examples of Soviet expressions of alarm at such a possibility, see V. Medvedev, *Pr.,* July 4, and N. Khokhlov, *Izv.,* July 8, 1958.
7. *Pr.,* July 16, 1958.

On July 16, the USSR and Communist China recognized the Iraqi Republic. Moscow, "unfailingly guided by the principle of self-determination of peoples and with profound respect for the legitimate national aspirations of the people of Iraq," expressed hope that the formation of the republican regime would contribute to the "strengthening of universal peace and the development of friendly relations between the USSR and Iraq."[8] It soon became obvious, however, that Moscow, unlike Cairo, was not prepared to go beyond moral and political backing of the revolutionary government.

The Iraqi revolution was widely hailed in both Cairo and Moscow as a landmark in the modern history of the Arabs. However, while Egypt stressed the importance of the Iraqi revolution for the improvement of inter-Arab relations,[9] Soviet publications, not unnaturally, emphasized the connection between the uprising and the deterioration of Western influence in the Middle East. P. Demchenko, for example, described the events of July 14 as a "cruel blow at the positions of American and British imperialism in the Near and Middle East."[10] More precisely, the Kremlin hailed the revolution as a "new and convincing proof of the strength of the national-liberation movement." The Iraqi masses had risen to defend the independence of their country and regain control of its national wealth, "plundered by foreign monopolies." The popular uprising had overthrown Nuri al-Sa'id, that "puppet of the imperialists who converted his country into a foreign military base, dragged it into the aggressive Baghdad Pact, and made it a weapon of the colonialists in their intrigues against other independent Arab states."[11]

Moscow was particularly impressed with Qasim's stated determination to pursue a neutralist foreign policy based on the principles of Bandung. Such a break with Iraq's previously close association with

8. Text in *ibid.*, July 17, 1958.
9. See editorials, *EG,* July 20 and 21, 1958, and Nasir's statement in *ibid.,* July 23, 1958.
10. *Pr.,* July 16, 1958.
11. Observer in *ibid.,* and editorial, "Iraq," *NT,* no. 29 (July 1958), p. 3. See also Commentator, "Rozhdenie respubliki," *Sovremennyi vostok,* no. 8 (August 1958), pp. 1–4.

the Western powers would deal US and British prestige and influence in the Arab East a serious blow. Moreover, Qasim promised also "to liberate [Iraq] from the rule of the criminals" and to proceed with the election of a government that would be both representative of and responsible to the people.[12] This implied restoration of a measure of political freedom to those groups that were supporting the "immortal republic," including the Iraqi Communist party.

Moscow continued to temper its joy with fear of a possible allied intervention in Iraq. For several days in mid-July, Soviet publications warned of an "impending aggression" against the newly proclaimed republic. It was becoming "increasingly evident," said *Pravda,* that Lebanon and Jordan would be used as springboards for an attack on Iraq and "other independent Arab states."[13] The primary blame for the "imperialist intrigues" in the Arab East was placed squarely on the shoulders of the Western "oil monopolies."[14]

Yet Moscow's propaganda campaign was more important for its omissions than for its general tone of joy. While a *Pravda* editorial on July 20 noted carefully that a Western or Western-sponsored intervention in Iraq would represent a "threat to world peace," it avoided any comment that could be interpreted as a promise to back Iraq in case of a showdown. This attitude was in keeping with the Kremlin's stand on the US and British landings in Lebanon and Jordan; since neither Soviet survival nor vital interests were directly involved, Moscow was once again reluctantly forced to demonstrate its inability to challenge the United States.

In any event, when Soviet pressure for a summit meeting to deal with the "increasingly explosive and dangerous situation" in the Middle East did not produce the desired results, Moscow's publications intensified their warnings against an impending Western aggression in the Middle East.[15] A July 31 *Pravda* editorial claimed that "in their

12. Editorial, "Iraq," *NT,* no. 29 (July 1958), p. 3.
13. Editorial, July 20, 1958. For more details, see Observer, "New Version of Suez," *NT,* no. 30 (July 1958), pp. 2–4, and "Middle East: What Next," *ibid.,* no. 31 (August 1958), p. 3.
14. Editorial, *Pr.,* July 20, 1958.
15. Observer in *ibid.,* July 30, 1958.

military staffs and at the diplomatic tables, the members of the aggressive pacts and blocs are feverishly working out plans for liquidating the Iraqi Republic." The first veiled threat to come to Qasim's assistance was contained in a TASS statement of July 31, some two-and-a-half weeks after the overthrow of Nuri al-Sa'id. Commenting on the July 28–29 London session of the Baghdad Pact Council, TASS asserted that Iraq and the UAR were the most likely targets of an imperialist attack. The USSR warned the Western powers that "if the aggression being prepared by the members of the Baghdad Pact is launched against the peace-loving people of Iraq, . . . other peace-loving peoples will come to the aid of the victim of aggression."[16] Even at this late stage, however, Moscow took great care not to promise *direct* Soviet intervention or to stipulate *what form* its support, if any, might take in case of an outside attack on Iraq.

The TASS statement was a skillful propaganda device, for if the Western powers did invade Iraq, Moscow, using some suitable excuse for its inaction, could claim that it had never promised specific assistance in the first place. Then, once it became reasonably certain that a Western or Western-sponsored military intervention in Iraq was not likely to occur, the Kremlin was able to insist that aggression had in fact been planned but that the United States and Great Britain had had to abandon the scheme in view of the firm attitude displayed by the "peace-loving nations," headed by the Soviet Union. More particularly, the "noble appeal" for an immediate convening of a summit conference, to be attended by the heads of state of the USSR, United States, Great Britain, France, and India, and the UN Secretary-General, "frustrated the plans of the inspirers and organizers of an armed intervention." Faced with such determination, the "official circles of the USA and Great Britain, which had openly proclaimed a course of destroying the young Iraqi Republic, were forced to quell their bellicose ardor and even recognize [the new regime]."[17]

The value to the Soviet government of these assertions must be

16. Text in *ibid.,* July 31, 1958.
17. Above section based on O. Orestov in *ibid.,* August 5, and editorial *ibid.,* August 12, 1958. See also editorial, "Baghdad Pact without Baghdad," *NT,* no. 32 (August 1958), pp. 2–3.

measured chiefly in terms of the propaganda advantages to be derived from them. In retrospect, it appears that the Agitprop outdid itself by being more pro-Arab than the Arabs themselves. While the pages of Soviet publications were being filled with anti-Western invective and no effort was being spared to discredit the Western powers, Cairo displayed much more moderation. True, there were occasional anti-American outbursts, but this was not surprising in view of such provocations as Dulles's remark that Nasir was not really an Arab nationalist and could, therefore, not claim to represent the movement.[18] Yet Egypt urged the Western powers not to regard the overthrow of Nuri as a "severe blow to [their] interests" in the Middle East.[19] The relative mildness of UAR press comments was an outward manifestation of a determination to forestall possible Western intervention by repeating Baghdad's assurances of tolerance and moderation. Thus a clash between the USSR and the United Arab Republic was inherent in the very perceptions of the nature of the international system held by their respective governments.

As soon as the Soviet government could be reasonably certain of both the Western intention not to invade Iraq and of Qasim's ability to control the country, the USSR embarked on a broad program of improving relations with the revolutionary regime. Soviet Ambassador Grigorii Zaitsev, who arrived in Baghdad on August 4, stated at a press conference that his country supported the national liberation movements in the Arab East and that the Soviet people "received with pleasure the establishment of the Iraqi Republic which courageously announced that it would follow an independent policy in agreement with the Bandung principles." Iraq, he noted, had in the USSR "an honest and sincere friend which guards peace and friendship among nations." As for other forms of support, Zaitsev made it plain that the extension of Soviet technical and economic aid to Baghdad merely awaited the pleasure of the Iraqi government.[20]

In contrast, the Iraqi revolutionaries approached relations with the

18. *Newsweek,* August 18, 1958, p. 41.
19. Editorial, *EG,* July 22, 1958.
20. *TIT,* August 6, 1958.

USSR very cautiously. As early as July 22, 1958, in a major speech outlining some of the principles of his foreign policy, Qasim stated that "friendship between Iraq and any other state must be based upon mutual interests and mutual esteem, and not on any form of dependence."[21] On August 1, Foreign Minister 'Abd al-Jabbar Jumard said that his government would accept Soviet technical aid but had no intention of acquiring Russian arms.[22] Although in early September it was reported that Radio Baghdad had adopted an anti-US and pro-Soviet view of world events,[23] Qasim told a delegation of religious leaders on September 14 that Iraq's foreign policy would be based on determination "to fight all sorts of imperialism, . . . because the exploiter and the foreigner will work incessantly to disunite our ranks and to use this as a pretext to interfere in our affairs." It is noteworthy that the Premier included Communism, along with Fascism and "American [and] English . . . ideologies," among foreign political theories that were held subversive and dangerous.[24]

However, Qasim's sentiments *vis-à-vis* Marxism-Leninism were not to influence his government's attitude toward relations with the USSR. Iraq, he promised, would seek the friendship of all the countries of the world and would cooperate with them "on the basis of mutual interest."[25] Addressing himself particularly to the problem of Iraqi-Soviet relations, Qasim noted that Moscow's early recognition had created a very favorable impression in Baghdad and prompted the revolutionary government to establish diplomatic relations with the USSR. The Premier also expressed an interest in widening cooperation between the two states, provided Russia abstained from interference in Iraq's internal affairs. He added that support of Iraq "in her struggle and in difficult situations" would gain the USSR "the confidence of the Iraqi nation."[26]

21. *NYT,* July 23, 1958.
22. *MEJ* 12, no. 4 (Fall 1958): 427.
23. *Ibid.,* p. 429.
24. *TIT,* September 16, 1958.
25. *Ibid.,* October 5, 1958.
26. Text of Qasim's interview with S. Kondrashov of *Izvestiia* in *TIT* (and *Izv.),* October 1, 1958.

The basis for economic cooperation between the two nations was laid when an agreement providing for the development of trade relations "on the basis of equality and mutual advantage" was signed on October 11, 1958.[27] Moscow's example was emulated by most of its East European satellites and, by end of 1958, Iraq had concluded similar agreements with Bulgaria, Rumania, Czechoslovakia, and East Germany. In early 1959, Poland, Hungary, and the Chinese People's Republic joined the ranks of the Communist nations extending aid to Iraq.[28] By February 1959, Dr. Ibrahim Kubba, Baghdad's pro-Communist Minister of Economics, was able to announce that the Soviet Union had consented to help in the construction of some thirty projects that would serve as a "foundation for the industrial future of the country."[29]

Economic cooperation was supplemented by numerous reciprocal exchanges of cultural and other delegations. Furthermore, despite earlier official Iraqi pronouncements, Moscow-Baghdad cooperation was extended in late 1958 to embrace military aid as well. On December 2, a British Foreign Office spokesman said that the USSR was supplying Qasim with "jet fighters, tanks, and other arms." Washington sources concurred.[30] In February 1959, the *New York Times* reported that in the past few months the USSR had doubled Iraq's heavy armor by the delivery of "100 to 150 tanks."[31]

Qasim appeared pleased with the Moscow-Baghdad cooperation. Laying the foundation stone for the new broad-gauge railway line between Baghdad and Basra, he praised Soviet support of the revolutionary regime, but insisted that Iraq would deal with other nations only "on the basis of mutual advantage. Our friendship with the Soviet Union is on this basis."[32] Commenting on the growing economic and technical ties between Iraq and the USSR, the *Economist*

27. Details in *Pr.,* October 13, 1958.
28. *MEJ* 13, no. 1 (Winter 1959): 84; and no. 2 (Spring 1959): 181. See also *TIT,* January 18 and February 2, 1959.
29. *Mideast Mirror* (Bayrut, henceforth referred to as *MEM),* no. 6 (February 8, 1959), p. 25 and no. 7 (February 15, 1959), p. 26, respectively.
30. *MEJ* 13, no. 1 (Winter 1959): 84.
31. *NYT,* February 10, 1959.
32. *TIT,* February 15, 1959.

noted that "the pattern of Soviet economic cooperation already established in Syria and Egypt" was about to be extended to Iraq. Yet the latter was in an infinitely better bargaining position—a major oil-producing country, Iraq would not become too dependent on Moscow as long as the West continued to purchase its "black gold."[33]

By late 1958, it had become apparent that Baghdad and Cairo were drifting further and further apart, forcing the Soviet government to choose between two Arab leaders, both of whom conducted foreign policies of which Moscow approved. Initial signs of awareness of the deterioration of UAR-Iraqi relations appeared in the Soviet press in mid-December 1958. In commenting on Undersecretary William Rountree's mission to explain Washington's position in the wake of the 1958 upheavals to the various Arab leaders, Moscow expressed confidence that "Arab public opinion" would not be misled by "soothing assurances" of American good will and an alleged desire to improve relations with the Arab states. Politically sophisticated Arabs would surely recognize that behind these assurances of good will, the United States was once again "concocting a new and dangerous game." Besides the pressure on Baghdad, which recently had assumed the form of an "unbridled campaign," Washington had significantly strengthened the military-strike capability of Israel. US propaganda efforts, it continued, fooled no one because, as in the case of Iraq, they were concealed behind warnings against an "imaginary Soviet threat" to the independence and sovereignty of the Arab states. "American propagandists," it was concluded, were determined "to sow dissension between the Arab countries, particularly between Iraq and the UAR."[34] A further attempt to explain the growing rift was contained in an article entitled "Middle East: Imperialist Comeback Plans," which appeared in the *New Times* in late 1958. Quoting Nasir's

33. *Economist,* February 14, 1959, p. 573.
34. S. Kondrashov, *Izv.,* December 14, 1958, and editorial, "Rountree in the Middle East," *NT,* no. 51 (December 1958), p. 21. Similar statements were made in the Iraqi Communist press. See, for example, 'Aziz al-Hajj in *Sawt al-Ahrar,* December 17, 1958. These views were not shared by Iraqi nationalist publications. *Al-Hurriya* said in an editorial on December 14 that Baghdad should refuse to take sides in the cold war and work for the "liberation of all Arabs."

November 22 interview with the *Scotsman* (Edinburgh) ("Arab nationalism now means that each Arab country must help the other if it faces difficulty, aggression or pressure, but [each] can [choose] . . . the form that help takes according to the time and the circumstances"), Moscow argued that "unity in the fight against imperialism" should be the main concern of Arab patriots. Unity at the present stage of historical development, it was held, had nothing in common with the desire of one Arab country to annex or control another. Moreover—and here Moscow went far beyond anything said by Cairo—since unity implied a joint "struggle against imperialism," "all social groups with different political attitudes and views" that favored the elimination of Western influence in the Arab East should be encouraged to cooperate in the implementation of this "noble task."[35] By questioning the "anti-popular" activities of the UAR government (i.e., the rigorous suppression of Egyptian Communists), the Kremlin made it unmistakably clear that in the growing rift between Nasir and Qasim it sided with the Iraqi Premier.[36]

Another early illustration of Russia's stand on the Baghdad-Cairo dispute was contained in an article by S. Kondrashov, published on January 1, 1959, accusing the UAR propaganda media, and particularly the newspaper *Akhbar al-Yawm,* of "close connections with American circles." How else, Kondrashov wondered, could one explain allegations about a "critical" situation in Iraq and the circulation of the "most fantastic fabrications . . . about the country's progressive democratic forces?" Some Cairo sources insisted, for example, that the "progressive forces of Iraq opposed friendly relations with the UAR." To top it all off, such assertions were "spiced with large doses of anti-Soviet slander." *Izvestiia* had no doubt that statements of this kind, intentionally or not, benefited only the imperialists, contributing as they did to the creation of an "atmosphere of artificial tension around Iraq." This was bound to "split the Arab countries'

35. Y. Zvyagin, "Middle East: Imperialist Comeback Plans," *NT,* no. 52 (December 1958), p. 10.
36. *Ibid.,* p. 8. For earlier endorsements of Qasim's "progressive measures," see P. Demchenko in *Pr.,* August 10, and S. Kondrashov in *Izv.,* September 27, 1958.

anti-imperialist front and, in the end, prepared favorable conditions for new conspiracies against the peoples of the Arab East."[37]

Writing a few days later, V. Borovskii noted that some (unspecified) UAR publications lent themselves to spreading "US-fabricated rumors" of a growing Communist threat to Iraq and even of an impending Soviet takeover of that country. The imperialists, the argument ran, were determined to hinder cooperation among the "liberated" Arab states through the use of the "reactionary slogan [of] . . . struggle against the so-called 'Communist danger.'" Their efforts, it was hoped, would be met with "resolute resistance."[38]

As the war of nerves between Cairo and Baghdad continued to intensify, Viktor Maevskii, one of Russia's leading journalists, attacked Haykal for his stand on both the problem of freedom of Communist activity in the United Arab Republic and Nasir's attitude toward Iraq. The tone of Maevskii's article, written at the height of the Cairo-Moscow crisis, was unusually strong. This might have been because Haykal's attack on Qasim appeared only one day after the publication of his "Open Letter to Khrushchev." The latter article, according to Maevskii, "grossly distorted the facts and was directed against the growing friendship between the peoples of the USSR and the UAR." In concluding his "Letter to Khrushchev," Haykal had asserted that the United Arab Republic was not in the habit of "throwing words to the winds" or "going beyond the bounds of our country to impose . . . [its] views [on others]." An illuminating example of Cairo's alleged restraint, Maevskii noted with irony, was provided by Haykal's "Open Letter to Qasim," which said, in part, that "the devil is trying to use . . . [the Iraqi Premier] as his weapon to disperse the forces of Arab nationalism and to destroy Arab solidarity." The "devil" he had in mind was an "alliance between the Communists and imperialists!" Maevskii exclaimed indignantly. To make this type of statement, he continued, "one must really have lost all sense of shame," for "thousands of Arab Communists have given their lives in the struggle against imperialism." To top it all off, Haykal

37. *Izv.*, January 1, 1959.
38. V. Borovskii, *Pr.*, January 6, 1959.

summoned Qasim to crush "the most steadfast and resolute fighters against imperialism [and] for the independence of the Arab countries [i.e., the Arab Communists]." Haykal's statements not only belied Cairo's assurances that the UAR would not impose its views on others, but in effect constituted an "unceremonious interference in the internal affairs of Iraq." Moreover, the "appeal for reprisals against the Iraqi Communists represented an encroachment on Arab unity, a blow at the national-liberation struggle of the Arab peoples, and complicity with the imperialist predators."[39]

Even though Soviet sympathies were clearly on the side of Qasim in the unfolding crisis between Baghdad and Cairo, the Kremlin was not prepared to abandon entirely its relatively close association with the UAR. This stand was crystallized by Khrushchev in his January 27, 1959, speech before the Twenty-first Congress of the CPSU. Commenting on the recent cooling in Moscow-Cairo relations, the Premier said:

> We, Communists, and all progressives naturally sympathize with those who are fighting for social justice. We do not deny that we and some of the leaders of the UAR hold divergent ideological views. But on questions of fighting imperialism, consolidating the political and economic independence of countries that have broken away from colonialism and are fighting the danger of war, our positions coincide with theirs.[40]

"The difference in ideological views," added the *New Times*, "should not impede the development of friendly relations between the countries which strive to strengthen peace and which are threatened by aggressive imperialist designs. The socialist countries will continue to play a big part in the life of former colonies and dependencies."[41]

39. *Ibid.*, February 19, 1959.
40. Text in *ibid.*, January 28, 1959.
41. Editorial, "Foreign Political Problems at the CPSU Congress," *NT*, no. 5 (January 1959), pp. 1–3. For detailed subsequent discussion of the Soviet view of the deteriorating relations between Baghdad and Cairo, see Dantsig, pp. 69–70.

Thus, approval and support of Qasim in his conflict with Nasir did not signify a decision in Moscow to break completely with the United Arab Republic or even to deprive Cairo of extensive Soviet political, military, and economic backing.[42] What it did mean was that in the growing dispute between the two Arab leaders, Russian *sympathies* were definitely, and for the time being, with the revolutionary leaders in Baghdad. This Soviet attitude, as already mentioned, no doubt contributed to the deterioration of Moscow-Cairo relations while serving as an additional impetus to Qasim to improve relations with the USSR as well as with the Iraqi Communist party by offering it more freedom of political activity.

Perhaps the most comprehensive Soviet analysis of Iraq's early post-revolutionary period was an article by Georgii Mirskii, one of Moscow's young and, at the time, influential theoreticians. Internally, the Qasim regime had introduced a series of far-reaching reforms that struck at the very heart of the established order. For example, soon after seizing power, the authorities ordered the dismissal of all government, army, and police officials who were found guilty of "collaboration with imperialism" (a formulation broad enough to encompass any undesirable elements), embezzlement, bribery, terror, and the like. The property of dozens of former dignitaries was expropriated. Many of these individuals were committed to trial, while political prisoners who had been detained by the old regime were released. The Qasim government struck also at the feudal class, above all the tribal shaykhs, who were hard hit by the abrogation of the so-called tribal law, which conferred upon them the right to try the members of their tribes, and the large landowners, who would lose most of their land upon implementation of a sweeping agrarian reform law, adopted on

---

42. See, for example, I. Aleksandrov in *Pr.*, February 22, 1959. It might be of interest to note, however, that a later Soviet publication, appearing at the height of the 1961 Moscow-Cairo crisis, accused the "leaders of the UAR" of "demanding [in 1958] that Iraq join the United Arab Republic on the same conditions that Syria joined Egypt." Vysshaia partiinaia shkola pri TsK KPSS, *Mezhdunarodnye otnosheniia i vneshniaia politika SSSR, 1917–1960* (Moscow: Izdatel'stvo VPSh i AON pri TsK KPSS, 1961), p. 464. Having been rebuffed, the "Egyptian bourgeoisie began interfering in the internal affairs" of Iraq. *Ibid.*, pp. 464–65.

September 30, 1958.⁴³ Concerned with the economic development of Iraq, the government was working on a broad industrialization plan in which major industrial enterprises would belong to and be controlled by the state. In its foreign trade relations, the government had made public its determination to break the "Western trade monopoly" and to broaden economic relations with the Communist countries.

Mirskii was equally pleased with Qasim's apparent willingness to proceed with the "democratization" of Iraq. Initially, the revolutionary regime did not oppose political activity by any of those parties which had been persecuted and driven underground by the Nuri government. By early 1959, however, the authorities increasingly disassociated themselves from the activities of those groups which Mirskii described as "tending to the Right," and, after the February 1959 cabinet reshuffle, the newly appointed ministers favored the "independent and democratic development" of Iraq. Equally encouraging was "the exceptionally high [degree of] political activity of the masses who are striving to consolidate the republic's independence and promote Arab unity in the struggle against imperialism and for the liberation of the Arab world from alien domination." Since this was also the aim of the authorities, Mirskii found it easy to understand why the government enjoyed the backing of "the people and the army."

In its foreign relations, Qasim's Iraq adhered to the policies of positive neutralism and Arab solidarity. Dealing a "heavy blow to imperialism," Baghdad virtually disassociated itself from the Baghdad Pact and recognized the Provisional Government of Algeria. It would have been unrealistic, Mirskii continued, to expect the Western powers not to react to "provocations" of such magnitude. Among their efforts "to poison relations among the Arab countries, to set them against one another and thus split the national-liberation front,"

43. For more details on Agrarian Law, see Zaki Hairi, "The Agrarian Reform Law in the Republic of Iraq," *World Marxist Review* (henceforth referred to as *WMR*), no. 4 (April 1959), pp. 55–60, and P. Demchenko, "Zametki ob agrarnoi reforme v Irakskoi respublike," *Sovremennyi vostok*, no. 2 (1959), pp. 24–25.

Mirskii singled out the accelerated campaign designed to drive a wedge between the "liberated" Arab states and the "socialist camp" on the one hand, and among the neutralist Arab governments on the other. The favorite ploy consisted of "hypocritical warnings . . . against the 'Communist menace' [both] facing Iraq and emanating from it." This imperialist plan, Mirskii thought, was "quite primitive" in that it "attempted to represent Iraq as the 'spawn of Communism,' to isolate her, deal her a blow and then turn . . . [the imperialist] guns against the Arab states that fall for this propaganda bait." Those "who spread lies about 'Communist plots,' " he concluded, were "merely helping the enemies of the national-liberation movement."[44]

With regard to Arab unity, Moscow's stand closely resembled the views expressed in the statement of Ibrahim Kubba at the 5th Session of the Arab League Economic Council in mid-January 1959:

> The Arab path to national unity is the path of their joint struggle against imperialism and Zionism, the path of struggle for closer solidarity. . . . Insofar as the strengthening of Arab ties is concerned, we must strive to achieve that by seeking and finding the most favorable and best forms and democratic methods of rapprochement in order finally to solve this matter in the interests of the Arab nation.

"Iraqi progressives," Mirskii added, "resolutely oppose the Arab unity variants that leave out of account the historical features of any one of the Arab countries and are detrimental to their democratic development."[45]

On March 8, 1959, an anti-government uprising led by Colonel 'Abd al-Wahhab al-Shawwaf broke out in Mosul, the largest city of northern Iraq. In an official proclamation, Shawwaf accused Qasim of "betraying the principles of the July revolution," and of handing the country over to the Communists. The revolt failed, for within a few days loyal units routed the insurgents. Some sixty officers who

---

44. For variations on this theme, see K. Smirnov in *Izv.*, February 21, 1959.
45. Unless otherwise indicated, the preceding paragraphs are based on G. Mirsky, "The Iraqi Republic Today," *NT*, no. 8 (February 1959), pp. 11–13. See also R. Palme Dutt, "Britain, Oil and Middle Eastern Liberation," *WMR*, no. 10 (October 1959), pp. 41–43.

participated in the attempted coup were reportedly executed without trial, while Shawwaf died of his wounds near the Syrian border.[46]

It is unlikely that the UAR or the Western powers participated in planning or executing the Mosul uprising. It was, rather, a poorly organized, emotional outburst, which testified to the frustration felt by the pro-Cairo officers in the Iraqi army at the direction in which Qasim was leading the country. There can be no doubt, however, that Nasir fully sympathized with the revolt after it had broken out.[47] Qasim's alleged association with the Communists soon became one of Cairo's favorite propaganda themes:

> Whereas before it could have been said that he was caught on the crest of a Communist-led wave and had to ride with it . . . if only as a price of maintaining order in Baghdad, it would be idle now to deny that he has chosen to go with the Iraqi Communists the whole way. . . . He has given his blessing to the Iraqi Communists, and in so doing has labelled himself an open opponent of the wishes of the majority of his own people and those of his Arab neighbors.[48]

Baghdad reacted by accusing the UAR government of organizing the Mosul uprising,[49] while Moscow, not unexpectedly and without reservation, sided with Qasim: "The suppression of the Mosul revolt," wrote the *New Times,* "is in the interests not only of the Iraqis, but of all the Middle Eastern nations fighting for national liberation."[50] "In crushing the revolt of the insurgents," seconded *Izvestiia,* "the Iraqi people have won an important victory in their historic development. By this victory they have further strengthened the country's national independence."[51]

---

46. For more information, see Michel Montserrat, "L'affaire de Mossoul," *Orient,* no. 9 (1959), pp. 23–30, and Arnold Hottinger, "Mosul—Failure of a Revolt," *Swiss Review of World Affairs,* (April 1959), pp. 16–17. See also the Egyptian press of March 9–11, 1959.
47. For details, see *President Gamal Abdel Nasser's Speeches and Press-Interviews, 1959* (Cairo, n.d.), pp. 121–58.
48. Editorial, *EG,* March 12, 1959.
49. *TIT,* March 18, 1959.
50. Y. Zvyagin, "The Mosul Plot," *NT,* no. 12 (March 1959), p. 10.
51. N. Khokhlov, *Izv.,* March 15, 1959.

Whereas Baghdad blamed Nasir, the USSR felt that the revolt was due to "imperialist machinations."[52] Nevertheless, Soviet publications noted that the UAR had sympathized with the insurgents and, in so doing, had played into the hands of the imperialist powers. In a variation on an old theme, the *New Times* noted that Nasir's "hostile attitude" toward Iraq stemmed from his "one-sided interpretation of Arab unity." Cairo had insisted that Iraq join the UAR but "the Iraqi people and government have their own opinion on that score and do not believe that Arab unity must necessarily take the form of amalgamation in a single state."[53]

The strongest Soviet endorsement of Qasim's stand was voiced by Khrushchev himself in an address to an Iraqi government delegation headed by Ibrahim Kubba: "When the clique of plotters recently started to overthrow the government of 'Abd al-Karim Qasim, the Iraqi people extended full support to their government and destroyed the plotters and the wicked plans of the reactionary forces." Cairo, he continued, had initially extended Qasim its unqualified support in the apparent hope that Iraq would merge with the United Arab Republic, but once it became evident that the revolutionary government had no intention of bowing to the will of Nasir, Egypt had adopted a policy of both overt and covert interference in the internal affairs of the Iraqi Republic. Khrushchev made no secret of the fact that the USSR government viewed Nasir's ambitions in the Arab East as "delusions," which Moscow, " not indifferent to what transpires in an area not far from . . . [its] borders," opposed.

Khrushchev did express confidence that common sense would prevail and that every effort would be made "to resolve this conflict and to prevent the imperialists from using it in their own interest." He also

---

52. As early as March 9, Radio Moscow charged that the United States "might have deliberately stirred up the Iraqi revolt." *MEJ* 13, no. 2 (Spring 1959): 182. It is noteworthy, however, that a subsequent publication tied Shawwaf with "imperialists as well as certain circles in the UAR." Akademiia nauk SSSR. Institut mirovoi ekonomiki i mezhdunarodnykh otnoshenii. *Mezhdunarodnyi politiko-ekonomicheskii ezhegodnik, 1960* (Moscow: Gospolitizdat, 1960), p. 178. See also Akademiia nauk SSSR. *Politika SShA* . . . , pp. 156–57.

53. See n. 50.

made it clear that, in the estimate of the Soviet government, Iraq was neither a Communist country nor even moving in that direction. But "progressive changes" were being introduced in Iraq and "a more advanced system" was being established than in the neighboring countries. "Naturally, our sympathies are with governments and states which consider the interests of their peoples."[54]

Words were backed by action. On March 16, 1959, the USSR and Iraq signed a far-reaching economic and technical aid agreement pledging, in part, $137 million in Soviet economic assistance.[55] On May 5, the two countries signed a cultural agreement, followed two days later by a similar accord between Iraq and Czechoslovakia.[56] On July 3, a Soviet-Iraqi Friendship Society was formed, followed on August 17 by the signing of an agreement on cooperation in the peaceful uses of atomic energy.[57]

As might have been expected, Cairo struck back immediately by accusing the USSR of a desire to "dominate the Arab nation." Khrushchev's speech marked the beginning of a new Soviet policy in the Middle East. Whereas, prior to March 1959, Moscow had relied on Arab nationalists to help eliminate Western influence in the region, the fiasco that the "imperialist" powers had suffered there in 1958, coupled with the Communist advent to power in Iraq, led the Kremlin to conclude that it could now center its attention on the "Arab nationalist, neutralist forces" that were determined to keep the region "outside foreign zones of influence."[58]

Soviet publications in turn deplored the violent anti-Qasim and anti-USSR statements emanating from the UAR. For example, quot-

54. Text in *Pr.,* March 17, 1959. See also Observer in *ibid.,* March 30, 1959.
55. See *MEJ* 13, no. 3 (Summer 1959): 290. For Soviet comment, see P. Maletin, "Beskorystnoe sotrudnichestvo," *Sovremennyi vostok,* no. 7 (1959), pp. 14–15. Text of the agreement in SSSR. Ministerstvo inostrannykh del, *SSSR i arabskie strany, 1917–1960* (Moscow: Gospolitizdat, 1961), pp. 694–700. Text of the joint communiqué of March 17 in *ibid.,* pp. 701–3.
56. *TIT,* May 6 and 8, 1959. Text of the Soviet-Iraqi accord in Ministerstvo inostrannykh del, pp. 704–6.
57. *TIT,* July 5 and August 21, 1959.
58. A statement by Middle East News Agency, as quoted in *MEM,* no. 12 (March 22, 1959), pp. 6–7.

ing the *Egyptian Gazette,* which expressed confidence that in the wake of the Mosul uprising "new leaders will arise to take the place of those who died," *Izvestiia* countered that such assertions were "inspired by anti-Arab propaganda from across the seas, propaganda that aims at fomenting quarrels among the Arabs and transforming the Near and Middle East into a permanent center of dangerous tension."[59]

Cairo's response to Khrushchev's statement was considered quite unsatisfactory, leading *Izvestiia* to conclude that "among the public of the UAR . . . the conviction is growing that it is time to sober up from the intoxication of short-sighted propaganda over which only the imperialists gloat and to approach this matter in a statesmanlike and mature manner." Should a constructive attitude be adopted, Moscow felt, it would "become clear that the aggravation of relations with Iraq is a course that runs counter to the genuine national interests of the UAR." *Izvestiia* expressed confidence that Khrushchev's appeal to Nasir would find "sympathetic response and understanding."[60] In the meantime, however, the Kremlin's sympathies remained with Qasim. The joint communiqué, published at the conclusion of Soviet-Iraqi talks of March 1959, expressed the desire of both countries "to develop friendly cooperation . . . based on mutual respect for sovereignty, equality, and noninterference in one another's affairs."[61]

On March 24, 1959, Iraq officially announced its withdrawal from the Baghdad Pact and was immediately praised by the Soviet press. Moscow was particularly pleased with the fact that the Western powers would no longer be legally entitled to use the air bases at Habbaniya and Shayba: "In denying the imperialists these bases, the Iraqi revolution had rendered inestimable assistance to all the forces battling against colonialism."[62] According to *Izvestiia,* Qasim's decision "knocked the trump card from the hands of [those] Arab circles that have been trying to accuse this country of collaboration with imperialism, on the ground that it formally remained a member of the Bagh-

59. N. Khokhlov, *Izv.*, March 15, 1959.
60. S. Kondrashov, *ibid.*, March 19, 1959.
61. Text in *Pr.*, March 17, 1959.
62. Editorial, "Baghdad and the Baghdad Pact," *NT,* no. 14 (April 1959), p. 3.

dad Pact." Lest there be any misunderstanding, it was explained that such "arguments were advanced by the official circles and the press of the UAR, waging an unbridled anti-Iraqi campaign."[63]

Moscow also hailed Iraq's unilateral abrogation of three treaties concluded between the royal government and the United States: the military assistance treaty of 1954, an agreement regulating the purchase and use of US military equipment, and Baghdad's undertaking to support the Eisenhower Doctrine. These measures attested to Qasim's determination to "eliminate all survivals of subservience to the imperialist powers." In an obvious reference to the United Arab Republic, Moscow insisted that by its "resolute action," Iraq taught "other independent Arab countries," leaning toward cooperation with the United States, an "object lesson. . . . By exposing the nature of the agreements which Washington imposed on the Royal government without the consent and knowledge of the people, the Iraqi republicans have shown what such 'cooperation' implies."[64] Equally laudable were Iraqi efforts to curtail the freedom of activity of foreign oil companies. *Izvestiia* praised Baghdad's determination to achieve gradually the "liberation of Iraq from foreign economic dependence."[65]

As noted by Mackintosh, "the Soviet Union had both gained and lost from the [July 1958] events in the Middle East."[66] On the credit side, Moscow no doubt profited from the bitter confrontation between the pro-Western and Arab nationalist forces in Lebanon and Jordan, culminating in the overthrow of Nuri al-Sa'id and the Hashimite dynasty in Iraq. Premier Qasim's subsequent decision to take Iraq out of the Baghdad Pact dealt a telling blow to the Western defense posture in the Middle East. At the same time, the Kremlin was caught by surprise by the decisiveness, speed, and efficiency with which the United States and Great Britain handled the deployment of their

63. S. Kondrashov, *Izv.*, March 26, 1959. See also M. Mikhailov, *ibid.*, March 29, 1959.
64. Editorial, "Object Lesson," *NT*, no. 24 (June 1959), p. 21.
65. *Izv.*, July 3, 1959.
66. J. M. Mackintosh, *Strategy and Tactics of Soviet Foreign Policy* (London: Oxford University Press, 1963), p. 237.

forces in Lebanon and Jordan in total disregard of the USSR and its insistence that major changes in the Middle East affected the vital interests of the Soviet Union. Western initiative and Moscow's inaction served as an additional indication of Soviet nuclear inferiority and of the Kremlin's unwillingness to risk a showdown with its American adversary over any issue arising in the Middle East. It may be safely assumed that this display of weakness in the face of US and British determination more than offset any of the indirect gains Moscow may have made as a result of the 1958 upheavals. The temporary emergence of the Iraqi Communist party does not alter this conclusion for, as will be seen below, in the long run the organization proved to be neither an effective political instrument nor an obedient tool of Soviet policy. In addition, as noted above, the Iraqi revolution brought into the open the latent conflict between Cairo and Baghdad, forcing the Kremlin to express a public preference for one of the parties to the dispute.

In the ensuing confrontation between Nasir and Qasim, Moscow initially sided with Iraq. Ideological considerations aside, the USSR may have hoped to increase its influence in the area by backing Qasim and benefiting from his weakness and the resulting need of Arab Communist and Soviet backing in the struggle against the Cairo-led forces of Arab nationalism. It appears also that the Kremlin supported Baghdad in order to divide the Arab nationalist ranks and, in so doing, to prevent the establishment in the Middle East of a unified Arab state. The latter, it may be safely assumed, was rather low on the list of Soviet objectives; Moscow was no doubt aware of the fact that influence over a relatively strong, united Arab state would be very difficult to attain. After all, the Soviet government found it almost impossible to exert any real control over the actions of a weak and seemingly dependent UAR.

PART II
COOPERATION AND RECRIMINATION, 1958-1963

6
The Egyptian Crises of 1959 and 1961*

During the first six months after the Iraqi revolution Moscow endeavored to maintain equally friendly relations with both the UAR and the Republic of Iraq. For example, a few days after it had signed the far-reaching trade agreement with Baghdad, the USSR consented to finance the construction of the first stage of Egypt's Aswan High Dam. Cairo's references to "common interests" and its subscription to Khrushchev's "peace program" constituted the price it was required to pay for Russian aid in building the Dam. But these allusions were skillfully blended with an emphasis on positive neutralism as the guiding light of Nasir's foreign policy.[1] The Soviet press, on the other

---

*Portions of this chapter are based on my "Moscow-Cairo Crisis, 1959," *Slavic Review* 22, no. 4 (December 1963): 713–26. Reprinted by permission of the publisher.

1. See *Pr.,* October 22, 1958. See also N. Khokhlov, *Izv.,* October 25, 1958. The determination of the UAR government to adhere to an independent position in the East-West conflict was reiterated by President Nasir. Speaking at Minia, he said: "We mean by Arab nationalism that we be independent, and that this independence emanate from our consciences. We must never be subservient to any country, or to imperialism, neither must we be part of any sphere of influence. That is Arab nationalism: union, unity, solidarity, but all that must be built on right, and on the interests of the Arabs, not on the interests of imperialism. . . ." Text in *EG,* November 14, 1958.

hand, used the occasion to contrast the respective economic policies of "imperialism" and "socialism." The new agreements allegedly once again demonstrated that while the West endeavored to keep the underdeveloped nations economically backward and militarily weak so as to facilitate their exploitation, the Soviet Union was determined to help them develop their economies and defend their independence against the common adversary.[2]

The Kremlin was probably gratified by the response of Egypt's influential *al-Ahram*, which praised Moscow's willingness to aid Cairo in the construction of the Aswan High Dam.[3] Nevertheless, the Soviet government must have noticed with misgiving that, despite his outwardly friendly relations with the USSR, President Nasir attempted to balance his rapprochement with Moscow by strengthening Egypt's ties with the Western powers.[4] For example, Cairo, in early 1959, directed to the Western powers an urgent appeal to strengthen ties with the United Arab Republic: "If the West wants friendship with the U.A.R. and is willing to accept the legitimate aspirations of the Arab nations, President Nasser is willing to accept that friendship within the framework of his policy of neutralism and nonalignment, and to do his utmost to remove obstacles to it."[5]

The Soviet press soon reflected Moscow's growing alarm at this development. Washington's alleged desire to improve relations with the Arab countries, coupled with promises of economic aid and compliments to Arab nationalism, "have never been anything but talk," *Izvestiia* asserted. In reality, the USA was concocting a "new and dangerous game." Israel was to be armed, pressure was to be applied against Iraq. "This unbridled campaign is being concealed under cries

2. See, for example, Khrushchev's speech, *Izv.*, October 22, 1958, and editorial, "The Aswan Problem," *NT*, no. 44 (October 1958), p. 2, and E. Pletnyov, "The Seven Year Plan," *ibid.*, no. 47 (November 1958), pp. 4–5. See also S. Kondrashov, *Izv.*, October 26, 1958; L. Teplyakov, "Unselfish Friend," *IA*, no. 12 (December 1958), p. 81; and L. Stepanov, "Helping Underdeveloped Countries," *NT*, no. 52 (December 1958), pp. 5–7.
3. Editorial, *al-Ahram*, October 25, 1958.
4. See, for instance, editorials, *EG*, October 23, and *EM*, December 13, 1958.
5. Editorial, *EG*, January 11, 1959.

of a 'Soviet threat.' " The United States was also accused of trying to "spawn an armed struggle" between different groups in Iraq and to "sow dissension between the Arab countries, particularly between Iraq and the UAR."[6]

During the second half of 1958, new complications entered the picture as the Syrian Communist party initiated a far-flung campaign designed to alter the administrative structure of the United Arab Republic. Though not overtly anti-UAR or anti-Nasir, the campaign was aimed at effecting changes that would obviously wreck the very foundation of the union envisaged by the UAR President and his Syrian supporters.[7] Stung by Soviet support of Qasim and the activities of the Syrian Communists, Nasir staged his first open, full-fledged counterattack in his Port Sa'id speech of December 23, 1958.[8] For the first time, Communism was equated with Western imperialism, and the UAR press supported him by unleashing a violent propaganda campaign against Arab Communists. Although initially Cairo refrained from direct attacks on the Soviet Union, it did warn against "insincere moves that may be made from any quarter appearing to support Arab nationalism but, in reality, aiming at its overthrow."[9]

Coupled though they were with assurances of Cairo's good will toward the Soviet Union, such attacks on Arab Communists were bound to arouse Moscow's indignation. Initially, the Soviet government mirrored Nasir's cautiousness. Occasionally, some Egyptian publications, notably *Akhbar al-Yawm,* accused of "close connections with American circles," were criticized for attacks on Syrian and Iraqi Communists or, to use the Soviet terminology, for spreading "fantastic fabrications" about Arab "democratic forces" in an effort to "split the anti-imperialist front . . . [and] prepare favorable conditions for

6. S. Kondrashov, *Izv.,* December 18, 1958. See also *ibid.,* December 10; and V. Borovskii, *Pr.,* December 14, 1958, and January 6, 1959.

7. See statements by Khalid Baqdash, Secretary-General of the Syrian Communist party, as quoted in *MEM,* no. 52 (December 28, 1958), pp. 2–3.

8. Text in *EG,* December 24, 1958. See also the statement by 'Abd al-Hamid Sarraj, *al-Ahram,* December 26 and editorial, *EG,* December 25; Ihsan 'Abd al-Quddus, *Ruz al-Yusif,* December 29; editorial, *al-Akhbar,* December 30, 1958.

9. Editorial, *EG,* December 30, 1958.

new conspiracies against the peoples of the Arab East."[10] But, as Cairo continued to insist on Communist determination to "deal a shattering blow to Arab nationalism" and condemned Arab Communists as traitors to the cause of unity and national aspirations,[11] Moscow struck back. In his speech before the Twenty-first Congress of the CPSU Khrushchev asserted that, "both as a Communist and as Chairman of the Council of Ministers of the USSR," he felt obliged to defend fellow Marxists in other countries who were being subjected to "unjust attacks": "Communists are bold and staunch champions of liberation from imperialist and colonialist oppression." However, while it could not be denied that Moscow and Cairo held "divergent ideological views," these differences should not impede the development of friendly relations between countries that strove to "strengthen peace" or were threatened by "aggressive imperialist designs."[12]

Although Khrushchev's speech was relatively mild, it was meant to serve as a reproach to Cairo for having carried its anti-Communist campaign too far and was received by the sensitive UAR government as an encroachment on its sovereignty. Muhammad Hasanayn Haykal wrote:

> We are not a rich people, nor are we a big country. Our entire wealth and value lies in our independent personality. . . . The greatest error we can ever make—both toward ourselves and our friends—would be to remain silent if ever we felt that the features and boundaries of our independent personality have been touched by any hand or trodden by any foot.

Arab nationalists did not love or respect the USSR for the sake of Arab Communists, Haykal concluded. They did so in spite of them, in appreciation of the Soviet attitude toward the United Arab Republic: "The people who love and respect the Soviet Union in this country are the same people who have faith in their Arab nationalism and

---

10. S. Kondrashov, *Izv.,* January 1, 1959. See also V. Borovskii, *Pr.,* January 6, 1959.
11. For example, see editorial, *al-Akhbar,* January 17, 1959.
12. Text in *Pr.,* January 28, 1959.

positive neutralism. They are the same people who do not believe in Communism as an ideology and a system suitable for their country."[13]

The Soviet press singled out Haykal for "grossly distorting the facts." Countering his allegation that the USSR was attempting to interfere in the internal affairs of the United Arab Republic in violation of the Bandung principles, *Pravda* observed that it was Cairo, not Moscow, which was guilty of such transgressions. Referring to another of Haykal's "slanderous articles,"[14] which warned Qasim of an "imperialist-Communist alliance" designed to isolate Iraq and to destroy Arab solidarity, *Pravda* accused the editor of *al-Ahram* of "unceremoniously interfering in the internal affairs of Iraq" and of "covering up this interference with talk about Arab nationalism, unity, and the struggle against imperialism." In reality, Haykal's appeal for reprisals against the Iraqi Communist party represented an "encroachment on Arab unity, a blow at the national-liberation struggle of the Arab peoples, and complicity with the imperialist predators."[15]

Nevertheless, both Moscow and Cairo made some attempts to ameliorate the situation. For a time the Soviet government shifted the blame on "imperialists and their Myrmidons"—meaning Tito, then visiting Nasir—for splitting the Arab states and driving a wedge between them and the Soviet Union. The Arabs were assured that Moscow's "policy of friendship and cooperation" would remain unchanged.[16] Nasir reciprocated, alluding to "imperialist attempts" to utilize ideological difference between the USSR and the United Arab Republic.[17] But deep-seated distrust and animosity continued to prevail. For example, a TASS statement of March 1, 1959, termed Arab press reports concerning the emigration of Soviet Jews to Israel[18] a "malicious provocational fabrication" and expressed regret that the

13. *Al-Ahram*, January 29, 1959.
14. *Ibid.*, January 30, 1959.
15. V. Maevskii, *Pr.*, February 19, 1959.
16. I. Aleksandrov, *ibid.*, February 22, and K. Smirnov, *Izv.*, February 21, 1959, respectively. See also editorial, "First Year of the U.A.R.," *NT*, no. 9 (February 1959), pp. 2–3.
17. Text of Nasir's speech of February 21 in *EG* of the next day. See also editorials, *al-Sha'b* and *EG*, February 24 and 26, 1959, respectively.
18. See editorial, *ibid.*, February 17, 1959.

Arab publications "provided grist for the mill of those who aspire to undermine the friendship between the Soviet Union and the Arab countries."[19]

The problem of mass emigration of East European Jews to Israel was of course only an outward manifestation of the tension. On March 16, the Soviet Premier touched on deeper issues in a speech honoring an Iraqi delegation that had arrived in Moscow to negotiate an economic agreement with the USSR.[20] Khrushchev said that the Iraqi revolution had met with the support of all "progressive forces" because it had made a major contribution to the Arab struggle against imperialism. Referring to Nasir's alleged insistence on the unification of Iraq and the UAR, he urged Cairo to display "wisdom and patience"; hasty action at this stage of historical development would undermine Arab unity, not promote it.

The Soviet Premier expressed regret at the deterioration of Cairo-Baghdad relations, but hoped that common sense would prevail and that the conflict would be resolved before the imperialists had a chance to utilize it for their own purposes. In the meantime, however, Moscow's sympathies were clearly on the side of Qasim. Khrushchev said that he had always been aware of Nasir's anti-Communist views. Yet he had hoped that "more tolerance . . . [and] more attention to the people's democratic demands" would be displayed by the UAR government in the course of the national liberation struggle, which required the "unity of all anti-imperialist forces." Unfortunately, Cairo had taken measures to suppress the "freedom-loving aspirations" of the Egyptian and Syrian masses. Qasim, in contrast, while not striving to "build socialism," had introduced "progressive changes" and a system "more advanced" than in any other Arab country. Gathering momentum as he went along, Khrushchev con-

---

19. *Pr.*, March 2, 1959.
20. A Soviet-Iraqi economic agreement, "without any political or other similar conditions that would affect the sovereignty and national dignity of Iraq," was signed in Moscow on March 16, 1959. In a communiqué, both parties professed a desire to develop friendly cooperation on the basis of "mutual respect for sovereignty, equality, and noninterference in one another's affairs." Details in *Izv.*, March 17, 1959.

cluded by warning Nasir that the USSR could not remain indifferent to developments taking place in an area so close to its frontiers.[21]

Khrushchev's speech was intended as a rebuff to Nasir's anti-Communist and anti-Qasim propaganda campaign, which had become especially violent in the wake of the abortive Mosul revolt.[22] The Kremlin may have hoped to pressure the UAR into relinquishing its propaganda activities by reminding Cairo of its dependence on the Soviet Union. If so, Moscow appears to have learned nothing from the past mistakes of the Western powers: Nasir was not likely to yield to outside pressure in instances where his interests were directly involved. Indeed, such external pressure seemed only to strengthen his resolve.

Nasir's reply was couched in strong and unmistakably hostile language: "The support [and defense] of Communists in our country . . . constitutes a challenge to the unanimous will of the people of our Republic." The United Arab Republic had always welcomed Soviet backing, but it could not tolerate Moscow's support of Arab Communists—a group that had "deviated from the Arab struggle for independence."[23] The UAR press described Khrushchev's speech of March 16 as an indication that "the stage which has started is a struggle between Communists, supported by Moscow, and neutralists and Arab nationalists who have faith in the complete independence of

---

21. Text of Khrushchev's speech in *ibid.* Speaking at the same reception, Ibrahim Kubba, head of the Iraqi delegation, said: "From the very first days of the revolution a new page of friendship was opened in the relations between Iraq and the Soviet Union. The noble position taken by the USSR with respect to our revolution and the immediate recognition of our Republic by the Soviet government have been of great importance in consolidating and developing these relations." *Ibid.*

22. See chap. 5. For more details, see Nasir's speeches of March 12 and 13, texts in Egyptian publications of the next day.

Scoring the UAR press for its anti-Qasim campaign in connection with the Mosul revolt, Soviet publications stressed even prior to Khrushchev's speech that the Arab states were taking but the initial steps on the path of strengthening their independence and national economy. The stronger the national independence of each Arab state, the stronger would be their unity in the face of the imperialists. "Everything else was of secondary importance." N. Khokhlov, *Izv.*, March 15, 1959.

23. Text of Nasir's speech in *EG*, March 17, 1959.

their country which should remain outside foreign zones of influence."[24]

In late March and April 1959, there was an exchange of personal insults between Khrushchev and Nasir. The Soviet Premier not only rejected the UAR President's accusation that Moscow had interfered in the internal affairs of various Arab states, but termed him a "passionate and hotheaded young man." Nasir countered by asserting that he was not the only one who was passionate and hotheaded and, in any case, had it not been for his passion, Egypt would long ago have been turned into a "rocket-base against the Soviet Union and the whole Communist world." The UAR President charged that Communism and imperialism had entered into an alliance against Arab nationalism and the United Arab Republic because "both parties realise that the obstacle which stands in their way is the belief of the Arab people in Arab nationalism." He pledged an all-out fight against "Communist interference" in UAR affairs.[25]

By the end of April 1959, the Soviet-UAR crisis had been allowed to subside. Anti-Soviet attacks gradually disappeared from the pages of Cairo's publications, but attacks on Arab Communists continued with undiminished vehemence. In turn, Moscow, apparently recognizing that continued friction with the United Arab Republic could benefit only the Western powers, toned down its anti-Nasir campaign. The Kremlin once again appeared intent on picturing itself as a disinterested friend of all Arabs, anxious to help them with advice and material aid in their struggle for complete political and economic independence.[26]

24. *Ibid.*, March 19. See also editorial, *ibid.*, March 18, 1959.
25. See Nasir's speeches of March 22 and 30; texts in *ibid.*, March 23 and 31, 1959, respectively. For Egyptian and Soviet press comments, see Mustafa Amin in *Akhbar al-Yawm*, March 29; editorial, *EG*, April 1, 1959. See also *Akhbar al-Yawm*, April 4, and *al-Ahram*, March 24; and Observer, *Pr.*, March 30, 1959.
26. For example, Moscow was not surprised when it became evident that the UAR wanted to reestablish economic contacts with the Western powers, broken off in 1956. "Indeed, it would be a good thing if . . . [Cairo] were to obtain economic assistance not only from the socialist nations, but from the Western powers as well." But the Soviet government appeared astonished at "some Cairo publications" alleging that the United Arab Republic had to

The events of late 1958 and early 1959 presented the USSR with both a political and an ideological dilemma. Cairo's persecution of local Communists had to be reconciled with Moscow's continued support of the United Arab Republic, and the Soviet position in the Nasir-Qasim feud had to be explained in ideological terms. To do this, a joint conference of the editorial boards of *International Affairs* (USSR) and *Shih-chieh Chih-shih* (Communist China) met in Moscow in January 1959. Although the discussions covered a wide range of topics connected with the national liberation struggle of the underdeveloped countries, the conference singled out certain problems that the "socialist camp" was facing in the Middle East, and the findings shed some light on Soviet policy in the region.[27]

In his paper entitled "The Bankruptcy of the Imperialist Colonial System and International Relations," E. M. Zhukov stated what may be considered the main theme of the conference: "the collapse of colonialism is an important and inseparable feature of the whole present-day epoch of the revolutionary transition from capitalism to Communism." He asserted that the process of the disintegration of the colonial system was inseparable from the movement for political emancipation on the part of former and present colonial peoples. However, the process of liberation in Asia and Africa was taking place very unevenly, as "varying internal and external circumstances" gave rise to different forms of the national liberation struggle, determining its slogans and demands, changing the "nature and character of its leadership," and influencing the degree of activity of "democratic forces."[28] The participants in the Moscow conference nonetheless

---

resume economic ties with the West because the Soviet Union was not "a reliable partner and might cut off economic assistance." There was no shred of evidence to support this, Moscow argued. E. Primakov, "U.A.R.—Economic Ties," *NT,* no. 21 (May 1959), p. 9.

27. Full text of the addresses in *IA,* no. 3 (March 1959), pp. 64–83. See also the findings of a seminar on the "National Bourgeoisie," held in the Leipzig Institute of World History in May 1959, in *WMR,* no. 8 (August 1959), pp. 61–81, and no. 9 (September 1959), pp. 66–81.

28. Zhukov in *IA,* no. 3 (March 1959), pp. 68 and 66, respectively. For more details, see V. V. Balabushevich, "O nekotorykh osobennostiakh rabochego dvizheniia v stranakh vostoka na sovremennom etape," *Problemy vostokovedeniia,* no. 2 (1959), p. 49 *et passim.*

agreed that "at any stage and in any form, the national-liberation struggle of the peoples of the East is of a profoundly progressive and revolutionary character in that it weakens imperialism and undermines the world capitalist system."[29]

Moscow held that the newly independent Asian and African nations should center their attention primarily on winning total emancipation from Western rule by means of the "final uprooting of colonialism." To achieve this, it was necessary to consolidate "*all* progressive, national and anti-imperialist forces, including the working class" (i.e., native Communists). Suppression of the Communist party or its exclusion from active political life was described as an "anti-popular program" benefiting only the imperialists.[30] Applied to the Middle East, this meant that Moscow would continue to back Qasim against Nasir. But it would not automatically withdraw its support from the United Arab Republic, for the "national-liberation struggle of the peoples of the East" was of a "profoundly progressive and revolutionary character."[31]

An assessment of the short-run success or failure of this policy is possible only in the light of the objectives that Moscow was pursuing in the Middle East in the late 1950s. If, at this stage of the game, the

29. Zhukov, p. 66. See also A. A. Guber, "Distinctive Features of the National-Liberation Movement in the Eastern Colonial and Dependent Countries," *IA*, no. 3 (March 1959), pp. 71–75, and "Osnovnye problemy sovremennogo razvitiia stran vostoka," *Problemy vostokovedeniia*, no. 1 (1960), p. 3 *et passim*.

30. As quoted by Zhukov, p. 68, Khrushchev stated in his report to the 21st Congress of the CPSU: "The struggle against Communist and other progressive parties is reactionary. The pursuit of an anti-Communist policy does not unite the national forces, but divides them and hence weakens the efforts of the entire nation in the defence of its interests against imperialism." For more details, see L. N. Chernov, "Kommunisty stran Azii i Afriki: V avangarde bor'by za svobodu i natsional'nuiu nezavisimost'," *Narody Azii i Afriki*, no. 5 (1961), pp. 15–31.

31. For subsequent elaboration of the Soviet view and the introduction of the concept of "national democracy," see "Dal'neishee razvitie marksistsko-leninskogo ucheniia o natsional'no-kolonial'nom voprose," *Problemy vostokovedeniia*, no. 1 (1961), pp. 3–12. See also "Proekt programmy KPSS i nekotorye problemy natsional'no-osvoboditel'nogo dvizheniia narodov Azii i Afriki," no. 5 (1961), pp. 6–7.

USSR was striving to turn Syria into a Soviet satellite and was extending aid to the neutralist Arabs in order to effect a pro-Soviet change in their foreign policy, then the Russians did in fact suffer a clear setback. However, if the Kremlin's support of the Arab nationalist movement (with two rival centers of power) was motivated basically by the desire to speed up the elimination from the Middle East of the "last vestiges" of Western influence—a preliminary step to making the area dependent on the USSR—then Moscow's efforts were crowned with considerable success, for in the late 1950s the West was steadily losing ground in the Arab East. Thus, even at the height of the crisis of 1959, the United Arab Republic (and later also Qasim's Iraq) was unwilling to abandon its neutralist position and adopt an anti-Soviet foreign policy.

Some have argued that Khrushchev suffered a serious defeat in that both Cairo and later Baghdad came close to destroying the Communist party and its affiliated organizations in territories under their control. It should be noted, however, that the tactical sacrifice of local Marxist organizations is a time-tested device justified in Communist eyes by the important objectives of the Soviet government in its all-out struggle with the Western powers.

On the other hand, if curbing Cairo's influence in the area had been one of the purposes behind Moscow's anti-Nasir campaign, as probably was the case, the 1959 crisis should be termed a political defeat. For some four months President Nasir, one of the leading exponents of neutralism, had attacked the USSR with a bluntness and vehemence that had previously been reserved for "imperialism and Zionism," and it may be assumed that his words were widely heard and weighed, not only in the Arab East but also throughout Asia and Africa.

The crisis illustrated the basic incompatibility of long-range Soviet-Egyptian policy aims. Though both sides sought the termination of Western influence in the Arab East, Cairo viewed this as a necessary prerequisite for complete independence from both the Western and Communist blocs and for the "unfettered" development of the "Arab personality," whereas Moscow regarded it as a preliminary step to establishing its own influence. As a result, when events occurred to mar the surface calm, illusions about the true nature of the Soviet-Egyptian rapprochement were soon shattered. Nasir and his adherents were forced to recognize and publicly admit that the Soviet Union could be relied upon to offer aid in combating imperialism but not to implement the political aspirations of Arab nationalists once full independence was attained. Khrushchev and his associates learned that the neutralist Arabs, in their effort to build up the economic and military potential of their respective countries, were determined to exploit the big-power rivalry while resolutely avoiding an alliance with either the Western or the Communist bloc. After the crisis no one could take too seriously future assurances of unencumbered friendship between the USSR and the United Arab Republic, whether made by Moscow or Cairo.

A period of relative calm in USSR-UAR relations followed the upheavals of late 1958-early 1959. Thus, in his note congratulating President Nasir on the seventh anniversary of the Egyptian revolution, Khrushchev expressed confidence that friendship and cooperation between Moscow and Cairo would "continue to develop in the interests of the peoples of both countries and in the interests of peace."[32] Even in late August 1959, at the height of the "Free Hellu" campaign (see below), Moscow announced the signing of a contract "on conducting exploration and survey operations prior to drafting a project for the irrigation of 100,000 hectars of new lands with the waters of the Euphrates."[33] Several days later, the UAR and the USSR signed a contract providing for Soviet technical aid in constructing the first stage of the Aswan High Dam.[34] The project was the most ambitious undertaking in the history of both modern Egypt and of the Soviet foreign aid program, and it was to dominate economic relations between the USSR and the United Arab Republic for many years to come.

32. *Pr.*, July 23, 1959. Text of Nasir's polite but noncommittal reply in *ibid.*, August 10, 1959.
33. *Ibid.*, August 29, 1959.
34. *Izv.*, September 9, 1959. See also *Pr.*, October 1, 1959. For Cairo's approval of the Soviet design for the first stage and Moscow's comments, see *ibid.*, July 3, 16, 30, 1959. See also L. N. Malyshev and I. Beliaev, *ibid.*, August 2 and 4, 1959, respectively.

the United Arab Republic and the Soviet Union." Their talks were reported to have been marked by a "spirit of mutual understanding and cordiality," confirming that "relations between our states are settling down on a firm and long-lasting basis." 'Amir, in contrast, was much more careful. Occasional references to "unshakable friendship" and "complementary long-range interests" notwithstanding, the UAR Vice-President, in his public pronouncements, preferred to concentrate on the "fierce struggle against imperialism and its agents" being waged in Algeria and the Congo. This was a very diplomatic and safe course to follow in that both Moscow and Cairo, for reasons of their own, supported the Algerian insurgents as well as Patrice Lumumba—the "legitimate" head of the Congolese state.[49]

However, while Moscow would not let Nasir's anti-Communism and his quarrels with Qasim affect relations between the USSR and the UAR, it clearly reserved for itself the right to criticize Cairo's treatment of Egyptian and Syrian Marxists. After a temporary lull, the campaign was intensified again in mid-1959, when it was reported that Farraj Allah Hellu, leader of the Lebanese Communist party, had been "illegally seized" in Damascus on July 25, 1959. The "Lebanese public," *Pravda* noted, protested against this "arbitrary act" and appealed to the UAR authorities "immediately to cease the tortures to which Hellu was being subjected" and to set him free.[50]

Additional pressure was applied later in the summer, when *Pravda* reported that a trial of 64 men accused of membership in the Egyptian Communist party and of an "attempt to overthrow the regime of President Nasir," had opened in the "highest state security court" in Alexandria on August 15, 1959. *Pravda* noted that there was an "unmistakable connection between the present trial and the overblown anti-Communist campaign conducted by the reactionary circles in the UAR."[51] The "trial of the 64" was succeeded by the "trial of the 48." Quoting *l'Unita*, official organ of the Italian Communist party, *Pravda* reported that the "persons on trial [were] . . . a small

49. *Pr.*, December 9, 1960.
50. *Ibid.*, July 30, 1959.
51. *Ibid.*, August 20, 1959. See also *ibid.*, August 25 and 31, 1959.

part of the 15 thousand democrats and Communists arrested in January and March, 1959, and thrown into dungeons where prisoners are cruelly tortured."[52] The protests against the persecution of the Marxists in the United Arab Republic were supplemented by demands for the release of Hellu.[53]

As in the past, this pressure soon led to a strong UAR reaction in the form of editorials in several influential newspapers, above all *al-Akhbar* and *Akhbar al-Yawm,* which rejected Moscow's concern over the fate of the native Communists as interference in the internal affairs of the United Arab Republic. Since *Pravda* did not believe that these publications reflected the attitude of the Arab public, it was concluded that they served the interests of those who, "unable to tolerate the growing Arab-Soviet friendship, would like to isolate the Arab people and to prejudice them against support from the socialist countries."[54]

Such Soviet political pressure, combined with efforts to improve Moscow-Cairo relations, did not prevent Nasir from refusing cooperation with domestic Marxists and from occasionally criticizing the USSR for pursuing policies that were at variance with Arab nationalism as defined by the UAR leaders.[55] Without implying that he envisaged a change in his relations with the USSR, Nasir simply served notice on all concerned that Cairo's close economic cooperation with both power blocs did not signify its readiness to subscribe to their respective political lines. Rather, he was as determined as ever to pursue an independent policy based on his own definition of Arab nationalism and its interests.

Nasir's recriminations were regularly followed by conciliatory gestures, such as expressions of gratitude to "the Soviet Union which is contributing to the development of our economy and which has, faithfully and sincerely, continued to carry out the economic agreement concluded between us in spite of the obvious and evident differ-

52. *Ibid.,* October 24, 1959. See also *ibid.,* October 10, 1959.
53. See *ibid.,* August 23, 25, 27, 29, 30, and September 4, 1959.
54. P. Egorov, *ibid.,* September 19, 1959.
55. See *President Gamal Abdel Nasser's Speeches and Press-Interviews, January-March 1960* (Cairo, n.d.), pp. 46, 63, 90.

ences in our social systems." Significantly, the UAR President reminded the Kremlin that cooperation was possible only under these circumstances or, as he put it, only so long as Moscow was pursuing this "noble and wise policy." Commenting on the future of Soviet-UAR relations, Nasir said: "We feel that the friendship which binds the Soviet people to the Arab people is strong and firm and cannot be obscured by passing clouds which might appear in . . . our relations due to differences of social and political ideologies."[56]

Nevertheless, in late 1960 and early 1961, the Soviet propaganda apparatus once again complained about what it called "a violent offensive [launched] against democratic freedoms and civil rights in the United Arab Republic."[57] In January 1961, *Pravda* quoted *l'Unita* reports that, in late December, the Egyptian authorities had ordered 200 Communists and Communist sympathizers arrested and exiled to a "region . . . where 800 other fighters for democracy . . . have been confined for several years." In view of the distressing nature of this news item, *Pravda* felt that it was obliged "to point out and condemn the contradictory nature of the policy pursued by the Egyptian government and President Nasir." While claiming to be a champion of the "struggle against imperialism and for complete liberation of Africa and Asia," he was persecuting the "best Egyptian patriots . . . thereby decreasing the effectiveness of this struggle and serving the forces that fight against the independence and progress of the Arab peoples."[58]

Another serious attack on the UAR government was mounted by Khalid Baqdash, the exiled leader of the Syrian Communist party. Commenting on the third anniversary of the creation of the United Arab Republic, he stated that the union between Egypt and Syria had "no sound basis" and that President Nasir was "wreaking havoc with the slogan of Arab unity and Arab nationalism." His real aim was to

---

56. *President Gamal Abdel Nasser's Speeches and Press-Interviews, April-June 1960*, p. 98.
57. *WMR*, no. 12 (December 1960), pp. 98–100. See also *ibid.*, no. 3 (March 1960), pp. 89–90; no. 6 (June 1960), pp. 84–86; no. 8 (August 1960), pp. 54–55; and no. 4 (April 1961), pp. 94–95.
58. *Pr.*, January 20, 1961. See also *ibid.*, February 5, 1961.

foster "Egyptian nationalism, which is the embodiment of the expansionist and jingo features of the Egyptian big bourgeoisie." Although Baqdash was not in principle opposed to the idea of Arab unity, he argued that it must be consummated on Communist terms. A basic prerequisite for an effective union was the creation of a "broad front of the workers and peasants, the progressive national bourgeoisie, youth, students, women—of all patriots and democrats."[59]

These statements did not provoke an immediate reply from the volatile UAR President, indicating that Cairo was not quite certain how much significance it should attach to them. If they represented but a tactical move designed to placate the increasingly intolerant Chinese, who were beginning to criticize Moscow's ideological laxity, it was wise to remain discreet. Nevertheless, in challenging Egypt's role as the leader of the Arab world, the Communists were striking at the very heart of the UAR President's philosophy and ambitions, and such pronouncements could not be allowed to pass in silence indefinitely.

The crisis point was reached innocently enough in late April 1961, when a UAR Parliamentary delegation, headed by Anwar Sadat, then Speaker of the National Assembly, arrived in Moscow at the invitation of the Supreme Soviet of the USSR. Judging from the statements appearing in the Russian press, the guests were given the red-carpet treatment, which included a tour of the country, receptions in the Kremlin, and meetings with Khrushchev, Mikoian, Leonid Brezhnev (then Chairman of the Supreme Soviet), and Mukhitdinov.[60] But it was probably no coincidence that the April 1961 issue of the *World Marxist Review,* which appeared prior to Sadat's arrival in the USSR, repeated earlier calls for a "solidarity campaign" to obtain the release of Communist prisoners detained in UAR jails.[61] In any case, the allegedly "warm and friendly discussion" between Khrushchev and Sadat soon was shown to have been a heated argument with pronounced ideological overtones.

59. *WMR,* no. 1 (January 1961), p. 62.
60. For details, see *Pr.,* April 29, 30, May 10, 11, 12; and *Izv.,* May 4, 1961.
61. *WMR,* no. 4 (April 1961), pp. 94–95.

Since Khrushchev's statement of May 3, probably the high point of the 1961 anti-Nasir campaign, has not been released by Soviet sources, it is necessary to rely on Haykal's version of what was said during the Kremlin reception given by the Soviet leaders for the UAR Parliamentary delegation. The initial part of the address, devoted to intergovernmental relations between the two countries, contained nothing new or extraordinary. The Soviet government had found itself in full sympathy with the aims and aspirations of genuinely neutralist nations and endeavored to contribute, to the best of its ability, to their social and economic development. However, this did not mean that the USSR approved of many "undemocratic," if not outright "reactionary," policies pursued by some neutralist leaders. Having set the stage, Khrushchev then proceeded to lecture Sadat and the members of the UAR delegation in the manner of a schoolmaster instructing his not-too-intelligent and obviously erring students. Nasir and his adherents, the Soviet Premier noted, were working to create a socialist society without understanding that socialism, as a "scientific phenomenon" in the historical development of human society, could only be viewed as a preliminary stage to Communism. He then proceeded to compare the Egyptian leaders to individuals who study the alphabet and who, upon learning the letter "A," refuse to admit that it is followed by the letter "B." Socialism, Khrushchev explained, was "A" while Communism was "B." "If you want socialism, you should not say that you oppose Communism. [Otherwise] you place yourself into an embarrassing position," a trap that the imperialists were certain to exploit. How that might be done, he did not explain.

Having lectured the Egyptians on doctrinal grounds, the Soviet Premier magnanimously offered to have history settle their ideological controversy. Whether intended or not, this part of Khrushchev's address also contained an element of insult. Since the Soviet people lived a better life under Communism than their Arab counterparts under socialism, how could the Arab leaders declare themselves against Communism, he asked? Just as King Faruq had been overthrown by a group of young officers determined to introduce progressive reforms, so Communism was bound to triumph in the future because it promised more by way of social and economic reform than the present UAR leaders were able to offer. "Therefore, victory will be ours. You cannot see it today, but . . . in the future you will see that you were wrong."[62]

No record of Sadat's verbal reply to Khrushchev's lecture is available. Since the Egyptian press has remained silent on this subject, it might be assumed that the UAR delegation was dumbfounded by the outburst and that its leader decided to reply after consultation with his colleagues in Cairo. Sadat made his reply to Khrushchev in writing, three days after the delegation's return to the United Arab Republic. Although it noted that there were indeed many issues on which the two governments had found themselves in complete agreement—the best example of Cairo-Moscow collaboration was provided by Soviet aid in constructing the Aswan High Dam—they did differ, at times fundamentally, in their approach to the solution of some of the basic social and economic problems facing their respective countries. Here Cairo reserved for itself the right to make its own evaluation and to introduce its own remedies, regardless of whether its views and actions fitted the "dialectical materialistic" mold or met with the approval of the Soviet authorities.

Sadat rejected Khrushchev's assertion that the UAR government would be swept away by the people because Communism was accomplishing more in the Soviet Union than Arab socialism in Egypt. Should this type of logic be applicable to comparisons between different socioeconomic and political systems, would not the United States have an equally convincing argument with regard to capitalism's superiority over Communism? In any event, the October 1917 revolution took place 45 years ago, while its Egyptian counterpart was only 9 years old. In addition, the Arabs devoted most of their energy to combating not only "internal oppression" but "foreign aggressors" as well. It was noted in conclusion that opposition to Western-style capitalism did not imply automatic approval of Communism simply because it had proved workable in some countries. Cairo "refused to

62. Haykal in *al-Ahram,* June 9, 1961. Bayrut's independent and well-informed *al-Nahar,* commenting on Haykal's article, said on June 10 that not all of Khrushchev's remarks had been released. An attack on President Nasir, too embarrassing to print, had allegedly been omitted.

be pushed into . . . a dilemma" of having to choose between two established social and economic patterns, but was determined to experiment and develop the system that would be best suited to its own peculiar problems and needs. This was not an impossible task, for "the intellectual horizon today is extremely vast."[63]

The relative mildness of Sadat's reply contrasted sharply with the occasionally bitter denunciations of the Soviet government that began to appear in various Egyptian publications in late May and early June. The Egyptian authorities evidently had had enough of the vociferous condemnations of the UAR by the Soviet radio and press and felt that silence was being interpreted as a sign of weakness. Writing in *al-Ahram,* Kamal Hamdi Abu Khayr, an Egyptian journalist of some renown, stated that the Soviet system could not possibly be considered "real socialism" for the simple reason that it was marked by the "deprivation of the individual's right to property and by the state ownership of production." He was seconded by Fikri 'Abaza, who concluded that in order for the relations between the "progressive" Arabs and Russia to remain "cordial" and "fruitful," the Kremlin had to demonstrate more respect for Arab nationalism and its aspirations. Mutually profitable relations could be continued only on the basis of complete respect and nonintervention in each other's internal affairs.[64]

The strongest denunciation of the Soviet campaign came from the English-language *Egyptian Economic and Political Review (EEPR).* Commenting on the Khrushchev-Sadat exchange, it blasted Moscow for its "misguided" policy in the Arab East. The Soviet leaders were guilty of mistaking Communism for "some sort of a divine message addressed to all men, to be disseminated by legions of Marxist-Leninist messiahs," and of underestimating Arab resistance to their ideology. They were equally erroneous in assuming that the relatively high degree of technological advancement achieved by the USSR made the Russians "more civilised" than their counterparts in the underdeveloped nations. These mistaken assumptions led Khrush-

63. Haykal, *al-Ahram,* June 9, 1961.
64. As quoted by Commentator, *Pr.,* May 31, 1961.

chev "to adopt patronising and paternalistic attitudes towards representatives of the UAR.... Being African, in Mr. Khrushchev's mind, was ... tantamount to being uncivilised and primitive."[65]

Moreover, *EEPR* felt that Khrushchev was not competent to judge the merits or possible shortcomings of "Socialist Co-operate Democracy," which the UAR leaders were allegedly trying to introduce to the developing Arab societies. For one thing, the Premier insisted on drawing comparisons between Communism and nationalism. In so doing, he spoke like a "XIXth century European bourgeois for whom Nationalism, in its European sense, was ... an artificial ideology based on racial and religious discrimination . . . [allowing] the imperialists to fight wars, occupy countries and generally serve the acquisitiveness of kings, tycoons and robber barons." To the Arabs, nationalism had a different meaning. It referred more to a community than a political entity. It stressed "traditions, principles and civilisations," rather than "territory, racialism and power concepts." Khrushchev's error was an understandable one, *EEPR* continued. Like his political mentors, Marx and Lenin, he was "the prisoner of the usual XIXth century clichés, . . . that afflict the Europeans, and especially the Marxist Leninists, in their attempt to interpret Arabism and Afro-Asian ways of thinking." While he was not, like his American counterparts, "likely to accept washing machines and refrigerators as justificatory symbols for ... [his] social doctrine," Khrushchev preached that Communism was superior to capitalism because Gagarin was the first to orbit the world in space and because Russian rockets were bigger and better than American missiles. Was this not an "adulation of power concepts" of the type exhibited by the Kaiser and Adolf Hitler?[66]

The seriousness with which the Kremlin viewed the situation was illustrated by the fact that a public rebuttal was delivered in the form of an article, entitled "Onslaughts of the Slanderers," which appeared in *Pravda* and was signed by "Commentator." The peoples of the

65. Editorial, "Civilisation and Colliwobbles," *Egyptian Economic and Political Review* (henceforth referred to as *EEPR*) (May-June 1961), p. 5.
66. Editorial, "Aria's in the Sky," *ibid.,* p. 24.

Soviet Union and the newly independent nations, it said in part, were linked by "indestructible fraternal friendship." The USSR, through its policy of "total support" of and noninterference in the internal affairs of other states, had proved to the emerging countries that it was a "loyal and reliable friend." It was therefore all the more surprising and regrettable that some individuals in the underdeveloped world were willing to collaborate with the imperialists in the "thankless and hopeless" task of slandering the USSR and belittling the magnitude of its efforts. "Commentator" singled out *al-Ahram* and *al-Musawwar* as falling into this category: they made their "pages available for the foulest anti-Soviet slander concocted by the old recipes of the imperialist propaganda kitchen." Khayr's equation of Communism, which had "triumphed on an enormous part of the planet," with the "bloody regime of Hitler's Germany" was but one illustration of such contemptible activity. The lengthy discourse closed with an obliquely worded but explicit warning directed at the Egyptian government. Having implied that Cairo bore full responsibility for the diplomatic crisis, the article advised UAR authorities not to "fell a tree which . . . [gave them] shade."[67]

"Commentator's" article had been preceded, on May 29, by a statement from the proscribed Lebanese Communist party informing the world of the death of Farraj Allah Hellu. Arrested in Damascus, he was allegedly "tortured to death" by the UAR secret police.[68] This incident was seized upon by Soviet publications as an additional proof of their contention that there was no political freedom in the UAR: "proven fighters for peace and democracy" were subjected to inhuman treatment. Soviet newspapers reproduced numerous statements from the International Committee for the Liberation of Hellu, foreign Communist, "progressive," and Soviet organizations condemning the "unjustifiable arbitrariness" of the UAR bourgeoisie, determined to protect its "egotistical class interests." These misguided efforts were doomed to failure because the people would eventually gain "broad rights and basic democratic freedoms" by whatever means neces-

67. *Pr.,* May 31, 1961.
68. See *MEM,* no. 22 (June 3, 1961), p. 15.

sary.⁶⁹ Finally, on June 5, the CPSU Central Committee expressed its official condolences on Hellu's death to the Lebanese Communist party.⁷⁰

Egyptian tempers not surprisingly reached a new pitch in early June 1961. The Middle East News Agency issued a statement asserting that Cairo's restraint in the face of the Communist campaign had been "misinterpreted" in the Kremlin. Instead of responding in kind, the Soviet government had encouraged its propaganda organs to step up the "flow of abuse" directed at the United Arab Republic. As a result, the campaign had reached a "pitch which could not be tolerated." MENA labeled the attacks an "obvious attempt to undermine relations" between the two states, advising Moscow to stop the "organized campaign of libel" or face unspecified "serious repercussions."⁷¹ Cairo then rejected Moscow's intervention on behalf of Syrian and Egyptian Communists, asserting that a country that interned and jailed "more than three million" of its citizens was in no position to criticize the UAR for measures designed to protect its security. If anyone had the right to protest against Hellu's death, it was Lebanon, the country of which he was a national, and not the USSR or any Communist organization.⁷²

The prevailing tenor of opinion voiced in the Egyptian press in early June was that a basic clash between Arab nationalism and Communism was inevitable. Arab nationalism was concerned primarily with the interests of the Arab nation and harmony of all classes, whereas the Marxists viewed nationalism as a "bourgeois and capitalist" notion which was but one of the roadblocks on history's "inevitable" march to Communism. Moreover, the Arab nationalists saw nothing inevitable about history and were even now working to establish what was termed "democratic and cooperative socialism."⁷³ Finally, the

69. *Pr.*, June 3, 1961. See also *ibid.*, June 2, 4, 7, 8, 10, 1961; and *WMR*, no. 7 (July 1961), p. 87.
70. See *Pr.*, June 6, 1961.
71. *Al-Ahram*, June 5, 1961.
72. Editorial, *al-Gumhuriya*, June 9; and Kamal al-Shannawi, *ibid.*, June 12, 1961, respectively.
73. "We have our own democratic socialism which differs from that of the USSR. It did not emanate from theoretical works but from our own needs,

Communists insisted on unrestricted freedom of Marxist propaganda and organization—an idea not acceptable to the nationalists—as a prime condition for their support of any future unity.[74]

Nevertheless, neither Cairo nor Moscow was interested in escalating the crisis to the point where it might imperil the foundation upon which their cooperation had been based, and so each took the necessary steps toward a verbal reconciliation. It was thus noted in Cairo that, present difficulties notwithstanding, "very solid friendship" still tied both the peoples and the governments of the two countries. The results of the UAR-Soviet cooperation were also of overriding international significance in that they served as "glowing examples of peaceful coexistence between fundamentally different regimes." But Cairo could not allow the Russians to carry out activities that were denied the Western powers. Otherwise, Egypt's "long and arduous battle against imperialism will have been in vain."[75]

Regrettable as the diplomatic confrontation was, it had one positive result, Cairo concluded. It helped to crystallize relations between the USSR and the United Arab Republic on the one hand, and the UAR and the Western powers, on the other. If Washington, London, and Paris believed that, by adhering to the policy of nonalignment, Egypt had moved closer to the Soviet Union and its allies, the current crisis refuted such assumptions. Similarly, if Moscow thought that Cairo's independent policy invited Communist penetration of the Arab East, its leaders should now know better. The region did not constitute a "vacuum of power" and could advance on its own, without too much reliance on either the East or the West.[76]

The Soviet reaction, rather slow in coming, took the form of an article entitled "Whose Interests Does This Serve" by I. Aleksandrov. He accused the UAR authorities of blowing up various relatively minor incidents out of all proportion and agreed with Egyptian publi-

---

environment, and traditions. It is a result of our conscience and history." Muhammad al-Taba'i, *al-Akhbar*, June 6, 1961.

74. See Melhem Ayashi, *ibid.*, June 11, 1961.

75. Kamal al-Shannawi, *al-Gumhuriya*, June 6, 1961. See also editorials, *ibid.*, June 5 and 9; and Yusuf al-Siba'i, *Ruz al-Yusif*, June 12, 1961.

76. Ibrahim Nawar, *al-Gumhuriya*, June 10, 1961.

cations that only "third parties" would benefit from the deterioration of relations between Moscow and Cairo. More precisely, Aleksandrov endeavored to prove that the "Commentator" article had been directed not against the UAR government or its political and economic programs, but against individual journalists. Without disclosing the true content of the "Commentator" article to the UAR public, MENA had subjected the Soviet press to a "ferocious attack," placing statements by USSR publications "on a par with imperialist actions." Having invented a Soviet propaganda war against the United Arab Republic, it had plunged into a "genuine propaganda campaign against the Soviet Union."

The Soviet government regretted the verbal clashes of recent weeks, Aleksandrov noted, admitting that a break-up of Moscow-Cairo relations would indeed represent a serious political setback to the USSR. But there was also no denying that the UAR, which relied heavily on Soviet military, economic, financial, and technical support, would be the biggest loser. "Imperialist circles in the West," interested in driving a wedge between the two states, would be the only winners. Aleksandrov concluded by stating that "Soviet-Arab friendship had withstood the test of time and had proved itself . . . to be a most important factor in strengthening the political independence and economic progress of the Arab peoples." The USSR cherished this friendship and would continue to promote it. "It must be assumed that the United Arab Republic will do likewise."[77]

As far as Moscow was concerned, the unpleasant diplomatic interlude came to an end in July 1961, when Khrushchev, congratulating Nasir on the anniversary of the Egyptian revolution, expressed "specific satisfaction" with the "continuous successful development" of relations between the two countries. The two governments were offering the world a "graphic example of mutually advantageous cooperation between states with different social and political systems, based on the principles of equality, mutual respect, and noninterference in internal affairs."[78] In a sense, the message represented an official

77. *Pr.*, June 17, 1961.
78. Text in *ibid.*, July 22, 1961. See also I. Beliaev, *ibid.*, July 23; and S. Kondrashov, *Izv.*, July 23, 1961.

apology for Khrushchev's treatment of the UAR Parliamentary delegation. The olive branch was accepted and, in his reply a few days later, Nasir expressed the conviction that good relations between the two countries would continue to develop. He noted that Cairo was determined not to "let anyone bring discord" into Soviet-UAR friendship.[79]

Generally speaking, it would appear that the crisis had been caused partly by the traditional duality of Soviet foreign policy toward the non-Communist nations. While extending numerous newly independent states economic, financial, technical, and, occasionally, military support, Moscow could not officially disclaim interest in the fate of its "co-believers" in these countries. It is very likely that in the majority of cases, including the United Arab Republic, the Soviet leaders did not much care about the fate of indigenous Marxists. The Kremlin was no doubt aware of the fact that most such organizations outside the Communist bloc were a liability, not an asset, because their advent to power tended to multiply rather than decrease Moscow's difficulties. (As illustrated by Castro's Cuba, in such instances the Kremlin was forced to assume a wide range of political, military, and economic obligations without being able to control its ally's policies.)

In any event, when confronted with the alternatives of aiding its fellow-Marxists or gaining the good will of the nationalist elites in the Third World, the USSR usually chose to work with the established anti-Communist governments. In the "good old days" of the 1920s and 1930s, when Stalin ruled over a relatively monolithic Communist movement with an iron hand, this dilemma did not exist. Communists, by definition, were those who executed Moscow's orders regardless of all other considerations. This is not to say that the USSR did not occasionally face embarrassing situations in its relations with foreign Communists, but simply that the latter rarely presented Stalin with any lasting problems.

In the early 1960s, in contrast, the Communist world had openly split into two feuding camps, as Moscow and Peking vied with each other for the allegiance and support of Marxist organizations

---

79. Text in *Pr.*, July 28, 1961.

throughout the world. Since it was unrealistic to expect the Soviet government to abandon leadership in the Communist world to its Chinese counterpart, it was only natural that the Kremlin would attempt to uphold its image as an ardent defender of the "true faith" in the face of Mao's ideologically couched accusations of doctrinal complacency *vis-à-vis* the capitalist world. More particularly, Chinese ideological pressure made it impossible for the USSR to remain silent to pleas from members of various Asian, African, and Latin American Communist parties to help defend the "innocent victims" of the bourgeois-nationalist terror.

There can also be no doubt, however, that intervention (even if only in terms of public statements) on behalf of fellow-Marxists constituted interference in the internal affairs of sovereign states and led to an increase in tension between these nations and the Soviet Union. In 1961, in particular, the Russians found themselves on the horns of a dilemma: they were attempting to wrest the ideological initiative from Peking, by posing as a powerful and determined leader of the movement, while persuading the heads of friendly neutralist states that, despite doctrinal differences, the emerging countries could rely on Moscow for aid in the pursuit of their national objectives.

Hence the intensification of Moscow's propaganda campaign was probably due, in part, to the exigencies of Sino-Soviet relations. Moreover, Khrushchev's surprisingly vituperative personal attack on Cairo also attested to his annoyance with the new meaning that the UAR and some of its neutralist friends were imparting to "positive neutralism."[80] The intention to pursue a more active policy with regard to both power blocs was announced by Nasir as early as September 1960. Addressing the General Assembly of the United Nations, the UAR President stated his opposition to summit meetings held outside the UN framework. Superpower exclusiveness, he noted, made it impossible for the neutralist countries to influence the solution of a number of problems, among them disarmament, which were of vital concern to all the nations of the world.[81] The Soviet leaders must also have

80. For some details, see Marcel Colombe, "Panorama du trimestre," *Orient*, no. 18 (1961), pp. 7–13.
81. Soviet reaction to Nasir's speech was predictably negative. Details in *MEM*, no. 40 (October 1, 1960), pp. 3–4.

viewed with disfavor Cairo's subsequent pronouncements, such as Haykal's article "On Positive Neutralism," in which he argued that the attitude of passivity and isolation from the mainstream of world politics, characterizing the policies of many noncommitted nations, did little to enhance the cause of peace and of socioeconomic progress. "Positive action" in international relations, aiming at the elimination of the cold war and the settlement of differences between the USSR and the United States was the new motto of the nonaligned nations.[82] Words were followed by action. On May 20, 1961, *al-Ahram* announced the decision to convene in Egypt a meeting of twenty neutralist nations to prepare the agenda for another "summit conference" of the nonaligned states, to be held in Belgrade in August 1961.[83] The noncommitted nations were thus openly preparing to assume the role of an active moral arbiter between Moscow and Washington.

Behind these assertions of independence from both power blocs, the USSR government detected the guiding hand of Yugoslavia's President Tito who, in the spring of 1961, was subjected to a renewed and violent Soviet campaign accusing him of "revisionism," a euphemism for ideological treason. Moscow was clearly alarmed that Belgrade's "right-wing Communism" might undermine its efforts to "sell" the Soviet brand of Marxism as the only viable method for accelerated socioeconomic development in the underdeveloped areas. Of even greater significance was the implication contained in the planned reassessment of nonalignment that placed the USSR on the same footing with the "imperialist" West. The "citadel of world Communism," too, could be found guilty of "immoral behavior," a distinction which, until then, had been strictly reserved for the capitalist countries. In this sense, the anti-UAR campaign could also be interpreted as an attempt to demonstrate the extent of Soviet disapproval of this new and, from Moscow's viewpoint, dangerous trend in Nasir's foreign policy.[84]

82. *Al-Ahram,* January 27, 1961.
83. The delegates of twenty countries opened the conference on June 5. Details in *Economist,* June 10, 1961, p. 1095.
84. For a good treatment of what was described as the transformation of "positive neutralism" into "nonalignment," see Simon Jargy, "Du Neutralisme positif au nonalignment," *Orient,* no. 18 (1961), pp. 15–22.

It would thus appear that the responsibility for initiating the 1961 crisis falls squarely on the shoulders of Khrushchev. An ideological campaign was the only approach open to him, since an open threat to cut off Soviet aid, the single trump card held by Moscow, would only have provoked Nasir, proud and all too conscious of his reputation as a strong, incorruptible Arab leader, to demonstrate that Khrushchev could not succeed where the Western powers had failed. Moreover, such a course of action would have exposed to the rest of the world the hollowness of Moscow's protestations concerning the "selflessness" of its aid to the emerging nations.

The debate, which was, in essence, only an intricate power-political gambit initiated by the USSR in an attempt to pressure Cairo into abandoning some of its basic policies, backfired. The discussion of the merits of Communism and Arab socialism attested to the wide ideological gap separating the USSR and the UAR and served as but another illustration of the basic incompatibility of their respective long-range interests. The Soviet government again discovered that its powers of persuasion were indeed much more limited than had apparently been believed by Kremlin leaders, and the ability to challenge his Soviet friends openly and successfully not only provided the UAR President with a potent propaganda weapon but undoubtedly increased Nasir's prestige among the Arabs as well as in the rest of the underdeveloped world. Basically, however, neither the USSR nor the United Arab Republic was interested in escalating such crises to the point where they might have endangered the mutually profitable political and economic foundation upon which their relations had been based. For this reason, the confrontations were relatively brief and resulted in no permanent damage to Soviet-UAR relations.

7
Disenchantment in Iraq

During the spring and early summer of 1959, the Soviet investment in Qasim seemed to be paying off. Judging by the rapidly increasing military, economic, and cultural ties between the two countries, Iraq appeared to be moving away from the West while tying itself more closely to the Communist states.[1] The public pronouncements of the Iraqi leaders, while stressing their determination to uphold the sovereignty and independence of their country, also asserted their desire to maintain close relations with the USSR and its allies. For example, on June 14, Minister of Economics Kubba said in East Berlin that Iraq, "as an anti-colonialist nation, belongs to the same camp as East Germany—the camp of peace, independence, and freedom."[2] At the same time public meetings, which turned into what was described as "striking demonstrations of Soviet-Iraqi friendship," were being held in Moscow.[3] Commenting on the first anniversary of the Iraqi revolu-

---

1. It is true that in late spring of 1959 Qasim negotiated an arms agreement with Great Britain. (For details, see Kenneth Love, *NYT,* May 12 and 17, 1959.) However, it was more than offset by a $100 million arms contract with the USSR, signed on June 25, 1959. *MEJ* 13, no. 4 (Fall 1959), p. 430.
2. *MEM,* no. 25 (June 21, 1959), p. 9. See also Qasim's statement, quoted in *ibid.,* no. 20 (May 17, 1959), p. 4.
3. *Izv.,* July 4, and *Pr.,* July 12, 1959.

tion, the Soviet press emphasized the "progressive" aspects of Qasim's regime, praising it for the reforms introduced in the political, economic, and social life of the country. Thus, the "toiling masses" of Iraq were for the first time being given an opportunity to organize trade unions. Similar freedom of action was afforded to "progressive" newspapers and periodicals; Moscow was particularly gratified by the fact that the Communist *Ittihad al-Sha'b* (Union of the People), the "most popular [newspaper] in the country, loved by the working people," was appearing regularly. In addition, Iraq's decision to leave the sterling zone and demand the closing of the USIA center in Baghdad was especially satisfying: "The grip of enslaving obligations which strangled the people for many years has been weakened even more."[4]

Yet certain events in Iraq during the same period annoyed both Moscow and the local Marxist organization. When the latter, under the pretext of helping to "preserve the gains of the Revolution," demanded the legalization of the Communist party and its representation in the cabinet, the Prime Minister refused. This led Moscow to warn Qasim not to suppress the "progressive elements." *Pravda,* calling for vigilance against the "plots of the imperialists and their agents," argued that the best method of protecting the revolution against the recurrence of efforts to unseat the government was through the "strengthening of trade unions, peasant associations, and the units of popular resistance." In Iraq, most of these were controlled by the Communists.[5]

Commenting on the first anniversary of Qasim's revolution, Georgii Mirskii insisted that the legalization and strengthening of the "National Unity Front," whose official recognition the Communists had demanded as a means of gaining a similar privilege for their own

4. P. Demchenko, *Pr.,* July 13, 1959. For more details, see editorial, *Izv.,* July 14; V. Osipov, *ibid.,* July 15; Y. Zhukov, "Anniversary of the Revolution in Iraq," *IA,* no. 8 (August 1959), pp. 14–18; and editorial, "V bor'be za natsional'noe edinstvo," *Sovremennyi vostok,* no. 9 (1959), pp. 5–8. For more details on internal developments, see also Akademiia nauk SSSR. Institut mirovoi ekonomiki i mezhdunarodnykh otnoshenii, *Mezhdunarodnyi politiko-ekonomicheskii ezhegodnik, 1960* (Moscow: Gospolitizdat, 1960), pp. 176–77, 179.

5. P. Demchenko, *Pr.,* July 13, 1959.

organization, was a basic prerequisite for the successful growth of the revolutionary regime. "The enemies of the Iraqi Revolution," Mirskii argued, had been endeavoring to split the Front because it constituted "the kingpin of the Republic's strength and development." Created in 1959, the Front was comprised of the left wing of the National Democratic party, the Kurdish Democratic and Communist parties, along with "numerous public organizations, such as the National Union of Peasant Associations, the Democratic Youth Federation, the National Peace Committee, the Society for the Defense of Women's Rights, and many prominent public leaders." Mirskii held that the support of the Front was indispensable to the government's efforts to solve "many complex problems" confronting the republic, above all "further consolidation of national independence based on solid unity of all patriotic forces."[6]

This implicit criticism of Qasim was coupled, however, with continued support of Iraq in its confrontation with the United Arab Republic. Moscow labeled Cairo's allegation that Baghdad had isolated itself from the rest of the Arab states an "absurd assertion." It was a well-known fact that the Iraqi government and people were working to "strengthen the solidarity of all Arabs in their struggle against imperialism."[7] When a high-level delegation, headed by Deputy Foreign Minister Vasilii Kuznetsov, arrived in Baghdad on July 12, 1959, to represent the USSR government at the festivities commemorating the first anniversary of the revolution, Kuznetsov expressed confidence that friendly relations between the two countries would continue to develop on the basis of "equality, mutual respect, and noninterference" in each other's internal affairs. Similar sentiments were also expressed by Khrushchev in his congratulatory telegram to Premier Qasim.[8]

Even as the Soviet delegation was attending the mass demonstra-

---

6. G. Mirsky, "Iraqi Republic: The First Year," *NT*, no. 28 (July 1959), p. 12. See also editorial, "V bor'be za natsional'noe edinstvo," *Sovremennyi vostok*, no. 9 (1959), p. 8. For more details, see Akademiia nauk SSSR, *Mezhdunarodnyi ezhegodnik, 1960*, pp. 176–77 and Akademiia nauk SSSR. Institut narodov Azii, *Noveishaia istoriia arabskikh stran (1917–1966)* (Moscow: Izdatel'stvo "Nauka," 1968), pp. 188–89.
7. P. Demchenko, *Pr.*, July 13, 1959.
8. See *ibid.*, July 13 and 14, 1959.

tion staged in Baghdad, however, blood was flowing in the streets of Kirkuk, the second largest city of northern Iraq. The disturbance, which began as a coffee-house brawl between the Kurds (a non-Arab Muslim people inhabiting northern Iraq) and the Turkomans (a wealthy, and therefore unpopular, minority engaged primarily in trade and business), soon deteriorated into a blood bath with definite political overtones. Local Communists seized this opportunity to settle old scores with the "reactionary elements." Dozens of anti-Marxists were dragged out of their homes and killed in the streets by units of the "Popular Resistance Forces." By taking the law into their own hands, the Communists had openly challenged Qasim's authority, leaving the Premier no choice but to reassert his control over them.[9]

It is noteworthy that, even though there could be no doubt as to the indigenous Communists' complicity in the massacre, the Soviet government washed its hands of the entire affair. The *New Times,* quoting Bayrut's Communist *al-Nid'a,* said that the "incidents" were but "a part of a fresh conspiracy against the Republic and Premier Kassem." The plot was allegedly "engineered by the US imperialists and their Turkish agents [i.e., the Turkomans] and was intended to sever the Kirkuk and Mosul oilfields from Iraq." The episode, it was concluded, demonstrated beyond the shadow of a doubt the need for "vigilance and stronger national unity."[10] Shedding "additional" light on the massacre, Moscow's *International Affairs* asserted later that the disturbances were intended to "split the ranks of the democratic, patriotic forces" and to "drive a wedge between the progressive circles" and the government.[11]

The Kremlin rejected subsequent attempts "to put the blame for the Kirkuk events on the progressive patriotic forces" and expressed regret that "reactionary circles" that were instrumental in spreading such rumors were "to a certain extent aided by some elements from

9. For more details, see my "Qasim and the Iraqi Communist Party: A Study in Arab Politics (Part One, 1958–1959)," *Il Politico* 32, no. 2 (1967): 301–4.
10. Editorial, "Kirkuk," *NT,* no. 31 (July 1959), p. 2.
11. S. Danilov, "Provocation in Kirkuk," *IA,* no. 9 (September 1959), p. 93.

the Iraqi administration who have not gotten rid as yet of memories of the Nuri Said regime."[12] Since Qasim was quite outspoken in his accusations of the Communists, there could be no doubt that Moscow's censure was directed primarily at him. The criticism served as an additional indication of the Kremlin's growing disenchantment with the Iraqi Premier.[13]

In any event, Qasim used the Kirkuk episode to bring the Iraqi Communist party under tighter government control. He accomplished this by publicly denouncing the "anarchists" (a newly coined phrase denoting the Communists) and by accusing them of efforts to topple the revolutionary government. In retrospect, it appears unlikely that the local Marxists were attempting to oust Qasim or to communize Iraq. Instead, they were trying to strengthen their organization and to spread its influence over the Iraqi masses. Aware of the limited nature of their objectives, the Premier had utilized the ICP to help stem the Arab nationalist tide and turned against them only after that immediate threat to his regime had been removed. Following several hastily called meetings of the Central Committee, the Iraqi Communist party, on August 3, 1959, publicly admitted that its leaders were guilty of "irregularities" and "tactical errors" committed in the organization's dealings with the government.[14] This was the beginning of the decline of the party, which during the spring of 1959 had reached what was to be the zenith of its political power and influence.

The feud between its ideological followers and Qasim presented the Soviet government with an unpleasant choice: the Kremlin could throw its support behind the Iraqi Communist party, thus vindicating Western and Arab nationalist claims that the USSR was in fact seeking to establish direct control over Iraq, or it could side with Qasim, thus opening itself to Mao's criticism that Russia placed the exigen-

12. *Ibid.*
13. Initially, however, Khrushchev apparently decided not to let the Kirkuk episode affect Soviet-Iraqi relations. On July 21 he invited Qasim to visit the USSR. The move was interpreted in Washington as an indication of Moscow's concern over anti-Communist developments in Iraq. Qasim accepted the invitation on August 5, but the visit never took place. *MEJ* 13, no. 4 (Fall 1959): 430.
14. Full text in *Orient,* no. 11 (1959), pp. 175–221.

cies of power politics over ideological affinity. Since neither alternative was acceptable, Moscow, as evidenced by its attitude toward the Kirkuk episode, initially tried to downgrade the issue. As time passed, however, and as relations between Iraq and the USSR cooled considerably, Soviet publications grew more vocal in their support of the "legitimate grievances" of the Iraqi Marxists.[15]

On January 6, 1960, after the government passed the so-called New Associations Law No.1,[16] which stipulated that parties that favored Iraq's independence and unity should apply to the Ministry of Interior for licenses, *two* Marxist groups sought recognition under the name of the Iraqi Communist Party. They were centered around two competing newspapers, *Ittihad al-Sha'b* (Union of the People) and *al-Mabda'* (The Innovator), edited by 'Abd al-Qadhir Isma'il al-Bustani and Dawud al-Sa'igh, respectively. Once the split was brought into the open, the two factions became embroiled in a bitter feud, devoting much of their time and energy to combating each other.[17]

The Kremlin abstained from comment until it could be reasonably certain of Qasim's stand on the matter. The issue was settled on February 9, when the Ministry of Interior granted licenses to the National Democrats, Kurdish Democrats, and the splinter faction of Dawud al-Sa'igh.[18] The authorities later explained that their decision against the Ittihad group was based on Article Four of the Associations Law, which prohibited licensing of parties that "spread disunity among Iraq's various nationalities, religions and beliefs," or conducted activities that were "incompatible with the country's independence and national unity."[19] An additional illustration of Qasim's concerted effort to undermine the strength and influence of the Iraqi Marxist organization was provided by the dismissal of Ibrahim Kubba, pro-Communist Minister of Agrarian Reform and Petroleum Affairs.[20]

15. See *Pr.*, August 17, 1959.
16. Text in *TIT,* January 6, 1960.
17. For details, see my "Qasim and the Iraqi Communist Party: A Study in Arab Politics (Part Two, 1960–1963)," *Il Politico* 32, no. 3 (1967): 530–35.
18. For more details, see Vito Priestley, "The Political Situation in Iraq," *Middle Eastern Affairs,* no. 5 (May 1962), pp. 141–42.
19. *TIT,* February 25, 1960.
20. *Ibid.,* February 17, 1960. Prior to the July 1959 cabinet reshuffle,

From information now available it is impossible to determine what steps, if any, the USSR government actually took, but the Soviet press left no doubt as to Moscow's preferences on these matters. *Pravda* printed statements from *Ittihad al-Sha'b* criticizing the Ministry of Interior, announcing its determination to combat Sa'igh's "opportunist clique," and assuring its followers that the proposed change in the party's name (from Communist to Ittihad al-Sha'b) to meet one of the objections raised by the Ministry of Interior in no way signified a change in the organization's policy.[21] It is possible that Moscow reluctantly took a stand on Qasim's treatment of the ICP, because silence would have been interpreted as an admission of guilt to the charges leveled by Peking and its ideological allies that the USSR was no longer concerned with the interests of the "international Communist movement." It was, therefore, necessary to express concern for the plight of the Iraqi Communist party without becoming entangled in Qasim's internal politics. This delicate task was accomplished by extending a measure of moral support to the Ittihad faction by simply publishing its statements on the pages of Soviet publications and letting these pronouncements speak for themselves. But aside from a few scattered comments that could be interpreted as mild and indirect reproaches to Qasim for his treatment of the Iraqi Communist party, the Soviet press, in early 1960, continued to emphasize the "positive aspects" of the achievements of the revolutionary regime.[22]

There were also other indications that the Kremlin was unwilling

---

Kubba headed the Ministry of Economics. After it was abolished, he became the Minister of Agrarian Reform and Petroleum Affairs.

21. See *Pr.*, February 13, 1960. For more details on Ittihad's position, see editorial, *Ittihad al-Sha'b*, February 16, 1960, and "Iraqi Communists Combat Opportunism," *WMR*, no. 4 (1960), pp. 63–64. A later publication attacked Qasim for supporting "a group of renegades and dummies headed by a certain Dawud al-Sa'igh. This testified to the determination of the Iraqi government to undermine the unity of the working class and the influence of the Communist party." O. E. Tuganova, *Mezhdunarodnye otnosheniia na Blizhnem i Srednem Vostoke* (Moscow: Izdatel'stvo "Mezhdunarodnye otnosheniia," 1967), p. 118.

22. For details, see P. Demchenko, *Pr.*, January 7; *Izv.*, January 14 and 20; and *Pr.*, January 24 and 26, 1960. See also the statement by S. Skachkov, Chairman of the USSR Council of Ministers' State Committee on Foreign Economic Relations, in *ibid.*, February 9, 1960; and Demchenko's articles in *ibid.*, February 16, March 18 and 24, 1960.

to let Qasim's treatment of local Communists affect its relations with Iraq. For example, in late January 1960, Moscow extended Baghdad its diplomatic and moral backing in the latter's dispute with Iran over territorial rights in the Shatt al-Arab, a river formed by the confluence of the Tigris and the Euphrates.[23] While the reproduction of some of the material from *Ittihad al-Sha'b* implied criticism of Qasim for his handling of internal politics, it is noteworthy that not a single Soviet commentary attacked the Iraqi authorities directly. Iraq's internal affairs, including the fate of the local Communist party, were of minor significance to the leaders of the USSR, who did not wish to strain relations with Baghdad.

There can be no doubt that, by 1959, the Soviet government had become strongly disenchanted with the intransigence of Nasir and was searching for ways of curtailing his influence in the Arab East. Qasim, an independent fellow-nationalist and neutralist, served, in Moscow's eyes, as a convenient counterweight to the influence that the UAR President had come to wield, an influence that the Kremlin felt was excessive. For this reason, the survival of an independent, strong, neutralist, and, preferably, "progressive" Iraq became one of the main planks of Russian policy in the Arab East.

It gradually became evident, however, that Qasim was losing ground in his competition with Nasir, and that Baghdad was slipping into a state of political isolation. Internally, the program of economic development, although heavily backed by the USSR, had brought few tangible results, largely because of the lack of energetic and, in some instances, qualified leadership among Qasim's economic advisers. Since, however, in the eyes of the Arabs, Iraq's economic progress was closely associated with the Soviet aid program, Moscow was often blamed for the country's lackluster performance.[24] Finally, whereas Qasim was initially willing to let native Communists operate without major restrictions, in January and February 1960 it looked more and more as if he were determined to prevent the "progressive elements"

23. S. Danilov, "Who Is Interested in the Iran-Iraq Conflict," *IA*, no. 2 (February 1960), pp. 89–90. See also *Pr.*, January 31, 1960.
24. For more details, see Richard P. Hunt, *NYT*, April 17 and 25, 1960.

from emerging as one of the leading political forces in the country.

On April 2, 1960, the Soviet press announced that Anastas Mikoian, one of Moscow's top trouble-shooters and Khrushchev's closest collaborators, would visit Iraq. *Pravda* expressed confidence that the Deputy Premier's trip would "further strengthen friendly relations between the two countries."[25] The delicate task of clarifying Qasim's intentions, of assessing his strength, and of gathering firsthand information had thus been entrusted to a man of vast experience and considerable diplomatic skill. While in Baghdad, he could also appraise Iraq's economic, financial, and technical needs with an eye to suggesting ways of improving the country's economic performance. Finally, Mikoian was probably instructed to explain to Qasim the Soviet attitude toward internal developments in Iraq.

Mikoian arrived in the Iraqi capital on April 8, 1960, ostensibly to open a Soviet industrial fair.[26] His public pronouncements stressed two basic themes. The first, continuously underlined by Khrushchev during his visits to underdeveloped countries, was that Asian and African peoples should avail themselves of Soviet experiences in the process of turning a backward, agrarian nation into a powerful industrial giant. The second and more pointed theme emphasized the "genuine" willingness of the Soviet Union to aid the Iraqi people and government in their efforts to protect the "gains of the revolution" and to strengthen the country's "freedom and independence." Mikoian repeatedly expressed hope that friendly relations between the two states would be strengthened "with each passing day." In no instance did he refer to the fortunes of the Iraqi Communist party. In their replies, Qasim and other local dignitaries expressed appreciation for Moscow's support of and respect for the aims of the July revolution. The republican regime, proclaiming its interest in seeking the friendship of all nations that respected the national interests of Iraq, was determined to maintain close relations with the Soviet Union.[27]

When Foreign Minister Hashim Jawad, at a meeting with Mikoian,

25. *Pr.,* April 2, 1960.
26. *MEJ* 14, no. 3 (Summer 1960): 301.
27. Texts of Mikoian's and Qasim's speeches at the opening of the Industrial Fair in *Pr.,* April 11, 1960.

stated that the Iraqi Republic adhered to a policy of positive neutralism intended both to strengthen world peace and to secure the country's national independence, the Deputy Premier, as if attempting to dispel any possible doubts that Moscow's espousal of the Ittihad might have created, said that the USSR was "in full sympathy and agreement with the principles upon which the foreign policy of Iraq is based." Moscow could be relied upon, he concluded, to "support fully the peaceful foreign policy of Iraq."[28]

The initial welcome in Baghdad apparently left nothing to be desired,[29] but one Soviet account of the "enthusiasm" with which Mikoian was met in Basra alluded to "certain things which left an unpleasant impression." As the "workers and young people" who chanted "peace and friendship forever" approached the cars to shake hands with the Soviet guests, policemen and soldiers "forced their way into the crowd and began to drive the demonstrators away, beating [them] . . . with clubs." Similar incidents took place as the motorcade proceeded along the streets of Basra. "What was the reason for the concentration of military forces?", *Izvestiia's* Kondrashov asked "with a feeling of regret and bewilderment." He later learned from other journalists that a similar welcome for the Soviet delegation was being prepared in center city and near the docks, where the visitors were never taken.[30]

The "overzealous" police administrators, however, were not the end of Mikoian's troubles. On April 15, 1960, the Deputy Prime Minister held a press conference, which opened with a lengthy statement to the effect that the USSR was anxious to work with all independent and peace-loving nations of the world in the cause of peace and prosperity. During the question-and-answer period that followed, Yunis al-Ta'i, editor of the nationalist *al-Thawra* and a personal friend of Qasim, thanked the "great Soviet Union for its friendly feelings toward the Arab peoples" and then proceeded to query Mikoian about Moscow's position on the Palestine problem. More precisely, if the USSR was indeed a friend of the Arabs, why did it

28. *Ibid.,* April 12, 1960.
29. For details, see S. Kondrashov, *Izv.,* April 9, 1960; P. Demchenko, *Pr.,* April 12; *ibid.,* April 13 and 14, 1960.
30. *Izv.,* April 15, 1960.

also back Israel? Visibly upset, Mikoian expressed his inability to understand why any Arab journalist would have "any use for all these lies, which distort the policy of the Soviet Union." The USSR, he continued, had not created the problem and was not responsible for the expulsion of the Arabs from Palestine. Moreover, Moscow had consistently supported the "legal right of the Palestinian Arabs to return to their homeland. . . . Must I really show an Arab, a literate man," he exclaimed in anger, "that the policy of the Soviet Union and its attitude toward the Arab peoples differs from the policy of the imperialist powers?" When al-Ta'i insisted that he was "not satisfied," Mikoian, obviously annoyed, said that he had "no magic charm that can leave everybody satisfied."[31]

Whatever else the Mikoian visit may have accomplished, it did bring about a temporary end to *al-Thawra's* occasionally violent anti-Communist attacks. Qasim may have felt that al-Ta'i's criticism of the USSR had gone too far, for it was announced in Baghdad, on April 18, that the newspaper would cease publication because of "printing difficulties" and unspecified "other reasons." Yet, when seeing Mikoian off, Qasim allegedly told his guest that *al-Thawra* was "patriotic" and "serving the country well."[32] A short while later, it reappeared, intensifying its "anti-anarchist" campaign.[33]

Judging by the subsequent comments in the Soviet press, Mikoian left Iraq convinced that Qasim's ability to counter Nasir's influence in the Arab East and to handle internal reforms had been overestimated by the Kremlin. In this sense, his visit could be regarded as a turning point in Moscow-Baghdad relations. This did not mean that the USSR would refuse to back Qasim in his feud with Nasir or cut off Soviet economic, technical, and financial support.[34] From the

31. *Pr.*, April 17 and 18, 1960.
32. As quoted in *MEM*, no. 17 (April 24, 1960), p. 12.
33. See editorials, *al-Thawra*, June 28, September 8 and 11, 1960.
34. As a matter of fact, Mikoian agreed to speed up Soviet economic aid to Iraq and reportedly denied rumors of impending changes in the Soviet loan agreement for 550 million rubles. While in Baghdad, he also expedited planning on "43 industrial and development projects specified in the agreement of March 16, 1959." In late May, the USSR consented to increase the above loan by an additional 180 million rubles. *MEJ* 14, no. 3 (Summer 1960): 301 and 302, respectively.

Soviet viewpoint, Qasim was still performing an invaluable service in helping to impede Cairo's progress toward domination of the Arab East. But he could no longer be regarded or treated as a "progressive" Arab leader worthy of full and unqualified political support.

Moscow's growing disenchantment became more evident in the summer of 1960. For example, commentaries on the second anniversary of the Iraqi revolution concerned themselves with such relatively innocent topics as the part allegedly played by the USSR in securing the success of the uprising and vague hopes that the two countries would continue their joint efforts to "safeguard peace, disarmament, and collaboration between all nations against colonial slavery."[35] Such statements, as well as the telegrams dispatched by Soviet dignitaries to their Iraqi counterparts on this occasion,[36] passed over in silence Qasim's relations with the Communist party and the problems of the nation's development, which were among the most significant issues facing Baghdad at the time. Since silence might have been interpreted as approbation, however, it seemed necessary to indicate occasionally that the state of Iraqi internal affairs was, from Moscow's standpoint, far from satisfactory.

One article argued that, though the revolutionary regime had successfully solved its first task, the gaining of national independence through the elimination of "colonialist" influence, this did not mean the attainment of "complete independence." Nor did it signify that the remaining political and socioeconomic problems would automatically be solved. In Iraq the "enemies of the revolution," tied to imperialist circles outside the country, had "hastened to utilize the differences which emerged among the initial members of the national front." Although the "devotion of the Iraqi masses to the goals of the revolution . . . [had foiled] the schemes of the plotters, . . . the criminal intrigues of the enemies of the revolution continue unabated." This led to the conclusion that new gains and the successful development of the republic could be secured only through the government's reli-

35. B. Vasil'ev, *Izv.*, July 14, 1960. See also P. Demchenko, *Pr.*, of the same date.
36. Text in *Pr.*, July 14, 1960.

ance on the "patriotic forces," acting through the "united national front." Suppression of the "most progressive elements in the Iraqi society," on the other hand, would be utilized by the enemies of the revolution to undermine the power of the regime itself. While it lacked the recriminatory tone of later comments, this was the first serious public indictment of Qasim and his policies to appear in the Soviet press.[37]

Despite the degree of outward friendliness and economic cooperation that was maintained throughout the rest of 1960 and most of 1961,[38] other frequent signs of mutual dissatisfaction and disenchantment also began to appear. In September 1960, for example, Radio Moscow attacked the nationalist newspaper *al-Hurriya* for its alleged anti-Soviet bias, only to have it reply that events that had taken place after the 1958 revolution had revealed the "dictatorial nature of international Communism." Since hundreds of Iraqi patriots had subsequently fallen victim to "Communist terror," the time had come to expose the "Communist danger threatening . . . [the country's] national existence." Previously, *al-Hurriya* had differentiated between the USSR, a state, and Communism as an "international movement urging local Communists to commit crimes."[39] This had proved incorrect, leading to the conclusion that Moscow, using Communism as a vehicle, was endeavoring to substitute "Soviet influence" for "imperialist influence"—an ambition most Iraqis were not prepared to tolerate.[40]

In early October, *Pravda* reported that the First Military Court had ordered the closing of *Ittihad al-Sha'b*.[41] The editorial comment that

37. A. Stupak, *ibid.*, July 13, 1960.
38. See, for example, *Izv.*, July 16 and *Pr.*, July 21, 23, and 26, August 27, September 3, 27, 28, 1960. An important new economic and technical aid agreement between the two states was reached on August 18, 1960. Among other things, the Soviet Union undertook to build a new broad-gauge railway between Baghdad and Basra. Details in *TIT*, August 21, 1960. Text in SSSR. Ministerstvo inostrannykh del, *SSSR i arabskie strany, 1917–1960* (Moscow: Gospolitizdat, 1961), pp. 726–27.
39. See editorials, September 5, 6, and 8, 1960.
40. Editorial, *al-Hurriya*, September 20, 1960.
41. *Pr.*, October 4, 1960.

appeared a few weeks later insisted that the newspaper was a "genuine defender of Iraq's national interests." It reflected the "aspirations of the working people . . . [and had] consistently exposed the plots of the imperialists and the machinations of the oil companies." Because of its "principled position," *Ittihad al-Sha'b* had been consistently exposed to efforts by the "reactionaries" to silence it.

For a while, the Soviet press refrained from openly associating Qasim with the intensifying anti-Communist activities in Iraq. Thus, Demchenko mentioned that 'Abd al-Qadhir Isma'il al-Bustani, editor of *Ittihad al-Sha'b,* had been released from prison on the orders of the Premier. It was hoped that this "enlightened approach" to an unfortunate occurrence would herald a reappraisal of the government's attitude toward the Iraqi Communist party before its enemies succeeded in inflicting serious damage on the republic.[42] Nevertheless, the anti-Communist drive continued to gather momentum. On December 16, 1960, a military court passed death sentences on thirty-eight men accused of crimes committed against "innocent citizens" during the Mosul uprising of March 1959. Later, as reported by the *World Marxist Review,* the death sentences of some "Communists and other democrats, trade union officials, leaders of the youth and student movement and army officers" were commuted to life imprisonment. Others were threatened with "immediate execution." These developments were described as the culminating point in the "reactionary" campaign that the authorities had initiated as early as July 1959. The *World Marxist Review* appealed to Qasim "to save the lives and secure the release of the heroes whose only crime is that of upholding the national independence of Iraq."[43]

While not addressing himself directly to the subject, the Iraqi Prime Minister nevertheless made his attitude clear by stating, in a widely publicized speech on January 6, 1961, that he worked for the benefit of the people as a whole and not for any of its various segments. For this reason, Qasim opposed the legalization of political parties and the

42. P. Demchenko, *ibid.,* November 4, 1960. See also A. R. D., "An Unjust Act," *WMR,* no. 11 (November 1960), pp. 96–97.
43. Aziz Kourdi, "Save the Lives and Release the Heroes of Mossoul," *WMR,* no. 2 (February 1961), p. 96.

activities of those groups which did not work for the benefit of the entire nation.[44] The Iraqi Communist party clearly, in his view, fell into this category.

Moscow was not prepared to abandon its propaganda pressure, however. In early February, *Pravda* reported that the "Iraqi public" had petitioned Qasim to release those political prisoners who were arrested without specific charges.[45] On February 12, TASS announced that the Organization of Soviet Trade Unions had dispatched a message to Qasim asking him to "free patriots, democrats, and trade union officials, and to end their persecution." While disassociating the Prime Minister from the "wrongful actions of anti-democratically inclined persons in positions of power," this appeal asserted that restoration of "democratic freedoms" would greatly contribute to the "consolidation of the genuine independence" of Iraq.[46]

In April, the *New Times* went on record as protesting the "persecution of Iraqi patriots." It explained that the Kremlin's initial hopes, that "having thrown off imperialist control, Iraq would follow the road of independence, democracy, and social progress," were now being dashed. The news coming out of Iraq demonstrated beyond doubt "that the patriotic and democratic elements in the country are being persecuted and sentenced to death [and] that the reactionaries are once more rampant."[47]

As might have been expected, Moscow's propaganda campaign provoked a strong reaction from the Iraqi nationalist press. *Al-Ahd al-Jadid,* for example, deplored the "anti-Iraqi attacks" emanating from the USSR and warned that they only served the purposes of the imperialists, who exploited these "poisoned and baseless" statements to sow dissension between the two countries.[48] The comments of *al-Mustaqbal* were even harsher. Those individuals whose interests the USSR was attempting to protect were but "murderers who shed

44. *TIT,* January 10, 1961.
45. *Pr.,* February 8. See also statement of the Soviet Afro-Asian Solidarity Committee in *ibid.,* February 10, 1961.
46. As quoted in *MEM,* no. 7 (February 18, 1961), p. 13.
47. Y.B., "Patriots Persecuted in Iraq," *NT,* no. 14 (April 1961), p. 20.
48. Editorial, February 11, 1961.

innocent blood and did great damage to the revolution." Moscow's "unjust campaign" constituted an "act of flagrant interference in the internal affairs of Iraq" and was "totally unacceptable."[49]

In a speech of February 20, Qasim, too, insisted that "foreign countries" had no right to interfere in the internal affairs of the Arab states,[50] and the campaign of repression against the Ittihad Communists continued unabated. The offices of Peace Partisans, a Communist front organization, were closed throughout Iraq on the orders of the Military Governor-General; Communist functionaries were arrested and detained without trial; and some Marxists had been sentenced to death for alleged complicity in the Kirkuk massacre.[51] When Fuad Nassar, a Jordanian Communist, writing in *Sovremennyi vostok*, labeled as "dictatorships" the regimes of both Nasir and Qasim,[52] *al-Ahd al-Jadid* warned Moscow that "such sensationalist reports" could seriously impair "good relations" between the two "friendly states at a time when both of them need these relations to be fostered for serving civilization and peace and for delivering the world from the evils of imperialism."[53] Other Iraqi nationalist newspapers accused the USSR of fomenting trouble both among the various Arab states and within Iraq. For example, Moscow was pronounced guilty of "driving its submissive slaves [i.e., the local Communists] to commit more acts of anarchy, rioting, and sedition. . . . The moves of the agents have unmasked the greedy designs of the masters."[54]

In reply, the *World Marxist Review* blamed Qasim for the persecution of the country's "democratic elements." Initially a proponent of "democratic reforms," the Prime Minister not only refused to punish "the instigators" of the Kirkuk bloodshed but ordered a campaign of "massive repression of genuine patriots." This led to the conclusion that Qasim had decided "to crush the popular movement and 'curb'

49. Editorial, February 13, 1961.
50. Text in *TIT*, February 21, 1961.
51. *MEJ* 15, no. 2 (Spring 1961): 190; *MEM*, no. 19 (May 13, 1961), p. 16; *TIT*, May 10, 1961, respectively.
52. As quoted in *MEM*, no. 19 (May 13, 1961), p. 13.
53. Editorial, May 18, 1961.
54. Editorial, *al-Fajr al-Jadid*, June 7, 1961.

the Communists and other progressives, . . . [while] giving more and more freedom of action to the reactionaries."⁵⁵

This was one of the first articles that placed responsibility for the anti-Communist "campaign of terror" squarely on the shoulders of Premier Qasim and his government: "The terror is obviously part of a master plan designed to intimidate the progressive forces, to crush the popular movement and to provoke the members of the Communist party and other democratic organizations to clash with the reactionaries, which in turn is used as a pretext for further reprisals." In the process of implementing the "master plan," "democratic freedoms won by the people" had been wiped out. Despite Qasim's assurances that the emergency situation would be ended and general elections held, "the extraordinary military tribunals [had] continued to operate." Government offices were being purged of "progressives . . . who had taken a resolute stand against the oil monopolies and the feudal elements . . . [and] top civil and military posts . . . [were being] given to supporters of the old regime and reactionary conspirators."⁵⁶

By early June 1961, Soviet-Iraqi relations in the post-revolutionary period had clearly reached an all-time low. They were not approaching a breaking point, however. For example, on June 16, Baghdad's newspapers printed the text of Khrushchev's cable to Qasim, occasioned by the Muslim New Year, expressing the perfunctory hope that "friendly relations between the two countries would be further strengthened." Similar sentiments were voiced by Qasim.⁵⁷ Of much greater importance, economic and trade relations between Moscow and Baghdad continued, with Soviet aid pledged for the construction of "one of the most powerful radio transmitters in the Middle East" and an agreement on economic and technical cooperation.⁵⁸ In mid-March 1961, P. Demchenko, reporting on progress in the construction of the Baghdad-Basra railway, spoke, significantly, of Soviet

55. Sami Mahmud, "Combatting the Terror in Iraq," *WMR*, no. 6 (June 1961), pp. 90–91.
56. *Ibid.*
57. Texts of the telegrams in *TIT*, June 16 and 22, 1961.
58. *Izv.*, December 8, 1960, and *Pr.*, January 11, 1961, respectively.

support of "the Iraqi people."[59] In late April, the two countries signed contracts whereby the USSR undertook the construction of plants manufacturing agricultural machinery, electro-technical products, and electric light bulbs.[60]

Nevertheless, there can be no doubt that whatever hopes the Kremlin might have harbored for the emergence of a "progressive" regime in Iraq had been shattered by mid-1961. Qasim's rule had "degenerated" into another, relatively unattractive, bourgeois-nationalist regime. In addition, Qasim's temporary rapprochement with Nasir, initiated in the summer of 1960,[61] must have heightened Moscow's disenchantment, since it had originally supported Iraq in an effort to counterbalance Cairo's expansionist ideology.

Yet the USSR was still not prepared to break openly with Baghdad. With or without Qasim, Iraq could be expected to play an important role in Arab politics and might therefore be of use to Moscow at a later stage. Furthermore, the important Soviet investment of economic, technical, financial, and, to a degree, military assistance, that had been made in Iraq could conceivably pay off in the future.[62] The Kremlin was no doubt aware that Qasim was slowly but surely sinking into the sort of political isolation that would eventually result in his downfall, and it probably felt that it would be relatively easy to cooperate with his successors provided that they, too, were unwilling to submerge themselves in Nasir's empire. Until then, it could continue to extend its support to Iraq without associating itself too closely with Qasim personally.

Similarly, there can be no doubt that the Iraqi authorities were annoyed with what the nationalist press correctly labeled as outside intervention in the internal affairs of the country. As noted by *al-Bayan,* however, Baghdad's annoyance should "not exceed the limits necessary to express in a reasonable way the denunciation and con-

59. *Pr.,* March 17, 1961.
60. *MEJ* 15, no. 3 (Summer 1961): 309.
61. For more details, see my "Nasir-Qasim Relations (July 1958-February 1963): A Study in Inter-Arab Politics," *Political Scientist* 5, nos. 1 and 2 (July-December 1968 and January-June 1969): 56–59.
62. For some details of Soviet military aid to Iraq, including the delivery of MIG-19 jet-fighters, see Harry B. Ellis, *Christian Science Monitor,* March 9, 1961.

demnation of the attacks by the Soviet side." Such moderation acknowledged the fact that the "interests of the Arab liberation movement require maintenance of good and close relations with the Soviet Union."[63] Qasim was not prepared to jeopardize his relations with Moscow, especially since his political neutralism revolved around his ability to play both sides against the middle. But he, like Khrushchev, was soon to face the Kuwayt crisis, which threw the Arab East once again into turmoil and confusion.

On June 19, 1961, Great Britain formally relinquished its 1899 treaty of protectorate over Kuwayt, an oil-rich shaykhdom situated on the Persian Gulf along the southern border of Iraq, and promised to help uphold its independence. Six days later, Qasim claimed that Kuwayt was an "integral part" of Iraq that had been usurped by means of an "illegal, forged and internationally unrecognized document," and promised to "free the people [from] the yoke of feudalism." Those who stood in his way would be regarded as "traitors."[64] Most Baghdad newspapers expressed confidence that Qasim's "courageous stand" would be wholeheartedly supported by the other Arab countries because his initiative engaged the Iraqi government in a "bitter struggle against imperialism."[65] Instead, in a statement of June 26, the Saudi government insisted that Kuwayt was a "part of Saudi Arabia." Negative responses came also from Jordan and the UAR.[66] The crisis became serious in late June, when it was reported that Iraqi troops were massing along the Kuwayti frontier, and, on July 1, at the request of the Shaykh British units began landing in the principality. On July 6, Qasim stated that while the "reunification" of Iraq and Kuwayt remained the official policy of the government, it would be pursued only by "peaceful means."[67]

In early August, the Arab League, strongly backed by the UAR, Jordan, and Saudi Arabia, agreed to the replacement of the British

63. Editorial, *al-Bayan*, June 14, 1961.
64. *TIT*, June 27, 1961.
65. See, editorials, *al-Ahd al-Jadid* and *al-Bayan*, June 27 and 28, 1961, respectively.
66. *MEM*, no. 26 (July 1, 1961), pp. 3–5.
67. *Ibid.*, no. 27 (July 8, 1961), p. 3.

units by a joint Arab force, a plan that also proved acceptable to the Shaykh. On September 10, the first contingents of the Arab force began arriving in Kuwayt.[68] Although Qasim hysterically insisted that Iraq was now exposed to "sure destruction from Kuwayt at any moment,"[69] there were no dramatic confrontations, and, by October 10, the withdrawal of the British units had been completed. On the same day, the United Arab Republic, followed, in quick succession, by most other members of the Arab League, recognized Kuwayt as a sovereign and independent state.[70]

The initial Communist reaction to Qasim's claim attested to the fact that the Marxists, along with the other Iraqi political groups, were caught off guard by the Premier's move. Their early statements omitted any reference to the validity of the Premier's claim to the principality and were deliberately vague on the problem of the future relationship between Iraq and Kuwayt. On June 29, however, *Sawt al-Ahrar* openly backed Qasim's claim, insisting that the Shaykhdom formed a part of Iraq and that its recognition by other states constituted an "act of aggression" against Baghdad. It argued that in the days of the Ottoman Empire the district of Kuwayt had been linked administratively to the province of Basra and that, in any event, the principality possessed no requisites for sovereignty. Did the support that the Shaykh received from the "imperialist powers" and some Arab states signify that "any tribal head in Iraq, Saudi Arabia, and Jordan can create for himself an independent state and seek membership in the Arab League and the United Nations simply because he has secured the backing of the British, French, and American imperialists?"[71]

While opposition to Qasim might have jeopardized the very existence of the persecuted Communist party, the Marxists may also have seen the crisis as an opportunity to regain some of their lost influence in Iraq. Thus, *Sawt al-Ahrar* held that the "military concentration in

68. See *ibid.*, no. 31 (August 5, 1961), p. 5, and *MEJ* 15, no. 4 (Fall 1961): 435, respectively.
69. *TIT,* September 12, 1961.
70. See *MEJ* 16, no. 1 (Winter 1962): 70–71.
71. Editorial, *Sawt al-Ahrar,* June 29, 1961.

Kuwayt" reinforced the "necessity of cooperation between the people [meaning the ICP] and the government and the creation of comprehensive national unity."[72]

Although Moscow also focused on the technical details of Kuwayt's independence,[73] the main thrust of Soviet propaganda efforts was predictably directed at the "unprovoked activities" of Great Britain.[74] There was no mention of the Shaykh's declaration that Qasim's statements and the Iraqi troop concentrations along the Kuwayti frontier attested beyond reasonable doubt to Baghdad's determination to annex the principality by force. Instead, publicity was given to Qasim's refutation of the assertion that troops were being massed and his claim that no orders had been issued for the army to cross the frontier. Since there was no justification for the British decision to land troops in Kuwayt, thus returning to the area they had left only a short while earlier, it was concluded that London was "clearly anxious to utilize the existing situation to increase tension in all of the Arab East and especially in the Persian Gulf and the Red Sea areas."[75]

In the Soviet view, the "British aggression against the Arabs" was backed by London's "NATO allies," above all the United States, partly because the Shaykhdom was reported to hold "first place in all the capitalist world in its wealth of 'black gold.' " In addition, the British government was hoping to utilize its military presence in Kuwayt to reach a "more equitable" understanding with its US competitors, who appeared equally determined to enlarge their own foothold in the principality. London was also using the opportunity to exert on Baghdad pressure for a more favorable attitude toward the Iraqi Petroleum Company, "another leviathan of the British oil empire in the Near and Middle East," which, since the spring of 1961, had been encountering difficulties in its dealings with the Iraqi govern-

72. Editorial, *ibid.,* July 9, 1961.
73. Subsequently, Soviet publications explained that independence was granted "under the pressure of the national-liberation movement." See "Colonial Possessions in the Arabian Peninsula," *IA,* no. 11 (November 1962), p. 109.
74. See *Pr.,* June 29, and *Izv.,* June 30, 1961.
75. *Pr.,* July 2, 1961. See also *ibid.,* July 3 and 4, and *Izv.,* July 2, 4, and 5, 1961.

ment.⁷⁶ The unfolding events had obviously placed Moscow on the horns of yet another dilemma which, if dealt with directly, would force it to make an unappealing choice between Baghdad and the other Arab states, led by the unlikely coalition of the UAR, Saudi Arabia, and Jordan.

It was for this reason that the Soviet Union never took an official stand on the legality of Qasim's claim to the Shaykhdom.⁷⁷ When on July 1 Kuwayt appealed to the Security Council to consider the threat to its independence, Valerian Zorin of the USSR, ignoring the legal aspects of Kuwayt's claim, concentrated his attention on rejection of London's assertion that British units were protecting the Shaykhdom against an "impending Iraqi attack." On the contrary, their presence constituted "a threat to peace in the region and throughout the whole world." In this respect, the Soviet position coincided with the stand taken by the United Arab Republic, except that Cairo, like Washington, supported the British and Kuwayti claim to the Shaykhdom's independence.⁷⁸

On July 7, the USSR vetoed a British draft resolution calling on all nations "to respect the independence and territorial integrity of Kuwait" and also summoning all concerned to "work for peace and tranquility" and "to keep the situation under review." The Soviet delegation then supported a UAR draft resolution that provided for the withdrawal of British forces from Kuwayt without mentioning the problem of the Shaykhdom's independence. When that proposal failed to obtain the required number of affirmative votes for passage, the President of the Council appealed to all concerned not to take any steps that might aggravate the situation, and there the matter was allowed to rest.⁷⁹

76. I. Beliaev, *Pr.*, July 13, 1961. For more details, see V. Fatisov, "Gunboat Tactics Again," *IA*, no. 2 (February 1962), pp. 94–95.
77. The closest Moscow ever came to an implicit recognition of the claim was to state that "under the Ottoman Empire the territory of Kuwait and the present Iraqi district of Basra formed a single administrative unit." A. Lyubanin, "What is Happening in Kuwait," *NT*, no. 29 (July 1961), p. 26.
78. See United Nations, *Yearbook of the United Nations, 1961* (New York: Columbia University Press, 1963), pp. 146–48.
79. *Ibid.*, p. 149. For texts of Zorin's speeches, see *Pr.*, July 7, 8, and 9, 1961.

Interestingly, this delicate balancing act earned Moscow the gratitude of some Iraqi newspapers. In addition to the Communist *Sawt al-Ahrar*, which noted that in the July 7 voting in the Security Council the USSR was the only great power to back Baghdad, the National-Democratic *al-Bilad* described the Soviet veto of the UK draft resolution as a "slap in the face of British imperialism. Once again the friend of peoples has demonstrated the importance of the veto in supporting the causes of liberation."[80] By and large, in addition to its continuing efforts to "expose" Western "imperialist ambitions," the Soviet press, in the ensuing months, expressed the hope that the dispute would eventually be settled by the Arabs themselves.[81]

In November, after the British units in the Shaykhdom had been replaced by the Arab League force, the Security Council met to consider the UAR proposal that Kuwayt be admitted to the United Nations. Cairo argued that Kuwayt had been recognized by a majority of the members of the United Nations, had been admitted to the Arab League, and was a member of a number of international organizations. The proposal was supported by nine members of the Council, including the United States, Great Britain, France, and China. In rejecting the UAR motion, the Iraqi delegation repeated its previous arguments that Kuwayt had never been a state "in the internationally accepted sense," and that it was "an integral part of Iraq," while remaining, "for all practical purposes, a British colony." Baghdad contended that "oil . . . and the enormous profits of the oil companies coupled with the Sheikh's billion-dollar investments in the United Kingdom were the basis for an unholy alliance between feudalism and colonialism."[82]

It was the Soviet attitude, however, that once again decided the issue. The USSR delegation recommended that the examination of Kuwayt's application be postponed, advancing in its arguments most of the views that it had expressed earlier and that were shared by the Iraqi government. While not labeling Kuwayt a British colony, the

80. Editorials, July 9, 1961.
81. I. Beliaev, *Pr.,* July 13, 1961. See also Lyubanin.
82. United Nations, pp. 168–69.

Soviet representative noted that as long as the Shaykhdom's defense agreement with Great Britain was in force, it "remained in a state of factual dependence on the United Kingdom and the way was open for any aggressive action against the independent Arab States of the area by British troops using Kuwait as a military base." In addition, there existed differences among the Arab governments on this issue, differences that, Moscow felt, should be resolved by the parties directly concerned. A decision at this point would "prejudge and predetermine the future course" of events, and this the USSR found to be highly undesirable.[83]

Neither the UAR nor the Soviet motions were adopted, and once again the Soviet stand evoked favorable comments in the Iraqi press. Said *al-Bayan*: "The Soviet veto has defeated the loathsome endeavors [of the imperialists to perpetuate the exploitation of the riches of the Arab peoples] and has cut the ground from beneath the imperialist attempts to secure the passage of their plans contrived against the peoples struggling for liberation." Moscow's attitude, it was concluded, was "in keeping with its declarations concerning the elimination of imperialism and ridding the world of its ills and wickedness."[84]

Outwardly, the USSR had seemed to favor Baghdad over its antagonists by withholding recognition from Kuwayt and, eventually, vetoing its admission to the United Nations. Yet Moscow had also backed the UAR in its demand for a speedy withdrawal of British forces from the Shaykhdom and, even more important, had refused to recognize Baghdad's claim to the principality. Moscow must have been aware that Qasim's position was dictated by domestic considerations: with the political base of the regime reduced to a dangerously narrow level after the defection of his erstwhile Arab nationalist, Communist, and Kurdish allies, the Premier was in desperate need of an issue that would appeal to the patriotic sentiments of most Iraqis, diverting attention from the political and economic stagnation that characterized Iraq in the summer of 1961. Simply by supporting Kuwayt and its Arab allies Moscow could have dealt Qasim a crush-

83. *Ibid.*, p. 169.
84. Editorial, December 4, 1961.

ing political defeat, and the decision not to exercise this power probably resulted from fear of the possible repercussions in Iraq. More precisely, with the Communists weakened and the Iraqi nationalists disunited, it was likely that the pro-Nasir Arab nationalist elements would have seized control. The Kremlin therefore contributed to saving Qasim's face but refused to go beyond what it considered the absolute minimum essential to attain this aim. It is noteworthy in this connection that once the Premier was overthrown in February 1963, the USSR quickly reversed itself: the Security Council unanimously recommended the Shaykhdom for admission on May 7, 1963, and one week later the General Assembly elected it to UN membership.[85]

Moscow's attitude could certainly have been interpreted as hostile to Cairo, though it is very unlikely that the crisis was ever viewed by the Kremlin exclusively or even primarily as a vehicle for snubbing Nasir. Zorin's speech justifying the Soviet veto of Kuwayt's admission to the United Nations carefully emphasized Moscow-Cairo friendship and noted that his government's decision in this matter was aimed exclusively at the "imperialists." Nevertheless, there was, from the Kremlin's standpoint, no overriding need to be particularly accommodating to Cairo at a time when the two governments were engaged in another of their recurring public quarrels.[86] It is not at all impossible that the Soviet authorities viewed the Kuwayt crisis, in part, as an opportunity to demonstrate to Nasir that their political support of Cairo was not unconditional.

Tension in the Persian Gulf area rose again during late 1961 and early 1962, when rumors of impending new landings of British troops in Kuwayt swept the Middle East, allegedly because the Shaykhdom had reason to fear an impending Iraqi attack and the Arab force would not suffice to block the takeover. Ridiculing London's contention that the measures were designed to cope with the "recent increase of tension" in the Middle East, Moscow agreed with *al-Gumhuriya*

---

85. *NYT*, May 8 and 15, 1963, respectively. Only several years later did a Soviet publication ascribe Qasim's claim to Kuwayt to "adventurist, national-chauvinist tendencies" displayed by the Premier in the latter half of his rule. Tuganova, p. 120.

86. For details, see chap. 6.

that the crisis had been fabricated in Britain as an excuse to exert renewed pressure on Baghdad and to strengthen its own position in the oil-rich principalities of the Persian Gulf.[87]

Following an abortive coup in late December by the National-Socialist party in Lebanon, the Soviet press accused the United Kingdom of a "two-pronged action" intended to restore a measure of waning British influence in the Middle East. In an obvious attempt to discredit the "colonialist" powers in the eyes of the Arabs, *Pravda* reminded them that the times of what was termed gunboat diplomacy were gone forever and that the Arab peoples were no longer to be frightened. "Life has shown that the imperialist provocations of recent years have invariably suffered a fiasco."[88]

Since no intervention followed and the matter was allowed to pass into oblivion, it appears that these two unrelated incidents were merely utilized by Moscow and Baghdad as an excuse to unleash new attacks against the Western powers. During a press-conference held on January 12, 1962, Qasim argued that "creation of the so-called state of Kuwayt" was tantamount to the establishment of an "imperialist base threatening all Arab countries, and particularly Iraq." In supporting the Shaykhdom, the Western powers were motivated by the desire to divert Baghdad's attention from its program of economic development and to force it to make concessions to the Western petroleum interests. In addition, Great Britain and the United States were seeking to establish an "iron curtain" between the Iraqis and their "brethren" along the Persian Gulf and in the south of the Arabian peninsula. As might have been expected, Qasim's pronouncements were given wide publicity in the Soviet press.[89]

Despite the Kuwayt problem, most of the comments in the Soviet press in the latter half of 1961 and early 1962 were devoted to Mos-

87. See I. Beliaev, *Pr.,* December 29, 1961.
88. *Ibid.,* January 3, 1962. On the abortive Lebanese coup, see P. Demchenko, *ibid.* See also *Izv.,* January 3; V. Kudriavtsev, *ibid.,* January 5; and *ibid.,* January 6, 1962. Similar sentiments were also expressed by Qasim (*Pr.,* January 8, 1962) and the Iraqi press. Editorials, *Sawt al-Ahrar, al-Bayan* and *al-Thawra,* January 2, 1962.
89. See *Pr.,* January 13, 1962.

cow's efforts to aid the economic development of Iraq. Even in discussing the third anniversary of the revolution, *Pravda's* inevitable praise for efforts to undermine Anglo-American influence in the Arab East and reminders of Soviet backing "in the hour of need" heavily stressed Russia's contribution to the economy.[90] Compared to the pronouncements on previous anniversaries, the article was yet another demonstration that the Kremlin's relations with Qasim were rapidly approaching their nadir. This conclusion was supported also by the cool, noncommittal tone of the telegrams exchanged between Khrushchev and the Iraqi Premier in connection with the anniversary.[91]

The degree of Khrushchev's disenchantment with a number of neutralist leaders became evident during his speech before the Twenty-second Congress of the CPSU, held in the fall of 1961.[92] Addressing himself to the problem of the "national-liberation struggle," the Prime Minister expressed satisfaction with the fact that most former colonial and dependent countries had freed themselves from "imperialist oppression" and had entered a "new stage" of their political and socioeconomic development. However, after that objective had been gained and they were confronted with the "tasks of ripping out the roots of imperialism and carrying out agrarian and other urgent social reforms, the differences in class interests were beginning to show more and more distinctly." Khrushchev felt that the "broad strata of the working people" as well as a "considerable part of the national bourgeoisie interested in the accomplishment of the basic tasks of the anti-imperialist, anti-feudal revolution" endeavored to proceed along the path of strengthening independence and socioeconomic transformations. Unfortunately, in many instances, they were opposed by "forces within the ruling circles of these countries" that refused to collaborate further with the "democratic, progressive strata of the nation."

Although Khrushchev used Pakistan as an example of this type of

90. See P. Demchenko, *ibid.,* July 14, 1961.
91. Texts in *ibid.,* August 9, 1961.
92. Text in *ibid.,* October 18, 1961.

a regime, there can be little doubt that his scorching remarks were directed, among others, at both Qasim and Nasir. It was certainly no coincidence that the text of the Premier's speech was banned in Iraq.[93] While a degree of outward reconciliation had been attained with Cairo, the Soviet government periodically continued to express its dissatisfaction with the methods employed by the UAR government to keep its "progressives" under control. In Iraq, the Ministry of Interior had by mid-August 1961 canceled the licenses of both *Ittihad al-Sha'b* and the pro-Communist weekly *al-Hadhara*. Bustani, the former's editor-in-chief, was reportedly sought by the police to answer libel charges before a civil court.[94] In early October, it was reported that the Basra police had uncovered "the most dangerous nest of the clandestine Communist party" and arrested many of its members. Also, "thousands of leaflets, hundreds of banned Communist books, firearms and very important instructions" were confiscated.[95]

A further example of Moscow's disillusionment with Qasim was contained in a lengthy and elaborate article that appeared in the *World Marxist Review* in the fall of 1961. It contended, among other things, that the Iraqi Communist party regarded the preservation of the republic as the main objective of all of the national forces of Iraq. Yet the government, "on the pretext of the need to 'restore equilibrium' in the political situation and combat 'anarchy,' . . . gave a free hand to the reactionaries and incited them against the democratic forces." Coupled with "submission to the economic and political pressure of the imperialists," this served as an obvious indication that "the revolution is being steered farther and farther away from its original course."[96]

Iraq's crackdown on the Communist party continued, despite such protestations. On August 1, it was reported that the police had uncovered an underground Communist cell and arrested a score of its

---

93. *MEM*, no. 42 (October 21, 1961), p. 23.
94. For more information, see *TIT*, August 22, 1961, and *MEM*, no. 34 (August 26, 1961), p. 18.
95. *MEM*, no. 41 (October 14, 1961), p. 12. For Iraqi Communist account of the government's "terror campaign," see Sami Mahmoud, "Iraq: The Facts Accuse," *WMR*, no. 11 (November 1961), p. 92.
96. Mohammad Salim, "Three Years After the Iraqi Revolution," *ibid.*, no. 10 (October 1961), pp. 35–37.

members.[97] On September 3, the Military Tribunal sentenced to death seven Communists charged with murdering two men during the 1959 Mosul revolt.[98] Early in December, *al-Sharq* reported the uncovering of a new Communist headquarters in Basra,[99] and, on December 11, the Tribunal sentenced to imprisonment another eleven "anarchists" accused of attacking men and plundering their homes in Mosul in March 1959.[100] Such acts of suppression were accompanied by periodic releases of the imprisoned members of the country's anti-Communist organizations.[101]

Izvestiia did not even mention the fourth anniversary of the Iraqi revolution, while *Pravda* published only a brief article—without a single reference to Qasim or the internal situation—and a photograph of Soviet machines employed in the construction of the Baghdad-Basra railway.[102] The inevitable telegrams between Khrushchev and Qasim were also extremely formal and correct.[103] However, the USSR continued to cooperate with Baghdad in the economic, cultural, and, to an extent, military spheres.[104]

By June 1962, over one thousand Soviet specialists were involved in many aspects of Iraq's economy, and Russian projects were pivotal in the process of development. Soviet consumer goods were being imported, with the Ministry of Commerce clearly favoring this trend by limiting the activities of Western importers.[105] Soviet equipment, including artillery, helicopters, MIG fighters, and IL bombers, dominated the military parade on July 14.[106] In early September, another

---

97. See *MEJ* 16, no. 4 (Fall 1962): 488.
98. See *MEM*, no. 36 (September 8, 1962), p. 16.
99. See *MEJ* 17, nos. 1 and 2 (Winter-Spring 1963): 114. For more details, see *MEM*, no. 51 (December 22, 1962), p. 16.
100. See *MEM*, no. 50 (December 15, 1962), p. 22.
101. See *MEJ* 15, no. 4 (Fall 1961): 423, and 16, no. 1 (Winter 1962): 67, respectively.
102. P. Demchenko, *Pr.*, July 14, 1962. For more details on the aid program, see B. Svechnikov, *Izv.*, July 27, 1962.
103. Texts in *Pr.*, July 28, 1962.
104. See *ibid.*, September 17, 1961, and January 11 and February 23, 1962; *MEM*, no. 49 (December 9, 1961), p. 18, and no. 52 (December 30, 1961), p. 19; *NYT*, December 30, 1961; and *TIT*, March 1, 1962.
105. See *NYT*, June 10 and 11, 1962.
106. See *MEM*, no. 29 (July 21, 1962), p. 11.

Iraqi military mission, headed by General 'Ali Ghalib 'Aziz, Deputy Army Chief of Staff, arrived in Moscow for a three-week visit.[107] On December 21, 1962, a civil aviation agreement was signed between the two countries, establishing a regular air service between Moscow and Baghdad.[108]

The doctrinal justification for such cooperation rested on the "alliance and struggle" formula fashionable in the Marxist-Leninist literature of the late 1950s and early 1960s.[109] The Central Committee of the ICP stated in early 1962 that "the Kassem regime . . . is still anti-imperialist by nature." More precisely, it took a "firm stand against the oil companies and has pursued in the main an anti-imperialist policy." While admitting that Qasim's prestige had declined sharply both with the "progressive elements" as well as the national bourgeoisie, the Central Committee held that the Premier warranted a measure of the party's backing: "Communist policy remains as before: support for the government against the imperialist intrigues and pressure, and struggle against its anti-democratic measures."[110]

In any event, by 1962 the political life of Iraq had come to a virtual standstill. Utterly disappointed, most political leaders of the country had turned away from the revolutionary regime, which had promised the people a "democratic" form of government but had instead deteriorated into an incompetent personal dictatorship. Once Qasim discovered that popular support was on the wane, he attempted to arouse public enthusiasm by means of artificial crises. His attempts to stage a public feud with the IPC and the Kuwayt episode belong in this category. In contrast, the Kurdish revolt that broke out in the fall of 1961 was genuine, and the Prime Minister, for all his political ingenuity, proved incapable of handling it.

107. See *ibid.*, no. 36 (September 8, 1962), p. 17, and no. 37 (September 15, 1962), p. 18.
108. *Ibid.*, no. 51 (December 22, 1962), p. 21.
109. For more details, see my "The Soviet Union and the Underdeveloped World (1955–1963): An Ideological Interpretation," *Il Politico* 30, no. 4 (1965): 810–11.
110. "Meetings of the Central Committees: Iraq," *WMR*, no. 3 (March 1962), p. 55. For a detailed discussion, see Salim, pp. 37–39; Aziz al-Hajj, *WMR*, no. 11 (November 1962), p. 52; and Sami, *ibid.*, no. 12 (December 1962), pp. 38–39.

The eruption of large-scale fighting between the Iraqi armed forces and the insurgents, led by Mulla Mustafa al-Barazani, was part of a long history of Kurdish relations with their Arab, Turkish, and Persian neighbors. The fierce nationalist sentiments of the Kurdish minority—which comprised approximately one quarter of the country's population and inhabited the northeastern provinces, among them the oil-rich Mosul area—had often led to outbreaks of violence between the Kurds and Iraqi forces. After a major uprising, headed by Barazani, had been subdued by the Iraqi army in 1944, a few hundred Kurds, including Barazani, found refuge in the USSR. When many of these men were allowed to return to Iraq in September 1958, numerous nationalist politicians were dismayed. Wild rumors of Kurdish warriors trained in guerilla tactics and armed to the teeth with modern Soviet weapons circulated in the Arab East.

The anxiety of both the Iraqi and Arab nationalists in Baghdad was easy to explain. The former feared, correctly, that the influx of a well-trained, armed, and disciplined Kurdish force meant nothing but trouble for the central government. The latter were more concerned with the pronounced anti-union sentiments of the Kurds. Barazani's view of the subject, too, was quite understandable: had Iraq joined the United Arab Republic or any other state, the Kurds would have been relegated to the position of an insignificant minority. For this reason, their primary concern was to prevent themselves from being submerged in an Arab sea while pressing the Iraqi government for autonomy and self-government.

It was precisely because of their pronounced opposition to any plans of merger with the United Arab Republic that both the USSR and Qasim favored Barazani's return to Iraq.[111] In addition, by encouraging or discouraging the Kurdish demands for autonomy, Moscow may have hoped to utilize Barazani as a lever of influence over Baghdad. If so, the Kremlin miscalculated, for successful manipulation of Kurdish nationalism was possible only in a situation short of open hostilities. Once the revolt had broken out, the USSR faced the unpleasant choice of either backing Qasim, of whose internal policies

---

111. For more details, see Georges Clin, "Situation de l'Irak," *Orient,* no. 8 (1958), pp. 35–36.

the Kremlin for the most part disapproved, or supporting the Kurds, thereby losing whatever influence the Soviet government still exerted in Baghdad. In addition, Moscow was fully aware of the fact that the Kurdish cause enjoyed no sympathy at all in the other Arab capitals, not to mention Ankara and Tehran. In view of these considerations, it is highly unlikely that the USSR approved of the creation of an independent Kurdish state, some contemporary statements to that effect notwithstanding.[112]

Barazani and Qasim had cooperated for a time in the crackdown on Arab nationalists. By 1960, however, it was becoming increasingly evident that Baghdad was not prepared to grant the Kurds the autonomy they had been promised under the terms of the temporary constitution of autumn 1958.[113] When discontent manifested itself in late 1960 and early 1961, Baghdad attempted to stifle it by arresting and deporting a number of Kurdish leaders. *Khabat,* the organ of the Kurdish Democratic party, calling on the government to stop such persecution, labeled Baghdad's action a "departure from the objectives of the July 14 revolution."[114] When the pro-Barazani tribes manifested their displeasure by initiating warfare against the pro-Baghdad segments of the Kurdish population in July and August 1961, the Iraqi army had little difficulty in "restoring order" in Kurdistani towns but encountered serious problems in the mountainous countryside, which was not accessible to heavy armament.[115]

It would appear in retrospect that the Kurds were not fighting for secession but for what the *Economist* termed "a fairer deal." The uprising was due to "the procrastination and tactlessness of the cen-

112. *Newsweek,* for instance, argued that an independent Kurdistan, dominated by the Soviet Union (in itself a not very likely proposition), "would bring Russia within easy reach of the Persian Gulf and the warm water ports it covets." June 8, 1959, p. 49.
113. As noted by Barazani at the time, the document provided for equality of rights and obligations for all Iraqi citizens. He interpreted this to mean that the "national rights" of the Kurds were guaranteed by the central government. *MEM,* no. 43 (October 26, 1958), p. 27.
114. Editorial, March 14, 1961.
115. There is a striking parallel between the relatively poor showing of the Iraqi army in Kurdistan and Cairo's subsequent inability to defeat the pro-royalist tribesmen operating in the mountainous areas of Yemen.

tral government." The Kurds were reportedly "irritated by the inefficiency of the land reform scheme, by the order to stop tobacco growing in the area, by the new tax laws and by the transfer of Kurdish officials to other parts of Iraq."[116] Baghdad's inflexible and antagonistic attitude toward the Kurds, on the other hand, was motivated both by a general unwillingness to make sweeping concessions that might be interpreted as weakness and lead to further demands, including secession, and by Qasim's inability to cope with the political problems of Iraq, as manifested by the difficulties he had encountered in dealing with Iraqi Communists. To offset a sharp decline in his popularity the Premier had sought rapprochement with Nasir, hoping that this would lead to partial reconciliation with Iraq's Arab nationalist elements on whose support he could then rely to counterbalance the disaffected Marxists. Since Cairo and its Iraqi adherents were strongly opposed not only to Communist activities but also to the aspirations of the Kurds, it made good political sense to show firmness in the face of their demands for a redress of grievances. With the eruption of the Kuwayt crisis, which once again had brought Qasim into a head-on clash with the Arab nationalists, he no doubt came to regret the antagonism that had been created in Kurdistan. By that time, however, it was too late. Any compromise could only be interpreted as a serious sign of weakness and indecision under pressure. Qasim, in his public pronouncements, insisted that he would not rest until the "rebellious elements" were forced to capitulate.

The fact that Barazani and his followers had found refuge in the USSR and been allowed to return to Iraq in the fall of 1958 illustrates conclusively that, as late as 1958, the Kremlin believed that the Kurds could perform useful services in the future.[117] Yet, in line with its policy of attempting to avoid entanglement in the internal problems of states with which the USSR endeavored to maintain friendly rela-

116. *Economist*, September 23, 1961, p. 1142. For a later authoritative Soviet account of the causes of the Kurdish-Iraqi hostilities, see Akademiia nauk SSSR, *Noveishaia istoriia* . . . , pp. 191–94. See also P. Demchenko, *Irakskii Kurdistan v voine* (Moscow: Gospolitizdat, 1963), pp. 24–38.
117. See editorial, "V bor'be za natsional'noe edinstvo," *Sovremennyi vostok*, no. 9 (1959), p. 6.

tions, the Soviet government, throughout late 1960 and most of 1961, refused to take sides in the dispute. As noted by the *Economist,* even the regular Kurdish broadcasts emanating from the USSR were "discreetly silent about the . . . revolt."[118] Along with the radio, most Soviet publications withheld comments on the hostilities that had broken out in northeastern Iraq. One notable exception was the *World Marxist Review,* which offered its pages to the statements made by Iraqi Communists and which, it may be safely assumed, did, to an extent, reflect the views of the Kremlin. Since Qasim's relations with the country's Marxist organizations had by then become very strained, it was not surprising that the tone of the comments was not complimentary to the policies pursued by Baghdad.

The Iraqi Communist party never tired of pointing out that the war had been precipitated by the ruling "Arab bourgeoisie," which "blindly refuses to recognise the right of the Kurds to self-determination and, in fact, foments national strife." The party initially demanded "complete equality" for all national groups in Iraq, including the rights to self-government and "to supervise their own national culture and education within the Iraqi republic," emphasizing at the same time "the need for a common struggle of the Arabs and the Kurds in order to win the essential rights attainable at the present time for the Kurds living in Iraq." To prevent misunderstanding, it added that while "directing its criticism against Arab chauvinism, the Party at the same time combats the nationalist-extremist tendencies among the Kurds."[119] Thus the ICP had a defense against possible criticism from both Arab and Iraqi nationalists who, for obvious reasons, had no sympathy for the Kurdish desire for autonomy, let alone independence. At the same time, the party expressed its strong dissatisfaction with the Qasim regime, using the Kurdish problem as a means of putting pressure on the government to revise its attitude toward the Communist organization.

118. *Economist,* September 23, 1961, p. 1142.
119. Salim, p. 40. See also Jabbar Ali, "The Iraqi Communist Party and the Kurdish Question," *WMR,* no. 8 (August 1962), p. 21; Saadi Ali, "The Events in Iraqi Kurdistan," *ibid.,* no. 3 (March 1962), p. 84; and *ibid.,* no. 7 (July 1962), p. 92.

According to a March 1962 statement by the ICP Central Committee, the Kurdish national problem—"an integral part of the struggle for democracy for all the Iraqi people"—could be settled only through "the establishment of self-government in Iraqi Kurdistan within the Iraqi Republic." Compliance with this "just national demand" was the more desirable in that it would strengthen "the unity of the Arab and Kurdish peoples . . . in the struggle against imperialism and reaction." It would also "have a powerful impact in the Middle East, especially in Turkey and Iran" by giving "strength and confidence to the Kurds there in their struggle against the reactionary regimes and the CENTO pact. The Kurdish national movement in all parts of Kurdistan would then become a powerful ally of the Iraqi Republic, helping it to combat the imperialist intrigues. . . . The unity of the Arab and Kurdish peoples" was particularly important in that "an enforced alliance even between two Arab peoples," as demonstrated by the experience of the UAR, could be "harmful." It would be especially true "in the case of two such distinct nationalities as the Kurds and the Arabs." In conclusion, "the final solution of the Kurdish national problem" would be provided only by "the working class. . . . As the experience of the Soviet Union, Czechoslovakia and other socialist countries has shown, such a solution of the national question is possible only under socialism."[120]

Except for reproductions of these Iraqi Communist statements in the *World Marxist Review,* the Soviet press passed in silence the events in Kurdistan until, in the fall of 1962, Dana Adams Schmidt of the *New York Times* traveled to northern Iraq and spent several weeks observing the war and interviewing a number of Kurdish leaders, including Mustafa Barazani. Upon his return to Bayrut, Schmidt published a series of reports that were less than complimentary to Qasim and his policy in Kurdistan. In addition, Schmidt concluded that Barazani had appealed to the United States for help, promising, in return, full cooperation in containing "Communist expansion" in the Middle East.

Such a serious "provocation" merited a Soviet reply. On November

120. Jabbar Ali, pp. 23, 24.

15, 1962, *Pravda* referred to comments on Schmidt's articles that had appeared in the Lebanese newspaper *al-Hadaf*. These were based on conversations with an anonymous "noted" Kurdish nationalist who "categorically" refuted the allegation that Barazani was determined to create a "united and independent Kurdistan" that would encompass territories in Turkey, Iran, Iraq, and Syria. Instead, he wished merely to gain the autonomy guaranteed the Iraqi Kurds by the Provisional Constitution of 1958. Schmidt and other Western reporters persist in presenting a "biased" and "false" picture of the events in Kurdistan because "the imperialists . . . are fully aware of Barazani's determination to prevent their return to this area." In wishing to pit Qasim against the Kurds, the Western powers were simply continuing adherence to their "ancient policy of 'divide and rule.' " The Kurds possessed enough weapons to continue the struggle for their rights for a long time to come, and it was unfortunate that the Iraqi Premier had fallen into the Western trap by labeling the Kurdish leader a "British agent." Though Qasim later reportedly had modified his stand, he continued to accuse Barazani of "subversive activities." In conclusion, *Pravda* expressed the hope that the Kurds and the Baghdad authorities would eventually reach an agreement, settle their differences, and return to cooperation in order to safeguard Iraq's independence.[121]

It should be mentioned that, while absolving the USSR from any responsibility for and complicity in the Kurdish revolt, Qasim regularly charged the United States and Great Britain with fomenting it. His foreign policy, in late 1961, was based on what the *Economist* termed "a trinity of anti-western accusations: neo-colonialism in Kuwait; oil imperialism; subversive activities in Kurdistan."[122] It is hardly possible that Moscow had any illusions as to the basically anti-Communist attitude of the Kurdish nationalists,[123] but it had no reason to be alarmed at or dissatisfied with their anti-government activities provided that they did not ally themselves with the Western

121. *Pr.,* November 15, 1962.
122. September 22, 1962, p. 1113. For more details on the Iraqi nationalist stand, see editorials, *al-Fajr al-Jadid, al-Thawra,* and *al-Mustaqbal,* September 17, 1961. Comments on Schmidt's articles in *al-Thawra,* October 7, 1962.
123. As quoted in *Economist,* September 22, 1962, p. 1113.

powers. Through the Iraqi Communist party, it extended the Kurds moral, but *not* (as far as can be ascertained) material, support. The Iraqi Kurds were not only putting pressure on the unwieldy Premier of an Arab state with which Moscow was endeavoring to maintain outwardly friendly relations, but also protecting their *legitimate* rights, guaranteed to them with Qasim's personal approval, under the terms of the Provisional Constitution. Moreover, their action just might inspire their Turkish and Iranian fellow-countrymen into rebellion against their respective governments—a development that, from Khrushchev's standpoint, would have been highly welcome.

Unfortunately for the Kurds, the Western powers were not likely to support them. In spite of some sympathy for their cause, both Washington and London refused to interfere because the backing of Kurdish nationalists in Iraq might have had very serious political repercussions not only in that country but also in Turkey and Iran, two of Washington's staunchest allies in the Middle East. More particularly, a military defeat at the hands of the Kurdish insurgents would probably spell the doom of Premier Qasim, and while such a turn of events might not, in itself, have been unwelcome to the West, there was no way of knowing who would succeed him and what kind of line Baghdad would pursue as a result.

Thus, no major power supported Qasim's efforts to "solve" the Kurdish problem. Both the Soviet Union and Iraq had grown progressively disenchanted with each other, and by 1962 it was obvious that a stalemate had been reached. When Qasim was killed, Moscow did not mourn its former friend but interpreted his fate as a lesson to others who might also be considering the suppression of Communism: "By driving the Communist and other progressive parties underground, Kassem deprived the masses of their revolutionary vanguard, damped and extinguished their enthusiasm, and ultimately wrought his own destruction."[124]

124. G. Mirsky, "The Coup d'Etat in Iraq," *NT*, no. 8 (February 27, 1963), p. 11. See also V. A. Zorin, ed., *Vneshniaia politika SSSR na novom etape* (Moscow: Politizdat, 1964), pp. 128–29. For an interesting subsequent denunciation of Qasim, see Akademiia nauk SSSR. Institut mirovoi ekonomiki i mezhdunarodnykh otnoshenii, *Mezhdunarodnye otnosheniia posle vtoroi mirovoi voiny (1956–1964)* (Moscow: Politizdat, 1965) 3:549.

8
Syria and Egypt after the Dissolution of the United Arab Republic

In the early morning hours of September 28, 1961, Syrian army units stationed in the vicinity of Damascus revolted against the union with Egypt. Within 48 hours, the three-year old United Arab Republic had ceased to exist.[1] To Nasir's astonishment and dismay, very few Syrians objected to the dissolution of what had once been described as the historic first step on the Arab march toward unity.

The stagnation of the economy, for which Cairo was held responsible, had been one of the primary reasons for dissatisfaction among varied strata of the Syrian population. In addition, many Syrians resented Nasir's efforts to control the political life of the Northern Region by outlawing the traditional parties, among them the pro-union Ba'th.[2] Utilizing this popular discontent, a group of Syrian officers, alarmed at what they perceived as "a deliberate policy to make them subservient to the Egyptian cadres," decided to seek re-

1. For more details, see *NYT*, October 1 and 8, 1961. The term "United Arab Republic" was kept by President Nasir as a beacon to all true Arab nationalists struggling for the attainment of the "eventual union."
2. For a detailed analysis of the causes for the dissolution of the UAR, see Monte Palmer, "The United Arab Republic: An Assessment of Its Failure," *MEJ* 20, no. 1 (Winter 1966): 50–67.

dress for their grievances. When Nasir turned down their demands for autonomy, the anti-union military proclaimed Syria an independent and sovereign state.³

From September 29, 1961, to March 8, 1963, when the Ba'th overthrew the cabinet headed by Khalid al-'Azm, Syria was governed by coalitions of conservative and moderate politicians enjoying the support of the anti-union officers, headed by Major-General 'Abd al-Karim Zahr al-Din, Commander-in-Chief of the armed forces. The provisional government, appointed by the Revolutionary Command Council on the day of the coup, was headed by Ma'mun Kuzbari, a wealthy lawyer. His cabinet contained "three leading bankers and the President of the Latakia Chamber of Commerce." A new order, it was announced, would be built on the principles of "economic prosperity, based on stabilization of currency and prices, a high standard of living, and respect for legitimate profits." After the elections of December 1, 1961, which entailed a reshuffling of personnel rather than a change in policy, Dr. Nazim al-Qudsi, a former conservative premier from Aleppo, was elected President of the Syrian Arab Republic (SAR). Ma'ruf al-Dawalibi, a "moderate radical" from Aleppo, became Prime Minister, while Kuzbari was given the honorable but insignificant post of Speaker of the Chamber of Deputies.⁴ The first two men belonged to the People's party, which in the past had advocated close cooperation with Iraq.

Efforts aimed at restoring the influence of the conservative groups, coupled with their determination to re-create an economic environment best suited for the accumulation of wealth, soon brought the new regime into a basic conflict with the country's left-wing forces, above all the Ba'th and the pro-Nasir Arab nationalist elements.⁵ After a wave of general unrest,⁶ Qudsi promised a new constitution, a referen-

3. Ivison Macadam, ed., *The Annual Register of World Events, 1961* (New York: St. Martin's Press, 1962), pp. 285–86.
4. *Ibid.*, pp. 291–92. See also *MEJ* 16, no. 1 (Winter 1962): 79, and no. 2 (Spring 1962): 208–9.
5. For some details, see *Economist*, January 20, 1962, p. 214, and March 24, 1962, p. 1127. Surprisingly, for reasons that will be discussed below, the Syrian Communists were not in the vanguard of the opposition to the regime.
6. For details, see *ibid.*, March 31, 1962, p. 1244, and April 7, 1962, p. 15.

dum on Arab unity, new elections, and the correction of some of the mistakes allegedly committed by the conservative cabinet, including such transgressions as corruption and misapplication of the agrarian law.[7] On April 16, Bashir al-Azmah was appointed Premier, presiding over a coalition cabinet comprised of members of most of Syria's political groups as well as a number of leading independents. But since the members could not agree on policies and were only too willing to air their differences in public, the Azmah government was soon forced to admit its inability to institute the promised reforms. In desperation, the majority of the Syrian legislators turned to a strong man, Khalid al-'Azm, a wealthy old-time politician, to form a new cabinet. 'Azm obliged on September 17, 1962, appointing Azmah to the post of Deputy Premier. One week later, the Parliament dissolved itself for one year, empowering 'Azm to rule Syria by decree. In late November 1962, the Prime Minister promised to restore constitutional democracy and political parties sometime in 1963.[8] 'Azm had no chance to implement his program. Serious disturbances, fomented in part by the pro-Nasir as well as Ba'thi elements, led to his overthrow on March 8, 1963.

With this brief background, it is possible to examine Moscow's reaction to both the break-up of the UAR and the emergence of the Syrian Arab Republic. As might have been expected, the anti-Nasir governments of Jordan, Turkey, and Iran had been the first members of the international community to extend recognition to the newly formed SAR. Their initiative, Cairo noted, spoke eloquently of the "unceasing determination of imperialism and reaction to destroy Arab nationalism."[9] Nevertheless, on October 5, in an abrupt bow to

---

See also *MEJ* 16, no. 3 (Summer 1962): 366-67; and *MEM*, no. 13 (March 31, 1962), pp. 2-5, 8; no. 14 (April 7, 1962), pp. 2, 24, 8; no. 15 (April 14, 1962), p. 2; and Dana Adams Schmidt, *NYT,* April 1, 1962.

7. *Economist,* April 21, 1962, p. 229; and *MEJ* 16, no. 3 (Summer 1962): 367. For more details, see Marcel Colombe, "La République arabe syrienne à la lumière du coup d'Etat du 28 mars," *Orient,* no. 21 (1962), pp. 11-18.

8. See Ivison Macadam, ed., *Annual Register of World Events, 1962,* p. 294. For more details, see *MEM,* no. 37 (September 15, 1962), pp. 2-3; no. 38 (September 22, 1962), pp. 3-6; and no. 50 (December 15, 1962), p. 6.

9. Melhem Ayashi, *al-Akhbar,* October 2, 1961. See also Bahay al-Din in *ibid.*

reality, President Nasir stated that Cairo would not object to Damascus's readmission to both the Arab League and the United Nations. On October 13, the Syrian Arab Republic took its seat in the UN and, on October 29, in the Arab League. Once Nasir had cleared the way, the Kremlin lost little time in recognizing the new Syrian government; it was announced in Moscow on October 7 that the USSR would establish diplomatic relations with the break-away regime in Damascus. This Russian initiative was followed by similar moves on the part of the Kremlin's East European satellites. [10]

While it may be safely assumed that the dissolution of the United Arab Republic had caught the USSR by surprise, Moscow was not likely to mourn its demise.[11] In recognizing Syria only nine days after the coup, much earlier than either Great Britain or the United States, the Kremlin was acting in the face of the provisional government's determination to continue the ban on the Syrian Communist party. Its reasons were obvious. As evidenced by the crises of 1959 and 1961, the Soviet government strongly disapproved of a number of Nasir's policies, among them his opposition to the legalization of the Egyptian and Syrian Communist parties and, more important, his determination to adhere to a more aggressive brand of nonalignment. Khrushchev had long felt that Cairo had to be taught a lesson, and seized upon this opportunity to once again remind Nasir of Soviet disenchantment with the direction in which he was moving. In more general terms, the Kremlin continued to oppose Nasir's seeming determination to bring other Arab countries under the hegemony of Egypt.

It is of interest to note that Cairo recognized the Soviet game for what it actually was. Noting the speed of Moscow's recognition of the break-away Northern Province, Haykal examined some of the reasons that, in his opinion, induced the USSR to follow the initiative of Jordan, Turkey, Iran, Nationalist China, and Guatemala—a company with which the Kremlin, as a rule, did not care to associate itself. The Soviet attitude, Haykal argued, was conditioned by the history of relations between the Arab nationalists and Communists. More

10. *MEJ* 16, no. 1 (Winter 1962): 79, 80.
11. For initial comments, see *Pr.*, September 29, and October 1, 2, 3, 6, and 8, 1961; and *Izv.*, September 30, 1961.

particularly, since 1955, during the period of the "great struggle against imperialism and military alliances," both Arab Communists and their Soviet masters had sided with Arab nationalists. The USSR, in particular, had backed Cairo in its determination to break the Western arms monopoly. However, all of this did not mean that the Marxists sympathized with Arab nationalism, but merely that the tactical goals of both groups had coincided at that particular time. Arab nationalists, Haykal continued, were fully aware of the temporary nature of their cooperation with the Communists and realized, even at that early hour, the necessity of erecting a "staunch barrier" between themselves and the Marxist elements. The Syrian-Egyptian union, according to Haykal, presented a "demarcation line" between two "fronts." This explained why Khalid Baqdash, Secretary-General of the Syrian Communist party and one of the better known Arab Communists, fled Syria soon after its merger with Egypt and why the USSR displayed such unseemly haste in welcoming the emergence of the Syrian Arab Republic.[12]

Such comments, however, did not affect Cairo's cooperation with the USSR. In his message congratulating Khrushchev on the 44th anniversary of the Bolshevik revolution, Nasir held that "traditional bonds of friendship" continued to exist between the two countries and expressed the hope that their cooperation would continue to flourish. Commenting on Nasir's message, *al-Ahram* noted that, despite obvious differences that separated Marxism-Leninism from the "philosophy of the Arab revolution," the friendship between Cairo and Moscow constituted one of the cornerstones upon which Egypt's "independent foreign policy" had been based.[13]

If further proof were needed of Moscow's delight at the serious political setback that Nasir had suffered at the hands of his erstwhile allies, it was supplied in the form of a "Statement by the Syrian Communist Party," which appeared in *Pravda* on October 7, 1961, the same day the Soviet government announced its decision to recog-

12. *Al-Ahram,* October 13, 1961. See also Muhammad al-Taba'i in *al-Akhbar,* October 14, 1961.
13. Text and editorial, *al-Ahram,* November 9, 1961.

nize the SAR.[14] The fact that the official organ of the Central Committee of the CPSU lent its pages to this pronouncement indicated beyond any doubt that the latter reflected the views of the USSR authorities as well.

The break-up of the United Arab Republic was described in the Statement as a "historic victory won by the Syrian people." It was bound to have wide repercussions throughout the entire Arab East and was applauded because the "anti-democratic" attitudes and actions of the UAR regime had led to the establishment in Syria of a "bloody dictatorship" responsible for "killing in torture chambers . . . hundreds of honest citizens." It was only natural that the Syrian people should organize "heroic resistance [against] the oppressors" and that the Syrian Communists should be "in the forefront of those who made sacrifices and fought against the dictatorship."

Turning from the past to the future, the Statement noted that the "best way of preserving the victory [was] through the establishment of a national, democratic, and anti-imperialist regime on the basis of free elections"; further, it should "base itself on the people and on their patriotic and progressive forces," meaning the Syrian Communist party. To bring such a regime into existence, the Statement recommended the organization of a "national front, including all the national forces and movements regardless of party affiliation."

Clearly, now that Cairo's influence in Damascus had been eliminated, the Syrian Communists hoped that the new regime would allow them freedom of political activity, including a chance for participation in the government of the Syrian Arab Republic. Their hopes were shattered a few weeks later when Khalid Baqdash arrived in Damascus on board a Czech airliner and was denied permission to disembark.[15] Commenting shortly thereafter on the situation in Syria, Baqdash said that the resignation of Premier Kuzbari, announced on November 20, indicated that the policies pursued by the "right-wing,

14. Text in *Pr.*, October 7, 1961. The statement, it was subsequently noted, was issued on October 4. Leningrad. Gosudarstvennyi Universitet, *Noveishaia istoriia stran zarubezhnoi Azii i Afriki* (Leningrad: Izdatel'stvo Leningradskogo universiteta, 1963), p. 567.
15. See *Pr.*, November 22, 1961.

conservative elements" were being challenged not only by the "popular masses," but also by "certain circles of the national bourgeoisie." Baqdash doubted that Syria would soon return to "normalcy," since the right-wing elements opposed the "unity of forces struggling against all forms of colonialism." They also were pursuing domestic and foreign policies which endangered the "economic achievements of the toiling masses" and could bring Syria into submission to the "large colonialist powers."[16]

Soviet publications were not nearly so outspoken in their criticism of the Damascus authorities. For example, reporting from Bayrut on the eve of the Syrian elections, P. Demchenko merely echoed some of the sentiments expressed by Baqdash: the problem of the "democratic freedoms" remained one of the cardinal issues facing the new government. Was it not advisable to restore the political climate of 1957-early 1958, when various parties were permitted to function without undue interference and when the press reflected the whole spectrum of political opinion? There also had existed at that time a "front of parliamentary solidarity" that united the "bourgeois and leftist" elements and "played a positive part in . . . strengthening national unity." It was regrettable that the present leaders not only refused to cooperate with the "democratic elements," but also procrastinated in releasing political prisoners and prevented Baqdash from running in the forthcoming elections.[17]

The mild tone of Demchenko's article indicates that the Soviet government, fully aware of the immense political and economic difficulties facing Damascus in the immediate post-union period, did not wish to contribute to them by exerting additional political pressure. It may also have been hoping to establish close relations with the new Syrian regime and, in so doing, to offset some of the political losses that the USSR had recently incurred in Egypt and Iraq. And in fact Premier 'Izzat al-Nus, who succeeded Kuzbari on November 20, stated in a radio broadcast that Syria would adhere to a policy of strict nonalignment. As noted by Demchenko, the Syrian public received

16. *Ibid.*, November 24, 1961.
17. *Ibid.*, November 28, 1961.

this reassurance with "great satisfaction." "The friends of Syria hope," he wrote, "that the Syrian Arab Republic . . . will remain faithful to these traditions which have emerged in the years of stubborn resistance against the imperialists and the colonizers."[18]

In repeatedly reminding the Syrians that the restoration of political freedom for the "patriotic" parties was indispensable for the broadening of the popular base of the new regime, and, in the long run, for ensuring the growth and well-being of an independent Syrian state, the Kremlin made no secret of its political preferences and of its desire to restore freedom of activity for the Syrian Communist party. However, its support of the conservative government in Damascus was significantly not made conditional upon the latter's acquiescence to the demands voiced by Baqdash. As long as the new government continued to undermine Nasir's influence in the Arab East and refrained from close political and economic cooperation with the West, it was in Moscow's interest to establish and maintain cordial relations with it. After Leonid Brezhnev, then Chairman of the Supreme Soviet, expressed the hope in a telegram to President Qudsi that the "traditionally friendly relations" between the two countries would be improved in the near future,[19] both sides agreed on the "desirability of strengthening . . . economic and cultural cooperation." Their relations were to be based on "the principles of peaceful coexistence, complete equality, and mutual respect for the interests of both parties."[20]

As might have been expected, the Syrian Communist party disapproved of Moscow's support of the conservative regime in Damascus. One of the more interesting indications of this attitude appeared in *Pravda* in March 1962. Strange as it may seem, Baqdash used the official organ of the CPSU as a forum for criticism of Khrushchev's foreign policy, though he was ingenious enough to conceal his attack in the discussion of a different (though related) subject. His article,

18. *Ibid.*, November 23 and 28, 1961, respectively.
19. Similar sentiments were expressed by Khrushchev congratulating Dawalibi on his appointment as Premier. Texts of the telegrams in *ibid.*, December 19, 1961, and January 25, 1962, respectively.
20. See *ibid.*, March 9, 1962. See also *ibid.*, December 22, 1961, and February 16, 1962.

entitled "The Program of the CPSU and the Contemporary Stage of the National-Liberation Struggle," commented on some of the current Marxist ideological formulations concerning the developing areas. The majority of the emerging nations, he argued, were governed by the "national bourgeoisie." Because of their "dual nature,"[21] the ruling elites favored certain "anti-feudal and anti-imperialist" reforms but refused to allow the "progressive elements" to work for sweeping socioeconomic and political transformation of their respective countries. Anti-Communism in the emerging countries, Baqdash concluded, inevitably rested on a "union between the right wing of the national bourgeoisie and elements connected with imperialist capital and the remnants of feudalism." Its adoption invariably rendered the national bourgeoisie a prisoner of foreign and domestic exploiters or, in other words, of "imperialism and reaction."[22] The Syrian Communist was thus clearly implying that the USSR government was not only pursuing a shortsighted policy, but was actually violating its own ideological precepts, as laid down in the new party platform.

Baqdash's implied criticism of the Kremlin for its support of the "national-bourgeois" elements echoed the Syrian Communists' dismay in late 1961-early 1962 at Damascus's refusal not only to grant them freedom of organization and expression but even to release those party members who had been imprisoned under the Nasir regime. Nevertheless, the Kremlin continued to adhere to a policy of cooperation with the Syrian Arab Republic. Its propaganda support of Damascus during the March 1962 border clashes with Israel was routine,[23] but when, on March 28, a group of officers temporarily overthrew the conservative government for the avowed purpose of "continuing the revolution of September 28, [1961]," Moscow must have been alarmed at their determination to seek "most cordial relations with all the liberated Arab states, *especially with beloved Egypt*

21. For more details, see my "The Soviet Union and the Underdeveloped World (1955–1963): An Ideological Interpretation," *Il Politico* 30, no. 4 (1965): 806–8.
22. *Pr.*, March 23, 1962.
23. For more details, see *ibid.*, March 20, 1962; and P. Demchenko, *ibid.*, March 27, 1962.

and brotherly Iraq."[24] Soviet apprehensions were dispelled on March 30, when a group of foreign correspondents, including V. Maevskii and P. Demchenko, were invited to attend a press conference held by General Zahr al-Din, Commander-in-Chief of the Syrian armed forces. The coup, the general said, was but a continuation of the action that began on September 28, "when Syria left the United Arab Republic." He also made it clear that union on Nasir's terms was not acceptable to him and his colleagues. While Zahr al-Din referred to the desire of the military to help build "genuine Arab unity . . . on correct and clear-cut foundations," no one bothered to explain the meaning of these phrases, and they could be dismissed as mere lip service to ideals that still enjoyed great popularity with the Arab masses.

Much in Zahr al-Din's statement was in fact bound to appeal to the Soviet government. For example, he complained that the 1961 revolution gradually had come under the control of the "big Syrian bourgeoisie" who, with the support of unnamed "imperialist forces," had gained the control of the government and the Constituent Assembly. They had discontinued the policy of "liberal economic reforms" and denied freedom of political activity to all but the conservative groups. They had been about to open Syria to "Western imperialist capital." Thus, Zahr al-Din announced that President Qudsi and Premier Dawalibi were under arrest, awaiting trial before a "popular tribunal."[25]

Applauding the removal of the conservative elements from the Syrian government, the Soviet press expressed hope that the upheaval would bring changes for the better, but noted that only the future would tell whether such optimism was justified. In the meantime, it was hoped that the ruling elements in Damascus were aware of the fact that only a regime that "heeded the lessons of the past" and did not "ignore the aspirations of the people" had a chance to succeed. The Syrian people, *Pravda* noted, in a clear indication of Moscow's own preferences, were determined "to strengthen the independence of

24. *Ibid.*, March 29, 1962. Italics added.
25. See V. Maevskii and P. Demchenko, *ibid.*, April 2, 1962.

their country [and] to achieve the stabilization of the economic and political situation." This goal could best be achieved through the "unity of national forces."[26] As political strife continued, however, Soviet publications warned the "dissident elements" that instability, whether fostered by pro-Nasir officers or their "pro-imperialist" colleagues, could only serve the interests of "international reaction."[27]

According to Maevskii, the coup of March 28 was "inevitable," because the "efforts of the reactionary forces to utilize the Constituent Assembly and the government for the purpose of pushing the country farther to the right could not but evoke protests among the people and the army."[28] Ironically, Maevskii's article appeared in *Pravda* on the very day that General Zahr al-Din once again sided with the conservative politicians and ordered the hopelessly divided army officers to return to their barracks. President Qudsi was restored to his office, and Bashir al-Azmah was appointed Prime Minister. Commenting on these events, Demchenko noted that the Constituent Assembly was dissolved because it failed to justify the hopes that the nation had placed in it. "The Syrian people," he concluded, "are fully aware of the fact that the imperialist threat to [their country] has not been completely eliminated."[29] The Soviet government, it appears, had no trouble reconciling itself to the changes that had taken place in Syria. In a congratulatory telegram to President Qudsi, Brezhnev reiterated Moscow's previously expressed hope that "friendly relations" between the two states would continue to develop "in the interests of universal peace."[30]

As time passed, the Soviet press noted with approval the seemingly genuine efforts of the Azmah government to liberalize the political and economic life of Syria. For instance, the new Premier announced his determination to introduce a number of far-reaching reforms, ranging from the legalization of political parties and guarantees of

26. *Ibid.*
27. Iu. Iasnev, *ibid.,* April 4, 1962.
28. *Ibid.,* April 13, 1962. For more details, see "Recent Events in Syria," *IA,* no. 7 (July 1962), p. 119.
29. *Pr.,* April 18, 1962.
30. *Ibid.,* April 21, 1962.

freedoms of speech, assembly, and organization to adherence to a "socialist path of development." In inter-Arab and foreign relations, Maevskii noted, Azmah reflected the Syrian people's resolution to prevent "imperialism and internal reaction" from imposing their will on the country. Great problems remained, he concluded, that could be solved only through close cooperation between the government and the "democratic forces of the people."[31]

Throughout the summer and fall of 1962, Soviet press comments were reserved for such nonpolitical items as the search for oil being conducted by Soviet geologists in northeastern Syria, the construction of a railway linking the Mediterranean port of Latakia with the country's eastern provinces, and the building of the Latakia-Aleppo highway,[32] with no mention of the widespread disturbances, strikes, demonstrations, bombings, and arrests that finally culminated in the downfall of Azmah and the advent to power of Khalid al-'Azm. Nor are there any references to the rapprochement between Syria and Iraq and to the serious political crisis leading to the Cairo-Damascus confrontation at the Arab League meeting, held in Shtura (Lebanon) in August 1962.[33] The Kremlin must have been fully aware of the political instability gripping Syria and saw no reason to associate itself closely with a regime that appeared to be living on borrowed time. Furthermore, having found itself embroiled in the Iraqi-Egyptian dispute, Moscow clearly wished to steer clear of a similar confrontation between Syria, Iraq, and Egypt.

In mid-September, the Soviet press reported that President Qudsi had asked Khalid al-'Azm to form a new cabinet.[34] Khrushchev's telegram congratulating 'Azm on his appointment expressed the hope that the new regime would be able to contribute to the growth of an "independent" and "democratic" Syria. In his reply, 'Azm, who had announced his determination to pursue a policy of "complete neutrality" and to work for the preservation of peace, thanked Khrushchev for "wishing success to the Syrian Arab Republic as a democratic and

31. *Ibid.*, May 25, 1962.
32. See *ibid.*, July 28 and 31, and August 21, 1962.
33. For some details, see *MEM*, no. 35 (September 1, 1962), pp. 2–5.
34. See *Pr.*, September 15, 1962.

independent state."³⁵ During the remainder of the year there were occasional references in Soviet publications to economic cooperation between the two countries and to "threats of Israeli aggression."³⁶ No attempts were made to evaluate the political situation in Damascus, however, or to shed any light on the intricacies of inter-Arab politics. Already disillusioned with its Arab friends in Cairo and Baghdad, the Russians should by then have realized that the imposition of long-range political stability in Syria was in all probability beyond the reach of even the most talented local politician.

In early 1963, Soviet publications did note the clashes between pro-government forces and dissident elements in Syria, warning against "imperialist-reactionary plots" intended to overthrow the Damascus regime. Commenting on the serious disorders staged by Ba'thi students and some military personnel in the major cities of Syria, *Pravda* remarked that the "toiling masses" opposed the "violators of peace and order." Such activities represented attempts by the "reactionary forces to prevent the introduction of democratic reforms." The Syrian Communist party went so far as to appeal to the people "to unite in the struggle to thwart any plots directed against the stabilization of the situation in the Syrian Arab Republic."³⁷ This attitude is understandable in view of the Soviet and Syrian Communists' awareness of the Ba'thi attitude toward Marxism and its Arab adherents. 'Azm, in spite of his numerous "shortcomings," was preferable to the Ba'th. The latter, however, was not to be denied and seized control of Iraq and Syria, in February and March 1963 respectively, opening a new chapter in Soviet relations with both Baghdad and Damascus.

Official Soviet pronouncements on the dissolution of the Egyptian-Syrian union were made only after the Ba'thi revolutions in Syria and Iraq. Most of the discussions published between 1963 and 1968 borrowed heavily from the Syrian arguments.³⁸ One of the most eloquent

35. *Ibid.*, September 20 and 23, 1962, respectively.
36. See A. Stepin, *Izv.*, October 28, and *ibid.*, December 20, 1962.
37. *Pr.*, January 23, 1963.
38. Only one of the latest authoritative volumes, published in 1968, expressed criticism of the Syrian bourgeoisie for aggravating the 1961 crisis by

examples, published by Leningrad University in 1963, contended that Cairo bore the basic responsibility for the breakdown of the union. Dissatisfaction with its activities in Damascus had reached a new high when the socioeconomic reforms of 1960–1961 were implemented "in conditions of a continuous sharpening of the class struggle and of the deepening conflict between labor and capital." The ensuing terror against the Syrian Communist party had resulted in the spread among the country's "toiling masses" of "deep resentment and disappointment." As a consequence, the "Syrian region became the center of opposition against the UAR government."

In addition, "numerous specific reasons" were cited for the dissatisfaction of the Syrian bourgeoisie with Cairo's policies. Chief among them were the dominant role that the Egyptian bourgeoisie played in the UAR government, reducing their Syrian counterparts to political posts that lacked power and responsibility. The Ba'thi politicians who initially had collaborated with Nasir soon followed their conservative colleagues into political oblivion. In 1960, most of the important positions in the Northern Region were held by professional military men who had no party affiliation and were subservient to the will of Cairo. Nasir had also endeavored to establish the Egyptian bourgeoisie as the dominant economic element in both regions, with the result that the Syrian bourgeoisie was reduced to a position of both political and economic inferiority. New customs regulations had cut Syria off from its traditional markets in Turkey, Iraq, and Jordan, and "large quantities of Syrian goods" had been transferred to Egypt in the form of "credits." Instances of repayment were rare and usually took the shape of subsidies, labeled as "aid to the Northern Region." Financially, the relatively stable Syrian pound had been tied to the volatile Egyptian currency and the exchange rate set was unfair to Syrian businessmen dealing with their southern counterparts.

The Syrian bourgeoisie was particularly appalled at the 1961 nationalization decrees. Though basically "progressive," these measures

---

seeking contacts and general accommodation with the imperialist powers. See Akademiia nauk SSSR. Institut narodov Azii, *Noveishaia istoriia arabskikh stran (1917–1966)* (Moscow: Izdatel'stvo "Nauka," 1968), pp. 75–77.

had resulted in the supplanting of Syrian businessmen by Egyptian bureaucrats and officers who, for the most part, were ignorant of local conditions and methods of production. "These actions of the UAR government," the study concluded, "were dictated by the great-power aims of the Egyptian bourgeoisie, its striving for supremacy [over and] hegemony in the Arab countries. Egyptian bourgeois nationalists began to conceive of Arab unity as subordination to the UAR of all the Arab countries."[39] Adopting a different theme, a later publication by O. E. Tuganova, a leading Soviet authority on the Middle East, noted that the break-up of the United Arab Republic was "one of the most striking expressions of the . . . deepening class demarcation in the Near and Middle East. . . . Simultaneously, it showed that Arab unity can be implemented only on a truly democratic basis, [and] that it must be a result of a wide movement of popular masses."[40]

The Leningrad University study contended that the Syrian military had not initially demanded the dissolution of the UAR but favored autonomy within the general union framework. They were turned down by Nasir, who was confident that the majority of the Syrian units had remained loyal to him. Only when his September 28 order to the Syrian army to crush the mutineers was ignored did the UAR President direct Egyptian naval units and paratroop commandos to move into the Northern Region. But the invasion was a "lamentable failure."[41] Tuganova, in contrast, was much more charitable to Cairo: "In having issued the order to stop military operations . . . , the UAR government placed the interests of the Arab peoples above considerations of prestige, averted bloodshed between two brotherly Arab peoples, and excluded the possibility of a new military intervention by the imperialist powers in the Arab East."[42]

The break-up of the United Arab Republic in September 1961 adds further support to the contention that the separatist tendencies preva-

39. Leningrad, pp. 564, 565, 566.
40. O. E. Tuganova, *Mezhdunarodnye otnosheniia na Blizhnem i Srednem Vostoke* (Moscow: Izdatel'stvo "Mezhdunarodnye otnosheniia," 1967), p. 142.
41. Leningrad, p. 566.
42. Tuganova, p. 142.

lent in the post-1945 Arab East could not be blamed exclusively on the Western powers. They were also due to the unwillingness of the local ruling strata to agree upon and implement a joint course of action. In Syria, as previously noted, there was a return to traditional instability initiated primarily by army officers motivated by both political ideals and lust for power. Egyptian reaction to the break-up of the UAR was a bit more complex. Following his reflex action of dispatching Egyptian paratroopers to Latakia and then ordering them to return in mid-flight (those units already in Syria were ordered not to resist the rebellious Syrians), President Nasir appears to have reconciled himself to the *fait accompli.* His "strangely candid friend," as the *Economist* called Muhammad Hasanayn Haykal, went so far as to suggest that the UAR fell apart because it was based on a "hero personality." The latter, Haykal noted, should never have become the foundation for Arab union. According to the *Economist's* reporter, "seldom have dust and ashes been scattered in Egypt with such precision."[43]

The serious blow that Syria's secession dealt to his ambitions in the Arab East forced Nasir to seek new points of departure for his domestic as well as his regional policies.[44] In refusing to deal with the secessionist regime in Damascus, in terminating the loose confederation with Yemen, in denouncing Saudi Arabia, and in breaking diplomatic relations with Jordan, Nasir seized the political initiative from his potential and actual adversaries, "putting them on the defensive in the eyes of their own populations." At the same time, by restoring the ideological purity of his regime, which the critics claimed he had lost in 1959, he "recaptured . . . the high-pitched enthusiasm from his hard core supporters that had been his at Suez and at the birth of the UAR." In the process, he abandoned the slogan "of a 'unity of ranks' . . . among Arab regimes of diverse internal orientation" in favor of

43. *Economist,* October 28, 1961, p. 320.
44. In July, it will be recalled, Cairo had embarked upon a massive program of nationalization and socialization. Briefly, the government obtained controlling interest in most large industrial and business concerns: limited the earnings from dividends, imposed a stiff income tax law, and cut in half the maximum of permitted landholding. For details, see Macadam, *1961,* p. 286.

"the notion of 'unity of purpose.' "⁴⁵ In practice, this meant that Cairo would no longer be required to respect the views of the "sisterly" Arab governments; it was free to pursue its objectives in open opposition to the other regimes.

His self-imposed moratorium on participation in inter-Arab politics and his seeming determination to concentrate on domestic affairs were of relatively short duration. By late 1962, Nasir responded to appeals for help from a group of Yemeni officers who had succeeded in staging a successful *coup d'état*. Having emerged from its "splendid isolation," Cairo once again threw itself into the thick of Arab politics, because this "progressive" Arab uprising against "imperialism and reaction" left it no other choice. However, the involvement came to constitute a drain upon Egyptian resources, which Nasir certainly did not anticipate and which ultimately made him more dependent upon the USSR than he would probably have wished to be.

Well aware of the fact that Cairo's relative isolation from inter-Arab politics and concentration on internal affairs (particularly on economic development) had made Nasir more than ever dependent on Soviet support, Moscow was not alarmed at the deterioration of Egypt's relations with the other Arab states. However, since the Kremlin was also interested in maintaining normal political and economic relations with both secessionist Syria and Qasim's Iraq, it is not surprising that the Soviet press did not devote a great deal of attention to, and refused to take sides in, these inter-Arab squabbles. Although some of his doctrinal formulations were criticized, Moscow, by and large, approved of Nasir's internal reforms. Commenting on the work of a preparatory commission charged with the summoning of the country's new parliament, *Pravda* held that the UAR government was in the process of revising some of its views as a result of the violent reaction with which the Egyptian and Syrian bourgeoisie had greeted the nationalization decrees of July 1961. Although Cairo had previously denied the necessity for a class struggle, President Nasir had begun to refer to it in his speeches of late 1961.⁴⁶

---

45. See Malcolm Kerr, *The Arab Cold War, 1958–1967: A Study of Ideology in Politics,* 2nd ed. (London: Oxford University Press, 1967), pp. 36, 37, 39.

46. I. Beliaev, *Pr.,* January 3, 1962.

On January 17, 1962, Nasir decreed the formation of the National Congress; the election of 1500 delegates to represent the peasants, the workers, the national intelligentsia, the national bourgeoisie, and the students was held a few weeks later. This move, in *Pravda*'s opinion, was of "great political importance." But of overriding significance was the fact that the current course of the Egyptian government was aimed at the "liquidation of big capital and of the landlords, the destruction of the last remnants of foreign domination in Egypt, [and] the activization of an anti-imperialist foreign policy." Since these measures implied nonparticipation in Western military blocs and a growing friendship with the "socialist bloc," they were enjoying the "widespread support of the broad masses of the UAR public."[47]

When the Congress that assembled on May 21, 1962, approved Nasir's so-called Charter of Arab Socialism, some of Moscow's ideological apprehensions concerning the future development of Egypt seemed justified. For this reason, initial Soviet comments on the Charter were confined to a mere description of some of its provisions, with no analysis at all.[48] Only in mid-July 1962, when the Soviet press, in keeping with its custom of the past several years, marked the anniversary of the Egyptian revolution, did V. Maevskii finally report President Nasir's rejection of some of the basic tenets of Marxism-Leninism (above all the notion of the "dictatorship of the proletariat") and his insistence on the intrinsic harmony between Islam and Arab socialism. These principles, Maevskii continued, had found their reflection in the Charter that had been adopted by the National Congress on June 30. As a result, the document mirrored not only the "transformations" that had taken place in Egypt after the 1952 revolution, but also the "contradictions" that were still very much in evidence in the country's socioeconomic development. Maevskii was not certain what kind of a political and economic system would emerge as the result of the Charter's application—another clear indication that the Krem-

---

47. *Ibid.,* February 17, 1962.
48. See *ibid.,* May 24. See also Akademiia nauk SSSR. Institut mirovoi ekonomiki i mezhdunarodnykh otnoshenii, *Mezhdunarodnye otnosheniia posle vtoroi mirovoi voiny (1956–1964)* (Moscow: Izdatel'stvo politicheskoi literatury, 1965), 3: 552–53. For some preliminary comments, see I. Beliaev, *Pr.,* May 11, 1962.

lin did not think very highly of Nasir's efforts at theorizing. Moreover, echoing an unnamed Cairo journalist, he asked what kind of socialism was being built in the UAR if "true socialists" were still kept in prisons.[49]

As might have been expected, the Egyptians were anything but elated by the sentiments expressed in *Pravda*. Replying to Maevskii, Galal Kishk of *Ruz al-Yusif* refused to recognize Moscow's insistence that Communists alone deserved to be called "true socialists" and that socialism could not exist outside the "Bolshevik church." In any event, it was time for the USSR to recognize that, in the Arab East, Arab socialism and not Arab Communism, was the driving force behind all the movements for "liberation, progress, and peace."[50]

Throughout the ensuing months, the Soviet press refrained from any analysis of the political developments in the UAR, apparently in the hope of keeping the lid on a potentially explosive situation. Similar treatment was also accorded to the nationalization of "all cotton and cotton ginning companies" and "pharmaceutical factories and distributing firms" in April and June 1963. It was not until mid-August 1963, when Cairo, "in the biggest operation since the 1961 decrees," took over "more than 200 industrial firms,"[51] that *Pravda* expressed its agreement with the policies of UAR Minister of Industry 'Aziz Sidqi. The decrees represented a "big new step on the path of strengthening the public sector" of Egypt's economy.[52]

During the second half of 1963, Moscow's official attitude toward the United Arab Republic warmed appreciably. An early indication of this impending change was contained in a *New Times* editorial devoted to the anniversary of the Egyptian revolution,[53] which stated flatly that Egypt had succeeded in wresting "complete and unhampered independence . . . [from] the imperialist powers." This, in turn,

49. V. Maevskii, *ibid.*, July 19, 1962.
50. *Ruz al-Yusif,* July 30, 1962.
51. Ivison Macadam, ed., *Annual Register of World Affairs, 1963,* p. 302.
52. *Pr.,* August 14, 1963.
53. The texts of Khrushchev's and Brezhnev's perfunctory telegrams to Nasir, stressing Cairo's "contributions to peace" and promising increases in Soviet aid are in *ibid.,* July 23, 1963.

enabled Cairo "to launch an ambitious programme of social and economic reforms," highlighted by the agrarian reform and the nationalization of industry. Most important of all, the editorial noted, significant changes were expected shortly in the political sphere as well. For President Nasir, in a recent interview with a correspondent of *Le Monde,* had said that the government had decided to "close all concentration camps and [to] enable citizens of differing political views to express them freely and share in the upbuilding of the country within the framework of the Arab Socialist . . . [Union]." Predictably, the *New Times* concluded that "the Soviet public welcome[d] these achievements of the Egyptian people."[54]

Words were soon followed by action. In mid-August, *Pravda* informed its readers that, in a special decree honoring the eleventh anniversary of the revolution, the UAR government had freed most of the country's political prisoners. World public opinion, *Pravda* noted, had received the decree with "great satisfaction."[55] The move, which removed an important ideological thorn from Moscow's side, led *Pravda* to conclude a few weeks later that "friendly relations between the Soviet Union and the UAR have improved considerably in the recent past."[56]

Soviet gratification made itself evident again in November 1963, when the Egyptian government ordered the nationalization of an additional 175 enterprises embracing "a wide range of manufacturing, transport, and storage firms."[57] Commenting on the nature of Cairo's recent economic and political reforms, *Pravda* described them as "serious measures," noting that the industrialization program went hand-in-hand with the elimination of private enterprise. Although shortcomings remained—particularly in agriculture, where the lack of cultivable land, capital, equipment, and water made development very difficult—the difficulties did not seem insurmountable, and substantial progress was expected in the near future. Problems also remained in streamlining and cleansing the state apparatus of "unrelia-

54. Editorial, "Egypt's 'Star Hour,' " *NT,* no. 29 (July 24, 1963), p. 4.
55. *Pr.,* August 16, 1963.
56. E. Primakov, *ibid.,* September 6, 1963.
57. Macadam, *Annual Register . . . , 1963,* p. 302.

ble elements" who were opposed to the government's socioeconomic and political reforms, because, "according to some Egyptian critics," the authorities were not moving far and fast enough. On balance, however, *Pravda* reached the ideologically important conclusion that Cairo's reforms were beginning to go *beyond* the framework of state capitalism and that, in Egypt, the groundwork was being laid for the transfer of the society to a "non-capitalist [i.e., socialist] path of development."

This was the first official reference to the fact that, in the eyes of the Soviet leaders, the UAR was moving to a "higher" level of development. Not surprisingly, the decisive criterion in determining the classification of the underdeveloped countries on Moscow's "capitalist-socialist" scale revolved around *political,* not socioeconomic, considerations. *Pravda* claimed that the final judgment on the status of the UAR would have to be reserved until such time as no doubts remained concerning the freedom of activity of the Egyptian Communist party. As Beliaev put it, Cairo would have to demonstrate that the "bold progressive measures . . . in the field of economics . . . would be combined with continuous care for the rise in the political activism of the toiling masses, [and that] all the patriotic, democratic strata of the country would be guaranteed an opportunity . . . to participate in the implementation [of the reforms]."[58]

Thus, after Nasir abandoned his anti-Communist campaign, Moscow's ideological campaign against Cairo ceased. It might be argued convincingly that, by the summer of 1963, the effectiveness of the Egyptian Communist party, after almost ten years of continuous and unrelenting government repression, had been reduced virtually to nil and that it no longer constituted any real or potential threat to Nasir. The lifting of restrictions against the Marxist elements may also have

---

58. I. Beliaev, *Pr.,* November 26, 1963. Georgii Mirskii, writing in early 1964, agreed: "Objectively, the reforms in the U.A.R. provide a basis for non-capitalist development. . . . [However,] they are a 'revolution from above' . . . and have not yet been attended by far-reaching democratization of public life." "The Changing Arab East," *NT,* no. 2 (January 15, 1964), pp. 5–6. For favorable subsequent comments, see Tuganova, pp. 142–50, and Akademiia nauk SSSR, *Noveishaia istoriia arabskikh stran,* pp. 423–31.

been designed to appease the Russians, who were concerned about Peking's accusations of ideological double-dealing.

Legitimate as these explanations might be, however, they do not fully explain the timing of Nasir's move, which was far more dependent on inter-Arab relations. Because tension and hostility between the UAR and Ba'thi-dominated Syria and Iraq had reached their highest level, an important area of overlapping interest between Cairo and the Syrian and Iraqi Communist parties was created: they were all hostile to the Ba'th and were actively working for its overthrow. Moveover, its ever-deepening alienation from the conservative Arab regimes, especially Jordan and Saudi Arabia, was intensified by Egypt's involvement in the Yemeni civil war. Since the royalist regime in Yemen also enjoyed a measure of Western backing, particularly from Great Britain, it was imperative for President Nasir to search for political reassurance and material support to aid the Yemeni republican forces. Once again the Kremlin was the logical place to turn, and the UAR leaders must have been fully aware of the fact that the release of Egyptian Communists was bound to make Moscow more receptive to Cairo's overtures.

As noted, Nasir's move was applauded in Moscow and led to a noticeable diminution of the ideological criticism of the United Arab Republic. This apparent cause-and-effect relationship makes it tempting to argue that the change in Soviet attitude was prompted solely by Cairo's initiative. The two were, of course, related. At the same time, part of Moscow's restraint in public criticism of the UAR as well as of most other developing nations was probably the result of growing awareness in the Kremlin that official Soviet backing of nonalignment (both in its traditional anti-Western form and, in the case of India, its anti-Chinese variation) was logically inconsistent with the denunciation of the "pseudo-socialist" tendencies of such "objectively progressive" leaders as Nasir, Ben Bella of Algeria, and Sékou Touré of Guinea. They and other recipients of Soviet aid usually reacted to such criticisms by accusing the USSR of interference in the internal affairs of their countries, and the resulting strains did nothing to improve Moscow's image as a "selfless" supporter of the developing nations.

In the particular case of the United Arab Republic, the decision to elevate it to the level of countries "embarking upon a non-capitalist path of development" may indeed have been facilitated by Nasir's lenience toward the local Communists. It may also have been dictated (though only if the decision to make the trip had already been made) by a desire to remove some of the ideological barriers between the two nations prior to Khrushchev's May 1964 visit to Egypt. On a more general level, Moscow may have wished to strengthen Nasir's hand in his feud with the Ba'th while also scoring propaganda points against its Chinese Communist rivals. To quote Georgii Mirskii:

> Analysis of the development of the U.A.R. shows that, dogmatist [i.e., Chinese Communist] views to the contrary, in our day of a world socialist system the prospects before former colonies . . . are infinitely wider and more diversified than before. . . . Initially, the Nasser movement leaned on the same social elements as the Al-Baath: the petty bourgeoisie, the intellectuals, the officers, the middle strata. But while the Baathist chiefs became servitors of the big bourgeoisie, the U.A.R. leaders proved equal to furthering the national interest.[59]

Since police surveillance over the released party members would be maintained and the government would crack down hard at the first sign of independent political activity, the release of the Communists was obviously of no practical political significance inside Egypt. Neither Cairo nor Moscow was in any way concerned about the fate of the prisoners; they simply formulated their policies as a matter of political expedience. When in late August 1963 the Egyptian weekly *al-Musawwar* subjected Arab Communists to a strong attack, Cairo may have already discovered that the Iraqi and Syrian Communists refused to cooperate with the Nasirist elements against the Ba'th. It is, however, also entirely possible that the outburst was aimed primarily at the Soviet Union and was intended to serve as a demonstration that the release of prisoners was not prompted by internal weakness and instability that could be used by the Kremlin to further its own interests in the UAR.

59. G. Mirsky, "The Changing Arab East," *NT,* no. 2 (January 15, 1964), p. 6.

In any event, it was probably no coincidence that the attack appeared in *al-Musawwar,* a periodical known for its strongly anti-Communist editorial policy,[60] and was written by Fikri 'Abaza, who charged that Arab Communists were "champions of neo-colonialism" and that the USSR had provided them with "money and weapons." While Arab Marxists were working for the overthrow of existing regimes in their respective countries, 'Abaza charged, Moscow also was endeavoring to force upon them its own brand of Communism.[61] *Pravda*'s reply would seem to indicate that Cairo's message was intended for Soviet rather than Arab Communist consumption—or was at least interpreted that way in Moscow. The UAR authorities were simply overlooked in the intimation that 'Abaza was insane. No rational man, *Pravda* argued, could accuse the Communists, "people who devoted their . . . [lives] to the . . . struggle against imperialism, colonialism, . . . [and] reaction," of backing neo-colonialism. Equally absurd were 'Abaza's charges concerning the alleged supply of Soviet money and weapons to the "Communist conspirators" in the Arab East, unless he was prepared to include the Egyptian government in this category.[62]

Despite such incidents, as long as Egypt, for whatever reason, pursued foreign policy objectives that clashed with Western political aims in the underdeveloped world, and as long as Cairo's activities in no way infringed on any vital Soviet interests, there was no reason why the USSR should not attempt to maintain friendly relations with it. At most, Khrushchev might criticize it as one of the many Asian and African nations that had eliminated outward political dependence on the West but nevertheless refused to get to the "roots" of their problems. Only by means of sweeping socioeconomic reforms could they settle the serious internal conflicts between "broad strata of the working people" and the conservative, pro-Western elements reluctant to part with their wealth and other privileges. Such nations, Khrushchev reported to the Twenty-second Congress of the CPSU,

60. For an earlier, heretofore-unmentioned exchange, see *al-Musawwar,* February 21, 1963. Soviet reply in editorial, "Anonymous Opus," *NT,* no. 9 (March 6, 1963), p. 21.
61. As quoted by E. Primakov, *Pr.,* September 6, 1963.
62. *Ibid.*

are often called neutralist, although they can be regarded as neutral only in the sense that they do not belong to any of the existing military-political alliances. But the majority of these countries are by no means neutral when it comes to the fundamental question of the day—the question of war and peace. As a rule, they take their stand for peace and against war.

The newly independent states had emerged as a "serious factor" in international relations. Hence the "basic issues of world politics can no longer be settled without regard for their interests."[63] In other words, the foreign policies pursued by the various neutralist governments were, for the time being, proclaimed of more importance to the Kremlin than their domestic politics.[64]

On balance, it would appear that, periodic mutual recriminations notwithstanding, Soviet-Egyptian relations were slowly but surely improving after their nadir at the time of the 1961 crisis. Not particularly noticeable in 1962, this trend gathered momentum in 1963 and finally "blossomed" into Khrushchev's visit to Egypt in May 1964. It is interesting to note, however, that even in the second half of 1962, when Cairo's political fortunes in the Arab East had reached an all-time low, Moscow refused to take sides in the Egyptian-Syrian tangle, though it did support Cairo's decision to intervene in Yemen's civil war on the side of the republican government—a position that no doubt influenced Egypt's unequivocal endorsement of Khrushchev at the time of the Cuban missile crisis.[65] The tone of Khrushchev's and Brezhnev's July 1963 telegram congratulating Nasir on the anniversary of the Egyptian revolution was unusually warm. It said, in part, that the Soviet people valued Egypt's "contribution to peace and the struggle against imperialism" and promised efforts to increase cooperation between the two countries because this "fully corresponds to the mutual interests of our people."[66] In his reply, Nasir agreed that their

63. Text in *ibid.*, October 18, 1961.
64. For elaboration of this theme, see the text of Khrushchev's telegram to Nasir on occasion of the fifth anniversary of Egypt's "victory" at Port Sa'id. *Ibid.*, December 24. See also E. Primakov, *ibid.*, December 23, 1961.
65. For details, see the Egyptian press of October 24, 1962, *et passim*.
66. Text in *Pr.*, July 23, 1963.

mutual relations were demonstrating the "reality of Soviet-Arab friendship and the strength of its foundations." In language that resembled Khrushchev's own phraseology, the UAR President referred to the Moscow-Cairo association as a "free revolutionary act in the struggle against imperialism for the sake of peace, prosperity, . . . and the liberation of man from all exploitation."[67]

It is significant in this connection that, while even as late as January 1963 Nasir occasionally reasserted his independence from Moscow, such references eventually disappeared from the pronouncements of Egyptian leaders and even from the pages of Egyptian publications.[68] It was not that Nasir and his colleagues had decided on a major shift in their policy, for they continued to adhere to nonalignment. However, as Egypt's inter-Arab fortunes continued to decline in mid- and late 1963 (the elimination of the hostile regimes in Baghdad and Damascus, far from improving Egypt's position in the Arab East, actually led to its further deterioration, and the Yemeni affair began to resemble quicksand swallowing Cairo's resources), Nasir found himself in an unenviable position. Since the Syrian and Iraqi Ba'th, in particular, had continued to accuse him of personal aggrandizement at the expense of Arab unity, Egypt's isolation had become almost as complete as it had been in the summer of 1962. Yet while the conservative regime in Syria and Qasim in Iraq had been easily written off as either pro-imperialist or just plain ineffective, similar accusations against the Ba'th made no sense at all. Its ideology was closely related to Nasir's philosophy, and its leaders were the same men with whom he on April 17, 1963, had agreed to form an Arab union. Hence he was forced to seek political and military backing from the Kremlin, which was extremely annoyed with the Ba'thi regimes in Baghdad and Damascus. Furthermore, because of the Western (primarily British) entanglement in the Yemeni civil war on the side of the monarchists, Moscow was glad to support Nasir's participation on the republican side. These circumstances merely

67. Text in *ibid.*, August 1, 1963.
68. For an example, see Nasir's address at the celebration of the third anniversary of the Aswan High Dam in early January 1963. I. Beliaev, *ibid.*, January 11, 1963.

served to make Cairo even more dependent on and theoretically more responsive to the USSR.[69] From the Kremlin's viewpoint, this was particularly desirable in late 1963–1964. Concerned with the deployment in the Eastern Mediterranean of US nuclear submarines, which brought most of European Russia within the range of Polaris missiles, Moscow decided to counter Washington's initiative by establishing there a permanent Soviet naval presence. To succeed, the Soviets had to secure facilities in the region, and Egypt was the logical place to do so.

Despite their occasionally strained political relations, the Kremlin continued to widen the scope of its economic and cultural cooperation with the United Arab Republic. Long-term trade and payments agreements with Egypt were signed not only by the USSR but also by Poland, Rumania, and Hungary.[70] There was further Soviet-UAR cooperation in the construction of the Aswan High Dam.[71] In short, by the spring of 1964, the extent of Soviet economic aid to Egypt had reached impressive dimensions.[72] Between 1962 and 1964, there was also a noticeable upsurge of Soviet military aid to the UAR,[73] as evidenced, in part, by the numerous visits of high Soviet and Egyptian functionaries to Cairo and Moscow, respectively. By the end of 1963, it had thus become evident that, partly as a result of the difficulties that the USSR as well as the UAR were encountering in their relations with Ba'thi-controlled Iraq and Syria and partly because of Nasir's involvement in Yemen, Moscow and Cairo were being drawn ever more tightly into the embrace of their marriage of convenience.

To put them in their proper perspective, the dissolution of the

69. For details of Moscow's support of Nasir's anti-Ba'thi campaign, see *ibid.*, October 26 and 31, 1963.
70. See *Izv.*, February 7, 1963; *Pr.*, June 24, 1962; *MEJ* 16, no. 4 (Autumn 1962): 505, and 17, nos. 1 and 2 (Winter-Spring 1963): 140, respectively.
71. See *MEJ* 16, no. 4 (Autumn 1962): 505; 17, nos. 1 and 2 (Winter-Spring 1963): 139; 17, no. 4 (Autumn, 1963): 442; and 18, no. 3 (Summer 1964): 349.
72. For more details, see *NT*, no. 19 (May 10, 1964), pp. 8–9, and *Pr.*, February 12, 1963.
73. *MEM*, no. 1 (January 5, 1963), p. 14, no. 52 (December 30, 1961), p. 11, and no. 42 (October 20, 1962), p. 19. See also *MEJ* 16, no. 4 (Autumn 1962): 505, and 17, no. 3 (Summer 1963): 310.

United Arab Republic and the ensuing tension between the various Arab states were not in and of themselves of overriding importance to the Kremlin. But they did once again illustrate the tenuous nature of the relationship between Moscow and its Arab clients. Moreover, they demonstrated the continuing inability of the USSR to use effectively the alleged influence that it had been so carefully cultivating in the Arab East since 1955.

PART III
THE LIMITS OF RAPPROCHEMENT, 1963–1964

9
The Ba'th Regimes in Iraq and Syria

When the military overthrew Premier Qasim on February 8, 1963, accusing him of "deviation from the principles of the July 14 revolution," most Iraqis hoped that the Revolutionary Command Council, headed by Colonel 'Abd al-Salam 'Arif, would provide the kind of enlightened leadership necessary to unite the country and move it out of the political isolation of the Qasim era.

These hopes proved short-lived since, for the next nine months, Iraq was ruled by one of the most bloodthirsty regimes in its modern history. The government was dominated by the Ba'th party, led by a triumvirate consisting of Brigadier Ahmad Hasan al-Bakr, the new Prime Minister; 'Ali Salih al-Sa'di, Deputy Premier, Minister of Interior (later of National Guidance) and Secretary-General of the Iraqi Ba'th; and Lieutenant-Colonel Salih Mahdi 'Ammash, Minister of Defense.[1] In its initial statements, the Revolutionary Command Council pledged to work for the attainment of "national unity" and "Arab-Kurdish fraternity" as well as for the realization of "Arab

1. Ivison Macadam, ed., *The Annual Register of World Events, 1963* (New York: St. Martin's Press, 1964), p. 311.

Union." Iraq's foreign relations were to be based on "anti-imperialism" and "respect for international obligations."[2]

By the summer of 1963, a deep split had developed in the ranks of the Ba'th, as the more moderate elements made known their objections to the mass terror being perpetrated by the so-called National Guard, a private army of the radical wing of the party headed by Secretary-General Sa'di, which gained widespread notoriety for arbitrary arrests, torture, and executions. While directed primarily against the Communists and, to a lesser extent, the Nasirites, the activities of the National Guard caused anxiety among all those who were opposed to the Ba'th.[3]

As the division within the Iraqi Ba'th became a matter of public knowledge, its fortunes declined steadily, and on November 18, 1963, General 'Arif staged his third successful *coup d'état*.[4] Not only had the party succeeded in alienating Cairo and Moscow, while reopening the bloody war against the Kurds and antagonizing all important segments of Iraqi society (including the army); it was also hopelessly divided by internal splits, intrigues, and power struggles. In addition, the Ba'th proved unable to implement the badly needed social and economic reforms.[5]

With the real power of the party temporarily broken, 'Arif reestablished close and friendly relations with Cairo and relatively close cooperation with the USSR. His success in negotiating a cease-fire with the Kurds was announced on February 10, 1964, and by the summer Baghdad appeared to have restored a measure of stability in the northern areas, as local administration was reinstated and promises were made to compensate and rehabilitate the victims of the war.[6] In early 1964, the government also turned its attention to economic

2. *Economist*, February 16, 1963, p. 577; and *MEM*, no. 6 (February 9, 1963), p. 3.

3. For more details, see E. F. Penrose, "L'Irak en 1963: une année de coups d'Etat," *Orient*, no. 28 (1963), pp. 22–26.

4. For details, see *MEM*, no. 46 (November 16, 1963), pp. 2–5; and no. 47 (November 23, 1963), pp. 2–7. See also *Economist*, November 23, 1963, pp. 745–46.

5. For a good general account, see Penrose, pp. 17–36. For more details, see *Economist*, July 6, 1963, p. 16.

6. For details, see *MEM*, no. 47 (November 23, 1963), pp. 2–7, and no. 7 (February 15, 1964), pp. 3–4 *et passim*.

and social reforms. On February 8, the authorities announced the formation of the Iraqi National Oil Company, empowered "to explore and develop oil throughout Iraq" with the exception of those areas leased to foreign oil companies,[7] and, in July, the government nationalized all banks, insurance companies, and the thirty-two leading industrial enterprises, with the exception of the Iraq Petroleum Company (IPC), the largest foreign concern operating in the country. Along with the establishment of the Arab Socialist Union, a political organization intended to harness the support of the masses behind the 'Arif regime and set up along the lines of its Egyptian counterpart, the nationalization move was intended to bring Iraq into line with Cairo's "progressive" and "forward-looking" orientation.[8]

Judging by its initial comments, the Kremlin was not particularly alarmed by the overthrow of the Qasim regime. On February 9 and 10, the Soviet press informed its readers that a group of officers had seized power in Iraq with the alleged aim of implementing the "real aims of the July 1958 revolution." It was also reported that Qasim and some of his close collaborators had been tried by a military tribunal, sentenced to death, and executed.[9] Despite the disquieting news that the Revolutionary Command Council had ordered the "elimination of Communists resisting the revolution,"[10] the USSR, along with the United States and Great Britain, recognized the Ba'thi regime on February 11, 1963. This decision was explained in terms of respect for the sovereign rights of other states and recognition of the right of each people to determine the form of government under which they wished to live. The Kremlin expressed the hope that "friendship and coopera-

---

7. *MEJ* 18, no. 2 (Spring 1964): 219. For details, see *Economist*, February 15, 1964, p. 636.
8. *Ibid.*, July 18, 1964, p. 238.
9. *Pr.*, February 9 and 10, 1963, respectively.
10. *MEJ* 17, nos. 1 and 2 (Winter-Spring 1963): 115. It might be noted parenthetically that the Ba'th's violent reaction was motivated, in part, by the armed resistance against the coup that had been staged by the Communists in Baghdad and other cities. As a noted Marxist subsequently disclosed, "When the coup was staged on the morning of February 8, our Party immediately called upon the people to resist it." For details, see Aziz Al-Hajj, "The Current Situation In Iraq." *WMR*, no. 11 (November 1963), p. 37. See also O. E. Tuganova, *Mezhdunarodnye otnosheniia na Blizhnem i Srednem Vostoke* (Moscow: Izdatel'stvo "Mezhdunarodnye otnosheniia," 1967), p. 123.

tion" between the two countries would be maintained and strengthened.[11]

The first public indication of Soviet displeasure with the turn of events in Iraq appeared on February 14, when *Pravda* reprinted a French Communist party statement protesting "bloody repressions against [Iraqi] democrats." The next day, it praised the Iraqi Communists as "staunch and heroic fighters against repression and oppression" and reminded the Ba'thi leaders that hundreds of Marxists had been imprisoned by the pro-Western regime of Nuri al-Sa'id. "They were subjected to inhuman tortures, but the executioners failed to break their fighting spirit," and they emerged "in the forefront of those who staged the July 1958 revolution." Now, the Ba'th was following Nuri's "tragic example" by endeavoring "to destroy . . . the most consistent fighters for the happiness of the Arab peoples."[12] On February 16, the Central Committee of the CPSU—in a move so rare that it attested to the degree of the Kremlin's annoyance—issued an official statement condemning the "bloody terror" against Iraq's Marxist elements. Repeating the arguments that had appeared in *Pravda,* the statement added that the "persecution of the Communists [was] in conflict with the . . . policy of national unity, freedom, democracy, and social justice" proclaimed by the Ba'th. In suppressing the "progressive elements," Baghdad only served the "cause of reaction" and weakened the "unity of the nation in the defense of its interests against the encroachments of imperialism." The CPSU, along with "all the Soviet people," was "alarmed" at the turn of events in Iraq but expressed confidence that the "policy of banditry and destruction of the best sons of the Iraqi people will collapse. The freedom-loving people of Iraq will find the strength to repel [this] brutal reaction through concerted and energetic action."[13]

In his first report from post-revolutionary Baghdad, P. Demchenko accused the Ba'th of "terrorist acts against the progressive elements," noting that the National Guard appeared to have been established for

11. Text in *Pr.,* February 12, 1963.
12. See also *Izv.,* February 15, 1963. For details of Ba'thi persecution, see *MEM,* no. 7 (February 16, 1963), pp. 3–4.
13. Text in *Pr.,* February 17, 1963.

the exclusive purpose of destroying the Communists and their sympathizers. Along with the army and the police, the Guard was acting on the strength of the National Revolutionary Council's "Declaration No. 13," which described the Marxists as "supporters of Qasim" and ordered their physical elimination. When questioning Foreign Minister Talib Shabib about the government's anti-Communist attitude, Demchenko was told that the revolutionary regime did not attempt to combat Marxism as an ideology but was merely trying to eliminate those who had actively backed Qasim and continued to oppose the Ba'thi government. In reality, commented Demchenko, this meant death to hundreds, perhaps thousands, of people.[14]

Moscow was particularly annoyed by the Western endorsement of the anti-Communist activities of the Ba'th. The fact that the *New York Times* and other prominent "capitalist" newspapers applauded Baghdad's "brave measures," testified beyond the shadow of a doubt that the "anti-Communist hysteria in Iraq plays into the hands of the reactionaries and imperialists—the enemies of the Arab national liberation movement."[15] Nevertheless, the USSR refrained temporarily from lodging any official protests with the Iraqi government. The Soviet embassy in Baghdad disclaimed any such intention as late as February 18, 1963.[16]

The most striking feature of the Iraqi response in the early stages of the propaganda tussle was its relative mildness—motivated, no doubt, by a desire to aggravate an already delicate situation no more than was necessary. The only newspaper allowed to appear in the early post-revolutionary period, *al-Jamahir*, avowed, on February 17, that the Communists were "irreconcilable enemies" of the Iraqi people and warned that it was not in "anyone's interest" to defend them. The Ba'thi "battle with Communism" was not motivated by ideological considerations; it was merely a struggle for self-preservation against the enemies of the Iraqi people. *Al-Jamahir* stated categorically that internal events were not designed or intended to affect Iraq's

---

14. *Ibid.*, February 18, 1963. For more details, see "Stay the Hand of Reaction in Iraq," *WMR*, no. 3 (March 1963), pp. 82–83.
15. E. Maksimov, *Pr.*, February 21, 1963.
16. *MEM*, no. 8 (February 23, 1963), p. 6.

relations with the Soviet Union: the Ba'th strongly believed in "maintaining the strongest ties with the Socialist states" and urged them "to take the initiative in establishing such ties."[17] On February 21, Prime Minister Bakr, in an interview with *al-Jamahir,* criticized the mounting Soviet campaign in defense of the Iraqi Marxists:

> Certain states are carrying out a reckless campaign against the government's measures against the Communists. The Soviet Government, along with all world states, recognized the revolutionary Iraqi Republic, and we thanked it for the move. A strange hostile campaign followed. The promoters of this campaign will bear reponsibility for worsening relations between the friendly Iraqi and Soviet peoples.[18]

When the Baghdad authorities intensified the campaign of terror against the country's Marxist elements—on February 24 "reliable sources" in the Iraqi capital announced that three leading Communists had been arrested and another one killed in an alleged "gun battle" with the police[19]—Moscow again warned the Ba'th not to play into the hands of the "imperialists" by persecuting the country's "progressive elements":

> The recent events in Iraq have once more confirmed one of the most indisputable lessons of the liberation movement of peoples; a split of national unity, the suppression of democratic freedom, the persecution of the progressive forces, inevitably jeopardize the newly attained national independence and are in irreconcilable contradiction with the vital interests of the young sovereign states. . . .
> The danger arises that imperialist forces, resorting to the tested

---

17. As quoted in *ibid.*

18. As quoted in *ibid.,* p. 7. Similar sentiments were expressed by Minister of State Hashim Jawad at a press conference of February 23. Details in *ibid.,* no. 9 (March 2, 1963), pp. 9–10.

19. Apprehended were Husayn Ahmad al-Radhawi, alias Salam 'Adil, the powerful Secretary-General of ICP; 'Abd al-Qadhir Isma'il al-Bustani; and 'Aziz al-Sharif, leader of the Peace Partisans, who had enjoyed considerable political influence in the early days of the Qasim regime. Sharif's deputy, Tawfiq Munir, had reportedly been killed while resisting arrest. See *MEJ* 17, nos. 1 and 2 (Winter-Spring 1963): 116, and *MEM,* no. 9 (March 2, 1963), p. 9.

methods of bribery, blackmail, and intrigue, will be able to push the country . . . onto the path of renouncing the policy of neutralism and of submitting to imperialist orders, and, specifically, to the orders of the oil monopolies.

Not to see the "grave consequences" of anti-Communism, *Pravda* concluded after an examination of Qasim's experiences along similar lines, was to be either politically blind or to serve as an "outright agent of imperialism."[20] Undaunted, the National Revolutionary Council, on February 28, appealed to the public to provide the authorities with "precise and disinterested" information on "anarchists and saboteurs."[21]

On March 9, Military Governor-General Rashid Muslih announced that three leaders of the Iraqi Communist party had been executed two days earlier[22] and this "monstrous act" prompted the Central Committee of the CPSU to express "anger and indignation at the bloody violence against prominent figures of the Iraqi Communist party . . . [and to] resolutely protest against this new act of barbarous repression."[23] Numerous protest meetings took place throughout the Soviet Union on March 12 and 13, culminating on March 14 in a mass demonstration before the Iraqi embassy in Moscow, where mobs vandalized the building.[24] The strongly worded protest note from the Iraqi government accused the Soviet authorities

20. *Pr.*, February 26, 1963. The same theme was sounded by G. Mirsky, "The Coup d'Etat in Iraq," *NT*, no. 8 (February 27, 1963), pp. 10–12. See also Ibrahim Saadi, "The February Events in Iraq," *WMR*, no. 4 (April 1963), pp. 37–39.
21. *MEM*, no. 9 (March 2, 1963), p. 10.
22. They were Husayn Ahmad al-Radhawi, Muhammad Husayn 'Abd al-'Ays, a Central Committee member, and Hasan 'Uwayni, the Central Committee's liaison officer. According to Muslih, a military tribunal had found them guilty of "conspiring to overthrow the government, inciting the people against the government and murdering civilians and soldiers." See *ibid.*, p.11.
23. Text in *Pr.*, March 12, 1963. Initial comment in *ibid.*, March 10, 1963. See also "In Memory of Hussein Ahmed Al-Radhawi (Salam Adil)," *WMR*, no. 4 (April 1963), p. 36.
24. *Pr., Izv.*, March 13 and 14, 1963. For an account of the March 14 demonstration, see *Pr.*, March 15. For general comment, see editorial, "Black Days in Iraq," *NT*, no. 12 (March 27, 1963), pp. 2–3.

of negligence in failing to protect the Iraqi embassy. Commenting on the note, Minister of State Hashim Jawad expressed the hope that the "information services in the Soviet Union and other socialist countries would discontinue their unjust attacks on Iraq" and would cease to support "a handful of hired killers who constituted the main pillar of the [Qasim] . . . regime."[25]

On April 5, the *Iraqi Times* reported that the property of the ICP had been impounded.[26] Finally, on May 14 a civil court in Baghdad "granted the government's request to dissolve the Iraqi communist party, and ordered the closure of party branches throughout the country and seizure of [its] property." The injunction said, in part, that the organization was an "agent party," as evidenced by its attitude toward the February 1963 revolution.[27] Secret trials and executions of Communists and their sympathizers continued into the summer and fall of 1963.[28] On one occasion, Khrushchev interceded personally on behalf of three Iraqi women who, according to *Pravda*, had allegedly been sentenced to death because of their membership in the Communist party.[29] In his reply 'Arif denied that the three women had been sentenced to death and asked Khrushchev not to believe "false reports against the national government of Iraq and Arab nationalism which are fighting imperialism."[30]

On July 3, the authorities announced that "a communist attempt to overthrow the Iraqi Government [had been] quickly and decisively crushed in the early hours" of that day. The leaders of the coup allegedly had planned to proclaim a Communist regime, to draw away from the United Arab Republic, to dissolve the National Guard, and

25. *MEM*, no. 12 (March 23, 1963), p. 15. See also *ibid.*, no. 15 (April 13, 1963), p. 15; and *MEJ* 17, no. 3 (Summer 1963): 297.
26. *Ibid.* For details, see *MEM*, no. 20 (May 18, 1963), p. 19.
27. *Ibid.*
28. For some details, see *MEM*, no. 23 (June 8, 1963), p. 20; *MEJ* 17, no. 4 (Autumn 1963): 424; *Pr.*, May 27, June 1, 2, 6; and *Izv.*, May 28, 1963.
29. *Pr.*, June 19, 1963. Text of Khrushchev's telegram of June 19, 1963, in *Izv.*, June 21, 1963.
30. *MEM*, no. 26 (June 29, 1963), p. 24. The receipt of 'Arif's telegram was not publicly acknowledged in Moscow, and its text did not appear in the Soviet press.

to restore the People's Resistance groups.³¹ As might have been expected, Moscow denied that the ICP was behind the July 2–3 disturbances at Camp Rashid, a military base in the vicinity of Baghdad. In reality, wrote *Pravda,* the riots had been caused by soldiers refusing to fight against the Kurds.³² The whole episode, it was argued, was not the result of any "conspiracy," but simply attested to the "profound dissatisfaction of the broad popular masses with the actions of the Ba'thi authorities."³³

Predictably, the Camp Rashid incident merely intensified the government's determination to destroy the power of the Iraqi Communist party. Dozens, perhaps hundreds, of Marxists and their sympathizers were executed during July and August 1963, including three members of the ICP's Central Committee alleged to have been involved in the "abortive coup" of July 3.³⁴ While the Soviet press unleashed a flood of protests concerning the "bloody reprisals" against Iraqi Communists and expressed the "horror and indignation" felt by "progressive mankind" over the murder of thousands of "fighters for peace and democracy,"³⁵ Baghdad, on July 27, publicly accused the First Secretary of the Bulgarian embassy of master-minding and supervising the disturbances at Camp Rashid.³⁶

Commenting on the "acts of unbridled terror," *Pravda* noted that, during the summer and early fall of 1963, the anti-Communist campaign in Iraq had reached its peak. "Outright annihilation," instituted in the wake of the Ba'thi coup of February 8, gave way, under the pressure of world public opinion, to executions ordered by the "legal" emergency military tribunals set up for the purpose of passing "mass

31. *Ibid.,* no. 27 (July 6, 1963), pp. 2–3.
32. Hostilities were reopened on June 10. Details below.
33. *Pr.,* July 9, 1963.
34. They were Jamal al-Haydari, 'Abd al-Jabbar Wahbi, and Muhammad Salih al-Abbasi. See *MEJ* 17, no. 4 (Autumn 1963): 426. For more details, see *MEM,* no. 30 (July 27, 1963), p. 18; and no. 36 (September 7, 1963), p. 17.
35. Details in the Soviet press of July 12 *et passim.* See also Ali Mohamed, "Call to Account the Murderers in Iraq," *WMR,* no. 7 (July 1963), pp. 88–89.
36. Secretary Nikolov, along with four minor embassy officials and an East German consular official, was expelled from Iraq on July 21. *MEM,* no. 31 (August 3, 1963), p. 10.

death sentences." According to the Iraqi press, more than 120 persons had been executed. That list, however, *Pravda* contended, was far from complete. Hundreds more had been executed secretly and hundreds had perished in prisons and concentration camps as a result of "barbarous torture."[37] The Soviet view of the Ba'thi regime in Iraq was subsequently summarized as follows: "In place of [Qasim's] dictatorship was installed a savage tyranny; a reactionary government was replaced by fascism."[38]

The Kremlin's unconcealed indignation was caused not only by the violent anti-Communism of the Ba'th, but also, at least officially, by Baghdad's war against the Kurds, which was renewed in June 1963. Interestingly, the Soviet government appeared reasonably certain of Baghdad's determination to settle the Kurdish problem by the use of arms as early as May 6, when an authoritative statement appeared in *Pravda*. "Commentator" went out of his way to emphasize that the Kurdish Democratic party and other "freedom-fighters" were not separatists but, "acting within the framework of the Iraqi Republic," were demanding the "right to have their own autonomous government and parliament [and] to express the will of the Kurdish people." In addition, the Kurds wanted fuller participation in the economic growth of the country because their region, though it was Iraq's chief oil-producing area, was among the nation's poorest and most backward provinces. Baghdad, while paying lip service to an alleged determination to implement the goals of the July 14 revolution, was pursuing a "policy of terror and repression against those who [had] contributed to the successes of the young Iraqi republic." The resulting division of national forces had weakened the "efforts of the entire Iraqi nation in the defense of its interests against the intrigues of imperialism." In view of these considerations, "Commentator" hoped that the Kurdish problem would "find a solution in the framework of the new federal government."

37. *Pr.*, October 6, 1963.
38. Editorial, "The Changing Arab East," *NT*, no. 2 (January 15, 1964), p. 3. For subsequent description, see Tuganova, pp. 125–26; and Akademiia nauk SSSR. Institut narodov Azii, *Noveishaia istoriia arabskikh stran (1917–1966)* (Moscow: Izdatel'stvo "Nauka," 1968) pp. 197–98.

On June 10, after the Kurds had rejected an ultimatum demanding their unconditional surrender within a 24-hour period, units of the Iraqi army began military operations. In its initial comment, *Pravda* accused Baghdad of a "treacherous breach of promise, . . . [of] persisting in its policy of anti-Communism [and of] smothering the democratic movement."[39]

On June 16, the Kremlin escalated its propaganda war against the Iraqi government, officially accusing it of genocide against the "defenseless peaceful inhabitants of Kurdish villages and towns," a policy that "contradicts elementary human rights [and] the Charter of the United Nations." The Ba'thi regime was warned that, "having adopted methods of terror and oppression," it had taken upon itself a "heavy responsibility for the consequences of its actions": the door was now open for the penetration of the country by the "imperialist forces," thus endangering peace in the whole of the Middle East. "For these reasons," the Statement concluded, "the Soviet Union cannot but display deep interest in everything which is happening in Iraq today."[40] In reply, a spokesman for the Ministry of National Guidance called the TASS Statement "a break with recognized practice and a flagrant interference in an internal affair which concerned only the Iraqi people."[41]

On June 20, 1963, another of "Commentator's" articles, entitled "Stop the Crimes in Iraq!," delivered a thinly veiled threat to cut off Soviet aid to Iraq if the government persevered in its policy of persecution of Communists and of war against the Kurds. The article was important in that it cast grave doubts on Moscow's claims of "unselfish and unconditional aid" to the Third World countries. Accusing the "nationalist-fascist" Ba'th of genocide against the Kurds and of "mass-murders" of Iraqi "patriots," "Commentator" repeated the

---

39. P. Demchenko, *Pr.,* June 12, 1963. For the Soviet view of the negotiations between the Kurds and the Ba'th, see F. Seiful-Mulyukov, "The Ba'thist War on the Kurds," *NT,* no. 25 (June 26, 1963), pp. 24–25. For general background, see P. Demchenko, *Irakskii Kurdistan v ogne* (Moscow: Gospolitizdat, 1963).
40. *Pr.,* June 16, 1963. See also *Krasnaia Zvezda* of the next day.
41. *MEJ* 17, no. 4 (Autumn 1963): 425.

Kremlin's earlier warning that the USSR could not "remain indifferent to the events unfolding in Iraq." Besides Moscow's "holy duty to aid the peoples struggling for national liberation," the Soviet government was alarmed at hostilities in "immediate proximity" to the borders of the USSR, a region which the "imperialists regard as a springboard for aggressive actions against the socialist countries."[42]

As military activities in northern Iraq continued to intensify, Mongolia, on June 29, requested that the United Nations General Assembly consider the "policy of genocide" being pursued by the Iraqi government against the Kurdish people, and on July 9, the USSR asked that a similarly worded item be included in the agenda of the UN Economic and Social Council. The Soviet motion was turned down because the majority of the Council members regarded the war in Kurdistan as a "purely internal" affair and "denied that there was sufficient evidence of genocide to justify the inclusion of the matter on the Council's agenda." On the same day, the USSR government dispatched a letter to the President of the Security Council informing him that should the situation continue to be aggravated, it might be forced to request the Council to "put an end to . . . the outside interference" which it alleged was now taking place in Iraq.[43] On July 10, Baghdad, in turn, protested against "unwarranted interference by the USSR in the internal affairs of Iraq," which, if continued, "could only have the gravest consequences for international peace and security." The letter to the Security Council insisted that only "limited military operations [were] being conducted in a small area . . . against a band of traitorous outlaws who were being supplied by foreign interests with the aim of dismembering the Iraqi State."[44]

In conjunction with its moves in the United Nations, the Kremlin

42. *Pr.*, June 20, 1963. For more details on the Kurdish situation, see the Soviet press of June 21 *et passim*. The Iraqi press brushed off the Soviet threat, while protesting against Moscow's "brazen and open interference in the internal affairs of Iraq." Details in *MEM*, no. 27 (July 6, 1963), p. 20.
43. United Nations, *Yearbook of the United Nations, 1963* (New York: Columbia University Press, 1965), pp. 74 and 73, respectively. See also D. Lozinov, *Pr.*, July 8, 1963. More on the alleged Western involvement in V. Petrov, *Izv.*, July 7, 1963.
44. See United Nations, pp. 73–74.

also lodged official protests with the governments of Iraq, Syria, Turkey, and Iran, objecting to what it described as the "interference of other states in the events taking place in northern Iraq. This interference," it was held, "represents a definite threat to the cause of maintaining peace in the Near and Middle East region." More specifically, in the statement handed by Gromyko to Iraqi Ambassador Faysal Haysaran, Moscow claimed to be in possession of information to the effect that "member states of the colonialist military bloc, the Central Treaty Organization, . . . have started out on a path of interference in the events taking place in the north of Iraq, even going so far as to implement measures of a military nature." Iraq, along with Turkey and Iran, the note insisted, had reached an agreement on "joint military operations against the Kurds," while the Syrian armed forces were already participating in the hostilities. The granting of bases near the Soviet border to "foreign forces that are linked with aggressive military . . . blocs" created a "threat to the security of . . . the USSR" and prompted the Soviet government to issue this "forewarning" in the "sincere hope" that Baghdad would "put an end to foreign interference" in Iraqi Kurdistan. The note ended with a conciliatory gesture: "The Soviet government takes this occasion to state that, given a reciprocal desire on the part of Iraq, it will in the future conduct a policy of developing good relations with the Iraqi Republic."[45]

In an article that appeared in *Pravda* on July 11, Viktor Maevskii disclosed some of the details of CENTO's alleged participation in the war against the Kurds. The border between Iraq on the one hand and Turkey and Iran on the other had been closed to prevent the escape of the "rebels" into the neighboring countries and to stop a possible flow of supplies from the Kurds living in Turkey and Iran. Iraqi military planes were free to cross into the neighboring countries. Finally, Turkish and Iranian forces were massed along the Iraqi frontier. All this activity enjoyed the backing of the imperialist powers, bent on creating a new military alliance by drawing both Iraq and

---

45. Text in *Pr.*, July 10, 1963. As already mentioned, similar notes were also handed to the Iranian, Turkish, and Syrian ambassadors. Text of the note to Iran in *ibid.*

Syria into the "aggressive" Central Treaty Organization. It is noteworthy that the Maevskii article concluded with a threat that the diplomatic notes did not contain: "The continuation of foreign intervention in the events of northern Iraq may make it necessary for other states to adopt measures designed to eliminate this intervention and to protect their security."[46]

As might have been expected, the Iraqi government rejected the Soviet note. On July 11, a Foreign Ministry spokesman stated over Radio Baghdad that Iraq would not tolerate any foreign quarter "establishing itself as a patron of the insurgents." He also denied allegations concerning Syrian and other foreign intervention on the side of government forces fighting the Kurdish rebels.[47] It is noteworthy that the statement brushed aside Moscow's apparent desire to normalize relations with Iraq.

This attitude of the Ba'thi authorities left the Kremlin no choice but to continue its propaganda barrage against Iraq in the hope that the strongly anti-Communist regime would eventually be overthrown by more moderate elements.[48] One important article, entitled "Behind the Baghdad Reign of Terror," published in the *New Times* in late August 1963, argued that the Ba'thi coup in Iraq (as well as in Syria) was not an "internal affair," but had been "instigated and prepared from outside, with the help of the American and British secret services." A series of detailed accusations led to the conclusion that "the 1958 revolution has been betrayed, the people deceived, Iraq's sovereignty sold out. The Baath Party has become a tool of imperialist policy in the Middle East."[49]

46. *Ibid.,* July 11, 1963. For more details on "imperialist involvement" in Iraqi affairs, see *ibid.,* July 17, and V. Petrov, *Izv.,* July 19, 1963.
47. *MEM,* no. 28 (July 13, 1963), p. 7.
48. For details, see the Soviet press for the period between mid-July and early November, 1963. See also editorial, "Soap Bubbles," *NT,* no. 32 (August 14, 1963), p. 22; M. Mairakov, "Stop the Atrocities against the Kurds," *IA,* no. 8 (August 1963), pp. 55–59; Amin Salimov, "Iraqi Coup: Cause and Effect," *ibid.,* no. 9 (September 1963), pp. 43–45; and Arabe Shamilov, "The Kurds, Their Past and Present," *NT,* no. 40 (October 9, 1963), pp. 26–27.
49. V. Katin, "Behind the Baghdad Reign of Terror," *NT,* no. 33. (August 21, 1963), p. 7. For subsequent discussion, see Tuganova, pp. 126–28; and Akademiia nauk SSSR, *Noveishaia istoriia . . . ,* pp. 199–200.

By the fall of 1963, although diplomatic relations between the two countries had not been broken off, the Soviet anti-Iraqi propaganda output was both substantial and vitriolic in content. The bitterness of the attacks was prompted by Moscow's frustration at the turn of events in Iraq (and Syria) and was reinforced by the exigencies of the Sino-Soviet dispute. It is highly doubtful that the Kremlin was seriously concerned with the fate of the Iraqi Kurds as such. But the very existence of the Kurdish problem provided some leverage on *any* Iraqi government, should the need for such pressure arise. What Moscow may have failed to realize—adding yet another item to its lengthening list of miscalculations—is that fanning and controlling a crisis are two different things; the ability to do one does not automatically confer power to accomplish the other. In any event, between February and November 1963, Moscow's ability to preserve the appearance of a "disinterested and unselfish friend" of those neutralist regimes which refused to tie themselves to the "imperialist chariot" was greatly strained.

Commenting on the events leading to 'Arif's third successful coup on November 18, which resulted largely from the split of the Iraqi Ba'th into three warring factions, Moscow asserted that "the Baath leaders fell victim to their own insatiable lust for power. This was the mainspring of all their actions; and the same goes for their ideology, based on reactionary nationalism and anti-communism. "[50] *Pravda* found it significant that power was now concentrated in the hands of a group of military leaders headed by 'Arif, who was described as not being a member of the Ba'th. Of "greatest importance" was the fact that the new government had ordered the dissolution of the National Guard which, by instituting in the country an "impossible situation," had threatened the very future of Iraq.[51] While *Pravda* expressed optimism that the "patriotic officers . . . [had] rejected the programs and terror" of the Ba'th, the *New Times,* having apparently learned to approach all changes in the Arab East with considerable caution,

50. Y. Bochkaryov, "Baathist Bankruptcy," *NT,* no. 47 (November 27, 1963), pp. 6–7. For more details, see E. Primakov, *Pr.,* November 14, and P. Demchenko, *ibid.,* November 16, 1963.
51. E. Primakov, *Pr.,* November 20; and *ibid.,* November 19, 1963.

warned that "it would be idle to speculate on the further pattern of events or probable policies of the new regime, for Iraq has so often proved unpredictable." Only one thing seemed certain: "the collapse of the Baathist regime in Iraq signifies the bankruptcy of Baathism as such."[52]

While the Soviet press initially refrained from commenting on the measures instituted by 'Arif, subsequent publications expressed approval of the new regime's program, which was announced on November 26, 1963. Internally, the government stated its determination to proceed with the implementation of "Arab Socialism," to guarantee "freedom, equality, and safety" to all citizens, to secure the election of a National Council, and to establish a National Oil Company. The only negative aspect (from the Soviet view) of the domestic program was the prohibition of political activity in the trade unions and the army. In its foreign relations, the government expressed its intention to abide by the principles of positive neutralism, to work for peace and against colonialism, to seek unity with the other Arab states (above all the UAR), and to restore normal relations with the Soviet Union and the other socialist countries.[53]

In the meantime, the Soviet press continued to subject to close scrutiny the attitude of the 'Arif government toward two problems that, in the past, had caused so much ill will between the USSR and Iraq: the fate of the "progressive elements" and Baghdad's relations with the Kurds. After *Pravda* reported in late December 1963 that military tribunals were sentencing scores of Communists to hard labor for membership in the proscribed ICP and for unspecified "subversive activities,"[54] the Soviet press protested against "Bloody Repressions in Iraq."[55] This campaign came to an abrupt halt in mid-January 1964, probably because the Iraqi authorities had in fact

52. Bochkaryov, p. 7.
53. Akademiia nauk SSSR, *Noveishaia istoriia . . .* , p. 201.
54. *Pr.*, December 20 and 27; and *Izv.*, December 31, 1963. For more details, including news of a trial of a former Iraqi military attaché in Moscow, accused of handing over secret maps to Soviet authorities, see *MEM*, no. 1 (January 4, 1964), p. 9. See also Ali Mohamed, "The Terror in Iraq Continues," *WMR*, no. 2 (February 1964), pp. 90–91.
55. See, for example, *Pr.*, January 2, 6, and 11, 1964.

considerably scaled down their efforts to destroy the Iraqi Communist organization. The 'Arif regime also proceeded to adopt a policy of reconciliation in its relations with the Kurds, and Soviet publications noted with satisfaction statements to the effect that the Kurds would enjoy equal rights with the other Iraqi citizens and that peace in northern Iraq would be rapidly restored by nonmilitary means.[56] In view of these circumstances, *Pravda* noted, the "Iraqi Kurds have the right to expect from the new government a peaceful and just settlement of the Kurdish problem."[57]

The extent of Moscow's gratification was reflected in Khrushchev's telegram to 'Arif, dated February 15, 1964. The Soviet Premier hailed 'Arif's decision to end the "fratricidal war" as a "statesman-like act" that was bound to "strengthen peace in the Near East" while raising the "prestige of the Iraqi Republic in the eyes of the peoples of the world." Respect for the aspirations of the Kurds would enable Baghdad to unite "all the healthy and progressive forces of the nation," to strengthen Iraq's independence, and to raise the living standards of its population. Khrushchev wished 'Arif success on this "correct path." In his reply, the Iraqi President thanked the USSR government for its concern and good wishes and expressed his determination to strengthen the "national unity" of Iraq. He assured Khrushchev that Arabs and Kurds had lived "as brothers for millenniums" and that "people who resort to intrigues will never succeed in bringing about a split between them."[58]

In early March, Soviet publications reported that the truce agreement of February 1964 was being implemented. The imperialist powers were nonetheless spreading lies and rumors in an effort to implant doubts about the feasibility of the Iraqi-Kurdish accord. These activities were understandable, it was held, for the colonialist nations had

---

56. *Ibid.*, November 23 and 26, 1963, respectively. See also *ibid.*, November 28 and December 26, 1963.

57. G. Sibiriak, *ibid.*, November 27, 1963. For more details, see *ibid.*, February 12; E. Primakov, *ibid.*, February 13, 1964. See also *Izv.*, February 12, 1964, and editorial, "End of the War in Iraq," *NT*, no. 8 (February 26, 1964), pp. 2–3.

58. Texts in *Pr.*, February 16 and 20, 1964, respectively.

used the war to keep Iraq weak and divided in order to be able to exploit its natural riches and, perhaps, to draw it into the sphere of Western political-military influence. Fortunately, *Pravda* concluded, the elimination of the Ba'th had terminated Iraq's dependence on the imperialists: "Peace in the country and settlement of the Kurdish problem are now in the hands of the Iraqi government and people."[59]

By March 1964, relations between Moscow and Baghdad had thus taken a definite turn for the better. The opening of the broad-gauge railway line between Baghdad and Basra on March 10, constructed with the aid of the USSR under the terms of the 1959 technical aid agreement, served as a clear demonstration of Iraqi-Soviet friendship. The ceremonies were attended by Prime Minister Tahir Yahya and the Soviet Deputy Minister of Communications and Development.[60]

The issue of Baghdad's treatment of the "progressive elements" still remained, however, and it is noteworthy that, in late March and early April 1964, Moscow felt obliged to warn 'Arif to cease the persecution of the ICP. In an article entitled "Not in the Interests of Iraq," *Pravda* hailed the decision to stop the war against the Kurds but noted that it now appeared that "some circles . . . , especially those connected with Ba'th . . . , want to divert the government from the correct path . . . [by] setting afire . . . a campaign of persecution against Communists and democrats." More particularly, the Ministry of Justice had organized trials against "democrats" on the basis of accusations "fabricated" during the fascist rule of the Ba'th at a time when "official circles" in Baghdad were contending that they sought friendship with the "socialist" countries. "Could it be," *Pravda* inquired, "that such a course is not to the liking of the functionaries of the Justice Ministry who advance . . . ridiculous accusations against democrats, active fighters for peace?" Surely, it concluded, persecution of the Communists was aimed at "splitting the patriotic forces of the Iraqi people" and was favored only by the "imperialists and their henchmen."[61]

59. I. Beliaev, *ibid.*, March 10, 1964. For more details, see *ibid.*, March 12 and 25; and *Izv.*, March 20, 1964.
60. Details in *MEM*, no. 11 (March 14, 1964), p. 18. For Soviet comment, see M. Arkhangel'skii, *Pr.*, March 10, and *ibid.*, March 12, 1964.
61. Iu. Potomov, *Pr.*, March 24, 1964. Similar arguments, stressing the

On May 4, 1964, the 'Arif regime promulgated a provisional Constitution that produced a notable lack of enthusiasm in the USSR.[62] This Soviet attitude was explained in a later publication: the document did not satisfy the Kurdish demands for autonomy; it was limited to a "declaration of equal rights to all the nationalities of Iraq." In addition, the constitution did not contain a guarantee of "freedom for political parties."[63] Nevertheless, the overall situation in Iraq must have been judged to be improving and thus deserving of renewed Soviet participation in its economic progress and interest in its military strength. In mid-May, Soviet Ambassador Mikhail Iakovlev stated in Baghdad that the USSR was prepared to provide aid to those "friendly Arab states" which wished to apply for assistance,[64] and, on August 18, after several conferences 'Arif said that the Soviet Union "would supply Iraq with all the modern arms it required." He also noted that offers for weapons had been received from some Western countries; Iraq, as "a neutral state [was] dealing with all on a basis of mutual interest and equality."[65] Among the steps taken by the new regime that met with Moscow's approval were the restoration of friendly (but not subservient) relations with the UAR; the implementation, in July 1964, of political and economic reforms resembling measures introduced by Nasir in 1961; and the nationalization of all Iraqi and foreign banks, insurance companies, and enterprises producing cement, asbestos, and cigarettes. In addition, the government was insured participation in the capital of all weaving and sewing mills, brickyards, footwear, and trade firms. Commenting on these and other economic measures, *Pravda* noted that Iraq's reforms were fashioned after those introduced in the United Arab Republic but were not quite so broad or far-reaching. In particular, Baghdad

---

alleged Ba'thi efforts to reopen the war against the Kurds, were advanced by V. Maevskii, *ibid.,* April 5, 1964.

62. *Izv.* of May 5 carried a small news item, while *Pr.* did not report it at all.

63. Akademiia nauk SSSR, *Noveishaia istoriia* . . . , pp. 201–2.

64. *Al-'Arab* (Baghdad) May 16, 1964, as quoted in *MEM,* no. 21 (May 23, 1964), p. 22.

65. *MEM,* no. 31 (August 1, 1964), p. 6, and *MEJ* 18, no. 4 (Autumn 1964): 464.

continued its refusal to tackle the problem of land tenure. However, the "progressive character of the measures [was] obvious," and it was hoped that they would serve as a basis for reforms in other branches of the Iraqi economy.[66]

To summarize, Iraq, along with Egypt and Syria, became during this period one of the areas of major Soviet interest in the Arab East. Following what is commonly regarded as the high watermark of Soviet influence in Iraq, in late 1958 and early 1959, relations between Moscow and Baghdad began to cool perceptibly. This was not due to the Kremlin's own actions but, rather, to the fact that Qasim's evaluation of Iraq's interests and how they could best be protected, no longer coincided with preferences expressed by the USSR. As their respective views diverged, and as Qasim began proving himself incapable of successfully manipulating the internal forces in Iraq and challenging Nasir's leadership in the Arab East, Khrushchev finally came to realize that he was backing the wrong horse.

At this point, the "unique leader" had become expendable in Soviet eyes, though it is highly doubtful that the Kremlin ever seriously considered contributing directly to his overthrow. Once he was eliminated, however, it soon became obvious that the Ba'th was equally, if not more, unacceptable to the USSR, because its terror campaign against the Iraqi Communist party had placed Moscow in an embarrassing position in its ideological struggle with Peking. The ever-mounting anti-Ba'th campaign, which culminated in July 1963, brought Moscow into open conflict with one of the most influential

---

66. I. Beliaev, *Pr.*, July 18, 1964. See also Akademiia nauk SSSR, *Noveishaia istoriia* . . . , p. 202; *Pr.*, August 13, 1964; and Y. Bochkaryov, "New Orientation in Iraq," *NT*, no. 37 (September 16, 1964), pp. 12–14. Moscow's stand was subsequently endorsed by the ICP. Details in *Pr.*, September 4, 1964. This may have been due to the visit to Moscow and the meetings with Boris Ponomarev, Secretary of the Central Committee of the CPSU, who was also in charge of CPSU's relations with foreign Communist parties, of Anwar Mustafa, member of the Politburo, and Jabbar Husayn, member of the Central Committee of the ICP, reported in *ibid.*, July 22, 1964. For details, see "Important Event in the Life of the Iraqi Communist Party," *WMR*, no. 11 (November 1964), pp. 85–87; and Mounir Ahmid, "The Situation in Iraq and the Policy of the Communist Party," *ibid.*, no. 12 (December 1964), pp. 37–41.

political groupings in the Arab East as well as with the government of an Arab country that had only recently been friendly. The ensuing mudslinging contest left both antagonists with somewhat tarnished reputations, causing Moscow, in a moment of anguish, to threaten the discontinuation of its aid to a country whose foreign policy continued to be based on positive neutralism.

After the overthrow of the Ba'th in November 1963, a degree of normalcy was restored to Soviet-Iraqi relations. The USSR resumed the delivery of military goods and acknowledged the "progressive" nature of most of 'Arif's reforms. But the basic question remains: what benefits did Moscow actually gain, first by establishing relatively close ties with Qasim and, later, by resuming more or less normal relations with 'Arif? It is true that Qasim as well as 'Arif (and, for that matter the Ba'th) pursued a basically neutralist policy and, in so doing, contributed to limiting Western influence in the Arab East, but was this necessarily a gain for the Soviet Union? To this question, one suspects, Khrushchev would have been rather hard pressed to provide a satisfactory answer.

As previously noted, the Soviet press paid little attention to the steadily deteriorating political situation that prevailed in Syria in 1962 and early 1963. In the end, the efforts of the conservative Premier Khalid al-'Azm to suppress both the Ba'th and the pro-Nasir elements proved futile. On March 8, 1963, following clashes between the loyal security forces and dissident army units joined by students from Damascus University, the 'Azm government was overthrown by a group of Ba'thi and pro-union officers. The National Revolutionary Command Council (NRCC), formed on the same day, announced its intention to implement the Ba'thi principles of "unity, freedom and socialism." In the meantime, the new regime promised alignment with the other "liberated" Arab states: the UAR, Iraq, Algeria, and Yemen.[67] After a period of political instability, dominated by union talks in Cairo (see below), the right wing of the Ba'th seized power in Damascus. In the ensuing cabinet shake-up, Brigadier Amin al-Hafiz

67. Macadam, p. 304. For more details on the revolution, see *MEM*, no. 10 (March 9, 1963), pp. 2–4, 26.

was appointed Minister of Interior and soon emerged as Syria's new strong man.[68] His advent to power temporarily ended efforts at reconciliation with Cairo and led to a rapprochement between Damascus and Baghdad, whose regime was then also dominated by the Ba'th. The policy of what was described as "bilateral union" between the two states appeared to have been crowned with success when, on October 8, Damascus and Baghdad announced the conclusion of "a military union agreement as a first step towards a full merger."[69] Their honeymoon was a brief one, however. After the Iraqi Ba'th was overthrown in November, no open break occurred, but relations between the two countries cooled perceptibly.[70]

Throughout 1964, Syria continued to encounter both political and economic difficulties.[71] In inter-Arab relations, the Ba'th remained isolated from both Egypt and Iraq,[72] while domestically Hafiz was forced to devote most of his attention to keeping the lid on the explosive and threatening political situation. On April 25, Premier Hafiz "decreed a new Provisional Constitution." A few weeks later, "executive power was transferred from the Revolutionary Council to the Presidential Council," a five-man body consisting of the leaders of the Syrian Ba'th, and to a nineteen-man cabinet, headed by Salah al-Din al-Bitar. The new Prime Minister (Hafiz relinquished the post to become the new President) promised political conciliation and endeavored to win the favor of the industrial and commercial circles by assurances of consultation prior to passing pertinent legislation.[73] Nevertheless, by November, Bitar had been ousted as Premier and

---

68. Macadam, p. 304. For details, see *MEM*, no. 28 (July 13, 1963), pp. 2–3; no. 29 (July 20, 1963), pp. 2–4, 5; no. 30 (July 27, 1963), pp. 11–13; and no. 31 (August 3, 1963), pp. 2–3.

69. *MEM*, no. 41 (October 12, 1963), p. 2. For more details, see *ibid.*, pp. 2–6. For contacts in the intervening months, see *ibid.*, no. 29 (July 20, 1963), pp. 6–7; no. 32 (August 10, 1963), p. 2; no. 34 (August 24, 1963), p. 9; no. 36 (September 7, 1963), p. 4; no. 39 (September 28, 1963), p. 2; and no. 40 (October 5, 1963), pp. 8–9.

70. For initial Syrian reaction, see *ibid.*, no. 47 (November 23, 1963), pp. 10–11. See also no. 48 (November 30, 1963), pp. 2–4 *et passim*.

71. On the latter, see *ibid.*, no. 2 (January 11, 1964), p. 12 *et passim*.

72. For details, see *ibid.*, no. 3 (January 18, 1964), p. 3 *et passim*.

73. Ivison Macadam, ed., *The Annual Register of World Affairs, 1964*, p. 298. For details, see *MEM*, no. 20 (May 16, 1964), pp. 12–13.

General Hafiz emerged as the undisputed ruler of Syria.[74]

With this brief chronology as background, it is possible to analyze Soviet reaction to the events in Syria. As might have been expected, Moscow's initial reaction to the coup of March 8, 1963, was noncommittal. For the first two days, Soviet publications limited themselves to straight reporting on the new regime, the arrests of the leading conservatives, and the order closing down most newspapers.[75] But a note of alarm was clearly detectable in the reports on the "campaign of terror against 'the reactionaries and the Communists'" that gripped Syria in the wake of the revolution. P. Demchenko alleged that more than two hundred persons, among them noted Communists, had been thrown into prison during the first three days of the new regime. "More and more clearly can one hear here the echo of the tragic events which have unfolded in Iraq," he concluded.[76] It soon became obvious, however, that the Soviet government was interested in establishing and maintaining normal relations with Damascus. Soviet Ambassador Anatolii Barkovskii declared that the USSR was prepared "to maintain and develop friendly relations between our countries in the interest of our peoples and of strengthening the cause of peace."[77]

For the next few months, the USSR followed carefully the Cairo negotiations aimed at bringing about a union between Egypt, Syria, and Iraq. Interestingly, Moscow initially viewed such efforts with misgivings and made no secret of its attitude. As early as mid-March 1963, it expressed renewed concern with what were termed "imperialist intrigues in the Arab East." On March 16, Viktor Maevskii ascribed to the United States a desire to create in the Middle East a "confederation of states" consisting of the UAR, Syria, Iraq, Kuwayt, Arab Palestine (to be carved out of Jordan), Saudi Arabia, Yemen, and the South Arabian principalities. The proposed new entity was to be subservient to Washington: its purpose was to unify "all the sources of Arab oil in the Near East" and to facilitate their exploitation by American monopolies. This, Maevskii argued, was *not* tantamount to

74. Macadam, *1964*, pp. 298–99.
75. I. Beliaev, *Pr.*, March 9, and *Izv.*, March 9 and 10, 1963.
76. *Pr.*, March 12, 1963.
77. *Ibid.*, March 15, 1963.

US support of Arab unity. On the contrary, to achieve its goal of securing unlimited control over the region's oil deposits, the United States endeavored to pit Arabs against each other, *"to undermine Arab unity in the struggle against imperialism, to substitute for it such 'union' as would be suited to the interests of Wall Street."* In so doing, Maevskii continued, Washington had succeeded in skillfully blending the time-tested policy of "divide and rule" with the principle of "unite and rule." Maevskii appeared particularly incensed at the fact that "anti-Communism" was emerging as an integral part of this "imperialist scheme" and warned that *"he who forms an alliance with imperialism on the basis of anti-Communism risks . . . being relegated to the garbage dump of history."*[78]

While references to a united Arab state embracing such unlikely candidates as the "ultra-progressive" UAR and the conservative Saudi Arabia and the South Arabian principalities were patently false, Maevskii's generally negative observations on Arab unity were of the greatest importance. Without being specific, they clearly implied that the Kremlin was opposed to Arab unity on the alleged ground that it was inspired by the United States and was designed to help perpetuate imperialist control over the Middle East. In the ensuing weeks, the Soviet press continued to inform its readers about the progress of the union talks, though without taking an editorial stand on the dramatic shifts and turns that accompanied the negotiations. This was no doubt a reflection of the realization in Moscow that it was, for all intents and purposes, powerless to influence Cairo, Damascus, and Baghdad in such matters.[79]

At the same time, the Kremlin kept a close watch over the turbulent events which were unfolding in Syria during the spring of 1963. In late March, *Izvestiia* reported that a group of conservative politicians were placed in what was described as "political quarantine" for their participation in the dissolution of the United Arab Republic.[80] What it neglected to disclose, however, was the fact that a number of promi-

---

78. *Ibid.* Italics in the original.
79. For details, see *Pr.*, March 18; K. Vishnevetskii, *Izv.*, March 21; and I. Beliaev, *Pr.*, March 23, 1963.
80. *Izv.*, March 28, 1963.

nent Communists were also included in the group described in Damascus as "pillars of secession."[81]

In the meantime, Soviet coverage was extended to the pronouncements of Syrian government representatives to the effect that the proposed "federal union" of the three "progressive" Arab states implied preservation of "independent regions" within one political framework,[82] and also included some of the details of the Cairo negotiations.[83]

By mid-April, when it was becoming apparent that some kind of agreement on the unified state comprising Egypt, Syria, and Iraq would soon be worked out, I. Beliaev, reporting from Cairo, noted that the proposed federation would guarantee a significant measure of internal control for the respective regional administrations and that only foreign relations, defense, overall economic development, educational policies, and customs would fall under the jurisdiction of the central government.[84] Commenting on the proposed union, V. Kudriavtsev, in a tactical shift of some significance, bowed to the inevitable by labeling the Arab quest for union as a "fully legitimate and well-founded aspiration," but warned Cairo, Damascus, and Baghdad to expect "difficulties on this path." More precisely, in line with Maevskii's earlier admonition, the Arabs were told to beware of the "neo-colonialists [who] are not averse to depicting themselves as advocates of such unity as long as it is devoid of anti-imperialist, democratic, and anti-colonial content." Kudriavtsev left no doubt that Arab unity was now welcomed by the USSR and other "progressive elements" provided that "patriotic, nationalist forces proceed in the implementation of unity with the view to strengthening the independence of the Arab countries, of increasing their resistance to imperialist pressure."[85]

81. For details, see *MEM*, no. 13 (March 30, 1963), pp. 6–8.
82. Statement by Jamal Atasi, Syrian Minister of Information, as reported in *Pr.*, March 26, 1963.
83. For details, see *ibid.*, April 8, 9, 10, 1963.
84. *Ibid.*, April 12. For details on the April 17 agreement, see *ibid.*, April 18, 1963.
85. *Izv.*, April 14, 1963. See also G. Mirsky, "The Problem of Arab Unity," *NT*, no. 16 (April 24, 1963), pp. 11–13.

At a round-table conference, held in the summer of 1963, the participants, including a number of noted Arab Communists, distinguished between the bourgeois-nationalist and revolutionary-democratic approach to the problem of unity. Adherents of the former held that unity could be attained only after several preconditions had been met: adoption of "a nationalist-chauvinist ideology," marked by "anti-communism and an attack on democracy"; "isolation of the Arab peoples from the socialist camp, and reconciliation with imperialism." Not that the proponents of this approach were prepared to subordinate themselves to the Western powers, or wished to break off ties with the "socialist camp"; rather, they were simply engaged in a balancing act, "maneuvering between the socialist camp and imperialism."[86] The proponents of the "revolutionary-democratic" approach, in contrast, insisted that "Arab unity should rest on a democratic foundation, and recognize the objective conditions obtaining in each country." Adherence to this approach would facilitate the establishment of "a close alliance between the fraternal Arab countries, an alliance in which the interests of each country would be recognized, while the federal state created on this basis would have clear perspectives for socioeconomic and political advance."[87]

It is interesting to note the differences and the similarities in the respective approaches to Arab unity of President Nasir, the Ba'th, and the Arab Communists, who reflected the views of the Soviet government. The fiasco of the first union experiment with Syria made Cairo reluctant to agree to anything but a tightly organized political structure that would guarantee that Egyptian wishes would be respected by the other partners in the union. This was unacceptable to both the Ba'th and the Arab Communists as well as the Kremlin. But while the Ba'th demanded autonomous status for Syria and Iraq and refused to share power with anyone, especially the Marxists, the latter, with Moscow's blessings, kept insisting on the creation of "democratic"

86. "Present Stage of the National-Liberation Movement of the Arab Peoples," *WMR*, no. 10 (October 1963), pp. 68–69.
87. *Ibid.*, p. 69. See also Fuad Nasser, "On Arab Unity," *WMR*, no.2 (February 1964), pp. 18–24; and "Problems of the National-Liberation Movement of the Arab Peoples," *ibid.*, no. 7 (July 1964), pp. 73–81.

fronts in which their legal existence would be officially recognized and through which they would be allowed freedom of action in organizational and propaganda matters. A subsequent Soviet publication dismissed the April 17 agreement to form a tripartite federated state as doomed to failure from the outset because of the opposing tendencies displayed by the Iraqi, Syrian, and Egyptian leaders. More precisely, it contended that the right wing of the Ba'th not only had opposed the far-reaching socioeconomic reforms instituted by President Nasir but was actually determined to prevent their spread in Iraq and Syria. Hence, in the Soviet view, the Ba'th was responsible for the ultimate result, namely, the breakdown of the Cairo talks.[88]

In the meantime, the Soviet press continued to report on the instability prevalent in Syrian politics. The releases were free of editorial comment, indicating that the Kremlin had no intention of becoming embroiled in a highly volatile situation over which it had no control.[89] In July 1963, attention was closely focused on the Ba'thi attempts to remove from power the independent Minister of Defense and Chief of Staff of the army, Ziyad Hariri.[90] While it is unlikely that the Kremlin felt any particular sympathy for Hariri and his associates, Moscow was opposed to Colonel Hafiz, who, at this juncture, was emerging as the new strong man of Syria,[91] and viewed the removal of Hariri as yet another move by Hafiz to consolidate his power. The reasons for Moscow's initial disapproval of the colonel are not entirely clear, but it would appear that his main "liability" was his association with and membership in the Ba'th. The fact that the party, having already gained power in Iraq, was now consolidating its grip on Syria, must have been viewed with a certain amount of uneasiness in the Soviet Union.

It is all the more noteworthy in this connection that certain aspects

---

88. Tuganova, p. 168.
89. See *Pr.*, May 10, 11, and 15, 1963, and editorial, "Cairo-Baghdad-Damascus," *NT,* no. 21 (May 29, 1963), p. 11.
90. For details, see K. Vishnevetskii, *Izv.,* July 6, 1963.
91. K. Vishnevetskii, quoting an unnamed Bayrut newspaper, described Hafiz as a man who would not be stopped by either "conscience or honor." *Ibid.,* July 11, 1963.

of the Ba'thi policy had met with Soviet approval. For instance, in late May, Syria was one of the few Arab (and, for that matter, Mediterranean) countries to approve Khrushchev's proposal for the creation of a nuclear-free zone in the Mediterranean.[92] As the party's official newspaper *al-Ba'th* expressed it:

> The imperialists use the argument that the reinforcement of their armed forces with nuclear weapons is necessary to stop the imagined aggression by the Soviet Union. However, it is not easy to fool . . . [the Arab] peoples who understand the true intentions of the West. These imperialist maneuvers are a direct threat to our people and to the peoples of this whole region.[93]

In addition, the Syrian leaders attempted to ingratiate themselves with the Kremlin by insisting that the "policy of the Ba'th has always been a policy of friendship with the Soviet Union." Like Cairo, the Ba'th based its relations with other states on the principle of positive neutralism, but this did not imply an "equal attitude toward both camps: we are closer to the socialist camp, we are closer to the Soviet Union. We are for an independent socialist policy."[94]

Nevertheless, by mid-July 1963, it was becoming increasingly clear that the Kremlin strongly disapproved of both the party's theoretical formulations and its actual policies. The initial Soviet tolerance of the Syrian Ba'th was probably motivated by a desire not to get engulfed in Arab politics at a time when outward appearances pointed to a strong possibility that some form of Egyptian-Syrian-Iraqi union would in fact be consummated. Now that the Arab "revolutionary ranks" had once again been split, the Kremlin, as might have been expected, extended its moral backing in the ensuing confrontation to the United Arab Republic. Nasir remained the outstanding Arab leader; Egypt was still regarded as the leading proponent of Arab unity; and the Soviet political, economic, and military investment in the UAR surpassed by far Moscow's commitments to both Syria and

92. Initial comment by K. Vishnevetskii, *ibid.*, May 24, 1963.
93. As quoted by K. Vishnevetskii, *ibid.*, June 7, 1963. See also *Pr.*, June 8, 1963.
94. As quoted by K. Vishnevetskii, *Izv.*, June 7, 1963.

Iraq. In addition, the "anti-popular" activities of the Iraqi Ba'th, as the Soviet government insisted by July 1963, had enjoyed the full support of its Syrian counterpart; the Damascus government was even extending military aid in the war against the Kurds. Moreover, while refraining from mass persecutions of Syrian Communists, the Syrian regime was effectively hindering their freedom of expression and activity. These considerations led *Pravda* to conclude that the Ba'thi leaders were pursuing a policy "directed against the interests of the Arab peoples." In so doing, they allegedly were playing into the hands of the imperialist powers.[95]

As a cumulative result of these developments in the summer of 1963, the Soviet propaganda apparatus mounted a sustained anti-Ba'thi campaign intended to discredit the party in the eyes of its followers and sympathizers.[96] The first serious attack was launched in an article entitled "Baathist Theory and Practice" by Georgii Mirskii, who argued that the principle of "socialism" in the party's ideological structure was "secondary and subordinate to nationalism."[97] A separate publication claimed that the Ba'th was not a socialist party—it simply used socialist slogans "to mislead the broad masses of [the] people and [to] divert them from the struggle for stronger national independence, progress and democracy. In its ten years, [the] Baath has shown itself to be a rabid and crafty enemy of the entire democratic movement in the Arab East."[98] Mirskii pointed to Iraq as the country in which

> Baathist theory and practice have run the full circle. . . . : the logical results of their opportunism, adventurism [and] rabid anti-Communism [were] a reign of fascist terror, a policy of war on democracy. Reaction veiled by pseudo-Left demagogy, counter-revolution disguised as revolution—such is the picture of the Baathist movement, which, contrary to its name, can only delay not hasten the renaissance of the Arab peoples.[99]

95. V. Maevskii, *Pr.,* July 11, 1963.
96. For an example of the publicity given in the Soviet press to Nasir's pronouncements, see *ibid.,* July 29, 1963.
97. For details, see *NT,* no. 27 (July 10, 1963), p. 12.
98. "The Baath Party," *IA,* no. 4 (April 1963), p. 121.
99. *NT,* no. 27 (July 10, 1963), p. 15.

To make certain that there were no doubts about the connection between the Iraqi and Syrian branches of the Ba'th, *Izvestiia* noted that Baghdad's policy was "closely tied to 'Aflaq's 'philosophy,' the philosophy of anti-Communism."[100] The Ba'th was also described as an instrument of the colonialist powers determined to maintain a degree of control over their former possessions and of the "frail Eastern capitalism" struggling to delay the "inevitable" march toward "genuine socialism." Mirskii, on a separate occasion, termed Ba'thism but "a specific form of capitalism in the Arab countries." As demonstrated by the events in Syria and Iraq, the party had proved itself incapable of solving the problems confronting the Arab East.[101]

The Soviet press paid close attention to the August-September visit to Cairo and Damascus by Iraqi President 'Arif. *Pravda* saw nothing surprising in the fact that the Ba'th was seeking to end inter-Arab tensions, since, as the July upheavals in Syria demonstrated, the party had been forced on the defensive by the pro-union elements and by the barrage of anti-Ba'thi propaganda emanating from Egypt. Now that, as *al-Ahram* asserted, the Ba'th had become isolated from the Syrian and the Iraqi peoples, 'Arif was forced to attempt a reconciliation between Egypt and the Syrian and Iraqi regimes.[102] But President Nasir was in no mood to compromise and, having failed in Cairo, 'Arif proceeded to Damascus. After lengthy negotiations, the Syrian and Iraqi branches of the Ba'th concluded an agreement to enter into an economic union, followed, on October 8, by an accord to join their military forces. The latter agreement, wrote a noted Iraqi Communist, was but "a refurbished form of the old plans of British imperialism," tantamount "to restoration of imperialist domination in Syria and Iraq. . . . It is proof of an attempt to extend fascist methods of government to the Arab world as a whole."[103]

100. V. Petrov, *Izv.*, August 8, 1963. See also Y. Bochkaryov, "Baathist Bankruptcy," *NT*, no. 47 (November 27, 1963), p. 7.
101. Georgi Mirsky, "Troubled Times in Syria," *NT*, no. 34 (August 28, 1963), p. 14.
102. P. Demchenko, *Pr.*, August 30, 1963.
103. Aziz al-Hajj, "The Current Situation in Iraq," *WMR*, no. 11 (November 1963), pp. 39–40.

In late October, Moscow stepped up the propaganda campaign against the Syrian Ba'th, accusing it of direct participation in "genocide" against the Iraqi Kurds. The "bloody, anti-democratic policy" of the Iraqi government, *Pravda* concluded, enjoyed the support of both the imperialist powers and the Syrian Ba'thi authorities.[104] Moscow's attitude toward the Ba'th and the proposed implementation of a Syrian-Iraqi union was also reflected in the Soviet comments on the party's policies. Demchenko noted that, although at the recently held Sixth Congress of the Ba'th, its leadership adopted a number of resolutions envisaging the creation of a "socialist system" in Syria and Iraq—the development of democratic institutions, the establishment of cooperatives in the countryside, and the organization of workers' administrative bodies in industrial enterprises—practice was diametrically opposed to theory. In Iraq, brute force was used to suppress the "toiling masses," who were deprived of the most elementary "democratic rights." While Syria had no equivalent to the National Guard and there were no mass executions of the Communists, the lack of freedom and democracy was evidenced by the deployment of armed units in the streets of Damascus and the other cities and towns.[105]

The downfall of the Iraqi branch of the party was applauded in Moscow not only because it removed from power one of the most "blood-thirsty" regimes in the modern history of the Arab East but also because it was bound to have serious repercussions on the Syrian Ba'th. In addition to the Iraqi setback, the Syrian branch was also facing grave economic problems, among them the scarcity of food and spiraling inflation. It was not without some glee that *Pravda* reported a growing rift in the ranks of the Syrian Ba'th: while some leaders continued to insist on preserving the party's political monopoly in Syria and on restoring to power in Iraq the group that had been overthrown, the majority faction, led by Prime Minister Hafiz, who replaced Bitar in November 1963, expressed interest in cooperating

---

104. E. Maksimov, *Pr.*, October 25. See also P. Demchenko, *ibid.*, November 3, 1963. For later references, see Tuganova, p. 169.

105. P. Demchenko, *Pr.*, November 3. For more details, see E. Primakov, *ibid.*, November 14, 1963. For a slightly different later interpretation, see Akademiia nauk SSSR, *Noveishaia istoriia.* . . , pp. 82–83.

with other political groups and even in forming a coalition government.[106] Another encouraging sign was the withdrawal from Iraq of Syrian units dispatched to participate in the war against the Kurds.[107]

In early 1964, Soviet publications continued to emphasize what was termed the political bankruptcy of the Ba'th and its inability to attend to Syria's serious socioeconomic problems. The party, a "synonym for brutality cloaked by shameless demagogy," no longer had any "clear-cut aims, . . . leaders of stature and influence, . . . [or a] convinced mass following." All of its important political schemes, such as the tripartite or even the dual (Iraqi-Syrian) union, proved failures, resulting in a fiasco even "on its self-chosen main front: Arab unity." Ba'thi economic reforms, particularly in Syria, had proved similarly ineffectual. Some land had been nationalized and distributed among landless peasants, who then found themselves unable to farm it because of "lack of money, implements and seed." In towns and cities, some private enterprises were also nationalized, only to find that the move was "a totally unprepared precipitate venture."[108]

Confronted with popular discontent and restlessness, the Ba'th turned to the army, only to find Syrian armed forces hopelessly split among various competing factions. According to the *New Times*, it was the party's "ideological fogginess, its lack of a clear-cut programme, its inherent opportunism" that enabled the Ba'th to "appeal at one and the same time to the most diverse and dissimilar social groups. The eclectic nature of their programme affords them rich opportunities for manoevring." As the old political parties in Syria and Iraq continued to disintegrate, the Ba'th temporarily emerged as "the spokesman of the bankers', the big merchants', the landlords' fear of social revolution, of communism and of Nasserism."[109]

In early March 1964, a new element appeared in the Soviet comments on the Ba'th and its activities. Whereas Moscow had never before made a meaningful distinction between the various factions within the Ba'th, *Pravda*'s commentary on the Seventh Congress of

106. P. Demchenko, *Pr.*, December 6, 1963.
107. See, for example, *ibid.*, November 28 and December 24, 1963.
108. Editorial, "The Changing Arab East," *NT*, no. 2 (January 15, 1964), pp. 3–4.
109. *Ibid.*, p. 4.

the party, held in Damascus in late February and early March, subjected to strong criticism only the right wing of the Ba'th. This first clear indication of a more flexible tactical approach to the organization suggested that the Kremlin was not averse to normalizing relations with what it described as the party's moderate and left-wing elements. More precisely, *Pravda* ridiculed the contention that by expelling 'Ali Salih al-Sa'di (former Secretary-General of the Iraqi branch) and some of his followers, the party had divested itself of the responsibility for the executions and mass repression of Iraqi "patriots and democrats" and for its "open servitude" to the imperialists. It concluded that the "change in tactics cannot absolve them from Arab hatred, cannot liquidate the abyss which separates the *right-wing leaders of the Ba'th* from their own people."[110]

A further indication that the Soviet attitude toward the moderate elements in the Ba'th in general and the Syrian strong man Hafiz in particular was undergoing a change was provided by the text of the telegram that Khrushchev dispatched to the general on April 16, 1964, on occasion of the "Evacuation Day" (a national holiday commemorating the withdrawal of French troops from Syria). In conveying the Kremlin's "congratulations and best wishes," Khrushchev expressed confidence that "relations between our two countries will develop . . . for the benefit of the Soviet and Syrian peoples." Hafiz's reply of April 20 which, significantly, was reproduced in *Pravda,* noted that the Syrian government was "rather touched by the friendly tone of [Khrushchev's] message." Hafiz, too, expressed conviction that relations between Syria and the USSR would continue to improve.[111]

By the summer of 1964, attacks on the Ba'th had disappeared from the pages of Soviet publications, and internal developments in Syria, if they were mentioned at all, were referred to in an objective, matter-of-fact fashion.[112] If further proof of Moscow's benevolence were re-

110. *Pr.,* March 5, 1964. Italics added.
111. Texts in *ibid.,* April 23, 1964.
112. For example, on April 29, *Izvestiia* reported the abrogation of the Iraqi-Syrian alliance; on May 4, *Pravda* noted that 21 participants in the anti-Ba'th demonstrations (previously reported by K. Vishnevetskii in *Izvestiia* of April 19) had been sentenced to death. One day later, in another noncommittal note, *Pravda* informed its readers that the death sentences had been commuted to prison terms.

quired, it was provided by the restrained official coverage of both the June 1964 plenum of the Syrian Communist party Central Committee and a visit to Moscow of a party delegation.

The plenum was not reported at all until mid-August, when *Pravda,* commenting on its decisions, noted that during an exchange of views on a number of Arab and international problems, much attention was devoted to Khrushchev's forthcoming visit to the UAR, the questions of Arab unity and the national liberation movement, and the situation in Syria (in that order). No further details of these discussions were given, but it was also reported that the plenum condemned Communist China for "splitting the ranks of the world Communist movement" and endorsed Moscow's call for an "international conference of the Communist and workers' parties" to deal with the activities of the "left-wing deviationists" from Peking.[113]

In reporting the conversations between the Syrian Communists and Boris Ponomarev, Secretary of the Central Committee in charge of relations with foreign Marxist organizations, *Pravda* noted that a number of questions had been raised. The most important among them were Khrushchev's visit to Egypt and the activities of the Chinese Communist party. Significantly, there was in *Pravda* no reference at all to the internal situation in Syria, although it may be safely assumed that the subject must have been among the crucial matters discussed.[114] In both of these instances the omission of references to the internal situation in Syria attested to the reluctance of the Soviet government to side openly with the Syrian Communists against the Hafiz regime in Damascus.

Finally, with an obvious sign of approval, *Pravda* noted, in early September, that the Syrian Presidential Council had announced a general amnesty for all political prisoners and political emigrés.[115] By the summer of 1964, Moscow-Damascus relations had obviously improved significantly, and it came as no surprise that a Syrian military mission arrived in Moscow on October 17.[116] Its purpose was clearly

113. *Pr.,* August 14, 1964.
114. *Ibid.,* July 4, 1964.
115. *Ibid.,* September 4, 1964.
116. *Ibid.,* October 18, 1964.

to secure Soviet arms and war material for the regime of General Hafiz.

In considering the reasons for the change in Moscow's attitude toward the Ba'th, it would appear that the Kremlin had taken full cognizance of and attempted to use to its own advantage the split that occurred in the party's ranks in late 1963 and early 1964. The discord had surfaced at the Seventh Pan-Arab Congress of the Ba'th, held in Damascus in early 1964, and it should be noted parenthetically that the Soviet interpretations of the Congress were quite misleading. As stated earlier, Moscow reported that the *right* wing of the Ba'th had endeavored to single out former Party Secretary Sa'di and some of his followers (who, according to the Soviet press, were also a part of the right wing) as the culprits in the Iraqi fiasco. In so doing, other "right-wingers," among them 'Aflaq, Bitar, and other leaders of the Syrian and Iraqi Ba'th, were allegedly attempting to divest themselves of responsibility for the mistakes committed in Iraq. Moscow claimed that the sacrifice of Sa'di (to which, incidentally, it did not object in principle) was not going far enough, for it was 'Aflaq and his collaborators in both Damascus and Baghdad who had issued directives, offered encouragement, and actually sent aid to those who were now being ostracized.

The reality was different. As tenuous and unsatisfactory as the application of the standard Western classification of a political scene (e.g., right-center-left) might be in terms of Arab politics, Sa'di and his group constituted the left, not the right, wing of the Ba'th.[117] Contrary to Moscow's assertion, it was this group which at the Seventh Congress voiced strong criticism of the 'Aflaq-Bitar leadership.[118] In any event, the Sa'di-'Aflaq clash was not prompted by any ideological considerations (and, in this sense, any allusions to "right" and "left" are probably misleading), but was rather a result of their respective efforts to affix the blame for the Iraqi fiasco on the other group.

By late 1963, the Russians must have been aware of the fact that

---

117. *Mideast Mirror* actually referred to them as "the extremist left wing of the party's regional leadership in Iraq." No. 10 (March 7, 1964), p. 9.
118. For some details, see *ibid.*

Amin al-Hafiz, who had emerged as Syria's new strong man, was basically, in spite of his protestations of loyalty to the ideology and principles of the Ba'th, a pragmatic individual whose primary concern was to keep himself in power. In order to accomplish this end, he was prepared to compromise, as his dealings with the other nonunionist groups in Syria made clear. Whereas initially he had been wooing the conservative elements, one might expect that, in time, he would be forced to seek the cooperation of the leftist, anti-union elements, above all the Syrian Communists. Once that occurred, Hafiz would definitely be on his way toward establishing a "progressive, national-democratic" regime.[119] In addition, he had also displayed a definite interest in improving relations with the USSR.

It is noteworthy that the negative Soviet attitude toward the Syrian Ba'th did not significantly affect Moscow's desire to maintain (and, in some instances, actually expand) economic and cultural cooperation with Damascus. In adopting this approach, the Kremlin leaders were not blazing any new trails but were simply adhering to a policy that had hitherto been implemented with varying degrees of success in Egypt, post-1958 Iraq, and post-UAR Syria. Put differently, disapproval (and, in the case of the Ba'th, open condemnation) of any given regime did not automatically lead to breaking off economic cooperation and cultural exchanges. This approach was based in part on the assumption (as well as the hope) that in the highly volatile political climate of the Arab East, and particularly in countries like Syria and Iraq, undesirable governments would eventually be succeeded by others, hopefully more amenable to Soviet wishes. In that case, the existing framework for economic and cultural cooperation could be utilized to improve relations and to strengthen ties. In the case of basically hostile regimes, such as the 1963 Ba'thi governments in Iraq and Syria, the Kremlin apparently felt that maintenance of a Soviet presence, no matter how precarious, was commensurate with its

---

119. For a subsequent discussion of the "objectively progressive" attitude and reforms introduced by Hafiz in early 1964, see Akademiia nauk SSSR, *Noveishaia istoriia...*, pp. 83–84. A less enthusiastic account in V.P. Viktorov, *Ekonomika sovremennoi Sirii* (Moscow: Izdatel'stvo "Nauka," 1968), pp. 52–53.

status as a superpower with legitimate interests in the Middle East and was therefore preferable to no relations at all.

Thus, new economic agreements were signed,[120] and, in early February 1964, the Soviet *Narodnyi* Bank announced its "willingness to provide credit and financial facilities to Syrian banks to help merchants to import primary goods, particularly sugar and rice."[121] It might be noted in passing that such cooperation was undeterred by the growing (though, admittedly, still limited) economic ties between Damascus and Peking.[122] Cultural relations also improved,[123] and the USSR extended its support to the Syrian regime in a number of UN deliberations growing out of frontier clashes with Israel.[124]

Soviet relations with Syria in 1963–1964 were thus conducted within the (by then) traditional framework of limited political, military, economic, and cultural cooperation with regimes of whose policies the Kremlin often disapproved but whose cooperation it sought in line with Moscow's general objectives in the underdeveloped world. Ideologically, this attitude was explained in terms of Soviet determination to frustrate the designs of the imperialist powers, whose main purpose it was to drive a wedge between the USSR and, in this instance, the Arab peoples struggling for "genuine national independence." More precisely, in pursuing its "neo-colonialist" policies in the Middle East, the United States was alleged to rely not so much on "the feudal chiefs and the pro-imperialist bourgeoisie" (a policy still characteristic of Great Britain) but on

120. See *Izv.*, April 2, 1963; *MEM*, no. 15 (April 13, 1963), p. 20; no. 23 (June 8, 1963), p. 19; and no. 38 (September 21, 1963), p. 21. See also *Pr.*, March 12, 1964; *MEJ* 18, no. 3 (Summer 1964): 347 and 19, no. 1 (Winter 1965): 87; and *MEM*, no. 34 (August 22, 1964), p. 17.

121. *MEM*, no. 7 (February 15, 1964), p. 19.

122. Thus, in 1963, Communist China granted Syria a loan of 70 million Swiss francs for the purchase of unspecified industrial and agricultural machinery. In addition, the possibilities of enlarging economic and cultural cooperation between the two countries were repeatedly discussed by the Syrian and the Red Chinese representatives. See *MEJ* 18, no. 2 (Spring 1964): 235, and no. 3 (Summer 1964): 345, 346, respectively.

123. See *MEM*, no. 6 (February 8, 1964), p. 21.

124. For details, see K. Vishnevetskii, *Izv.*, August 21 and 22, and *Pr.*, August 22, 1963. See also K. Vishnevetskii, *Izv.*, September 17, 1964.

the new social strata of the national bourgeoisie and part of the intelligentsia who subscribe to the slogans of nationalism, Arab unity and even socialism. The neo-colonialists, while pretending to sympathize with the liberation movement of the Arab peoples, seek to direct this movement into anti-democratic channels, towards agreement with imperialism. In so doing they strive to split this movement, prevent the formation of a united national front and isolate the Arab peoples from their natural ally—world socialism.

It obviously became incumbent upon the USSR to stifle these "neo-colonialist intrigues" by demonstrating the Kremlin's desire and determination to support and aid the Arabs in the defense of their legitimate rights and aspirations. However, this attitude did not prevent the Soviet government from expressing its views on the policies pursued by the various Arab states, among them Ba'thi controlled Syria and Iraq.[125]

At the same time Moscow claimed that it was under no illusion as to the transitional nature and the limited scope of its cooperation with the Ba'th. The latter, it was held, was committed to the idea of Arab unity based on "anti-Communism, . . . an attack on democracy, a nationalist-chauvinist ideology, isolation of the Arab peoples from the socialist camp, and reconciliation with imperialism." However, from the standpoint of the USSR, the party's redeeming feature was its fear of falling under direct imperialist control. Because of this, the Ba'th was "reluctant to break completely with the socialist camp." In pursuing its objectives, the organization was "constantly maneuvering between the socialist camp and imperialism,"[126] a phenomenon that, as Soviet commentary unintentionally makes clear, the Kremlin was endeavoring to use for its own purposes.

125. "The Present Stage of the National-Liberation Movement of the Arab Peoples," *WMR*, no. 10 (October 1963), p. 62.
126. *Ibid.*, pp. 68–69.

10
The Grand Finale: Khrushchev's Visit to Egypt

By late 1963, in view of Egypt's increasing isolation from the mainstream of Arab politics, coupled with its involvement in the Yemeni civil war and the Kremlin's growing concern over the imminent deployment of Polaris submarines in the Eastern Mediterranean, close tactical cooperation between Moscow and Cairo appeared desirable to both capitals. The degree of their rapprochement made itself evident in two unrelated developments. The first, the visit to Cairo of Chinese Prime Minister Chou En-lai, served as an excellent illustration of Nasir's circumspect approach to the problem of Egypt's relations with the USSR. The second, the dispute between Israel and its Arab neighbors over the distribution and utilization of the Jordan river waters, was a good indication of the fashion in which Khrushchev, then in the twilight of his political career, handled his Egyptian clients.

"The distinguished visitor from Asia," as *al-Ahram* referred to the Chinese Premier, arrived in Cairo on December 14 and during his week-long visit had several meetings with President Nasir and other Egyptian dignitaries.[1] There can be no doubt that the visit, which was undertaken on Chinese initiative, was from Cairo's standpoint ill-

---

1. *MEM*, no. 51 (December 21, 1963), p. 8.

timed. For one thing, it occurred at the height of the Sino-Soviet dispute, when racial overtones had first been introduced into the public mudslinging contest between the two Communist giants. More precisely, Peking was denouncing Moscow, on which the UAR depended heavily for military and economic aid, as but another white, European, colonialist nation, which should be ostracized from the councils of the Afro-Asian countries.[2] In addition, it was feared in Cairo that Chou would attempt to drive a wedge between Egypt and India, China's main Asian antagonist but a close political ally of the United Arab Republic.[3]

In a sense, then, the visit was an embarrassment for Nasir, and the very fact that the UAR President was visiting Tunisia at the time of Chou's arrival illustrated the extent of Cairo's displeasure. On the other hand, Egypt could not possibly deny the Chinese Premier its hospitality: it was, after all, a nonaligned country that had no quarrel with the People's Republic. But the Egyptian leaders were no doubt hoping that their Chinese guest would have enough courtesy and common sense not to embarrass them publicly. Fortunately, Chou's only *faux pas* was a remark in his December 18 speech at Aswan that the construction of the High Dam demonstrated that the Asian and African peoples were "not only able to drive out imperialism and colonialism but . . . [also] to wrest more wealth from nature through *their own efforts.*"[4] It is noteworthy that Chou's statement was made after President Nasir, at a banquet honoring the Chinese visitors, hailed the "most noble aid of the Soviet Union" in the construction of the Aswan High Dam.[5]

The joint communiqué, issued at the conclusion of the visit on

---

2. Thus, Chou attempted to persuade Nasir and other African leaders to hold another Bandung-type conference instead of a meeting of nonaligned states *à la* Belgrade favored by the UAR. The former would enable China to attend, while barring Soviet participation. A conference of nonaligned countries, in contrast, would bar both Moscow and Peking.
3. It will be recalled that the latter backed New Dehli in its 1962 Himalayan confrontation with Red China.
4. As quoted in *MEM,* no. 51 (December 21, 1963), p. 9. Italics added.
5. *Pr.,* December 17, 1963. The latter, incidentally, was the only reference to Chou's visit to appear in the Soviet press.

December 21, attested to the continuing divergence of views between the two governments on many of the problems that were of particular interest to the Chinese. As might have been expected, the questions of Soviet-Chinese and Soviet-Egyptian relations were not mentioned. For the most part, general and harmless references to the "evils of imperialism" were combined with pledges to work for the eradication of its "last vestiges." Peking supported "legitimate" Arab claims to Palestine and favored the refugees' return to their "usurped homeland." Reciprocating, Cairo backed Red China's admission to the United Nations and Peking's right to Taiwan. Both countries agreed also to work for "complete disarmament, a final ban on nuclear weapons and the destruction of their stockpiles." In conclusion, the Chinese endorsed Cairo's "policies of peace, neutrality and non-alignment."[6]

Chou's circumspect behavior may have succeeded in winning friends in Egypt and elsewhere on his African tour, but it was clearly evident that he had failed to influence the Egyptian leaders. Apart from other considerations, it simply made no sense for Cairo to abandon its relatively close association with the USSR (and even India) in favor of a similar relationship with Communist China, for the latter was in no position to satisfy Egypt's steadily increasing requirements for capital, industrial goods, technological know-how, and war-materiel. The Kremlin, seemingly sensitive to the delicacy of Nasir's position, refrained from criticizing either Cairo or the Chinese Prime Minister and his activities in the UAR. In this sense, Moscow's reaction to Chou's visit was but another illustration of Soviet good will toward Egypt.

This attitude was prominently displayed again during the controversy surrounding Israel's decision to utilize a portion of the river Jordan waters for irrigation purposes. Since the various UN efforts to resolve the problem, which had been building up for years, had proved futile, Tel-Aviv, in late 1963, announced its decision to proceed unilaterally: the waters were to be diverted from Lake Tiberias, their natural storage basin, as soon as the work on the installation of the pipelines

6. *MEM*, no. 52 (December 28, 1963), pp. 11–12.

was completed. Nasir must have recognized immediately that passivity would result in an inestimable loss of prestige and influence among his followers throughout the region, but Egypt was deeply immersed in the Yemeni operation and in no position to take on Israel. Thus, circumstances forced Nasir to call (albeit reluctantly) upon his conservative, moderate, and revolutionary counterparts in other Arab countries to deal with what he described as the Israeli "threat" to the entire Arab nation. This proved to be a brilliant tactical move.[7]

The thirteen Arab governments that attended the summit conference in Cairo between January 13 and 17, 1964, agreed to coordinate their efforts to prevent the planned Israeli action by diverting the Jordan waters before they reached Lake Tiberias, "with the object of reducing the available supply to Israel from 327 million to 90 million cubic metres a year."[8] The Soviet Union expressed itself in favor of Nasir's diplomatic initiative and of the Arab summit conference. Since, however, the meeting signified Cairo's abandonment of the "unity of purpose" approach to Arab politics (which Moscow favored) and a return to cooperation with the conservative and pro-Western governments, such as Saudi Arabia and Jordan (which Moscow opposed), the change in the Kremlin's approach to Arab politics testified to both Khrushchev's awareness of the difficulty of Nasir's position and his determination to be as accommodating to his beleaguered Egyptian client as possible. One of the striking features of Moscow's reaction was the extensive coverage given to the conference, described by *Pravda* as the "most representative meeting of the leaders of the Arab countries to have taken place anytime in history."[9]

It is of interest to note, however, that the importance ascribed to the conference by Soviet and Egyptian journalists differed significantly, foreshadowing the divergence of opinion that would mark

---

7. For further details, see Malcolm Kerr, *The Arab Cold War, 1958–1967: A Study of Ideology in Politics* (London: Oxford University Press, 1967), p. 130.

8. Ivison Macadam, ed., *The Annual Register, 1964,* (New York: St. Martin's Press, 1965), p. 293.

9. P. Demchenko, *Pr.,* January 14, 1964. See also K. Vishnevetskii, *Izv.,* of the same date, *passim.*

Nasir's and Khrushchev's statements during the latter's May 1964 visit to the UAR. While Egyptian commentators emphasized the importance of the summit in terms of inter-Arab and Arab-Israeli relations, their Soviet counterparts found the "anti-imperialist content" of the meetings and their impact on the "national-liberation struggle" of the developing countries of primary interest. For example, to V. Kudriavtsev the summit was a "significant landmark in the history of the national-liberation struggle of the Arab East" and the chief villain was not Israel but the Western powers that stood behind it and prodded it to strike at the Arabs in order to undermine their struggle for genuine independence.[10]

Kudriavtsev noted also that the effectiveness of the "anti-imperialist" countermeasures depended on the Arabs' ability to settle their disputes. By and large, the Soviet press, echoing Nasir's current line, appeared rather confident that most inter-Arab disputes could be resolved and that a degree of harmony could be restored to relations among the feuding Arab governments. Quoting Moroccan *al-Alam* ("The most important step taken at the conference is the normalization of relations among the Arab countries"), Kudriavtsev agreed that inter-Arab relations had indeed improved substantially in the summit's wake and said that "in this respect, the ... conference was highly successful."[11] What Kudriavtsev overlooked, however, was brought up by the *New Times,* which noted that the recent summit resolutions notwithstanding, the Cairo-Damascus feud "evidently stands little chance of settlement at the present time." Moreover, despite the fact "that there was a clear desire to solve all issues peacefully, ... it would be naive to believe that the Cairo meeting put an end to all differences between the Arab states. The contradictions, some of which relate to social problems, are not easily smoothed out."[12]

Moscow may have early recognized in the Jordan waters affair

10. V. Kudriavtsev, *Izv.*, January 26, 1964. For the Egyptian view, see P. Gevorkyan, "Cairo Summit Meeting," *IA*, no. 3 (March 1964), p. 86.
11. V. Kudriavtsev, *Izv.,* January 26, 1964.
12. Editorial, "The Arab Summit Conference," *NT,* no. 4 (January 29, 1964), p. 3. See also V. Kudriavtsev, *Izv.,* January 26, 28, and 29, 1964; and E. Primakov, *Pr.,* January 28; and P. Demchenko, *Pr.,* January 30, 1964.

another of those typical Arab crises which consume a great deal of time and energy and produce much verbiage but little action. The Kremlin could also be reasonably certain that Cairo could not and therefore would not become engulfed in a military effort to prevent Israel from proceeding with its plans even if the other Arab governments insisted on this course of action. Since it may also be confidently assumed that the problem of the Jordan waters as such was of no significance to Moscow, it would appear that the Kremlin simply regarded it as an excellent opportunity to demonstrate once again to Nasir its benevolence at no cost to itself.

The fact that, by seizing the diplomatic initiative, Nasir had succeeded in improving his position in the Arab world mattered little to Moscow. It must have been understood that the basic cleavage separating the UAR President from his Ba'thi and conservative counterparts in the Arab East remained as deep as before and that he was still very much dependent upon Soviet moral and material support. It was in these circumstances that the Egyptian press announced on March 11 the impending visit to the United Arab Republic of Nikita Khrushchev.[13]

In the months preceding Khrushchev's arrival President Nasir made a noticeable effort to remove from the Egyptian political scene any possible irritants that might displease his guest and lead to diplomatic complications. His Unity Day speech of February 22, honoring the creation of the United Arab Republic, lashed out against imperialism and neo-colonialism and demanded the liquidation of foreign military bases "all over the world." He said that the Arabs were well aware of the "serious threat" to their security emanating from the British bases in Cyprus and US bases in Libya and called for their early elimination. Needless to say, these sentiments were reported in the Soviet press with satisfaction and gratification.[14]

Moscow appeared equally pleased with internal political developments in the UAR. For instance, many of the basic principles underly-

13. *Pravda* first mentioned it on March 20.
14. See, for example, *Pr.*, February 24, 1964. See also Nasir's speeches of April 6 and May 1, as referred to in *MEJ* 18, no. 3 (Summer 1964): 348, 349.

ing Egypt's new electoral laws met with Soviet approval. One of the more important provisions, it was felt, was the stipulation that not less than half of the 350 deputies to the National Assembly were to consist of workers and peasants. *Pravda* noted that the "implementation of this principle [in the wake of the March 10 elections] . . . should be considered a major political event." The new parliament was thus being established on a "new social basis." Therefore, despite the fact that the local branches of the Arab Socialist Union, Egypt's only political organization, had not yet worked out a "clear definition as to who belongs to the category of workers and peasants, the new situation represents a definite improvement over the past . . . [and] testifies to the continuation of the [Egyptian] revolution."[15]

Finally, following up on Nasir's 1963 promise, the Egyptian government announced on March 19, 1964, that it intended to release in the near future all those political prisoners who had not been tried by the courts.[16] In early April, President Nasir declared that the state of emergency in Egypt had been lifted and that no one who had not been convicted by the courts remained in prison.[17] Commenting on the reported release of 450 political prisoners and on the closing of the detention camps in the UAR, *Pravda* lauded these measures as an "important step in the process of democratization of political life in the United Arab Republic."[18] The stage for Khrushchev's visit had thus been set.

The Party Secretary arrived in Alexandria aboard the liner "Armenia" on May 9, and was met by President Nasir and other Egyptian dignitaries. During his 16-day visit, Khrushchev was invariably extended red-carpet treatment far surpassing the normal courtesies reserved for such occasions. Tumultuous crowds, waving banners and shouting laudatory slogans, greeted him wherever he went. He was

15. P. Demchenko, *Pr.,* March 10, 1964. On the results of the elections, see *ibid.,* March 23. For comments on the Constitutional Proclamation of March 23, which replaced the Provisional Constitution of 1958 and the Constitutional Declaration of 1962, see R. Arutyunov, "The New U.A.R. Constitution," *NT,* no. 16 (April 22, 1964), p. 28.
16. *Al-Ahram,* March 19, 1964.
17. *MEJ* 18, no. 3 (Summer 1964): 348.
18. *Pr.,* April 4, 1964.

asked to attend numerous social functions, addressed the UAR National Assembly, and was awarded the Collar of the Nile, the country's highest decoration. The Party Secretary reciprocated by conferring the title of "Hero of the Soviet Union" on Nasir and 'Amir. (Until late April 1964, when similar privilege had been accorded Algeria's President Ben Bella, such distinction was reserved for Communist dignitaries.) The highlight of the visit was the ceremony marking the completion of the first stage of the Aswan High Dam: on May 14, Khrushchev and Nasir together set off a dynamite charge that opened a channel to divert the Nile waters.[19]

It might be noted marginally that Khrushchev's visit to the UAR was regarded by some observers at the time as an indication that Nasir was a "a stooge of the Kremlin" working to facilitate a Soviet takeover of Middle Eastern oil.[20] As was to be expected, Cairo's publications took strong exception to such statements. While sparing no praise for Khrushchev and the USSR, the Egyptian press kept on insisting that the Party Secretary's visit was but another "living example of the policy of peaceful coexistence between countries with different . . . [political and social systems, based on mutual] respect for the national sovereignty of each country."[21]

One of the more important and constantly recurring themes associated with the visit was the necessity for the struggle against imperialism. In his pronouncements on this topic both before and during the Khrushchev visit, Nasir came close to a wholesale adoption of the Soviet line. His display of militancy may have reflected an awareness of the fact that Khrushchev's visit to Egypt was intended, in part, to justify to his constituency in the Kremlin his initial decision to embark upon an ambitious policy in the Third World. Thus, following the presentation to Khrushchev of the Collar of the Nile, President Nasir

19. For details, see *MEM*, no. 20 (May 16, 1964), p. 1 *et passim*.
20. A statement by Senator Ernest Gruening of Alaska, as quoted in *MEJ* 18, no. 3 (Summer 1964): 349.
21. *Al-Ahram,* May 9, 1964, as quoted in *MEM*, no. 20 (May 16, 1964), p. 11. See also *al-Gumhuriya,* as quoted in *ibid.,* and an article by Khalid Muhiy al-Din, Deputy Chairman of the UAR National Assembly, in *Pr.,* May 9, 1964.

FINALE: KHRUSHCHEV'S VISIT TO EGYPT 271

stated that the two countries were working together

> in the struggle for peace and progress. We united our efforts in the struggle against colonialism in all of its forms and manifestations, in the backing of the liberation movements in Asia, Africa, and Latin America, in the struggle for disarmament, the liquidation of foreign bases, the banning of nuclear weapons; in the struggle against racial discrimination, [and] for peaceful coexistence among the nations.

In the same speech, Nasir also accepted Moscow's current ideological dictum (something he had not done before) stipulating that the achievement of "political independence" was not tantamount to "complete independence." (The latter, the Soviet ideologists insisted, could be reached only by breaking off *economic* relations with the imperialist powers.) Needless to say, Nasir's pronouncement did not imply that Cairo was about to terminate its extensive economic contacts with the Western world. Verbal endorsement of an important plank of the Soviet ideological platform was designed merely to please the guests and its implementation was not seriously contemplated in the near or distant future. Nasir's speech was also significant in that, while thanking the USSR for its support of Egypt, it reminded Khrushchev that the relationship between the two countries had by no means been one-sided. It had been, after all, Cairo's refusal to associate itself with the Baghdad Pact that had prevented the transformation of the Middle East into a military base directed against the Soviet Union.

Nasir also emphasized that Egyptian society had discarded its "feudal-capitalist" character and was currently engaged in "building socialism." In addition to economic reform, he continued, the "efforts of the people are directed toward the implementation of the democratization of the sociopolitical sphere." In pursuing this course, Nasir insisted, Egypt was not only "building a socialist society for its people" but was also "setting an example for the establishment of a new society for the entire Arab nation." Finally, as might have been expected, Nasir used the opportunity to blast Israel as an "imperialist base ... in the middle of the Arab homeland." As evidenced by its latest "aggressive move" (the decision to proceed with the diversion of the Jordan waters), Tel-Aviv, with the encouragement of the Western powers, was forever bent on expansion.[22]

In his speech of May 9, Khrushchev refrained from commenting on a number of these issues raised by Nasir. He joined the UAR President in condemning "imperialist provocations" and praised Cairo's support of the USSR at the time of the Cuban missile crisis. The Soviet government noted with pleasure Egypt's endorsement of recent measures designed to reduce international tension, among them the Nuclear Test-Ban Treaty, and its adherence to "anti-imperialist attitudes and policies." In conclusion, Khrushchev noted his government's determination to maintain and broaden the policy of cooperation and friendship with the United Arab Republic.[23]

While imperialism, neo-colonialism, and the necessity of eliminating their influence in the underdeveloped world remained one of the main themes of most of Khrushchev's speeches in Egypt, his May 10 address before a youth rally in Cairo contained his first references to the internal situation in the UAR. The Party Secretary expressed his admiration for the "freedom-loving" Egyptian people, who had "successfully revolted against capitalist exploitation" and, in so doing, established an "independent national economy—a base for the country's development along the socialist path." Khrushchev described the socioeconomic changes that had taken place in Egypt as a proof that the "people of the UAR have rejected the capitalist system of oppression and are proceeding in the struggle for their social liberation."[24] Thus, while Nasir continued to speak in terms of an *established* socialist system in Egypt,[25] his Soviet guest deliberately refrained from conferring upon the UAR this "high distinction." Thus Khrushchev continued to adhere to the official Soviet line that some under-

22. Text quoted in *Pr.*, May 10, 1964.
23. *Ibid.*
24. *Pr.*, May 11, 1964.
25. Khrushchev actually did refer to Egypt as a "democratic socialist state," but *Pravda,* in reproducing his speech, was careful to place the phrase in quotation marks, indicating that he was using the language adopted by the UAR government. *Ibid.*

developed nations have merely "embarked upon the path of socialist construction," meaning that they have taken only the initial (albeit important) step in the direction of socialism.

Meaningless as these verbal exercises may appear to be, they indicated that the Party Secretary had important reservations about some of the ideological claims advanced by the UAR President. Khrushchev no doubt continued to regard Nasir as a "pseudo-socialist," a view he had propounded openly in 1961, and he may also have been motivated by the considerations of his ideological controversy with Peking. Finally, his behavior may also have been dictated by a desire not to appear as Nasir's mere equal: their respective "social standings" dictated a certain amount of aloofness, and by stressing the differences between the two systems (and, by implication, also between the two men) the Party Secretary may have hoped to make clear some of the ground rules he expected to govern their relations during his visit.

Nasir appears to have sensed the implication contained in Khrushchev's remarks. In his May 11 speech before the UAR National Assembly (which both men were invited to address), the President lavished praise on his guest—"one of the leaders of a great revolution" —and on the Soviet experience, which "liberated hundreds of millions of people from feudalism and exploitation, from the rule of imperialism, [and] paved their way into the age of the atom and the cosmos in the name of man."[26] But Nasir also reminded his audience that they could be proud of their achievements. The two revolutions, though seemingly unrelated at first glance, had much in common, he continued, and were equal in their importance to their respective peoples.[27] There can be no doubt that these remarks were directed primarily at Khrushchev and that they were designed to convey politely but firmly the message that Nasir rejected any implicit or explicit notions of the superiority of Russia's revolutionary experience. Moreover, the UAR President intimated that he regarded himself as a revolutionary hero—a distinction Khrushchev could not possibly

26. *Pr.*, May 12, 1964.
27. As quoted in *MEM*, no. 20 (May 16, 1964), p. 7.

claim for himself—and that he, in his own independent fashion, was striving to achieve for Egypt some of the gains allegedly attained by the Soviet leaders in Russia. Just as the Russians were free to decide their own destiny, so the Arabs would not settle for less. Implicitly rejecting the Marxist notion that Communism constituted the "way of the future," Nasir insisted that the "entire Arab nation . . . is itself deciding its fate and choosing its path into the future."[28]

Khrushchev's address to the National Assembly attests to his awareness of the undercurrents that characterized Nasir's speech. The Soviet government, he said, had no intention of interfering in the internal affairs of any country. At the same time, the Party Secretary had no intention of giving ground on any of the other issues. The Soviet people, he continued, applauded Cairo's efforts to create a socialist system and felt that these endeavors had in fact been crowned with a measure of success. The USSR government was particularly pleased with this turn of events because the Soviet people were the *"first* to raise the banner of the struggle against the exploiters, the banner of socialism." The nationalization of industry was followed by the collectivization of land, Khrushchev said, and "from an economically backward country, we emerged as a most powerful industrial nation." All of these victories, he concluded, were gained because the Soviet Union "proceeded along the path of socialism, as indicated by the great Lenin. We have proceeded, do proceed, and will proceed to follow this the only correct path."[29]

In reasserting his previous insistence on the superiority of the Soviet ideological experience and material achievements, Khrushchev implicitly rejected Nasir's egalitarian approach to revolutions. The UAR President was being none too subtly reminded to keep both his revolution and his own role in it in a proper historical perspective. As for Egypt's socioeconomic transformation, Moscow clearly approved of many of the measures introduced since 1952 and wished Cairo luck in their continued application; however, the Kremlin refused to label them as "socialist" and insisted, as it had in 1961, that independent

28. Text quoted in *Pr.,* May 12, 1964.
29. Text in *ibid.* Italics added.

experimentation was senseless and that the Marxist-Leninist (i.e., Soviet) method was the only valid approach to "meaningful" socialist development.

Switching to inter-Arab problems, Khrushchev unequivocally supported Nasir's appeal for the liquidation of foreign military bases in the Middle East, above all in Aden, Libya, and Cyprus. The Soviet government also endorsed Arab demands for Israel's compliance with UN resolutions on Palestinian refugees and called upon Tel-Aviv to desist from "imperialist projects aiming at the diversion of the river Jordan."

Khrushchev's remarks on Arab unity were of particular interest, since that subject, in a few days' time, was to give rise to the liveliest public controversy of the entire visit. In his speech of May 11, the Party Secretary insisted that the USSR had "always [and] with deep understanding approached the idea of Arab unity, based on the principles of mutual defense . . . , maintenance of peace . . . , and raising the well-being of all the Arab peoples." The strengthening of cooperation among the Arab countries on an "anti-imperialist, anti-colonial basis," he continued, deprived the colonial powers of an opportunity to utilize for their own purposes the differences that divided the Arabs. At the same time, returning to an old theme, Khrushchev reminded his listeners that a successful defense of the gains made by the Arabs and victory for those who were still engaged in the "struggle for freedom" depended on the "unity of all revolutionary, progressive forces of the world." He also warned his hosts that they would be harming their own interests if they preferred groupings based on the color of one's skin or religious convictions to the "unity of all revolutionary forces."[30]

Khrushchev's main pronouncements on the subject were made at Aswan on May 16, and in Cairo a few days later. At a mass rally dedicated to the presentation of awards to the workers and engineers engaged in the construction of the High Dam, Khrushchev became annoyed at some of the remarks made by Iraq's President 'Arif. Referring to the day of the closing of the Nile as the "day of Ara-

30. *Ibid.*

bism," 'Arif described the meeting at Aswan, which was also attended by President Ben Bella of Algeria, as an "expression of Arab unity."[31] In typical Arab oratorical style, 'Arif also thanked the Almighty that he and his friends were Arabs and expressed willingness to make unspecified sacrifices "for the sake of the Arabs. . . . Imperialism and its henchmen are still attempting to implement their schemes aimed at splitting our ranks. . . . I swear to you before God that we, advocates of unity, will strive for unification. . . ."[32]

When his turn to speak came, the Secretary discarded his prepared remarks and, according to the Soviet account, inquired whether the audience preferred him to be pleasant or to speak "from the heart." Having been "encouraged" to do the latter, Khrushchev proceeded to reprimand his hosts for having made the Russians feel unwanted ("If you take this position, it might seem that we . . . have nothing to do here . . . and should pack and go home"). Taking the offensive, he then attacked "certain speakers" who had used the occasion to speak only of Arabs and *their* unity, while in reality only unity based on a "labor and class basis" made any sense at all in terms of the national liberation struggle.

Moreover, Khrushchev continued, the USSR had no intention of helping the Arabs in general. It had come to the assistance of the Egyptian people, "engaged in the struggle against imperialism and colonialism . . . so that the working class, the peasantry, the laboring intelligentsia, and all the progressive forces of the nation might move more rapidly in building a new life." This, the Party Secretary said, was an application of Lenin's philosophy that had triumphed in the Soviet Union and would eventually triumph "in many other countries when the peoples of the former colonies develop and unite on a wider basis."

Khrushchev concluded by appealing for a modification of the term "Arab unity" to mean "fraternal unification of all Arab toilers, all people of labor against the imperialists, the exploiters, the colonialists, the monopolies, and for the victory of labor." In short, he suggested that the slogan "Arabs, unite!" be made more precise:

31. *Pr.*, May 18, and *MEM*, no. 21 (May 23, 1964), p. 3, respectively.
32. *Pr.*, May 18, 1964.

Arab workers, Arab peasants, Arab intelligentsia, all people of labor must unite in the struggle for freedom and independence, for a better life, for their rights against the exploiters. Given such unification, a place will be found for the Russians, . . . for the representatives of other nations, for all those who live by their labor, who fight for freedom, a better life, and the happiness of the people.[33]

Khrushchev's off-the-cuff remarks required a rebuttal, and President Nasir delivered it on May 20 at their joint meeting with the representatives of Egypt's trade-unions. The UAR President insisted that Arab unity was not a "racist slogan" but a reflection of "deep historical reality." The Arabs, his argument ran, had always formed a single nation marked by a "unity of material existence, a single conscience, and a single world view." The political and administrative divisions, relatively recent in origin, had been imposed by the imperialist powers, who "thrust upon the Arabs a situation which contradicts the nature, history, and the will of the people and coincides only with the interests of a tiny handful of exploiters who greedily reach out for thrones . . . for the sake of plunder and exploitation."

Nasir agreed with Khrushchev that "imperialism," aware of the Arabs' desire for unity, sponsored what Cairo regarded as "false unity projects." Needless to say, these "distorted ideas" were rejected by the Arab masses. An appreciation of their sentiments led the Egyptian government to adopt the "slogan of the unity of purpose as the basic condition of unity . . . among the working forces of the people." Nasir concluded his remarks on a conciliatory note, saying that there was no place for "feudalism and capitalism" in a unity that would eventually be based on "freedom and socialism."[34] The UAR President did not elaborate on the meaning of these terms. In this particular instance, as on many other occasions, high-sounding rhetoric enabled him to conceal basic differences of substance. He also succeeded in rebuffing his Soviet guest while creating an impression of outward harmony and understanding.

But the Party Secretary was not to be denied. Replying to Nasir,

33. Text in *ibid.*
34. *Pr.,* May 21, 1964.

and again departing from his prepared text,[35] Khrushchev said that he had listened to his host with "great attention and satisfaction." He conceded that the problem of Arab unity was indeed "truly important" and that "some differences" in its interpretation remained between the Soviet and the UAR governments. The former conceived of unity "somewhat more broadly, not merely as unity within a national framework . . . but as unity with all the peoples for building a socialist and a Communist society." Therefore, had Arab unity been consummated on the basis of the "unification of the working people against the exploiters," it would complement the "common struggle of the peoples of all countries . . . for a better future, for the building of a Communist society, if the term does not frighten you." Then, in an apparent tactical shift, Khrushchev proceeded to confer his blessings on Arab unity, as interpreted by President Nasir:

> We are heartily in favor of your unification, of your being a force, of your being the owners of your riches. Not only does this not contradict our policy, it fully conforms to our interests. [For] if the strength and might of the Arab people is added to the economic might of the Soviet Union, these two forces will operate more actively against the enemies of peace and the enemies of socialism.[36]

In view of the Kremlin's previous pronouncements on Arab unity, it is tempting to regard this statement as a significant public concession to Cairo. But upon closer examination it becomes evident that the USSR not only had not changed its basic approach to the problem (as indeed Khrushchev never tired of pointing out) but that the conditional acceptance of Nasir's position was predicated upon his abandonment of nonalignment in favor of a close association with Moscow. Their joint purpose was to work for the establishment of the Communist order throughout the world! Since the UAR was not about to commit itself to the Kremlin to such an extent, however, Khrushchev's endorsement of Arab unity simply helped to under-

35. *MEM*, no. 21 (May 23, 1964), p. 4.
36. *Pr.*, May 21, 1964.

score the deep ideological and long-range political gap separating the USSR from its Egyptian clients.

Aware of the unpleasant undercurrents that had almost surfaced during the visit, the two leaders went out of their way to dispel any appearance of disharmony at its conclusion. In a speech at a banquet that he gave in Nasir's honor on May 24, Khrushchev announced that the Kremlin was granting Egypt another long-term loan of over 250 million rubles.[37] The Party Secretary said also that in his conversations with President Nasir "an identity of views on the solution of international problems" had been achieved and thanked his host for making the visit "a success." Reciprocating, Nasir expressed Egypt's appreciation for Soviet aid and noted that Cairo's friendship with Moscow rested not only on practical considerations but also on a similarity of goals: "We and the Soviets are partners in building the future world of peace."[38]

The official communiqué, published at the conclusion of Khrushchev's visit, underscored Moscow's and Cairo's mutual desire to maintain an outward appearance of harmony and good relations within the limits of their rapprochement. Thus, their respective approaches to some of the "cardinal international questions" were reportedly "coinciding." (The fact that the term "identical" was not used is in itself quite revealing.) Among them were the questions of rendering assistance to peoples engaged in the national liberation struggle and of adhering to the principle of peaceful coexistence in relations between countries with different social and political systems. The two sides also condemned "imperialist efforts to impose their influence and domination on countries which have embarked upon the path of independent development," and demanded the liquidation of foreign military bases all over the world.

After singling out the UAR for its contribution "in serving the cause of freedom and the defense of world peace," Khrushchev offered Soviet support for the "struggle of the Arab states against the

---

37. The loan, it was reported at the time, was "in addition to the $1 billion in military aid and $500 million in economic aid that the Egyptians have received from the Soviet Union." *MEJ* 18, no. 3 (Summer 1964): 349.

38. *MEM*, no. 22 (May 30, 1964), p. 5.

aggressive intrigues of the imperialist forces." He promised to back efforts to settle the Palestine question "in conformity with UN decisions and with due regard for the legitimate and inalienable rights of the Palestinian Arabs." Finally, the Soviet side supported the Arab position on the utilization of the Jordan waters and saluted the Algerian and Yemeni peoples, who were waging a "national-liberation struggle" against "foreign aggressors." In return, Cairo subscribed to the Soviet position on the questions of the German peace treaty, Cuba, and the reorganization of the UN Secretariat. Turning to the problem of Soviet aid to the UAR, the communiqué expressed both parties' satisfaction with the successful implementation of the various economic and technical agreements, while Nasir noted his government's gratification at Moscow's willingness to supply Cairo with modern military equipment.

Significantly, the document passed in silence a number of questions raised in the speeches of Khrushchev and Nasir, including the problem of Arab unity and of the socioeconomic and political development of the UAR. The talks between the two leaders were described as "cordial, frank, and friendly," but since, in Communist parlance, these terms (especially "frank") are usually used to indicate wide areas of disagreement between the negotiating parties, it might be concluded that the conversations held between Khrushchev and Nasir were not so fruitful as the Kremlin may have hoped beforehand. The questions raised directly by the communiqué are, in fact, less significant than the issues omitted.[39]

In a highly unusual procedure, Khrushchev reported on his trip in a TV-radio speech on May 27, only one day after his return to Moscow. His comments reinforce the impression that he had been aware of the criticism (both in and outside the Kremlin) to which his policies in the underdeveloped world in general and Egypt in particular had been subjected. Since he used this opportunity to rebuff his critics, it may be safely assumed that he also sensed the rising dissatisfaction in party circles with his leadership and felt that he was in need of some concrete example of the wisdom of his important policy decisions.

39. Full text in *Pr.*, May 25, 1964.

Thus, it was not surprising that in his report he devoted considerable attention to the Aswan High Dam and to Moscow's role in implementing this gigantic project. In brief, he referred to the construction of the Dam as an "outstanding page in the history of modern Egypt," and as a "symbol of Soviet-Arab friendship." The success of this undertaking, Khrushchev noted, depended entirely upon the wholehearted support and cooperation of the USSR. Although the Party Secretary avoided an outright declaration on this point, his speech definitely implied that the decision to help Egypt was his and that the success of the Soviet personnel and equipment had been guaranteed by his brilliant leadership.

Judging from Khrushchev's remarks, some of the criticism he was encountering must have been directed at the magnitude of his foreign aid program. A revealing remark conceded that the extensive Soviet material backing of a number of underdeveloped countries had not, after all, been motivated by altruism: "We want the efforts of the socialist world, of the national-liberation movement, and of the revolutionary forces of the working people of the capitalist countries to unite in the struggle against imperialism.... We thereby strike a blow against the plans of the imperialists." Khrushchev admitted that in aiding the developing nations the USSR was limiting the resources needed for its own use. But, he insisted, "we would be poor Communists, poor internationalists, if we thought only of ourselves," and he claimed that the assistance that was rendered to the countries of the Third World would be repaid "a hundredfold."

In addressing himself to the problems of socioeconomic and political development in Egypt, Khrushchev appeared to be answering his Chinese and other "left-deviationist" critics, who charged that the Soviet government was extending massive material aid to governments that, far from being Marxist, had persecuted Communists and had pursued policies in conflict with the interests of "international Communism." In approaching the problem "with complete frankness," the Party Secretary admitted that the "journey along the road of socialist development upon which the United Arab Republic is embarking is not a simple or easy matter." "Great efforts" would be required "to overcome obstacles and to find the correct path of development." Of overriding importance, however, was the fact that Cairo appeared to be genuinely searching for "new paths." Nasir's anti-Communism in particular, Khrushchev felt, was definitely a thing of the past. Needless to say, this too served to vindicate the Secretary's wisdom and foresight; it was, after all, he who had predicted peaceful evolution of "national-democratic" states along the lines of "socialist construction."

Khrushchev's defensive posture was underscored by his discussion of Arab unity. Specifically, he denied that any "basic differences" existed between Moscow's and Cairo's respective views on this subject. In his references to Arab unity, Khrushchev said, he had emphasized Communist support for "unity of the working peoples, regardless of race, nationality, religion, or geographic location." He also insisted that "such an approach to unity . . . [did] not contradict the striving of the Arab people for unification in the struggle against the imperialists, the colonizers, and the exploiters."[40]

Some of the views expressed by Khrushchev in his TV and radio speech had been expounded in a *Pravda* article signed by Chief Editor Pavel Satiukov (a functionary who was generally regarded as one of Khrushchev's clients and collaborators) and by correspondents I. Beliaev and P. Demchenko, on May 24. The authors argued that "life and the logic of the class struggle" had confronted the Egyptian revolution with the necessity of solving the latent conflict between the exploiters and the exploited. Once President Nasir had decided to proceed with his program of "radical reforms" and announced that socialism was the "main goal in the struggle of the people," he had become convinced that his main support came from the "broad popular masses, the toilers."[41] Hence, the authors felt, it was not really surprising that among the important recent changes that had taken place in the UAR were the decisive attempts to implement a socialist program and to introduce a radical change in the concept of Arab unity. In support of this claim, *Pravda* cited Nasir's statement to the

40. Full text in *ibid.*
41. For an elaborate commentary on this theme, see Observer, "Roots of Soviet-Arab Friendship," *NT,* no. 22 (June 3, 1964), pp. 1–3.

FINALE: KHRUSHCHEV'S VISIT TO EGYPT

effect that "Arab unity . . . will be created on the basis of freedom and socialism," and also quoted excerpts from an article by Ahmad Bahay al-Din: "The unity to which we aspire . . . must be based on the support of the toilers and not on the interests of reaction and imperialism." This led to the conclusion that "this interpretation by the Egyptians of the problem of Arab unity . . . [was] a step forward leaving behind it the stage where the sentiments of 'Arab nationalism' were utilized by the Arab bourgeoisie for their own benefit."[42] On the question of anti-Communism, the authors had no doubt that if Nasir meant what he said about adherence to socialism, he had no choice but to seek the cooperation of the Egyptian Communists: "President Nasir's internal policy demonstrates that all progressive forces must become allies in the struggle against imperialism, for socialism."[43]

The overall picture that emerges from Khrushchev's speeches and the comments of the Soviet press is that of a great leader who had initiated a policy of collaboration with the developing countries and continued to maintain close relations with them even when their internal policies left a great deal to be desired. Further, the impression was conveyed that Khrushchev's wisdom and foresight had now been rewarded, for, as a *Pravda* editorial noted on May 11, the "powerful revolutionary forces of the present—the world socialist system . . . , the struggle of the proletariat in the capitalist countries, and the national-liberation movement"—had "merged into one stream." Together, they dealt "decisive blows against the imperialist and colonialist system. The unity of these forces, their continuing strength and development, are a dependable guarantee for the creation of a new world in which there will be no place for war and for the exploitation of man by man."

The fact that Khrushchev and his associates seemed to have accepted Nasir's own interpretation of Arab unity and of the tranformations that were allegedly taking place in the UAR reinforces the suspicion that they were simply looking for a justification for the

---

42. On Arab unity, see also editorial, "Visits of Peace and Friendship," *IA*, no 7 (July 1964), p. 4.
43. *Pr.*, May 24, 1964. See also Observer, "Roots of Soviet-Arab Friendship," *NT*, no. 22 (June 3, 1964), pp. 1–3.

Secretary's initial premise that the process of change in the Third World constituted a net gain for the Soviet Union. This was a relatively momentary change, however, for Soviet publications soon reverted to their previous propaganda lines. With a few important exceptions, references to Cairo's embarkation upon the "path of building socialism" all but disappeared from their pages, along with allusions to the "progressive" nature of Nasir's reforms. Instead, emphasis was once again placed upon the "community of views and purposes" with regard to the solution of important international problems. Leading among them were "the consolidation of peace and international security, general and complete disarmament, creation of nuclear-free zones, elimination of foreign bases . . . , peaceful settlement of territorial . . . disputes, consistent pursuit of the policy of peaceful coexistence as the basis of relations between states with different social systems, [and] struggle against imperialism and colonialism."[44]

It was obvious that Khrushchev had arrived in the UAR "with many powerful advantages," as the *Economist* put it. In the eyes of many Egyptians, he was the man who had taken grave risks in an effort to halt the tripartite aggression of 1956. He also had extended to Egypt large-scale economic and technical aid, enabling the country to embark upon an ambitious industrialization program. He had agreed to underwrite the costs and to provide Soviet personnel for the construction of the Aswan High Dam. Finally, it was he who had been responsible for supplying the Egyptian armed forces with up-to-date weapons and advisers, designed to turn them into a modern, powerful instrument of war.[45]

It would appear that these considerations should have ensured Khrushchev a warm welcome, making it quite unnecessary for him to appease his hosts by means of additional concessions. Yet he not only promised Nasir a supply of additional military equipment and granted Egypt a large new loan but also expressed approval of most

44. Editorial, "Visits of Peace and Friendship," *IA*, no. 7 (July 1964), p. 3.
45. *Economist*, May 16, 1964, p. 705.

of Nasir's domestic and foreign policies and implied that Cairo was free to pursue its own path toward socialism. In relation to Middle Eastern politics, the Party Secretary endorsed (albeit with reservations) the principle of Arab unity, backed Nasir's demands for the withdrawal of foreign bases from the area, condemned Israel as an "imperialist base," and supported the Arab position on the Jordan waters problem.

Most of these pronouncements were in line with the Kremlin's previously held positions, of course, and it would not be fair to say that Khrushchev was motivated by a simple desire to accommodate Nasir. But it is clear that one of the primary factors behind Khrushchev's attitude was to be found in Soviet *domestic* politics: the Secretary was almost certainly endeavoring to improve his deteriorating position in the Kremlin by means of a "triumphant" tour of Egypt. The visit was to serve as a vindication of his innovative policy in the Third World. Success, Khrushchev may have hoped, would help him recoup the loss of confidence in him attendant upon such political failures as Berlin and Cuba, and, in so doing, silence some of his opposition, at home and abroad.

As impressive as Khrushchev's reception in Egypt actually was, there were occasional signs of strain and discord. The Party Secretary, for all his apparent determination to be as polite as possible, had brushed aside restraint and spoken "from the heart" on a number of delicate issues, above all Arab unity. (It might be noted marginally that the oppressive heat of the Egyptian summer no doubt contributed to his short temper.) Khrushchev's brusque dismissal of Western economic aid to the developing nations was particularly unfortunate, since Egypt was vitally dependent on US wheat shipments and other forms of assistance.[46] And references to socialism as a preliminary (and inevitable) step to Communism were hardly acceptable to the Egyptian leaders, who never tired of pointing to the "originality" of the Arab socialist experiment.

46. As a matter of fact, the International Monetary Fund had announced on May 27 its decision to lend Cairo $40 million "on liberal terms." *MEJ* 18, no. 3 (Summer 1964): 349.

Though such outbursts were bound to irritate Nasir, he succeeded in controlling his temper and, as in the case of the Arab unity discussion, developed a formulation that would not be offensive to Khrushchev. On May 26, however, only one day after the Secretary's departure, Nasir and 'Arif (with whose views on Arab unity Khrushchev had found himself in total disagreement) signed an agreement establishing a joint presidential council and military command. These moves were promptly described in Cairo and Baghdad as "a step towards unity between the two countries"[47] but were in addition a none-too-subtle rebuff to Khrushchev for what Nasir no doubt considered his meddlesomeness.

In any event, it would appear in retrospect that Khrushchev's trip to Egypt did not secure for the Party Secretary advantages significant enough to offset the political losses that he had suffered over the previous years. He was removed from office less than half a year later, and it may be safely assumed that some of his Egyptian escapades, including his ideologically indefensible attempt to establish kinship between Communism and Arab socialism, were held against him along with an impressive list of other "transgressions and deviations." This is not to say that the trip proved a decisive factor in his overthrow but that, rather than halting the slide in Khrushchev's political fortunes, it probably helped to accelerate the process that resulted in his downfall.

During the months immediately following the visit, the Soviet Union and the UAR continued to maintain outwardly friendly relations and cooperation in the economic and technical fields. In his perfunctory telegram on the eve of the twelfth anniversary of the revolution, Khrushchev praised Egypt as a country "now embarking on the path of socialist development," a development that created the most favorable conditions for raising the national economy, as well as "the culture and the well-being of the people." He also assured Nasir that the "people and the government of the United Arab Republic . . . [could] be confident of Soviet support in their noble struggle for peace and in their construction of socialism."[48] In his reply, Nasir expressed

47. *MEM*, no. 22 (May 30, 1964), p. 2.
48. Text in *Pr.*, July 23, 1964.

confidence that the "principles of freedom, socialism, and unity" that formed the basis of Egypt's struggle for liberation represented a "vital contribution to the cause of peace and progress."[49]

Interestingly, *Pravda* noted that socialism had emerged as the "main goal of the Egyptian revolution." Whereas until recently there could be no certainty about Cairo's intentions, the far-reaching reforms instituted in the UAR, coupled with recent negotiations between Algeria's NLF and Egypt's ASU, had demonstrated that "both countries are filled with the determination to build socialism on a *scientific* [i.e., Communist] basis."[50] Actually, one could attribute such a meaning to Nasir's statements and actions only by taking the wildest interpretive liberties.

The Soviet government also backed Cairo in its diplomatic undertakings, the most notable being the meeting of the heads of African countries, which convened in the Egyptian capital in mid-July,[51] and the second Arab summit, which met in Alexandria in early September 1964. In spite of the fact that the latter represented an outgrowth of Nasir's original concept of the "unity of ranks" and was thus completely devoid of ideological considerations, Khrushchev sent "warm regards and greetings" to the participants and alluded to the meeting as a "new proof of the growing unity of the Arab countries and peoples." He also pledged to the Arab leaders continued Soviet support in their "noble endeavors."[52]

The last important event in Soviet-Egyptian relations of the Khrushchev era was the visit to the USSR of Prime Minister 'Ali Sabri, undertaken for the ostensible purpose of working out the details of the use of the one-quarter-billion-ruble loan promised by Khrushchev during his stay in the United Arab Republic. The Sabri visit, marked by the customary red-carpet treatment reserved for an impor-

49. *Ibid.*, August 4, 1964.
50. I. Beliaev, *Pr.*, July 23, 1964. See also K. Vishnevetskii, *Izv.* of the same day, and editorial, "Youth of an Ancient Land," *NT,* no. 30 (July 29, 1964), p. 5. Italics added.
51. For some details, see P. Demchenko, *Pr.*, July 23, and editorial, "African Summit," *NT,* no. 29 (July 22, 1964), pp. 2–3. The text of Khrushchev's telegram to the Chairman of the conference in *Pr.*, July 17, 1964.
52. Text in *Pr.*, September 6. For editorial comment, see I. Beliaev, *ibid.*, September 16 and N. Khokhlov, *Izv.*, September 17, 1964.

tant dignitary of a friendly country, included meetings with high Soviet officials and a tour of the Central Asian republic of Uzbekistan. In their speeches at a Kremlin dinner party on September 15, both Sabri and Khrushchev hailed the friendship between their two countries and emphasized the desirability of further improving and widening their cooperation. The Party Secretary reiterated Soviet support of Arab unity and repeated his earlier assertion that Egypt was "embarking on the path of socialist development." This historic departure lent "new substance" to the Moscow-Cairo friendship, Khrushchev concluded, noting that the USSR was prepared "to discuss in detail all questions connected with further expansion of Soviet-Arab economic and technical cooperation."[53]

The joint communiqué of September 23, 1964, specified some of the projects to be undertaken in Egypt with Soviet aid. The largest among them was "an iron and steel complex with a capacity of more than a million tons a year." The USSR would also build "a 200,000 kilowatt electrical power station near Alexandria and, within the next three years, a lubricating oil plant at Suez with an annual output of 69,000 tons." In addition, Moscow undertook the construction of "machine tool and heavy machinery works," along with a number of training centers for industrial workers. Agreement was also reached on "Soviet aid in reclaiming land, especially in the western desert."[54]

The Egyptians appear to have been pleased with the agreement. In a press interview given prior to his departure from Moscow, Sabri said that the economic and technical aid agreement "marked a new stage in the strengthening of friendly and fruitful ties between the Soviet and Egyptian peoples and opened vast new horizons for joint work." [55]

Another important by-product of the Sabri-Khrushchev negotiations was the apparent attempt by both governments to establish close working relations between the CPSU and the Arab Socialist Union. Since information on this significant new departure in Moscow-Cairo

53. Texts of Khrushchev's and Sabri's speeches in *Pr.*, September 16, 1964.
54. *MEM*, no. 39 (September 26, 1964), p. 2. Text of the communiqué in *Pr.*, September 24. For editorial comment, see *ibid.*, September 25, 1964.
55. *MEM*, no. 39 (September 26, 1964), p. 3. For selected comments by the Egyptian press, see *Izv.*, September 25, 1964.

relations is practically nonexistent, it is impossible to determine the exact origin of initiative for extended contacts between the two organizations. In view of the fact that the Kremlin had previously endeavored to establish similar contacts with the official political parties in Algeria, Mali, and Guinea,[56] however, it is entirely possible that Moscow seized the initiative in this case as well. Yet it should also be borne in mind that President Nasir, who for years was concerned with the weakness and inefficiency of his regime's political base, might have been interested in drawing upon the organizational expertise of Soviet party functionaries.

In any event, some contacts on the party level apparently took place during the Sabri visit. *The Mideast Mirror,* for example, reported that "a surprise meeting has been arranged for . . . [Sabri] with officials of the Soviet Communist Party's central committee."[57] It was also rumored that, upon his return to Moscow from Uzbekistan, Sabri discussed with Khrushchev "relations between the Soviet Communist Party and the U.A.R. Socialist Union."[58] But nothing of substance was accomplished before the Party Secretary's ouster in mid-October 1964. With his abrupt "retirement," an eventful and important period in Soviet-Arab relations came to an end.

56. *MEM,* no. 38 (September 19, 1964), p. 8.
57. *Ibid.*
58. *Ibid.,* no. 39 (September 26, 1964), p. 2.

Conclusion
The Ultimate Failure of Khrushchev's Policies

As early as 1954, in a major departure from Stalin's post-World War II policy, Moscow had embarked upon an ambitious and far-flung campaign designed to undermine and, wherever possible, eliminate Western positions in the underdeveloped world, while drawing some of the newly independent nations into the Soviet sphere of influence. Ideologically, the policy was justified in terms of the desirability of creating and establishing the so-called zone of peace, based on an alleged community of interests between the USSR and those former colonies and dependencies which were genuinely interested in gaining "complete independence" from the Western imperialist powers. Khrushchev's "peace offensive" usually took the form of extending Soviet political, economic, technical, financial, and, in some instances, military aid to those governments in the Third World which, for reasons of their own, were prepared to accept Moscow's cooperation. The degree of support and the quantities of funds, goods, supplies, and other forms of assistance differed from one recipient to another, depending, among other factors, on general exigencies of Soviet policies at any given time and the relative importance to the USSR of the leaders and policies of the countries in question.

In the Middle East, Khrushchev's determination to compete with the "capitalist" West was augmented by what he perceived as the necessity of neutralizing Western military presence in the area. More precisely, the creation of the Baghdad Pact, tied to NATO and SEATO through Turkey and Pakistan, respectively, was viewed by the Kremlin as the culmination of Washington's efforts to surround the USSR with a ring of Western bases. In so doing, Washington had reinforced the traditional "encirclement complex" of the Soviet leaders.

Khrushchev's initial efforts at penetration of the Arab East were relatively successful because of a uniquely favorable turn of events that Moscow had done little to bring about and over which it had no control. More precisely, the consummation of the 1955 arms agreement with Egypt was made possible by the decisive clash of Nasir's interests with those of the Western powers, which, in their determination to create a "position of strength" in the Middle East, had found in Nuri al-Sa'id of Iraq, Cairo's chief rival for the leadership of the Arab world, a ready client and ally. On the tactical level, however, Khrushchev deserves due credit for recognizing that the Middle Eastern situation of the 1950s could be utilized by the Kremlin to its own advantage.

That the USSR chose Cairo as its gateway to the Arab East was no mere coincidence. In surveying the Middle Eastern scene, Khrushchev must have been impressed by Nasir's ability to tackle a number of Egypt's pressing foreign and domestic problems. In his handling of them, the young Premier had displayed considerable energy, tenacity, and forcefulness—some of the important attributes of effective leadership. Nasir had also expressed himself in favor of positive neutralism, and, in so doing, had exhibited a determination to remain aloof from entangling alliances with the Western powers. By openly espousing and implementing a policy of opposition to Washington's determination to organize a regional defense alliance, Nasir was not only undermining Western influence and prestige in the Middle East but was also setting an example that some other Arab governments might be tempted to emulate. In addition, the Soviet leaders were aware of the military, political, and economic potential of Egypt, having recognized it as historically the most important link in the Arab chain.

Between 1955 and 1958, in an effort to establish an operational base in the area, the Kremlin extended to Cairo its full political and moral backing, coupled with massive military, technical, and economic support. The most notable manifestation of this policy was the decision to participate in financing and constructing the Aswan High Dam, the most ambitious project in the history of the Soviet foreign aid program. Yet Russian support of Nasir was hardly unqualified, and relations between Moscow and Cairo remained less than uniformly close and cordial. Indeed, after 1958, while it still cooperated with Cairo, Moscow not only did not object to, but sometimes actually welcomed, Nasir's increasing difficulties with his fellow-Arabs, particularly his quarrels with the Iraqis and Syrians and, after the Yemeni revolution, his massive involvement in the south of the Arabian peninsula.

Another distinctive feature of Khrushchev's policy in the underdeveloped world was an early recognition of the fact that "benevolent" (i.e., anti-Western) neutralist governments were a greater asset to the USSR than Communist-controlled satellites, for whose security and progress Moscow would be responsible but whose actions would be difficult to control. Hence the Kremlin not only did not favor but had actually opposed Communist takeovers in the countries of the Arab East. It should, of course, be noted that the lack of Soviet enthusiasm for the activities of the Arab Communist parties was based, in part, on an appreciation of the fact that nowhere in the region, not even in pre-1958 Syria and post-1958 Iraq, were the Marxist organizations strong enough to seize and hold power. But even if the Communists were somehow to gain control over some Arab country, they could be expected to make public demands for massive Soviet assistance without conferring upon Moscow the right to dictate their policies. The Kremlin would then be forced to shoulder all the liabilities of a great power-satellite relationship without enjoying many of its important assets. Moreover, open Soviet backing of the local Communist organizations was bound to create additional tensions in the government-to-government relations between Moscow and the neutralist Arab states. Finally, the establishment of a Communist regime (or regimes) in the Arab East would most assuredly have encountered general opposition from the surrounding Arab states. Not only would such a regime be extremely difficult to maintain in power even with Soviet backing, but such a "success'" would be certain to incur the wrath of Moscow's erstwhile non-Communist friends and clients. Feeling threatened, they could be expected to seek protection in a closer association with the West, thus dealing a decisive blow to positive neutralism—the very policy Khrushchev had worked so hard to encourage and support.

The Kremlin repeatedly appealed for respect of the right of the Marxist organizations to operate free from government restrictions and, ideally, to participate in state affairs. The Soviet attitude was usually expressed in terms of the desirability of establishing "democratic and anti-imperialist" regimes based on "national fronts" of "patriotic forces." At the same time, in addressing the various Communist parties in the underdeveloped world, Moscow openly objected to the tendency displayed by some Marxist leaders to pursue the ideologically pure but less-than-practical line of noncooperation with their bourgeois counterparts. Soviet calls for Communist moderation were based on the assumption that the "national bourgeoisie," despite its proverbial "dual nature," was carrying into effect some "basically progressive" reforms and should therefore be supported by the Marxists-Leninists.

Regardless of the ideological merits of its position, the Kremlin's attitude represented a thinly veiled attempt to dictate to the Arab Communists and to subordinate them to the requirements of Soviet policymakers. Not unexpectedly, the desire to direct and control their actions led to occasional difficulties with some of Moscow's Arab followers, notably the Iraqi and Syrian parties. While the former frequently disregarded Soviet appeals for moderation, Khalid Baqdash, leader of the Syrian Communist party, opposed cooperation with the conservative government in Damascus in the wake of the dissolution of the United Arab Republic at a time when Moscow favored such a course of action. The ideal state of affairs (from the Kremlin's standpoint)—the recognition of the legitimacy of Arab Communist parties and freedom of political and organizational activities, including participation in the decision-making process—was never fully attained in any Arab state during the Khrushchev era.

In retrospect, it seems likely that Khrushchev initially regarded his task in the Arab East as relatively simple: in supporting Egypt's strong man Nasir in his conflicts with the Western powers, Israel, and the pro-Western Arab governments (above all Iraq, Jordan, and Saudi Arabia), the Kremlin would contribute to the weakening of the West's positions while also establishing and cultivating its own influence in Cairo. There can be no doubt that at least during the earlier phase of its involvement (1955–1958) Moscow was primarily concerned with the Western strategic threat emanating from the Middle East and attempted to utilize the various levels of regional conflicts to limit and eventually eliminate Western military presence from the region. For this reason, the Kremlin leaders were not initially averse to help aggravate Arab-Israeli and inter-Arab tensions. At no time, however, was the Soviet government prepared to become directly involved in crises that could lead to a military confrontation with the United States.

Khrushchev must have discovered fairly early in the game, however, that even this relatively cautious approach to Middle Eastern problems was not without its serious drawbacks. For all of its apparent desire to be of assistance to Nasir and other like-minded Arab leaders, the Soviet government had little, if any, control over their policies and actions. Therefore, in a very important sense, the Kremlin found itself at the mercy of its Arab clients. The Suez crisis is a good illustration of such a dilemma: Khrushchev had not been consulted before Nasir's nationalization of the Suez Canal Company and had not even been apprised of the move. Nevertheless, he had to back Nasir or risk losing whatever influence the USSR had painstakingly built in Cairo during and following the period of the arms agreement. During the ensuing confrontation, as in the Lebanese and Iraqi crises of 1958, Khrushchev must have impressed his Arab clients as a man who was prepared to talk, argue, and even threaten, but not to act.

The overthrow of the pro-Western government in Iraq, the emergence of Qasim, and the ensuing rift between the neutralist regimes in Baghdad and Cairo represented the first serious challenge to the USSR's newly won position to emerge from within the region itself. When, after an initial (and unsuccessful) attempt at tightrope walking, the Kremlin clearly expressed its preference for revolutionary

Iraq, relations between Moscow and Cairo cooled perceptibly. Whereas, prior to 1959, the USSR had simply identified itself with the "objectively progressive" nationalist elements led by President Nasir and proceeded to make what political and propaganda capital it could out of their clashes with the West, Israel, and the pro-Western Arab governments, the Cairo-Baghdad feud affected the very foundation of Soviet policy. In its efforts to curb the growing influence of Egypt's "unreliable" leader, Moscow sided with Qasim and, in 1961, proceeded to back the conservative elements in Syria. In so doing, the Soviets departed from their position of 1959. For, whereas it could be argued that Qasim was after all "more progressive" than Nasir, the leaders of the Syrian revolt did not merit such a description. It could, of course, be argued that, in the case of the dissolution of the United Arab Republic, Moscow was applauding the play and not the players. Nevertheless, the fact remained that, as in the case of the Nasir-Qasim feud, the USSR once again had sided with a group opposing its Egyptian clients. This did not signify a total abandonment of Cairo; it meant merely that the Soviet government was endeavoring to keep Nasir in what to Khrushchev appeared to be his proper place.

Such tactical shifts and turns were based on Khrushchev's appraisal of the general situation and of his country's interests in the Arab East. More particularly, the relative closeness of Moscow's relations with Cairo and, to a lesser extent, Baghdad and Damascus, rested upon a coincidence of their tactical, short-range interests—above all, the mutual desire for weakening Western influence in the Arab East. Reinforcing this parallel interest were the Egyptian, Iraqi, and Syrian need for, and Moscow's willingness and ability to supply, military, economic, technical, and financial aid. In return, the Kremlin depended upon its Arab clients to serve as "proof" of the sincerity of its approach to the developing nations.

But coincidence of tactical goals was not equivalent to an identity of long-range, strategic interests. On that broader level, the Kremlin seems to have favored the elimination of the Western presence in the area, while the "progressive" Arabs, fully aware that such a turn of events would leave them at the mercy of their Soviet backers, were unwilling to undercut Western interests to the point where they would be completely withdrawn. Applying a Communist ideological formula to the temporary and limited convergence of Soviet-Arab nationalist interests, it is possible to speak of a "unity and conflict" of their respective policies toward each other and with regard to the West. This formulation would explain both their cooperation and the occasional flare-ups which, as Cairo was fond of saying, helped to "clear the air" in relations between Egypt and the USSR. It would also explain why, in times of strain, the two sides did not seriously contemplate breaking off what both obviously regarded as a mutually beneficial arrangement.

A basic area of conflict that attested to the incompatibility of long-range interests between the Soviets and the neutralist Arabs was exposed by the protracted controversy revolving around the concept of Arab unity, one of the main planks of Nasir's political platform. Even when, in 1963–1964, the Kremlin expressed what appeared to be guarded approval of Arab unity, Soviet spokesmen, including Khrushchev, continually expressed preference for a "single, anti-imperialist, democratic front of the Arab countries," an idea quite foreign to Nasir's own notions. The USSR continually attempted to undermine any efforts aimed at creating a large Arab state, because it realized that it would be very difficult, if not impossible, to control or even to influence a relatively strong and stable power in the Arab East.

The verbal portions of the 1959 and 1961 disputes between Moscow and Cairo, which openly demonstrated the limits of Soviet ability to influence the decisions of its clients in the Third World, were couched in ideological terms: the former crisis concerned the fate of the "progressive elements" in the United Arab Republic, whereas the latter revolved around the respective merits of Communism and "Arab socialism." At first glance, it may appear surprising that the two governments, in their efforts to cause each other to modify policies, would resort to ideological arguments. Upon closer examination, however, it becomes obvious that this was the only meaningful avenue for demonstrating displeasure and exerting pressure that the parties to the dispute were willing to use. Other possibilities, such as the discontinuation of Soviet aid programs (or even threats to do so) had to be dismissed for fear of demonstrating to its actual and potential clients the hollowness of Moscow's insistence on the "unselfish" nature of its assistance. (It will be recalled that, in the Arab East, such a threat was made only once, and even then, since it was carefully contained in a journalistic analysis rather than in a diplomatic communication, it was rightly disregarded by the Ba'thi government of Iraq.) Conversely, it made no sense at all for Nasir to refuse Soviet support of a type he badly needed.

No attempt to describe the framework within which Khrushchev's Arab policy operated would be complete without consideration of the West. It is thus possible to picture a trio of partially intersecting circles each representing the interests of one of the parties concerned; Arab, Soviet, and Western. While mutually conflicting on numerous obvious counts, their respective positions also fractionally overlapped, forming what can be described as areas of partial agreement. The interplay between these areas sheds additional light on the nature of Middle Eastern politics during the period under discussion, and it should be noted parenthetically that a similar situation of overlapping interests still obtains in the region.

Thus, it is possible to speak of an area of partial agreement between the neutralist Arabs and the USSR in their common anti-Western attitude and opposition to the creation in the Middle East of a Western-sponsored defense alliance. At the same time, however, their motivations were entirely different. The Kremlin was opposed not only to Western but also to Arab attempts to create a "situation of strength" in the area, while the neutralist Arabs were primarily interested in maintaining an independent, and, if possible, strong position in the big-power conflict.

Nasir probably realized better than most that a close association with the Soviet Union would eventually result in the Arabs' loss of sovereignty and independence, the very goals with which the Egyptian government identified itself. This explains Cairo's (and later Baghdad's and Damascus's) stress on positive neutralism and nonalignment, and their appeals to both power blocs to respect their desire to remain above big-power rivalry and to conduct their policies in the light of what they conceived to be Arab interests.

A similar area of partial agreement may also be said to have existed between the neutralist Arabs and the Western powers, in that both opposed an unlimited spread of Soviet influence and Communism in the Arab East and were interested in the stability and economic well-being of the area. However, here too we find only a kind of contentious agreement, for they differed in their interpretation of these terms. While the Western powers approached the problem of defense of the Middle East in terms of possible Soviet encroachments, the Arab states were primarily fearful of an Israeli aggression. Furthermore, the Western allies conceived any potentially successful program of intra-regional development as taking the form of Arab-Israeli cooperation. To the neutralist Arabs, on the other hand, a program of regional economic development would be acceptable only if it excluded Israel.

Finally, it is also possible to speak of an area of partial agreement between the Western powers and the USSR. For one thing, neither Washington nor Moscow exhibited a willingness to engage in a nuclear (or even a conventional) war for the sake of any Middle Eastern prize. Similarly, both displayed opposition to the establishment of a strong and united Arab state. Their attitude is quite understandable, because no matter how vigorously the neutralist leaders might insist on their determination to adhere to an independent course of action, there could be no guarantee against the eventual absorption of such a state by one of the blocs to the serious detriment of the other.

When drawing three circles in such a way that each intersects the other two, if the areas of overlap are at all substantial in size, there will also be a fourth area of simultaneous overlap among all three. This characteristic of the geometric model points to a final aspect of the relations between the three contending parties in the Arab East: all of them have, by and large, worked for the preservation of peace in the area. ("Peace" here means the absence of overt military hostilities between states and does not include the operations of, say, Palestinian guerrillas.) While all have also been interested in the economic development of the area, the Soviets may have been more concerned with the appearance than with the substance of progress. Truly significant economic gains might have strengthened local regimes to such an extent that they would lose most of their dependence on the Kremlin and thus inhibit the spread of Soviet influence in the Arab East.

On balance, it must be noted that during most of the Khrushchev era the USSR and the neutralist Arabs found in each other valuable allies who, for admittedly different reasons, often followed similar and complementary policies. In the process, each attempted to exploit the other for its own purposes. And, while the Arabs may have been taking far bigger risks—it was, after all, they who were gambling with the possibility of dependence on Moscow—Russia's entry into Middle Eastern politics was by no means an unqualified success.

It would appear that in his decision to enter the Middle Eastern scene Khrushchev had both grossly overestimated Moscow's capacity to influence the recipients of his aid programs and underestimated the Arab affinity for factionalism and strife. As a result, in the ensuing years the Kremlin found itself confronting a number of problems and crises over which it had relatively little control. In the context of Middle Eastern politics such crises could be classified in two general categories: (1) those initiated by Israel and the West or those in which the West had seized the initiative (Suez and Lebanon, respectively), leaving Khrushchev no choice but to display Soviet weakness and to adjust to a new situation; and (2) those initiated by Moscow's own clients. The "cold war" between Nasir and Qasim, as well as Egypt's relations with post-secessionist Syria, could be cited as examples in this category.

Since in crises in which the West was directly involved Khrushchev had no intention of challenging the United States, the alternative was an implied admission of Moscow's inferiority *vis-à-vis* Washington and a concurrent loss of prestige. In crises involving only his clients, Khrushchev's position was similarly ineffective: the Kremlin could remain neutral and be accused of insincerity by both feuding factions or side with one and incur the wrath of the other. In either case, the Soviet Union lost some prestige and influence—commodities that Khrushchev had worked hard to acquire. As a result, the USSR was often forced on the defensive, which explains why it was usually careful not to contribute to the outbreak of serious crises and why it often pursued a policy of relative noninvolvement after one had occurred. The only major exception to this rule was Khrushchev's backing of Qasim in the latter's 1958–1959 confrontation with Nasir. It will be remembered, however, that in this instance the Soviet attitude was dictated by what were, from Moscow's point of view, more important considerations. (It could, of course, be argued that the Soviets had benefited from Israeli victories in 1956 and 1967. Yet both of these conflicts represented a "loss of control" situation that no doubt made the Kremlin very nervous at the time.)

In short, once the basic decision to enter Middle Eastern politics had been implemented and potential friends had been transformed into actual clients, the Kremlin discovered that it had not acquired a great deal of additional leverage. Furthermore, it had actually lost some freedom of maneuver and was often forced to swim with the tide. Khrushchev may have found some consolation in the thought that, during his years in office, Western influence in the Arab East had been greatly reduced. But this did not alter the fact that Moscow's own ability to influence its clients had not been greatly affected by the Western decline. (Moreover, it is not always clear that Soviet actions were of any great significance in contributing to that decline; often Russia's most important contribution lay in simply *being* an available rival power.) It ultimately became apparent that politics in the Middle East is not a zero-sum game after all. In light of these considerations it could thus be argued that, far from gaining much in concrete terms, the Kremlin, after a considerable outlay of energy and resources, had little to show for its efforts: in crises that affected them directly, the Western powers and Israel acted without much regard for the USSR, while Moscow's Arab clients usually conducted their policies independently of Soviet wishes.

Some analysts have nevertheless concluded that, by the late 1950s-early 1960s, Moscow's efforts in the Arab East had in fact been crowned with success—Western influence had been significantly reduced by the events taking place in Jordan, Syria, Lebanon, and, above all, Iraq. On the military-strategic level, too, Soviet fears had been alleviated as US Jupiter missiles stationed in Turkey and Italy became obsolete and were removed in the wake of the Cuban missile

ULTIMATE FAILURE OF KHRUSHCHEV'S POLICIES 301

crisis. It was soon hereafter, however, that a new major strategic threat—the Polaris nuclear submarine—made its appearance in the Eastern Mediterranean. Constituting floating nuclear bases, the Polaris fleet provided the United States with a major new strategic weapons system and what appeared to be an untouchable second-strike capability, which greatly enhanced Washington's lead in the race for nuclear supremacy. The Kremlin had no choice but to attempt to counter this new threat to its security. Attempted permanent deployment of the Soviet fleet in the Mediterranean in 1964 makes sense only in the light of this strategic necessity. It is no exaggeration to state that *eskadra*'s primary initial function was to try to neutralize the nuclear threat created by Polaris submarines and thereby to enforce the credibility of Moscow's claim to nuclear parity with the United States.

While the initial decision to involve the USSR in Middle Eastern politics and to deploy a naval squadron in the Mediterranean was made by Khrushchev, the main burden of coping with the strategic nuclear threat represented by Polaris fell on the shoulders of his successors. The policies of Brezhnev and his colleagues are outside the scope of this dissussion but no appreciation of their activities in the late 1960s and early 1970s is possible without an understanding of Soviet policy in the Stalin and, above all, Khrushchev periods. Its origins are deeply rooted in the ever-present fear of the nuclear superiority of the United States.

In addition to strategic considerations, by entering the underdeveloped areas and by reorienting their trade toward the USSR, the Soviets had no doubt hoped to restrict commensurately investment and profit-making opportunities for Western capital. In so doing, they would presumably aggravate economic difficulties in the leading capitalist countries and intensify competition for the remaining outlets, leading to further divisions, friction, and conflict in the capitalist world. Therefore, if the desire of the new nations for complete independence could be encouraged by the USSR, Moscow hoped, in time, not only to weaken the West substantially but, by stepping in as an "unselfish" friend and ally of the developing countries, to acquire influence over them.

As far-fetched and unrealistic as this type of reasoning may appear in the 1970s, it should be remembered that, in the 1950s, Khrushchev appeared convinced of his ability to emerge victorious in peaceful competition with the Western world. His anticipation of dancing at the grave of capitalism (the literal meaning of his famous "We will bury you!") is an apt illustration of this line of thought, and it stands to reason that his belief in the basic weakness of the Western position in the Third World was one of the reasons for his unbridled optimism.

Moreover, Khrushchev was deeply conscious not only of Russia's steadily growing might but also of her definite inferiority to the United States in the ability to deliver a telling nuclear blow. In an attempt to conceal this weakness, Khrushchev was hard at work creating an image of the USSR as a superpower equal, if not superior, to its American counterpart. The use of giant rocket boosters in space exploration and explosions of mammoth nuclear devices were but some of the manifestations of his efforts. Khrushchev initiated his ambitious political and economic offensive in the underdeveloped world, particularly in areas where the West had already been forced on the defensive, as an integral part of this effort. His celebrated "peace offensive," the move into the Third World, was thus in some part a bid to confirm Moscow's "Big Power" status with global commitments and interests.

An added incentive to establish and maintain a Soviet presence in the Arab East may have been contributed by the growing rift between Russia and China, which began vying with each other in the early 1960s for the allegiance and support of the neutralist governments in Asia and Africa. For this reason, Khrushchev had to maintain reasonably close relations with the members of the neutralist (later—nonaligned) club or face the risk of being outflanked by his Peking rivals. To drop Nasir and other "progressive" regimes was tantamount to leaving them prey to Chinese blandishments and to undermine seriously Soviet claims to leadership in both the Communist movement and the Third World.

Another consideration that must have weighed heavily in Khrushchev's decision to embark upon his relatively bold and novel policy in the newly independent countries was the need to deliver "tangible" successes to the home audience. Absent under Stalin, this dimension

ULTIMATE FAILURE OF KHRUSHCHEV'S POLICIES

of Soviet politics called for substantive results in foreign as well as domestic affairs as a means of forestalling incipient challenge from contending circles within the Kremlin. This novel element of Soviet political life, which has been largely disregarded in the West, ultimately reduced foreign expansion to a function of domestic politics. It is instructive in this connection that, in 1963–1964, when he must have felt his position increasingly threatened as a result of the growing pressures within the Kremlin power structure, Khrushchev made a desperate attempt to vindicate his Third World policy by claiming that the United Arab Republic and Algeria were the first tangible achievements in his effort to steer "national-democratic" countries onto the "path of socialism."

After he became deeply engulfed in Middle Eastern politics, Khrushchev may have come to regret his initial decision and may even have questioned some of the basic premises upon which it had been based. But it was unrealistic to expect him to admit publicly that his "game had not been worth the candle." On the larger, more impersonal plane, the USSR had committed itself to maintaining the appearance of a great power with "legitimate" interests in the Middle East, a stand that the Kremlin could not relinquish without a most serious loss of prestige. Moscow was equally averse to writing off the relatively large-scale military, political, and, especially, economic investments made in a number of Arab countries. Thus, in striking out so boldly in the Third World, Khrushchev's policy had in an important sense maneuvered the Soviet Union into a position that compared unfavorably with that formerly held by the imperialist powers and even with its own position under Stalin. Whereas the West, upon a certain outlay of resources, had usually been able to control or exploit its colonies and dependencies, the USSR acquired clients who behaved more like contentious tenants accustomed to dealing with the landlord as a functionary at the mercy of their whims. It may safely be concluded that this highly unsatisfactory state of affairs in the Third World contributed to Khrushchev's downfall in October 1964.

Selected Bibliography

Newspapers and Periodicals

Akhbar al-Yawm (Cairo)
Al-Ahali (Baghdad)
Al-Ahd al-Jadid (Baghdad)
Al-Ahram (Cairo)
Al-Akhbar (Cairo)
Al-Ba'th (Damascus)
Al-Bayan (Baghdad)
Al-Fajr al-Jadid (Baghdad)
Al-Gumhuriya (Cairo)
Al-Hurriya (Baghdad)
Al-Masa' (Cairo)
Al-Musawwar (Cairo)
Al-Mustaqbal (Baghdad)
Al-Nahar (Bayrut)
Al-Qahira (Cairo)
Al-Sha'b (Cairo)
Al-Thawra (Baghdad)

Al-Thawra (Damascus)
Cahiers d'Orient Contemporain (Paris)
Christian Science Monitor (Boston)
Chronology of International Events and Documents (London)
Current Digest of the Soviet Press (New York)
Department of State Bulletin (Washington)
Economist (London)
Egyptian Economic and Political Review (Cairo)
Egyptian Gazette (Cairo)
Egyptian Mail (Cairo)
International Affairs (Moscow)
Iraqi Times (Baghdad)
Ittihad al-Sha'b (Baghdad)
Izvestiia (Moscow)
Krasnaia Zvezda (Moscow)
Le Monde (Paris)
Manchester Guardian (Manchester)
Middle East Journal (Washington)
Middle Eastern Affairs (New York)
Mideast Mirror (Bayrut)
Mirovaia ekonomika i mezhdunarodnye otnosheniia (Moscow)
Mizan Newsletter (London)
Narody Azii i Afriki (Moscow)
New Times (Moscow)
New York Times
Newsweek (New York)
Orient (Paris)
Oriente Moderno (Rome)
Pravda (Moscow)
Problems of Communism (Washington)
Problemy vostokovedeniia (Moscow)
Royal Central Asian Journal (London)
Ruz al-Yusif (Cairo)

Sawt al-Ahrar (Baghdad)
Sovetskaia Rossiia (Moscow)
Sovetskoe vostokovedenie (Moscow)
Sovremennyi vostok (Moscow)
Swiss Review of World Affairs (Zurich)
Times (London)
Trud (Moscow)
Vneshniaia torgovlia (Moscow)
World Marxist Review (London and Toronto)
World Today (London)

Books and Surveys

Abu Jaber, K. S. *The Arab Ba'th Socialist Party: History, Ideology, and Organization.* Syracuse: Syracuse University Press, 1966.

Adams, M. *Suez and After: Year of Crisis.* Boston: Beacon Press, 1958.

Akademiia nauk SSSR. Institut mirovoi ekonomiki i mezhdunarodnykh otnoshenii. *Mezhdunarodnye otnosheniia posle vtoroi mirovoi voiny, 1945–1964.* 3 vols. Moscow: Politizdat, 1962–1965.

Akademiia nauk SSSR. Institut mirovoi ekonomiki i mezhdunarodnykh otnoshenii. *Mezhdunarodnyi politiko-ekonomicheskii ezhegodnik.* 1958–1964. Moscow: Gospolitizdat.

Akademiia nauk SSSR. Institut narodov Azii. *Noveishaia istoriia arabskikh stran (1917–1966).* Moscow: Izdatel'stvo "Nauka," 1968.

Akademiia nauk SSSR. Institut narodov Azii. *Politika SShA na Arabskom Vostoke.* Moscow: Izdatel'stvo vostochnoi literatury, 1961.

Akademiia nauk SSSR. Institut narodov Azii. *Sovetsko-arabskie druzhestvennye otnosheniia.* Moscow: Izdatel'stvo vostochnoi literatury, 1961.

Akademiia nauk SSSR. Institut vostokovedeniia. *Araby v bor'be za nezavisimost'.* Moscow: Gospolitizdat, 1957.

Andreasian, R. N. and El'ianov, A. E. *Blizhnii Vostok: neft' i nezavisimost'.* Moscow: Izdatel'stvo vostochnoi literatury, 1961.

Beal, J. R. *John Foster Dulles: 1888–1959.* New York: Harper, 1959.

Becker, A. S. and Horelick, A. L. *Soviet Policy in the Middle East.* Santa Monica: The RAND Corporation, 1970.

Ben-Gurion, D. *Israel: Years of Challenge.* New York: Holt, Rinehart and Winston, 1963.

Berger, M. *The Arab World Today.* Garden City: Doubleday, 1962.

Binder, L. *The Ideological Revolution in the Middle East.* New York: Wiley, 1964.

Bromberger, M. and S. *Secrets of Suez.* London: Pan Books, 1957.

Bulganin, N. A. and Khrushchev, N. S. *Rechi vo vremia prebyvaniia v Indii, Birme i Afganistane.* Moscow: Gospolitizdat, 1956.

Calvocoressi, P. *Suez: Ten Years After.* New York: Pantheon Books, 1967.

Campbell, J. C. *Defense of the Middle East: Problems of American Policy.* Rev. ed. New York: Praeger, 1960.

Caractacus. *Revolution in Iraq.* London: Gollancz, 1959.

Copeland, M. *The Game of Nations: The Amorality of Power Politics.* London: Weidenfeld and Nicolson, 1969.

Cremeans, Ch. D. *The Arabs and the World.* New York: Praeger, 1963.

Dagan, A. *Moscow and Jerusalem.* New York: Abelard-Schuman, 1970.

Dallin, D. J. *Soviet Foreign Policy after Stalin.* Philadelphia: Lippincott, 1961.

Dann, U. *Iraq under Qassem: A Political History, 1958–1963.* Jerusalem: Israel Universities Press, 1969.

Dantsig, B. M. *Irak v proshlom i nastoiashchem.* Moscow: Izdatel'stvo vostochnoi literatury, 1960.

Dayan, M. *Diary of the Sinai Campaign.* London: Weidenfeld and Nicolson, 1966.

Demchenko, P. *Irakskii Kurdistan v ogne.* Moscow: Gospolitizdat, 1963.

Dzelepy, E. N. *Le complot de Suez.* Paris: Les editions politiques, 1957.

Eden, Sir A. *Memoirs: Full Circle.* London: Cassell, 1960.

Eisenhower, D. D. *Waging Peace, 1956–1961.* Garden City, N. Y.: Doubleday, 1965.

Finer, H. *Dulles over Suez.* Chicago: Quadrangle Books, 1964.

Fisher, S. N. *The Military in the Middle East and Problems in Society and Government.* Columbus: Ohio State University Press, 1963.

Fleming, D. F. *The Cold War and Its Origins, 1950–1960.* 2 vols. Garden City, N. Y.: Doubleday, 1961.

Foot, M. and Jones, M. *Guilty Men, 1957.* New York: Rinehart, 1957.

Hurewitz, J. C. *Diplomacy in the Near and Middle East.* 2 vols. Princeton: Van Nostrand, 1956.

―――――. *Middle East Politics: The Military Dimension.* New York: Praeger, 1969.

―――――, ed. *Soviet-American Rivalry in the Middle East.* New York: Praeger, 1969.

Institut mezhdunarodnykh otnoshenii. *Istoriia mezhdunarodnykh otnoshenii i vneshnei politiki SSSR, 1917–1963.* 3 vols. Moscow: Izdatel'stvo "Mezhdunarodnye otnosheniia," 1961–1964.

Issawi, Ch. *Egypt in Revolution.* London: Oxford University Press, 1963.

Johnson, P. *The Suez War.* London: Pan Books, 1957.

Joshua, W. and Gibert, S. *Arms for the Third World: Soviet Military Aid Diplomacy.* Baltimore: The Johns Hopkins Press, 1969.

Kerr, M. *The Arab Cold War, 1958–1967: A Study of Ideology in Politics.* 2nd ed. London: Oxford University Press, 1967.

Khadduri, M. *Republican 'Iraq: A Study in 'Iraqi Politics since the Revolution of 1958.* London: Oxford University Press, 1969.

Khrushchev, N. S. *Otchetnyi doklad Tsentral'nogo Komiteta KPSS XX-mu s'ezdu partii.* Moscow: Gospolitizdat, 1956.

―――――. *The National Liberation Movement.* Moscow: Foreign Languages Publishing House, 1963.

Kirk, G. E. *Contemporary Arab Politics.* New York: Praeger, 1961.

Klieman, A. S. *Soviet Russia and the Middle East.* Baltimore: The Johns Hopkins Press, 1970.

Kotlov, L. N. *Iordaniia v noveishee vremia.* Moscow: Izdatel'stvo vostochnoi literatury, 1962.

Lacouture, J. and S. *Egypt in Transition.* New York: Criterion Books, 1958.

Laqueur, W. Z. *Communism and Nationalism in the Middle East.* New York: Praeger, 1956.

———. *The Soviet Union and the Middle East.* New York: Praeger, 1959.

———. *The Struggle for the Middle East: The Soviet Union in the Mediterranean, 1958–1968.* New York: Macmillan, 1969.

Lenczowski, G. *Oil and State in the Middle East.* Ithaca: Cornell University Press, 1960.

Leningrad. Gosudarstvennyi universitet. *Noveishaia istoriia stran zarubezhnoi Azii i Afriki.* Leningrad: Izdatel'stvo Leningradskogo universiteta, 1963.

Lilienthal, A. M. *There Goes the Middle East.* New York: Devin-Adair, 1957.

Linden, C. A. *Khrushchev and the Soviet Leadership, 1957–1964.* Baltimore: The Johns Hopkins Press, 1966.

Little, T. *Egypt.* New York: Praeger, 1958.

Love, K. *Suez: The Twice-Fought War.* New York: McGraw-Hill, 1969.

Macadam, I., ed. *The Annual Register of World Events.* 1956–1964. New York: St. Martin's Press.

Mackintosh, J. M. *Strategy and Tactics of Soviet Foreign Policy.* London: Oxford University Press, 1963.

Marlowe, J. *Arab Nationalism and British Imperialism: A Study in Power Politics.* New York: Praeger, 1961.

Mirskii, G. I. *Armiia i politika v stranakh Azii i Afriki.* Moscow: Izdatel'stvo "Nauka," 1970.

Murphy, R. *Diplomat among Warriors.* Garden City, N. Y.: Doubleday, 1964.

Nasser, G. A. *The Philosophy of the Revolution.* Cairo: Information Department, n. d.

Nikitina, G. S. *Gosudarstvo Izrail'.* Moscow: Izdatel'stvo "Nauka," 1968.

Nutting, A. *No End of a Lesson: The Story of Suez.* New York: Potter, 1967.

Orlov, E. and Sashko, N. *Gosudarstvennyi stroi Iordanii.* Moscow: Gosudarstvennoe izdatel'stvo iuridicheskoi literatury, 1961.

Page, S. *The USSR and Arabia.* London: Central Asian Research Institute, 1971.

Patai, R. *The Kingdom of Jordan.* Princeton: Princeton University Press, 1958.

Pethybridge, R. *A Key to Soviet Politics.* New York: Praeger, 1962.

President Gamal Abdel Nasser's Speeches and Press-Interviews. 1957–1964. Cairo: Department of Information.

Protopopov, A. S. *Sovetskii Soiuz i suetskii krizis 1956 goda.* Moscow: Izdatel'stvo "Nauka," 1969.

Qubain, F. I. *Crisis in Lebanon.* Washington: The Middle East Institute, 1961.

Ra'anan, U. *The USSR Arms the Third World: Case Studies in Soviet Foreign Policy.* Cambridge: The M.I.T. Press, 1969.

Robertson, T. *Crisis: The Inside Story of the Suez Conspiracy.* New York: Atheneum, 1965.

Safran, N. *From War to War: The Arab-Israeli Confrontation, 1948–1967.* New York: Pegasus, 1969.

Sayegh, F. A. *Arab Unity: Hope and Fulfillment.* New York: Devin-Adair, 1958.

———. *The Dynamics of Neutralism in the Arab World.* San Francisco: Chandler, 1964.

Seale, P. *The Struggle for Syria.* London: Oxford University Press, 1965.

Shepilov, D. T. *Suetskii vopros.* Moscow: Gospolitizdat, 1956.

Shwadran, B. *Jordan: A State of Tension.* New York: Council for Middle Eastern Affairs Press, 1959.

Spector, I. *The Soviet Union and the Muslim World, 1917–1956.* Seattle: University of Washington Press, 1956.

SSSR. Ministerstvo inostrannykh del. *SSSR i arabskie strany, 1917–1960.* Moscow: Gospolitizdat, 1961.

Stephens, R. *Nasser: A Political Biography.* New York: Simon and Schuster, 1971.

Stewart, D. *Turmoil in Beirut.* London: Wingate, 1958.

Tatu, M. *Power in the Kremlin: From Khrushchev to Kosygin.* New York: Viking Press, 1969.

Thomas, H. *Suez.* New York: Harper and Row, 1967.

Torrey, G. H. *Syrian Politics and the Military, 1945–1958.* Ohio State University Press, 1964.

Trevelyan, H. *The Middle East in Revolution.* Boston: Gambit, 1970.

Tuganova, O. E. *Mezhdunarodnye otnosheniia na Blizhnem i Srednem Vostoke.* Moscow: Izdatel'stvo "Mezhdunarodnye otnosheniia," 1967.

Ulam, A. *Expansion and Coexistence: The History of Soviet Foreign Policy, 1917–1967.* New York: Praeger, 1968.

United Nations. Department of Public Information. *Yearbook of the United Nations,* 1954–1964. New York: Columbia University Press.

US Department of State. *The Sino-Soviet Economic Offensive in the Less Developed Countries.* Washington: G. P. O., 1958.

US Department of State. *The Suez Canal Problem, July 26-September 22, 1956: A Documentary Publication.* Washington: G. P. O., 1956.

US Department of State. *United States Policy in the Middle East. Documents.* Washington: G. P. O., 1957.

Viktorov, V.P. *Ekonomika sovremennoi Sirii.* Moscow: Izdatel'stvo "Nauka," 1968.

Vysshaia partiinaia shkola pri TsK KPSS. *Mezhdunarodnye otnosheniia i vneshniaia politika SSSR, 1917–1960.* Moscow: Izdatel'stvo VPSh i AON pri TsK KPSS, 1961.

Watt, D.C., ed. *Documents on the Suez Crisis, 26 July to 6 November 1956.* London: Royal Institute of International Affairs, 1957.

Wheelock, K. *Nasser's New Egypt.* New York: Praeger, 1960.

Wint, G. and Calvocoressi, P. *Middle East Crisis.* London: Penguin Books, 1957.

Wynn, W. *Nasser of Egypt: The Search for Dignity.* Cambridge: Arlington Books, 1959.

Zorin, V. A., ed. *Vneshniaia politika SSSR na novom etape.* Moscow: Politizdat, 1964.

Name Index

A.R.D., 170n
'Abaza, Fikri, 139–40, 147, 217
al-Abbasi, Muhammad Salih, 233n
'Abd al-'Ays, Muhammad Husayn, 231n
'Abd al-Nasir, Gamal, 23, 24n, 25–26, 28–33, 34, 37–42, 48, 51, 53, 59, 74, 75n, 76–82, 84, 88–89, 94, 95, 103, 104n, 107, 110–12, 114, 117–18, 120, 122, 125–32, 133–38, 141–45, 146n, 152–53, 154–56, 164, 167, 172, 174, 181, 184, 189, 194–98, 201, 202, 203, 204, 207–9, 210, 211, 212, 213, 214, 215, 216, 218, 219, 220, 243, 244, 250, 251, 252, 253n, 254, 264, 265–67, 277–80, 282–87, 289, 291–92, 294–97, 299–300, 302, 310, 311, 312
'Abd al-Quddus, Ihsan, 38n, 127n
Abu Jaber, K. S., 307
Abu Khayr, Kamal Hamdi, 147, 149
Abu Nuwwar, 'Ali, 60
Adams, M., 307
'Adil, Salam. *See* al-Radawi, Husayn Ahmad
'Aflaq, Michel, 62, 63n, 254, 259
Ahmid, Mounir, 244n

Akopian, G., 27n
Aleksandrov, I., 23n, 87n, 114n, 129n, 151–52
Ali, Jabbar, 190n, 191n
Ali, Saadi, 190n
Amin, Mustafa, 24n, 76–77, 78n, 132n
'Amir, 'Abd al-Hakim, 75, 140–41, 270
'Ammash, Salih Mahdi, 225
Andreasian, R. N., 307
Ardatovskii, V., 69n
'Arif, 'Abd al-Salam, 225–27, 232, 239–43, 245, 254, 275–76
Arkhangel'skii, M., 242n
Arutyunov, R., 269n
al-'Asali, Sabri, 62n
Atasi, Jamal, 249n
Ayashi, Melhem, 151n, 196n
'Aziz, 'Ali Ghalib, 186
al-'Azm, Khalid, 64, 195, 196, 205, 206, 245
al-Azmah, Bashir, 196, 204–5

Bahay al-Din, Ahmad, 196n, 283
al-Bakr, Ahmad Hasan, 225, 230
Balabushevich, V. V., 133n
Baqdash, Khalid, 62n, 127n, 143–44, 198, 199–200, 201–2, 293

313

al-Barazani, Mulla Mustafa, 187–89, 191, 192
Barkovskii, Anatolii, 247
Baturin, A., 72n
Beal, J. R., 307
Becker, A. S., 308
Beliaev, I., 87n, 136n, 139n, 152n, 178n, 179n, 182n, 210n, 214, 219n, 242n, 244n, 247n, 248n, 249, 282, 287n
Ben Bella, Ahmad, 215, 270, 276
Ben-Gurion, David, 45, 46, 50, 51, 86, 308
Berger, Morroe, 308
Binder, Leonard, 308
Biryuzov, V., 86n
al-Bitar, Salah al-Din, 62, 63n, 246, 255, 259
al-Bizri, 'Afif, 65
Bochkaryov, Y., 23n, 45n, 54n, 75n, 77n, 97n, 99n, 171n, 239n, 240n, 244n, 254n
Borovskii, V., 61n, 87n, 112, 127n, 128n, 138n
Bozhenko, A., 43n
Brezhnev, Leonid I., 144, 201, 204, 212n, 218, 301
Bromberger, M. and S., 44n, 308
Bulganin, Nikolai A., 25n, 43, 45, 46, 47, 51, 52, 69, 308
al-Bustani, 'Abd al-Qadhir Isma'il, 162, 170, 184, 230n

Calvocoressi, Peter, 44n, 308, 312
Campbell, John C., 44n, 55n, 308
Caractacus (pseud.), 308
Caruthers, Osgood, 67n
Castro, Fidel, 153
Chernov, L. N., 134n
Chou En-lai, 29, 263–65
Clin, Georges, 187n
Colombe, Marcel, 154n, 196n
"Commentator," 23n, 104n, 147n, 148–49, 152, 234, 235–36
Copeland, Miles, 308
Cremeans, Charles D., 308

Dagan, Avigdor, 308
Dale, Edwin L., 52
Dallin, David, 25n, 47n, 70n, 78n, 308
Danilov, S., 160n, 164n
Dann, Uriel, 308
Dantsig, B. M., 102n, 113n, 308
al-Dawalibi, Ma'ruf, 195, 201n, 203
Dayan, Moshe, 308
De Gaulle, Charles, 92, 106
Demchenko, P., 72n, 86n, 87n, 104, 111n, 115n, 158n, 159n, 163n, 168n, 170, 173, 182n, 183n, 185n, 189n, 200–201, 202n, 203, 204, 228–29, 235n, 247, 254n, 255, 256n, 266n, 267n, 269n, 282, 287n, 308
al-Din, Nizam, 65
Djilas, Milovan, 76n
Dulles, John Foster, 25n, 28, 37, 38n, 40, 55, 63, 65–66, 68, 84, 87, 107, 307, 308
Dzelepy, E. N., 44n, 308

Eden, Sir Anthony, 35, 43, 45–46, 50–52, 308
Egorov, P., 142n
Eisenhower, Dwight D., 35, 44n, 45n, 46, 51–52, 55, 65, 66n, 91n, 93, 96–97, 98, 106, 308
El'ianov, A., 307
Ellis, Harry, 174n

Faruq, King, 23, 145
Fatisov, V., 178n
Faysal, King, 103
Finer, Herman, 44n, 52, 308
Fisher, Sidney N., 309
Fleming, D. F., 52n, 309

Foot, Michael, 309
Fuzeyev, V., 86n

Gagarin, Iurii, 148
Gevorkyan, P., 267n
Gibert, S., 309
Goebbels, Joseph, 76
Grigoryan, Kh., 82n
Gromyko, Andrei, 68, 72, 99n, 237
Gruening, Ernest, 270n
Guber, A. A., 134n

al-Hafiz, Amin, 245–47, 251, 255, 257, 258, 259, 260
Hairi, Zaki, 115n
al-Hajj, 'Aziz, 110n, 186n, 227n, 254n
Hammarskjöld, Dag, 36, 44, 91–92, 98, 106
Hariri, Ziyad, 251
al-Hawrani, Akram, 62
al-Haydari, Jamal, 233n
Haykal, Muhammad Hasanayn, 30n, 50n, 75n, 89n, 102n, 103n, 112–13, 128–29, 137, 145, 146n, 147n, 155, 197–98, 209
Haysaran, Faysal, 237
Hellu, Farraj Allah, 136, 141–42, 149–50
Henderson, Loy, 65, 67
Hitler, Adolf, 148, 149
Horelick, A. L., 308
Hottinger, Arnold, 117n
Hunt, Carew, 76n
Hunt, Richard, 164n
Hurewitz, J. C., 40n, 309
Husayn, Jabbar, 244n
Husayn, King, 60–61, 86, 90

Iablochkov, L., 138n
Iakovlev, Mikhail, 243
Iasnev, Iu., 204n

Issawi, Charles, 309
Ivanov, K., 30n

Jargy, Simon, 155n
Jawad, Hashim, 165, 230n, 232
Johnson, P., 44n, 309
Jones, M., 309
Joshua, W., 309
Jumard, 'Abd al-Jabbar, 108

Kallas, Khalil, 72
Karami, Rashid, 100
Karev, N., 54n
Kassem. See Qasim, 'Abd al-Karim
Katin, V., 238n
Kerr, Malcolm, 210n, 266n, 309
Khadduri, Majid, 309
Khayr. See Abu Khayr
Khokhlov, N., 86n, 103n, 117n, 120n, 125n, 131n, 287n
Khrushchev, Nikita S., 16–17, 24–25, 28, 33, 34, 39, 47n, 49–50, 64, 68n, 69–70, 76, 80–81, 89, 91n, 92–94, 106, 112–13, 118–20, 125, 126n, 128, 130–32, 134n, 135–36, 137–38, 140, 144–49, 152, 153, 154, 156, 159, 161n, 165, 173, 175, 183–84, 185, 197, 198, 201, 205, 212n, 216, 217, 218, 219, 232, 241, 244, 245, 252, 257, 258, 263, 266–87, 288–89, 290–97, 299–303, 308, 309, 310, 311
Kirk, George E., 309
Kishk, Galal, 212
Klieman, Aaron S., 309
Kondrashov, S., 38n, 72n, 77n, 79n, 85n, 86n, 99n, 101n, 108n, 110n, 111, 120n, 121n, 126n, 127n, 128n, 138n, 139, 152n, 166
Kosygin, Aleksei N., 311

Kotlov, L. N., 61n, 309
Kourdi, Aziz, 170n
Kraminov, D., 67n, 73n, 96n, 98n
Kubba, Ibrahim, 109, 116, 118, 131n, 162, 163n
Kudriavtsev, V., 23n, 32n, 182n, 249, 267
Kuzbari, Ma'mun, 195, 199–200
Kuznetsov, Vasilii, 42n, 159

Lacouture, J. and S., 309
Laqueur, Walter Z., 23n, 53n, 78, 309–10
Lenczowski, George, 310
Lenin, Vladimir I., 24, 148, 276
Leont'ev, B., 56n
Leontyev, L., 95n
Lilienthal, Alfred M., 44n, 310
Linden, Carl A., 310
Litoshko, E., 91n
Little, Tom, 26n, 310
Lodge, Henry Cabot, 48
Love, Kenneth, 44n, 157n, 310
Lozinov, D., 236n
Lumumba, Patrice, 141
Lyubanin, A., 178n, 179n

Macadam, Ivison, 195n, 196n, 209n, 212n, 213n, 225n, 245n, 246n, 247n, 266n, 310
Mackintosh, J. M., 25n, 30n, 47n, 59, 60n, 65n, 70, 89, 121, 310
Macmillan, Harold, 92, 106
Maevskii, Viktor, 73n, 87n, 100n, 112, 129n, 203, 204–5, 211–12, 237–38, 243n, 247–48, 249, 253n
Mahmud, Sami, 173n, 184n, 186n
Mairakov, M., 238n
Maksimov, E., 229n, 255n
Maletin, P., 119n
Malik, Charles, 83, 84, 87

Malyshev, L., 136n
Mao Tse-tung, 94n, 154, 161
Marlowe, John, 310
Marx, Karl, 24, 148
al-Matni, Nasib, 84
Medvedev, V., 27n, 42n, 103n
Menderes, Adnan, 69
Menzies, Robert G., 40, 42
Mikhailov, M., 121n
Mikoian, Anastas, 139, 140, 144, 165–67
Mirskii, Georgii, 55n, 103n, 114–16, 158–59, 193n, 214n, 216, 231n, 249n, 253, 254, 310
Mirsky, G. *See* Mirskii, Georgii
Mohamed, Ali, 233n, 240n
Mollet, Guy, 43, 45, 46, 50, 51
Montserrat, Michel, 117n
Muhiy al-Din, Khalid, 75n, 270n
Mukhitdinov, Nuritdin, 139, 144
Munir, Tawfiq, 230n
Murphy, Robert, 52, 310
Muslih, Rashid, 231
Mustafa, Anwar, 244n

al-Nabulsi, Sulayman, 60, 61
Nagib, Muhammad, 23
Nassar, Fuad, 172, 250n
Nasser. *See* 'Abd al-Nasir, Gamal
Nasser, Fuad. *See* Nassar Fuad
Nawar, Ibrahim, 151n
Nehru, Jawaharlal, 25, 28–29, 45, 47, 106
Nekrasov, V., 43n
Nikitina, G. S., 310
Nikolaev, S., 61n
Nikolov, 233n
Nuri. *See* al-Sa'id, Nuri
al-Nus, 'Izzat, 200
Nutting, Anthony, 44n, 310

"Observer," 23n, 26n, 27n, 43n, 70n, 79, 91, 93, 97, 103, 104n,

NAME INDEX

105n, 119n, 132n, 138–39, 282n, 283n
Orekhov, F., 55n
Orestov, O., 26n, 99n, 106n
Orlov, E., 61n, 310
Osipov, V., 100n, 158n

Page, Stephen, 310
Palme Dutt, R., 116n
Palmer, Monte, 194n
Pastukhov, N., 70n, 72n
Patai, Raphael, 60n, 310
Penrose, E. F., 226n
Pethybridge, Roger, 311
Petrov, V., 236n, 238n, 254n
Pletnyov, E., 126n
Plyshevskii, I., 69n, 70n
Ponomarev, Boris, 244n, 258
Potomov, Iu., 242n
Priestley, Vito, 162n
Primakov, E., 133n, 138n, 213n, 217n, 218n, 239n, 241n, 255n, 267n
Protopopov, A. S., 311

Qasim, 'Abd al-Karim, 94, 103–9, 112–22, 127, 129–31, 133–35, 141, 157–64, 165–69, 170–75, 176–78, 180–83, 184–86, 187–90, 192–93, 210, 219, 225, 227, 229, 230n, 231, 232, 234, 244, 245, 294–95, 299, 300
Qubain, Fahim, 84n, 311
al-Qudsi, Nazim, 195, 201, 203, 204, 205
al-Quwatli, Shukri, 64, 79n

Ra'anan, Uri, 30n, 311
al-Radhawi, Husayn Ahmad, 230n, 231n
Robertson, Terence, 44n, 311
Rockefeller, David, 98

Rokossovskii, Konstantin, 69
Rountree, William, 110

Saadi, Ibrahim, 231n
Sabri, 'Ali, 287–89
al-Sadat, Anwar, 30, 31, 144–47
al-Sa'di, 'Ali Salih, 225, 226, 257, 259
Safran, Nadav, 311
al-Sa'id, Nuri, 71, 86, 87, 102–4, 106–7, 115, 121, 161, 228, 291
al-Sa'igh, Dawud, 162–63
Salam, Sa'ib, 83
Salim, Muhammad, 184n, 186n, 190n
Salimov, Amin, 238n
Sarraj, 'Abd al-Hamid, 127n
Sashko, N., 61n, 310
Satiukov, Pavel, 282
Sa'ud, King, 66n
Sayegh, Fayez A., 311
Schmidt, Dana Adams, 191–92, 196n
Seale, Patrick, 61n, 63n, 65n, 78n, 311
Seiful-Mulyukov, F., 235n
Shabib, Talib, 229
Shamilov, Arabe, 238n
Sham'un, Kamil, 83–87, 90, 101
al-Shannawi, Kamal, 150n, 151n
al-Sharif, 'Aziz, 230n
al-Shawwaf, 'Abd al-Wahhab, 116–17, 118n
Shepilov, Dmitrii, 38n, 41, 42n, 45, 48, 63, 68n, 311
Shihab, Fu'ad, 99
Shwadran, Benjamin, 98n, 311
al-Siba'i, Yusuf, 151n
Sibiriak, G., 241n
al-Sidqi, 'Aziz, 212
Skachkov, B., 138n

Skachkov, S., 163n
Smirnov, K., 76n, 116n, 129n
Sobolev, Arkadii, 55
Spain, James W., 25n
Spector, Ivar, 311
Stalin, Iosif V., 16, 24, 153, 290, 302, 303
Stepanov, L., 126n
Stepanov, M., 72n
Stephens, Robert, 311
Stepin, A., 206n
Stewart, Desmond, 83n, 311
Strel'nikov, B., 54n, 96n, 98n
Stupak, A., 169n
Sturua, M., 99n
Sukarno, 25, 28, 45, 47
al-Sulh, Sami, 83
Svechnikov, B., 185n

al-Taba'i, Muhammad, 151n, 198n
al-Ta'i, Yunis, 166–67
Tatu, Michel, 311
Teplyakov, L., 126n
Thomas, Hugh, 44n, 311
Tito, Iosif Broz, 28–29, 129, 155
Tolmachov, P., 91n
Torrey, Gordon, 61n, 65n, 78n, 311
Touré, Sékou, 215
Trevelyan, Sir Humphrey, 311
Tuganova, O., 73n, 101n, 163n, 181n, 208, 214n, 227n, 234n, 238n, 251n, 255n, 311

Ulam, Adam, 312
'Uwayni, Hasan, 231n

Vasil'ev, B., 168n
Viktorov, V. P., 260n, 312
Vishnevetskii, K., 248n, 251n, 252n, 257n, 261n, 266n, 287n
Vishnevskii, S., 61n
Voroshilov, Klimentii E., 45, 47

Wahbi, 'Abd al-Jabbar, 233n
Walz, Jay, 138n
Watt, D. C., 312
Wheelock, Kenneth, 312
William II, Kaiser, 148
Wint, Guy, 44n, 312
Wynn, Wilton, 38n, 312

Y. B. *See* Bochkaryov, Y.
al-Yafi, 'Abdallah, 83
Yahya, Tahir, 242
Yermashov, I., 71n
Zahr al-Din, 'Abd al-Karim, 195, 203–4
Zaitsev, Grigorii, 107
Zhukov, E., 133n, 134n
Zhukov, V., 98n
Zhukov, Y., 158n
Ziadeh, Nicola A., 61n
Zorin, Valerian, 101n, 178, 181, 193n, 312
Zvyagin, Y., 100n, 111n, 117n, 138n, 139n

Subject Index

Author's Note—Only those periodicals actually cited in the text have been included in this index; those mentioned in footnotes have been omitted.

Aden, 275
Africa, 50, 81, 133, 134, 135, 143, 148, 154, 156, 217, 264, 265, 271, 287, 302
Agitprop, 107
Aleppo, 195, 205
Alexandria, 141, 288
Algeria, 82, 115, 141, 215, 245, 270, 276, 280, 287, 289, 303
'Amman. *See* Jordan
Ankara. *See* Turkey
Arab League, 86, 116, 175–76, 179, 197, 205
Arab nationalism, 10, 32, 53, 62, 73, 77, 84, 102, 107, 111, 115, 126, 128, 132, 143, 144, 148, 150–51, 161, 187, 189, 190, 195–98, 219, 232, 248–49, 250, 253, 256, 258, 262, 276–78, 282–83, 285–87
 Soviet Union and, 41, 53, 60, 70, 81, 116, 119, 122, 127, 129–31, 135, 136, 142, 148, 198, 248, 275, 296
Arab Socialism, 145, 146, 156, 211–12, 240, 253, 271, 272–74, 282–83, 285, 286, 287, 296
Arab unity. *See* Arab nationalism

Arabian Peninsula, 182, 247, 248, 292
Arab-Israeli conflict, 17, 26, 29, 35, 36, 44, 62, 202, 261, 267, 268, 271, 275, 298
 Soviet Union and, 24, 64, 138–39, 206, 280, 285, 294, 295, 299, 300. *See also* Jordan River Waters Dispute; Suez Crisis
Asia, 50, 81, 133, 134, 135, 143, 148, 154, 165, 217, 264, 271, 302
Aswan High Dam, 35, 38, 80, 125, 126, 136–38, 140, 146, 220, 264, 270, 275, 281, 284, 292

Baghdad. *See* Iraq
Baghdad Pact, 17, 25–26, 28, 29, 32, 35, 71, 103, 104, 106, 115, 120, 121, 271, 291. *See also* Central Treaty Organization (CENTO)
Baghdad-Basra railway, 109, 173, 185, 242
Bandung Conference, 29, 45, 103, 104, 107, 129
Basra, 166, 176, 184, 185
Ba'th Party, 10, 215, 216, 220, 250, 251–57, 259, 260, 262
Iraqi, 62, 206, 219, 225–26, 228,

319

229, 230, 233–36, 238, 239, 244, 246, 251, 253–55, 257, 259, 262
Syrian, 61–63, 66, 78, 194–96, 206, 207, 215, 219, 245, 250–56, 259, 260, 262
Bayrut. *See* Lebanon
Berlin, 16, 285
"Bourgeois nationalism," 16, 23, 25, 33, 63, 154, 174, 202, 208, 250, 262, 293
Bulgaria, 109, 233

Cairo. *See* Egypt
Central Treaty Organization (CENTO), 237, 238. *See also* Baghdad Pact
China, Nationalist, 94, 179, 197, 265
China, People's Republic of, 35, 37, 63, 64, 94, 104, 109, 133, 263, 264–65, 302. *See also* Sino-Soviet Dispute
Cold War, 15, 24–25, 29, 33, 34–36, 75, 95, 121–22, 155, 157, 261–62, 290–91, 294, 297, 300–302
Columbia Broadcasting System, 51
Communism, 16–17, 24–25, 75–76, 108, 112, 113, 116, 127–29, 133, 145–51, 155, 156, 169, 198, 211–12, 217, 229, 250, 256, 262, 274–75, 278, 281, 282, 285–87, 292, 293, 296, 297. *See also* Communist Party; "National Liberation Struggle"
Communist Party:
  Arab Communists, 127, 128, 131, 132, 197, 198, 216, 217, 250, 292, 293
  Egyptian, 111, 131, 133, 135, 141–44, 150, 197, 214–16, 283
  French, 228

Iraqi (ICP), 105, 113, 114, 122, 127, 129, 135, 158–64, 168, 170–73, 176, 184–86, 189–93, 215, 216, 226–34, 240–41, 244, 254, 292, 293
Italian, 141
Lebanese, 141, 149, 150
Soviet Union (CPSU), 150, 201, 202, 206, 228, 231, 288–89
Syrian, 62–63, 66, 77, 78, 80, 82, 127, 135, 141, 143, 150, 197–99, 201, 202, 206–7, 215, 216, 247–49, 255, 258, 260, 292, 293
Congo, 141
Cuba, 153, 280
Cuban Missile Crisis, 218, 272, 285, 300–301
Cyprus, 268, 275
Czechoslovakia, 64, 109, 119, 191, 199
  Arms deal (1955), 23, 28, 30, 58, 291

Damascus. *See* Syria
Developing nations. *See* Third World

East Berlin, 157
East Germany, 64, 109
East-West Conflict. *See* Cold War
Egypt, 24, 26, 31, 34–58, 209–21, 263–89, 291, 302
  Domestic politics, 30, 210–11, 212–14, 216, 268–69
    Arab Socialist Union, 213, 269, 287–89, *see also* Communist Party, Egyptian; Syrian Crisis; and United Arab Republic
  Economic development, 74, 75, 80, 210, 220, 265, 279–81, 284, 285, 287, 292, 295, *see also* Aswan High Dam

SUBJECT INDEX 321

Iraq and, 205, 220, 233, 243, 247–51, 254, 286, 291, 292, 294, 295, 299, 300, see also Inter-Arab politics; United Arab Republic, Iraq and
Jordan and, 35, 60, 209, 215, 266, 294
Syria and, 35, 69, 202, 207–9, 218, 220, 245–51, 254, 256, 267, 292, 299, see also Syrian Crisis; United Arab Republic
Soviet Union and, 17, 30–32, 34–38, 61, 71, 74–82, 117–22, 125–32, 197, 198, 200, 205, 206, 212–21, 244, 252, 263–89, 291, 292, 294–96, see also United Arab Republic, Soviet Union and; Kuwayt Crisis, UAR and; Lebanese Crisis, UAR and; Suez Crisis
Eisenhower Doctrine, 35, 56, 57, 83, 121
Euphrates River, 136, 164

France, 25, 61, 67, 69, 70, 92, 106, 151, 179, 257. See also Suez Crisis, France and
"Free Hellu" campaign, 136, 141–42, 149–50

Gaza, 29
Geneva, 92
Great Britain, 25, 30, 31, 67, 69, 70, 87, 91–94, 96–100, 102–6, 121–22, 151, 192, 193, 197, 215, 219, 227, 238, 261, 268. See also Kuwayt Crisis; Suez Crisis, Great Britain and
Guatemala, 197
Guinea, 215, 289
Gulf of 'Aqaba, 54

Habbaniya, 120
Hashimites, 102, 121
Hungarian Revolution (1956), 47, 48, 50, 93
Hungary, 109, 220

India, 25, 29, 92, 106, 215, 264, 265
Indonesia, 25
Inter-Arab politics, 10, 11, 17, 26, 104, 127, 206, 207, 215, 219, 246–54, 259, 266–68, 294, 295, 299. See also Arab nationalism; Arab Socialism
Iran, 25, 70, 164, 188, 191, 192, 193, 196, 197, 237
Iraq, 27, 28, 58, 65, 66, 86, 87, 89, 94, 95, 102–22, 126, 129, 175–83, 192, 193, 225–45, 247, 275, 294, 300. See also Iraqi Revolution
Domestic politics, 102–3, 114–15, 158–62, 169–72, 180–81, 184–93, 225–29, 233–41, see also Ba'th Party, Iraqi; Communist Party, Iraqi
Kirkuk Massacre, 160–61, 162, 172
Kurdish Problem, 186–93, 226, 234–41, 253, 255, 256
Mosul Uprising, 116–18, 120, 131, 170, 185
Qasim's fall, 225, 227
Economic development, 108–10, 115, 119, 130, 164, 165, 168, 173–74, 182, 183, 185–86, 227, 234, 243–44, 295, see also Baghdad-Basra railway
Egypt and, see Egypt, Iraq and; UAR, Iraq and
Oil, 110, 121, 177, 186, 187, 227, 240
Soviet Union and, 61, 71, 103–22, 125–26, 134, 135, 157–75,

182–84, 200, 205, 206, 210, 220, 227–45, 252, 259, 260, 262, 275, 276, 294, 295, 297
Syria and, 61, 65, 66, 73, 195, 203, 205, 207, 245–51, 253–56
Iraqi Revolution, 10, 82, 87, 91, 101, 102–10, 125, 157, 159, 168, 294
  Great Britain and, 102–6
  Jordan and, 103, 105
  Lebanon and, 103, 105
  Soviet Union and, 103–10, 168
  United Arab Republic and, 103, 104, 106, 107
  United Nations and, 103
  United States and, 102–7
Islam, 211
Israel, 35, 42, 86, 126, 299. *See also* Arab-Israeli conflict; Jordan River Waters Dispute; Suez Crisis, Israel and
East European immigration, 129–30
  Egypt and, 17, 44
  Soviet Union and, 37, 167, 300
  Syria and, 138, 202
  United States and, 65, 110
Italy, 17, 69, 300

Jordan, 35, 58, 59, 60–61, 62, 65, 66, 71, 73, 103, 105, 121, 175, 178, 197, 209, 215, 247, 266, 294, 300. *See also* Jordanian Crisis; Lebanese Crisis
Jordan River Waters Dispute, 263, 265–66, 267–68, 272, 275, 280, 285
Jordanian Crisis (1957), 60–61

Korea, 97
Kremlin. *See* Soviet Union
Kuwayt, 62, 192, 247
Kuwayt Crisis, 175–82, 186, 189

Arab League and, 175–76, 179
Great Britain and, 175–82
Iraq and, 175–82
Jordan and, 175, 178
Saudi Arabia and, 175, 178
Soviet Union and, 177–82
United Arab Republic and, 175, 178–81
United Nations and, 176, 178–80, 181
United States and, 177

Lake Tiberias, 265–66
Latakia, 195, 205, 209
Latin America, 154, 271
Lebanese Crisis, 10, 82–101, 103, 294, 299
  Great Britain and, 87, 91, 92, 93, 94, 96–100
  Iraq and, 86, 87, 94, 95
  Jordan and, 86, 87, 89, 90–94, 97, 98
  Soviet Union and, 84–91, 92–95, 96–101
  United Arab Republic and, 84–89, 94, 96, 98, 99
  United Nations and, 86, 88, 90–94, 96, 97, 98, 99
  United States and, 84–91, 92–101
Lebanon, 58, 62, 65, 66, 71, 73, 103, 105, 121, 150, 300. *See also* Lebanese Crisis
  Domestic politics, 83–84, 99–100, *see also* Communist Party, Lebanese
Libya, 17, 268, 275
London. *See* Great Britain

Mali, 289
Marxism-Leninism. *See* Communism
Mediterranean Sea, 42, 43, 65, 84, 85, 205, 220, 252, 263, 301

SUBJECT INDEX 323

Middle East News Agency (MENA), 103, 150, 152
Middle East oil, 46, 91, 97, 177, 179, 182, 186, 247, 248, 270. *See also* Iraq, oil
Mongolia, 236
Morocco, 17
Moscow. *See* Soviet Union

"National liberation struggle," 45, 71, 88, 91, 97, 101, 107, 115, 117, 129, 133–34, 183, 202, 258, 262, 267, 271, 276, 279–81
Neutralism, 16, 17, 28–29, 33, 53, 62, 75, 81, 98, 104, 115, 125, 126, 129, 135, 137, 145, 151, 154, 155, 164, 166, 197, 205, 215, 218, 219, 240, 245, 252, 265, 278, 291, 292, 293, 297
Nonalignment. *See* Neutralism
North Africa, 45
North Atlantic Treaty Organization (NATO), 15, 52, 177, 291
Northern Region, UAR. *See* Syria

Organization of Soviet Trade Unions, 171
Ottoman Empire, 176

Palestine. *See* Arab-Israeli conflict
Palestinian refugees, 36, 59, 167, 265, 275, 280
Pakistan, 17, 25, 26, 29, 183, 291
Panarabism. *See* Arab nationalism
Paris. *See* France
Peking. *See* China, People's Republic of
Periodicals:
 Akhbar al-Yawm, 9, 111, 127, 142
 Al-Ahd al-Jadid, 171, 172
 Al-Ahram, 9, 37, 126, 129, 147, 149, 155, 198, 254, 263
 Al-Akhbar, 37, 76, 142
 Al-Alam, 267
 Al-Ba'th, 10, 252
 Al-Bayan, 174, 180
 Al-Bilad, 179
 Al-Gumhuriya, 9, 37, 38, 96, 181
 Al-Hadaf, 192
 Al-Hadhara, 184
 Al-Hurriya, 10, 169
 Al-Jamahir, 229, 230
 Al-Mabda', 162
 Al-Musawwar, 149, 216, 217
 Al-Mustaqbal, 171
 Al-Nid'a, 160
 Al-Sharq, 185
 Al-Telegraf, 84
 Al-Thawra (Baghdad), 9, 166, 167
 Al-Thawra (Damascus), 10
 Economist, 10, 109, 188, 190, 192, 209, 284
 Egyptian Economic and Political Review, 147, 148
 Egyptian Gazette, 10, 120, 137
 International Affairs, 9, 133, 160
 Iraqi Times, 10, 232
 Ittihad al Sha'b, 9, 158, 162–64, 169, 170, 184
 Izvestiia, 9, 32, 111, 117, 120, 121, 126, 166, 185, 248, 254
 Khabat, 188
 Le Monde, 213
 L'Unita, 74, 141, 143
 Middle East Journal, 10
 Mideast Mirror, 10, 289
 New Times, 9, 72, 97, 100, 110, 113, 117, 118, 160, 171, 212, 213, 238, 239, 256, 267
 New York Times, 10, 52, 69, 109, 191, 229

Orient, 10
Pravda, 9, 41, 43, 45, 54, 67, 71, 98, 105, 129, 141–43, 148, 158, 163, 165, 169, 171, 182, 183, 185, 192, 212–14, 217, 228, 231–35, 237, 239–43, 253–58, 266, 269, 282, 283, 287
Ruz al-Yusif, 9, 212
Sawt al-Ahrar, 9–10, 176, 179
Scotsman, 111
Shih-chieh Chih-shih, 133
Sovremennyi vostok, 172
Times (London), 10
World Marxist Review, 144, 170, 172, 184, 190, 191
Persian Gulf, 62, 175, 177, 181, 182
Poland, 64, 109, 220
Port Sa'id, 51, 127
"Positive neutralism." *See* neutralism

Radio Baghdad, 108, 238
Radio Moscow, 169
Red Sea, 45, 177
Rumania, 64, 109, 220
Russia. *See* Soviet Union

Saudi Arabia, 17, 35, 71, 175, 178, 209, 215, 248, 266, 294
Shatt al-Arab, 164
Shayba, 120
Shtura, 205
Sino-Soviet dispute, 144, 153–54, 161–62, 163, 215, 216, 239, 244, 258, 264, 265, 273, 281, 302
South Arabia. *See* Arabian Peninsula
Southeast Asian Treaty Organization (SEATO), 291
Soviet Union. *See also* Arab nationalism, Soviet Union and; Arab-Israeli conflict, Soviet Union and; Communist Party, Soviet Union; Israel, Soviet Union and; Jordanian Crisis; Kuwayt Crisis, Soviet Union and; Lebanese Crisis, Soviet Union and; Sino-Soviet Dispute; Suez Crisis, Soviet Union and
Domestic politics, 280–81, 285, 286, 289, 302–3
Egypt and, *see* Egypt, Soviet Union and
Foreign aid, 17, 32, 34, 64, 72, 73, 75, 80, 107, 109, 119, 136–40, 156, 164, 167, 185, 186, 215, 220, 235, 243, 245, 259–61, 279–81, 284, 285, 287, 288, 290, 292, 295–98, 303, *see also* Aswan High Dam; Baghdad-Basra railway; Czechoslovakia, Arms deal (1955)
Foreign policy, 15, 24, 27, 33, 34, 39, 56–57, 59, 82, 133–36, 164, 270, 280, 281, 283, 284, 290, 292–94, 299–303, *see also* Cold War; Sino-Soviet dispute; Third World
Iraq and, *see* Iraq, Soviet Union and
Military affairs, 69, 109, 220, 271, 300–302
Syria and, 32, 63–70, 71–74, 76, 135, 200–206, 210, 220, 237, 247–49, 251–62, 295, *see also* United Arab Republic, Soviet Union and
Trade, 63, 64, 109, 140
United States and, 36, 46, 48–49, 67–68, 89, 121–22, 294, 298, 300, *see also* Cold War
Straits of Tiran, 55
Suez (city), 288

SUBJECT INDEX 325

Suez Canal. *See* Suez Crisis
Suez Crisis, 10, 34–58, 60, 101, 209, 284, 294, 299
  Constantinople Convention (1888), 39, 40
  France and, 39–53, 56
  Great Britain and, 35, 39–53, 56
  Israel and, 35, 42, 44–51, 53–55
  Soviet Union and, 39–57, 284, 294
  Suez Canal Company, 35, 38, 39, 40, 41, 58, 294
  Suez Canal Users' Association, 40, 42, 43
  United Nations and, 41–48, 54, 55
  United States and, 35, 36, 40–57
Sweden, 91
Syria, 58, 60–73, 138, 192–209, 238, 245–62, 300
  Domestic politics, 61–63, 65, 66, 77, 195–96, 199–200, 202–4, 206, 246–49, 251, 252, 255, 258, 260, *see also* Ba'th Party, Syrian; Communist Party, Syrian; Syrian Crisis; United Arab Republic
  Economic development, 205, 255, 256, 260–61, 295
  Egypt and, *see* Egypt, Syria and
  Iraq and, *see* Iraq, Syria and
  Soviet Union and, *see* Soviet Union, Syria and
Syrian Crisis (1957), 10, 61–74
  Henderson Mission, 65–67
  Iraq and, 61, 65, 66, 74
  Jordan and, 60, 65, 66, 74
  Lebanon and, 65, 66, 74, 83
  Soviet Union and, 63–65, 66, 67–71, 71–74
  United States and, 63, 65–71, 74

Taiwan, 265. *See also* China, Nationalist

TASS News Agency, 47, 106, 129, 140, 171, 235
Tawafiq, 138
Tel-Aviv. *See* Israel
Tehran. *See* Iran
Third World, 16–17, 24–25, 33, 81, 89, 133–34, 149, 153–54, 183–84, 218, 235, 261, 270, 272–73, 280, 281, 283, 284, 285, 290, 293, 296, 301–3
Tigris River, 164
Truman Doctrine, 15
Tunisia, 264
Turkey, 17, 25, 26, 27, 58, 65, 66, 69–70, 72, 160, 188, 191, 192, 193, 196, 197, 207, 237, 291, 300
Twenty-first Congress of CPSU, 113, 128
Twenty-second Congress of CPSU, 183, 217

USSR. *See* Soviet Union
Underdeveloped nations. *See* Third World
United Arab Republic (UAR), 10, 74–84, 84–89, 94–96, 98, 99, 127, 136–39, 175, 178–81, 191, 198, 250. *See also* Egypt; Syria
  Creation of, 74, 76–79, 209
  Dissolution of, 194–95, 199, 220, 248, 293, 295
  Iraq and, 98, 103, 104, 106, 107, 110–14, 117–22, 130, 131, 161, 164, 167, 181, 232
  Soviet Union and, 76–77, 78–80, 81, 125–26, 127–32, 134–56, 184, 196–200, 206–9, 220
United Kingdom. *See* Great Britain
United Nations (UN), 69, 103, 197, 236, 261, 265

SUBJECT INDEX

UN Charter, 68, 87, 90, 235
UN Economic and Social Council, 236
UN Emergency Force (UNEF), 48, 54
UN General Assembly, 45–48, 72, 92–94, 96–99, 154, 181, 236
UN Secretariat, 280
UN Secretary-General, *see* Hammarskjöld
UN Security Council, 35, 36, 43–44, 45, 48, 55, 86, 90, 91–94, 178, 181, 236, *see also* Kuwayt Crisis, United Nations and; Lebanese Crisis, United Nations and; Suez Crisis, United Nations and

United States (US), 26, 61, 63, 65–71, 74, 110, 151, 192, 197, 238, 247, 248, 298
Foreign aid, 84, 139–40, 285
Military affairs, 15, 17, 65, 84, 85, 120–21, 220, 263, 291, 300–301. *See also* Cold War; Iraqi Revolution, United States and; Kuwayt Crisis, United States and; Lebanese Crisis, United States and; Soviet Union, United States and; Suez Crisis, United States and
Polaris submarines, 220, 263, 301
Sixth Fleet, 15, 65, 85
United States Information Agency (USIA), 158
Uzbekistan, 288, 289

Washington. *See* United States
Washington Declaration, 35

Yemen, 32, 35, 82, 209, 215, 218, 220, 245, 247, 263, 266, 280, 292
Yugoslavia, 28, 103, 155

Zionism, 67, 116, 135. *See also* Arab-Israeli conflict